N

Professi

Managing the Professional Practice

in the built environment

Edited by

Hedley Smyth

Senior Lecturer in the Bartlett School of Construction
and Project Management
The Faculty of the Built Environment
University College London

A John Wiley & Sons, Ltd., Publication

This edition first published 2011. © 2011 by Blackwell Publishing Ltd.

Blackwell Publishing was acquired by John Wiley & Sons in February 2007. Blackwell's publishing programme has been merged with Wiley's global Scientific, Technical, and Medical business to form Wiley-Blackwell.

Registered office
John Wiley & Sons Ltd, The Atrium, Southern Gate, Chichester, West Sussex, PO19 8SQ, UK

Editorial offices
9600 Garsington Road, Oxford, OX4 2DQ, UK
The Atrium, Southern Gate, Chichester, West Sussex, PO19 8SQ, UK
2121 State Avenue, Ames, Iowa 50014-8300, USA

For details of our global editorial offices, for customer services and for information about how to apply for permission to reuse the copyright material in this book please see our website at www.wiley.com/wiley-blackwell.

The right of the authors to be identified as the authors of this work has been asserted in accordance with the UK Copyright, Designs and Patents Act 1988.

Library of Congress Cataloging-in-Publication Data

Managing the professional practice: in the built environment /
edited by Hedley Smyth.
     p. cm.
  Includes bibliographical references and index.
  ISBN 978-1-4051-9975-9 (pbk. : alk. paper) 1. Construction industry–Management.
I. Smyth, Hedley.

  HD9715.A2M298 2011
  624.068–dc22   2010031869

A catalogue record for this book is available from the British Library.

This book is published in the following electronic formats: ePDF (9781444392340); Wiley Online Library (9781444392364); ePub (9781444392357)

Set in 10/12pt, Palatino by Thomson Digital, Noida, India
Printed and bound in Malaysia by Vivar Printing Sdn Bhd

1   2011

Contents

v

Preface

There is beginning to be a considerable body of resources on how to manage the professional practice that goes beyond the homogenous texts on practice management that rather imply that they are all the same and that there is one route to success. Two early contributions, which broke the mould, are undoubtedly Donald Schön's 1983 book, *The Reflective Practitioner*, and David Maister's work, especially his 1993 book, *Managing the Professional Service Firm*. Yet there are many important issues that remain to be explored in the first place or in greater depth, and this book aims to make a contribution to that development. Diversity in firm structure, strategy and tactical practice are evident in the market, which I have aimed to reflect in the contributions presented here.

My motivation is a long-standing interest in the management of firms in the built environment by direct experience and through academic research, including a period of over ten years working in professional practices, especially architects and design consultants. The more immediate motivation is teaching on masters courses a module called, *Managing the Professional Practice*, and it is for those students that this book is particularly dedicated as they represent the next generation of practice founders and senior management in their countries and around the increasingly globalised professional consultants in the built environment.

At the time of writing, the professions in the built environment have been experiencing one of the worst global downturns, yet are on the cusp of the upturn. Management will be looking to develop further depth to their services or grow their practices or even both by the one leading to the other. The shape in which practices entered the downturn, especially in resources terms, heavily influences the scope for development into the upturn. The vision that management have for the future will prove critical in relation to the value demanded and desired by clients and other stakeholders. How these combine to locate the market position of each practice will be important for each organisation and will aggregate with other practices to shape the professional practice by size, location, market segments and discipline.

H.S.
London, UK

About the authors

Summary details are provided about each author, arranged in alphabetical order.

Professor Antti Ainamo is part of the Department of Social Research, University of Turku in Finland.

James Barrett works as a change consultant and was the Knowledge Transfer Associate, UCL, working with engineers Silcock Dawson.

Professor Tim Dixon is Director of the Oxford Institute for Sustainable Development and Professor of Real Estate at the Department of Real Estate and Construction Management, School of the Built Environment, Oxford Brookes University.

Andrew Edkins is Senior Lecturer in the Bartlett School of Construction and Project Management, the Faculty of the Built Environment, UCL, London.

Junko Iwaya, of Yoshinobu Ashihara Architects & Associates in Tokyo, is a former architect at Nightingale Associates in London.

Miles Keeping is Director and Head of Sustainability at real estate consultants GVA Grimley.

Sofia Kioussi undertook research and her Masters in Project and Enterprise Management with UCL, joined ISV, with particular responsibilities for marketing, and is currently a practising architect and project manager in Athens.

Larry Malcic is Design Director for international architects HOK in their London practice.

Beatrice Manzoni is in the Department of Management, University Bocconi in Italy, and is undertaking a PhD in the Bartlett School of Construction and Project Management, the Faculty of the Built Environment, UCL, London.

Kate McGhee is an independent strategy & research consultant and, at the time of writing, was a client director at the brand consultants, BPRI, which is part of WPP plc.

Robert McIntosh is Executive Director for CB Richard Ellis Hotels Asia Pacific.

Andrew McSmythurs is Director of Project Management at cost consultants, Cyril Sweet.

Jim Meikle was formerly a partner of Davis Langdon LLP, establishing their management consultancy division. He is currently a non-executive director of AMA and a member of a number of UK industry bodies. He is a visiting professor in the Bartlett School of Construction and Project Management, UCL.

Makoto Nanbuya works with Okada & Associates, architects, engineers and planners in Tokyo.

Mike Nightingale is founder of healthcare and education architects, Nightingale Associates.

Shinichi Okada works with Okada & Associates, architects, engineers and planners in Tokyo.

Dr Stephen Pryke is Senior Lecturer and Course Director for the MSc in Project and Enterprise Management in the School of Construction and Project Management, the Bartlett Faculty of the Built Environment, UCL, London.

Kathy Roper is Associate Professor and Chair of Integrated Facility Management, Georgia Institute of Technology, School of Building Construction, Atlanta.

David Shiers is Senior Lecturer and Researcher, Department of Real Estate and Construction in School of the Built Environment, Oxford Brookes University.

Dr Ken Shuttleworth founded Make Limited in 2004, having built up a considerable portfolio of experience as a partner at Foster and Partners, and is a visiting professor at De Montfort University and Nottingham School of Architecture, and a member of several public and private design review panels.

Dr Hedley Smyth is Senior Lecturer in the Bartlett School of Construction and Project Management, the Faculty of the Built Environment, UCL, London.

David Stanford was one of the founding directors of Geoffrey Reid Associates and is currently a group director of 3DReid, responsible for integration and continuous improvement across the practice.

Professor Jeremy Watson, Global Research Director at Arup, a global firm of engineers, designers and planners, is responsible for Arup's Research Strategy. He is Chief Scientific Advisor to the Department of Communities & Local Government.

Professor Graham Winch is Professor of Project Management and Director of the Centre for Research on the Management of Projects at the Manchester Business School, University of Manchester.

Introduction

Aims

There are few books exploring this topic of managing the professional practice. Those that exist have tended to set out some general guiding principles for the professions or for a particular discipline. Thorny issues and major challenges cannot always be adequately addressed in this way. Many of the major management decisions arise from the specific internal characteristics of practices and from the contextual circumstances that practices are operating within at the time. This book addresses many of these topics, such as the step-changes associated with growth, developing capacity as a large international practice, the succession problem as founders retire and securing the future for the next generation. It also addresses issues that are sometimes misperceived, frequently poorly understood and inadequately managed, such as marketing, the development of technical knowledge and innovation, and core competencies.

Most senior practice managers are from their operational discipline. They have not been extensively educated or trained in management. This is both a strength and a weakness. Large practices employ experts in support, yet it is the architect, engineer, surveyor, project manager and so on who form the core of most decision-making in managing the professional practice. It is hoped that this book makes a contribution to inform better management for the current generation of reflective practitioners and for the future generation of founders and senior managers who are about to embark on their careers.

The management of the professions or the management of particular disciplines have tended to treat firms as homogeneous. Individual firms are different, the differences frequently giving rise to the degree of comparative success and to fitting into the markets in which they operate. Firms are also different within their boundaries. The market profile may not always echo the internal operations, and the organisational culture may have several hues across teams, functions or offices, and so on. Therefore one **aim** of this book is to embrace the diversity of management across the professions and in the disciplines within the built environment. There are different ways in which professional practices can successfully manage themselves, management approaches being part of the palette for differentiating the practice. Differentiation embraces two possibilities:

1. Management to help manage the market so as to avoid or minimise the extent of competition.
2. Management to help effectiveness and efficiency so as to be more competitive than the competition.

A second **aim** of this book is to consider the management of particular aspects of professional practices by function rather than discipline. In other words, rather than dealing with the ideas of being good engineers within a discipline or of improving design management, the functional focus of the book is managing tangible and intangible resources, managing marketing, managing social capital; hence, also managing such issues as innovation, collaboration or branding.

A third **aim** of this book is embodied in the title. 'Managing' is dynamic and thus is in flux and under constant review. Both internal and external issues impact upon the way in which firms evolve consciously and unconsciously. An aim of management is to be more aware of this dynamic and its impact. Whilst intuitive responses frequently work well, the danger is being ill-informed or reactive using poor judgement. Informed decisions that combine intuitive experience with conscious appraisal are more likely to succeed in the long run. Managing the professional practice involves assessing whether intuitive responses are appropriate, whether previous solutions still apply and what new measures are needed that are robust under emergent conditions.

The diversity of management practice and options cited above implies that there are distinctive practices. Founders of new practices tend to wish to mould the practice in their image, as this is what feels comfortable. Established practices tend to copy the success of others, being far less adventurous and more risk-averse. It is getting a balance between applying what is tested and introducing the new that is important. Moulding a practice in your own image does not necessarily mean that it will be successful in the market. Copying what others do may lead to losing ground against those competitors who anticipate new trends and forge their market position more rigorously. In other words, celebrating the diversity of management in the professional practice is not a relativist argument that 'anything goes'. There are distinctive management approaches that prove significant. There are patterns of general management activity that endure for particular disciplines, markets and professional conditions. These can be copied and adapted to both serve practice efficiency and serve the distinct elements that make practices effective. In other words, the general and the particular need moulding, arising from internal and external factors. It is the moulding that gives rise to the distinctive profile of each firm and its success in the market. It is hoped that this book will provide a set of academic and practitioner chapters that are a rich source of experience from professional practice. The book cannot provide a substitute for experience in the field, but it can enrich our understanding so that decisions in the future are informed by, and improved as a result of, the experience of others.

Management operates at a number of levels. Culture, strategic planning and decision-making, formal systems and procedures, tactical actions, and finally informal routines and norms, which both emanate from and inform the culture provide the levels and their interaction are all part of the management domain. The discipline provides the reason to be. Institutes and professional certifications provide guidance on the discipline. Marketing provides the strategy to secure the work, finance the oil in the wheels and enables the people to do the work. Legal and other issues are added in, but the discipline of operation, marketing, financial control and human resources are essential elements without which survival is impossible. Even practices that do not seem to overtly take one or all of these seriously – for example marketing – have implicit strategies and tactical implementation. The danger is that the lack of awareness of what they do may leave them vulnerable to competition, eroding profitability. Explicit awareness and understanding are important. Those in business primarily for profit, rather than love of the discipline per se, tend to be more aware of management issues. Yet to be primarily motivated by profit means that the firm must be good at their discipline to survive and seek to reinforce success through management functions. Those in business primarily for the love of their discipline must be good at management in order to be able to keep on being an architect, cost consultant, engineer and so on. Management is unavoidable. Management should be an important strength for any practice, yet it can act as a constraint. The aim is therefore to ensure that it is a strength that improves operations whether the main motivator is the love for the work or the desire to be highly profitable.

This book therefore aims to provide some means and guidance to strengthen managing the professional practice in the realm of the built environment.

Objectives

This book will explore some of the key issues of managing the professional practice for the built environment. Given the remit already set out, it is impossible to cover every aspect of management or every approach to management. The objectives are to provide sufficient information and analysis to inspire and guide professionals setting up or running their practices. There are a number of issues that are addressed in this book, for example the structure of the professions in the built environment, with practices typically being smaller than their counterparts in other sectors.

Two **objectives** are particularly important: managing practices in their totality and managing particular processes within practices, and these are covered in **Sections** I and II respectively; different practitioner chapters in **Section III** cover both objectives. **Section III** meets a further **objective**, that is, to combine theoretical exploration and conceptual exposition with practice as experienced on the ground. Thus, the book covers theoretical analysis and empirical research and is combined with experiential reflection. Thus, academics and leading practitioners in their fields have written chapters. The chapters from industry are supplemented by **postscript comments** from academics to provide some analytical support and locate the experience in the broader industry and management literature. In this way, it is hoped that the book provides a depth of analysis and insight.

The focus is upon established practices, particularly growing practices and large ones operating in both national and international markets. These are the ones where management is most critical, because more sophisticated forms and approaches are needed. Growing practices move from implicit to explicit forms of management, as founders no longer have the span of control to manage by example or direct guidance. These issues are particularly important for certain groups. The book is primarily targeted to the next generation of practice founders and management, to today's reflective practitioner and to the research community. It will therefore appeal to researchers, postgraduate students, some final year students as they graduate and pursue professional qualification and to the ambitious professional who wishes to have an informed and rounded view of their sphere of work.

The content

The book is divided into two halves. The academic contributions make up the first half, which is subdivided into **Sections** I and II, covering management of the practice totality and managing particular processes within practices in sequence. The practitioner contributions make up the second half, **Section III**.

Sections I and II are those with an emphasis upon managing the organisation as a whole. The section gives an overview by providing insight into the scope and context of managing the professional practice.

Chapter 1 addresses markets, organisational structures and relationship issues across the sector that managers address. It explores the way in which market structures are clustered and how practices are differentiated in their structure. The economic forces in the market also shape the ways in which successful practices manage resources over the economic cycle. These combinations of structures in the market and processes over the economic cycle give rise to certain management requirements. According to these internal and external structural factors, and in an interactive way between structure and operations, the degrees of creativity and routinised work are further dimensions that shape management and practice by discipline. A great deal is made of social capital – 'people are our main asset' – in the sector, yet this is infrequently reflected in strategic investment in people and particularly the value arising from relationships and how these are managed. The focus upon discipline can lead to overlooking how people create and add service value, which provides the final theme of this chapter.

In **Chapter 2**, Graham Winch addresses the economic leverage amongst architectural practices to survive and to compete as firms in markets of project ecology and globalisation of services. This concerns inputs, for example in the form of staff and suppliers of subcontracted work, and also deals with serving different types of international clients. These trends are explored according to a management model that characterises architectural practices along two axes: *project complexity* and *quality preference*. The analysis is illustrated with a series of vignettes from international and local practices, mainly from the USA and across Europe. The analysis brings into focus a series of important issues, including the outsourcing of design and production information given emergent ICT, BIM and parametric design capabilities, the role of the management in relation to professional values especially for the large global practices and ownership forms, and the tactics used to tackle recession through economic leverage by size of firm and staff leverage.

Antti Ainamo theoretically considers cross-functional working in design teams. In **Chapter 3**, he draws upon the work of others where design is considered the 'product'. He brings a perspective from research on design in information and telecommunications, retail and fashion design, conceptually exploring these lessons in the context of engineering and consulting services. The chapter especially explores creativity in participative structures and the role of marketing and design-led approaches to facilitating the process. Whilst architecture and engineering practices in the built environment follow design-led structures in the main, the marketing dimension is more challenging and this links with the findings presented in **Chapter 7**.

Growing from a small-to-medium-sized engineering consultancy to a large-scale player provides the focus for **Chapter 4**. Andrew Edkins, James Barrett and Hedley Smyth explore the human resource aspects in making a step-change. Organisational stretch is necessary, yet it can lead to a reduction of quality; and expansion too brings with it issues of maintaining the culture and coherence of quality delivery that have provided the basis for past success and for sustaining future growth. Selecting and inducting new staff are key issues, but retention and development of existing staff are also vitally important in periods of expansion, requiring careful management. Silcock Dawson, a multi-office firm of UK building services consulting engineers, provides a case-study example.

In **Chapter 5**, David Shiers, Tim Dixon and Miles Keeping consider some of the far-reaching practice management implications of sustainability issues. Sustainability can be construed as an operational issue but it fits best in **Section II**. The chapter teases out matters that have more fundamental implications, that is beyond the issues the significance of which are therefore more strategic than much management has yet to embrace, in other words how practices are managed as well as the environmentally related service per se. They review sustainability practices and legislation, placing them in the institutional context of the Royal Institution of Chartered Surveyors (RICS), corporate social responsibility (CSR) and whole-life-cost service issues, and look at implementation through a case study.

Section II covers issues at a more detailed level. **Chapters 6 to 9** address particular issues that are more concerned with managing operational processes from strategic and tactical perspectives.

Chapter 6 is by Beatrice Manzoni, who addresses the performance of architects in project teams. She selects architecture practices undertaking competitions as her focus and the Italian market in particular for conducting her research. She explores a series of factors, including age, nationality and reputation of the architects or practices involved, which might be expected to be critical to performance according to the literature. She examines these in the field, finding that the age of the practice is not a good predictor for success in competition entry. Local firms are still the most successful, despite trends towards internationalisation and 'strong idea' firms or 'archistars' from one location competing or entering alliances to compete in other locations. Therefore the 'strong ambition practice' is not a function of age or practice longevity (cf. **Chapter 2** by Graham Winch), thus further work is needed to open this 'black box' of keys to success in competitions.

Chapter 7 handles the intangible issue of client identification and endeavours to articulate the processes that lead to clients identifying with the designs and architecture practices. Hedley Smyth and Sofia Kioussi examine how client identification relates to brand and relationship marketing and management. Reputation and brand emanate from the designs produced by the practice. Clients that identify with the reputation and the brand are drawn to practices and individual architects. Commissioned designs will reinforce this process, but further identification is induced through the relationships built up between the architects and their clients. Relationship marketing tends to be implicit and poorly understood by architects, especially in 'strong idea' practices. Managing market reputation and hence the brand is therefore not merely a matter of developing robust relationship marketing processes, but relationship management is also a means for improving design.

Chapter 8 is by Kathy Roper, who considers the facilities manager practitioner. Facilities management sometimes lies in the grey area between being a pure consultant in the sense of acting as an advisor or contractor management consultant and being a direct provider of operational services. Does it neatly fit into the category of professional? Certainly, there has been a drive to professionalise the service and secure institutional recognition in a growing number of countries. However, the 'grey areas' are also deliberately configured through alliances in order to serve particular market needs as Kathy Roper sets out in her exposition of being lean and creative in competitive markets in terms of cost and quality. She explores three avenues in particular: client–contractor relationships; cost minimisation and value maximisation; and managing scope creep with a customer-service orientation.

In **Chapter 9**, Stephen Pryke revisits innovation in quantity surveying. He provides a review of conceptual approaches to innovation and then reviews practice in two stages. First he summarises previous work conducted on innovation in the QS practice. He then considers developments of recent years, particularly those that have led to service diversification and the increasing disjuncture between innovation in practice and the role of the professional institution. A primary conclusion is that innovation is becoming a key source of survival in the current recession, and that this contrasts with common wisdom that it is a costly source of competitive advantage.

Section III reflects upon practice. The remaining chapters are by practitioners, each with a 'postscript comment' from an academic, to place the practical reflection in a wider theoretical context, including the relevant literature to facilitate a deeper understanding of the conceptual issues being faced in practice.

Ken Shuttleworth, founder of *Make architects*, addresses creativity in the design studio and, in particular, how this is managed and enhanced through an architecture practice, which has been set up as a trust, where all the employees are owners of the practice. This is the focus of **Chapter 10**. With considerable high-profile international experience in architecture over a long period of time, it is a challenge to adopt a completely different management model. The chapter commences by setting down the aims and values envisaged from the start of the company and goes on to show these have effected ways of working both at a practice level – for example how reduced workloads can be managed under such a structure – and at studio level in terms of design. Working in and for the broader community is also addressed in the chapter, linking the practice aims and design operations. A **postscript comment** is provided by Graham Winch, who points out some of the issues that the practice will face as it grows and tries to retain leverage in the marketplace.

Larry Malcic in **Chapter 11** outlines the issues faced in design for an international practice. A small executive group, based in San Francisco, provides the overall strategic values and objectives, in which the regional offices operate. The London office of HOK covers the European, African and Middle East regions. Each local office is encouraged to operate as an entity, yet processes are in place to encourage sharing of expertise and staff across the region. Larry Malcic describes a fairly fluid process of creativity, where the practice aims to put negotiated outcomes ahead of efficiency. This is a matrix organisation, although perhaps looser than the traditional understanding of 'matrix' as a system whereby the horizontal and bottom-up negotiation is core to the creative process. Beatrice Manzoni provides a **postscript comment** that considers the challenges to a global design practice in producing good design for its markets. The first challenge is about design to embed a building in its local context. The second challenge is related to ways of coordinating work to maintain creativity.

Arup has been significant in design and technology innovation and development over a long period. Jeremy Watson considers innovation in construction and professional practices in particular in **Chapter 12**. Through reviewing the sector and influences from other sectors he sets out the ways that professional practices innovate, and ways in which they can increase their role as innovators technically, of products and services, thus adding to the trend of diversified services provided by consultants, especially at the upper levels of the market – see also **Chapter 9** by Stephen Pryke. Jeremy Watson also provides examples of innovations that have started with particular initiatives and projects, yet have proved to have broader application both as creators of value for clients and as sources of income streams for the professional firm. Antti Ainamo provides a **postscript comment**, exploring how creative engineering capabilities are important for architects to realise their creative aesthetic ambitions and the management challenges of maximising capabilities and transferring them into broader application.

The balanced scorecard has become a popular means to manage activities, ranging from projects to companies. In **Chapter 13** Andrew McSmythurs demonstrates how a firm of cost management consultants employs the balanced scorecard approach across the business of cost consultants Cyril Sweett, and in particular how the approach operates within the project management division for which he has responsibility. He takes both a top-down and bottom-up approach in the sense that, on the one hand, the approach provides general guidance and a model within which performance is monitored and strategic decisions taken, and on the other hand the activities of the division contribute to guidance on operational performance and resources to be managed, especially cashflow for the business as a whole. These top-down and bottom-up management process are mirrored at the project management divisional level for projects and clients. Stephen Pryke considers the strategic and leadership implications from a socio-psychological perspective in his **postscript comment**.

Robert McIntosh of CB Richard Ellis examines capacity development in an emergent market in **Chapter 14**. Charged with responsibility for developing specialist hotel consultant services for the Asia Pacific region he examines the options for so doing, the location from which to coordinate the service and constituting the service that extends beyond development and investment valuation and appraisal to in-depth understanding of the hotel and related business environment and the range of business models applicable. Capacity is being developed using existing staff in the region and drawing upon global expertise within the firm from other offices. Capacity development therefore involves core competencies arising out of multidisciplinary team working that cut across traditional service silos. David Shiers and Hedley Smyth provide the **postscript comment**, which analyses the underlying issues of building capacity, especially issues of culture, competency development and decision-making routines.

Kate McGhee writes about the importance of branding from the perspective of BPRI, a brand research organisation that is part of the WPP advertising and media group. **Chapter 15** therefore looks into the realm of built environment professions as a dispassionate observer, drawing attention to the lack of focus on branding in this sector in management terms and the benefits of taking brand management as part of a practice business model. Brand originates with the reputation of the service, yet is also part of who the practice are. Going on to manage branding is part of who the management are and Kate McGhee shows that it is a matter of mindset that is a primary barrier to explicit management. It is this lack of awareness of practitioners that is picked up by Hedley Smyth in the **postscript comment** and is placed in the wider domain of marketing and market management.

Mike Nightingale, founder of the healthcare, education and science architects Nightingale Associates, provides, in **Chapter 16**, a personal account of the vision and entrepreneurial mission to develop a practice from scratch to a leader in its field. The account shows the value of practice role models and previous personal experience for the new practice. It also shows the importance of contextual issues that, whilst specific to time and circumstance, are faced by all new practices in their own way. The overall management lesson is the way in which entrepreneurial vision is combined with, and harnesses, experience in the circumstances to shape a successful practice. The consistency of application has led in the case of Nightingale Associates to establishing a leading UK practice that is rapidly internationalising with the support of its parent at the time of writing, Tribal plc. **Postscript comment** is provided by Andrew Edkins, who poses alternative growth strategies of being corporate in approach or cloning offices and 'franchised' entrepreneurial units. Adhering to the core values, the practice chose a more corporate approach, first through organic growth, second through acquisition and third by aligning with a larger enterprise.

Chapter 17 comes from Shinichi Okada and Makoto Nanbuya (translated by Junko Iwaya). They describe the approach of Okada & Associates to the master planning and design of a large hospital project in Tokyo. In Japan, long-term business-to-business relationships are commonplace, yet this project has longevity in national terms. The management of the office for this project (and other projects) is set out in the chapter, covering design, resource and marketing dimensions of management. In his **postscript comment** Andrew Edkins covers three areas: how the work for the client constitutes the management of a programme, the significant role of relationships in delivering complex projects within the programme; and the challenge of managing knowledge, particularly imparting tacit knowledge within the practice.

In **Chapter 18**, David Stanford, a director of 3DReid architects, explores the thorny issue of succession when the founder and major shareholder retires from a practice. This is frequently an ill-considered issue but is best tackled in principle from set-up. He suggests that there are three options. Ownership remaining with the founders even though they have retired is one option. A second is the transfer of ownership to the practice, for example through a management buy-out, setting up an employee trust or share ownership scheme. The third option is to transfer ownership outside the practice. This was the option pursued by Reid Architecture in the acquisition and merger with 3D to form 3DReid. The chapter continues by developing some of the issues addressed in integrating the two practices, for example cultural fit, systems and procedures, and communications. A **postscript comment** is provided by Hedley Smyth, who places this case in a wider context to explore how such changes affect the market position and culture of the organisation in ways that will change the practice but may threaten its ability to compete.

In **Chapter 19**, Jim Meikle takes a look at how one professional service firm, Davis Langdon, developed at the end of the last century and into the new one. Davis Langdon grew to be the largest quantity surveying and cost consultant practice, diversifying the range of their services as they grew. Mergers and acquisitions were a major component of that growth and a part of the continuing consolidation and growth of firm size at the top end of the professional market. The **postscript comment** is provided by Hedley Smyth, who considers the importance of large multidisciplinary practices with global reach having a base in the leading world cluster for the professional practices in London.

The **Conclusion** tackles a selection of key issues distilled from the book and presents them as overarching issues that managers of the professional practice and the research community respectively could probably find themselves addressing over the coming years. These could even be issues that they should address as the book provides a weight of evidence that can be used to suggest this.

Overview in Scope and Context of Managing the Professional Practice

1 Structures, management and markets

Hedley Smyth

Introduction

The professions have a long history, including clerics, medics and lawyers, with varied modern origins, for example in the western part of the globe in the nineteenth century. Modern professional practice is typically defined by exclusive expertise captured in a body of knowledge (BoK). Such bodies are usually regulated institutionally and prescribe values, including:

- trustworthiness;
- formal association, certification and registration with the relevant professional body;
- serving the public interest.

The knowledge and codes of professional conduct provide a basis for operation that in many other areas of industry and practice would need to be established through management within the organisation (cf. Mintzberg, 1979).

The built environment professions, the focus of this book, are similar in these respects. Architects, engineers including various specialisations, surveyors in various forms and land use planners are established disciplines recognised by the institutional arrangements described, although the planning profession largely has its origins in the public sector activity rather than commercial activity, although recent times have seen a growth in private professional practice in this discipline. Project management and facilities management are emergent professions. For project management, there are several BoKs – for example the project execution emphasis of the Project Management Institute's PMBoK®, the more strategic BoKs of the Association of Project Management and the International Project Management Association and the Japanese ENAA demonstrate a diversity of approaches and BoKs that are

Managing the Professional Practice: in the built environment, First Edition. Edited by Hedley Smyth.
© 2011 by Blackwell Publishing Ltd. Published 2011 by Blackwell Publishing Ltd.

'thin' compared to those of medicine or architecture. Therefore, practice is dynamic and diverse according to the maturity of the profession, and is also affected by the regulatory and market conditions by nation and professional institution.

In recent decades there has been a crisis in the professions, which has been evident within the built-environment professions too. Society has generally become more educated and confident to challenge professional 'expertise' (e.g. O'Neill, 2002a), which is reinforced by a multitasking mentality and a greater 'DIY culture' in some nations. In the built environment, there have been different challenges in different places. In China, for example, large municipal design institutes have been subjected to increasing commercial rigour and have also been evolving new forms of provision. In the UK, as another example, in the late 1980s and throughout the 1990s several changes were of note. The built environment professional fee scales became subject to competitive bidding, perceived poor project management from architects and poor marketing and financial control of professional practice were becoming critical whereby change became inevitable. Architects have narrowed their focus in the UK – as in many countries – on the creative aspects. There has recently been migration 'up the food chain' to put increased emphasis upon master and urban planning amongst some practices. Concurrently traditional quantity surveying practices transitioned to cost consultant and project management activities. Financial management, especially cashflow management, has improved, although marketing remains poorly understood, especially by architects. Human resource management is underdeveloped. Despite the common cry that 'people are our greatest asset', practice does not always match the rhetoric. Investment in people is low, which although understandable given labour market mobility and the multiplicity of firms, is also a real challenge, given how much effort practices make to keep clients compared to keeping good staff. More surprising is the lack of investment in social capital, specifically the knowledge and skills that are spread and embedded across the practice, frequently called core competencies that add value (e.g. Hamel and Prahalad, 1996) and dynamic capabilities that improve effectiveness and efficiency (Teece *et al.*, 1997). This is surprising considering that professional practice is essentially a knowledge-based industry, much of the knowledge being embedded as tacit knowledge and skills derived from experience that comprise competency and core competencies.

These trends have led to less reliance upon professional expertise in the sense of being willing to pay for a basic service, especially where intangibility weakens bargaining positions: the effort and value of the inputs; the awareness of the contribution that the finished facility (outputs) will make to organisational (including household) well being and performance; and the value to wider society as onlooker and end-user. Bargaining positions are not strengthened for practices delivering high value, because added value from intangibles such as tacit knowledge and core competencies are difficult to assess at any time, especially before delivery. This is not helped by clients, even sophisticated ones, who switch from seeking firms with a differentiated focus in boom times, to having a price focus for selection under slump conditions.

New procurement forms have added to the mix over the decades, changing the power relationship between client and professional. Design and build, construction management contracts, various design-build-finance-operate forms of contract, including PFI and PPP contracts, tend to increase contractor power at the expense of the professions.

Yet buildings and built environment facilities are becoming more complex, and client demands more sophisticated. Value, especially added value, is in demand, particularly amongst clients where certain facilities form a vital element for their competitive advantage or public profile. Part of sophistication has been the focus upon accountability, especially performance measures. This is a double-edged sword – essential, yet if dominant over the trustworthiness ascribed to professionals adds to the challenge in that it conveys the message, 'we don't trust you', or as Anora O'Neill stated, 'In the end, the new culture of accountability provides incentives for arbitrary and unprofessional choices' (2002b).

Professionals end up concentrating resources and effort into satisfying key performance indicators (KPIs) rather than delivering what is really required – value and added value. This, coupled with the form filling to be placed on corporate and public sector panels of suppliers, plus satisfying procedures for prequalifying for competitive bids has a net corrosive effect. Whilst it makes reasonable sense for individual orga-nisations to make such demands, the sum adds significantly to costs while margins are forced down by competition. The consequence is higher long-term prices, or compromises in quality – the very thing that clients are trying to reassure themselves about or insure themselves against. One solution is growth of the professional practice into larger companies to obtain economies of scale and scope in managing the growing set of bureaucratic demands, increasing the competence base in breadth and depth to meet complexity requirements and taking advantage of cost differences in different national markets – another notable trend of the past decade or so.

Geographical diversification of large practices has been a major trend, coupled with mergers and acquisitions. The peak of the recent boom saw a considerable number of mergers and takeovers as cash reserves were employed and pooled to increase market penetration and geographical spread. Large multidisciplinary practices have emerged in this trend. A further wave of takeovers has occurred near the bottom of the recession, 2009–10, as well-placed firms, which managed cash flow and built up reserves in the boom are buying up struggling practices, even large ones, as they reposition themselves with higher market share for the return of growth market over the coming years.

This corporatisation of professional practices carries its own problems. Increased market power and reduced national allegiance has the effect of reducing reliance on professional institutional requirements and norms. It also tends to render the firms more self-interested rather than their pursuing independent judgment on behalf of clients (cf. Chapter 2 by Graham Winch). Furthermore, it can distance them from the ethical issue of serving public interest. This is exacerbated by some professional bodies becoming more introverted and thus failing to adequately serve their members' interests, which is not an easy task where the disciplines are redefining their roles, as cited earlier for quantity surveyors in the UK (cf. Ormrod Committee, 1971).

There are a number of general trends – institutional context and the value of professional expertise, deregulation and intensity of competitive forces, new forms of procurement and market power, accountability and trustworthiness, self-interest versus broader stakeholder and societal interests, the importance of social capital and concentration at the top into large practices undertaking increasingly complex projects – that have led to considerable change in the professions, which have been, and are being, expressed in different ways in different regions and nations. These affect the way professional practices are structured and managed and hence operate in the market. The market too affects the management and structuring of professional practice. These trends will continue and be reconfigured as part of change. In other words, an ideal state does not exist, but that is not to say that people should not pursue ideals in their discipline and in managing professional practice. The important point is to be aware of the trends and prevailing conditions, and to pursue goals that will work in the current and emerging context, and that are informed by ideals and aspirations. The chapter will consider each of the main dimensions – markets, structures and relationships, and their implications for management – starting with markets.

Markets and management

Services in general account for 70% of employment and value added in OECD countries (OECD, 2005, cited in Jewel *et al.*, 2010). Growth is concentrated in the G7 countries (Brook, 2008; Jewel *et al.*, 2010). Markets are further clustered into centres of activities.

World clusters

Many sectors of economic activity are concentrated in centres of global excellence, often referred to as world clusters. The most well-known world cluster is probably Silicon Valley in California where expertise in IT development resides. World clusters typically embody forces of competition and cooperation in the market. Being in a climate of creativity, access to expertise in general and the benefits from drawing upon a labour market with specific expertise in domains of specialisation are key factors feeding off each other in self-reinforcing ways.

Where are the world clusters for the built environment professions? Los Angeles, New York, London and Tokyo are consistently recognised as such. Chicago was a key location but has lost a premier position, whilst Shanghai is arguably in the ascendancy. As will be argued below, world clusters are not defined by large international firms located in one place, although it is instructive to cite Knox and Taylor (2005) on the location of international architecture firms, who show London as the dominant location with nearly twice the score from their calculations of New York, with San Francisco, Singapore and Los Angeles following and Tokyo ninth; and, according to ENR data, over the past decade the UK generally has consistently captured 12–13% of the international design market in the built environment (Hetherington, 2008). Attention has also been drawn to detailed design and production information being undertaken in branch offices or outsourced to other practices in low-cost international locations (Tombesi, 2001; Tombesi *et al.*, 2003; see also Chapter 2 by Graham Winch).

The reasons for geographical clusters in the built environment include:

- regional and national-level competitive advantages based on world cities as both strong domestic markets and links to global markets;
- network effects of each location as global financial hubs and skill concentration based upon cultural factors of creativity and communities of practice.

For example, London, as a cluster, was thought to finance, design or project manage up to 25% of global projects (Ive and Winch, 1999). Based upon ENR data (1999), they estimated 19 of the top 200 design professions were located in New York, and 12 were located in London. Therefore, the location of the projects is secondary to the mobilisation of resources to service and realise projects in the world cities and across the globe. Changes in technology and corporate strategy of leading multinationals in this sector tend to increase the proportion of these activities in the world clusters for the built environment, although the pressure to relocate routine activities, especially production information, to lower-cost locations will increase (Ive, c. 2001). This will potentially create discontinuity of service and may dislocate some key skills and could also inhibit knowledge transfer along the labour market chains that is necessary for maintenance and reinvigoration of the competitive advantage in the longer term. Ive states that much of the training and many of the skills are embodied in employees from overseas. This may be an important inhibiting factor to sustaining the competitive advantage of London in the long run without additional indigenous initiative and capacity development, but reinforces such centres as places to gain experience and enhance résumés or curriculum vitae amongst each new generation of professionals.

Evidence of innovation within professional firms, specifically the top 25 cost management consultants, was recently tested for the London cluster. A total range of innovation was present, and collaboration between the practices and service providers to them was found to be significant, although purely confined to very specific areas and organisations. Surprisingly, very few innovations were driven through clients, professional institutions and the influence of competitors (Page *et al.*, 2003), a factor confirmed in revisiting this issue (see Chapter 9 by Stephen Pryke).

The health and future success of these clusters for the built environment is therefore economically dependent upon the following factors:

1. Cluster factors:
    - The ability of firms to exploit their respective markets.
    - The ability to develop their capacity and competencies through a comprehensive set of integrated networks – project networks, communities of practice and industrial networks, which create links in the cluster yet also linkages beyond the immediate cluster.
2. Regional factors:
    - The development of the economic, institutional and social infrastructure to support the clusters for the built environment.
    - The maintenance of each cluster as a world city.

These factors are closely related, requiring the institutional bridge-building that adds value to the existing institutional structures, personal networks and discipline networks, including communities of practice (Wenger, 1998). The cluster factors are worked out through a combination of competition in the market, both on the broad scale and amongst themselves, and collaboration. Profitability, market share and other performance measures are all outcomes of successful innovation, application of knowledge and judgement, and other activities that add value. Collaboration is facilitated through networks, professional and trade bodies, as well as through research and higher education institutions. The scope of collaboration is limited within a cluster by the resources available and by market functions. Resource constraints in the market are not the only ones. Competitive advantage from the perspective of the firm is also a limiting factor. Many firms, especially some the internationally prominent consultants, believe that they must protect their market position and knowledge. Competitive advantage is quickly eroded and the lifespan of factors of advantage has been decreasing over recent years, as innovations become generic solutions and later

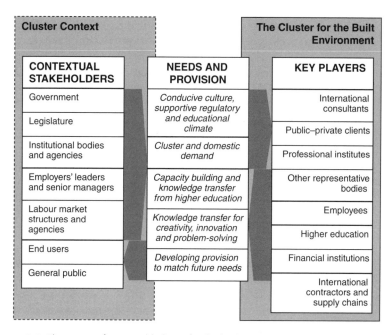

Figure 1.1 The context for a world cluster for the built environment

routinised applications. However, the most powerful players are inter-nationalising through organic growth and acquisitions to have a major office in several of the world clusters.

A world cluster does not simply comprise practices undertaking global projects. A wider infrastructure is required beyond these players and the institutional context, including SME consultants, international construc-tion groups, specialist employment agencies, financial institutions and agencies lending in the project/built environment sectors and strategic higher education linkages. High levels of knowledge transfer are needed within practices, between practices, through the employment market, imported from outside and via higher education institutions – see Figure 1.1.

Size of professional practices

Why are built environment professional firms typically smaller than other professional practices, such as law and accountancy? Is it a management or market factor? It is partly a function of market size and demand patterns, but it is also a management issue as will be explored in the next section. As a market, demand is less for the built environment professions than for many other professions, for example medical and accountancy professional services. Demand is also lumpy and subject to greater severity in booms and slumps compared to accountancy and legal services, which experience reasonably high demand levels even in a recession. The effects of boom and slumps are developed further below.

It is also a function of the demands of managing creativity and problem-solving. Management requires shorter spans of control to manage resources, whilst teams need flat structures of intense interaction and knowledge sharing to generate high-quality creative inputs and to lever tacit knowledge in problem-solving for complex tasks and project working in environments of high levels of complexity and uncertainty. This is characterised by the studio model in architecture, which contrasts with the more routinised practices of accountancy where departments and teams are large and management operates with large spans of control, or the more independent and cellular activities of legal firms where work is more self-regulating in management terms. These management dimensions are also developed further below.

Built environment professional practices continue to grow as projects become more complex. Growth occurs both organically and through acquisition. Acquisition achieves economies of scale and scope. Geographical diversification within a discipline and diversification by acquiring specialist areas of expertise as well as by discipline are commonplace. Acquisitions are presented as mergers of practices or takeovers. In practice, all mergers tend to become takeovers as certain cultural norms and management practices emerge as dominant by default if not by design post-merger. Table 1.1 is a snapshot of engineering-related takeovers and mergers reported at the peak of the boom at the upper end of the market in the UK in order to illustrate the prevalence of this type of activity.

Some practices pursue takeovers as a keystone of growth, for example Atkins and Scott Wilson (Table 1.1), and WSP in the UK. Takeovers are particularly pursued towards, and at, the peak of booms. Professional practices are essentially cash generators in financial terms, therefore reserves and liquidity are high as economic growth conditions prevail, provided that owners do not draw down profit and dividends to the maximum limits. Practices may sell to other firms for several reasons, some of the main ones being (i) the succession problem where existing partners or shareholders cannot, or do not want to, buy out principal equity owners as they leave or retire – a particular problem amongst architects (see Chapter 18 by David Stanford); (ii) where partners or directors wish to pay themselves at a premium rate yet want cash injection to survive and go to the next stage of development; (iii) where privately owned companies would rather be acquired by another private organisation rather become a public company for the next growth phase; and (iv) where practices are weak in the market through overstretched management, overextending their financial reach.

Takeovers are not only prevalent at the peak of the market. They commonly occur at the bottom of the slump and into the upturn, as financially strong practices acquire weaker ones in order to build market

Table 1.1 Engineering growth by takeover and merger reported 2007

Acquiring company	Acquired company
AKS Ward	two civil and engineering practices
Atkins	MSL Engineering and Mantrix Associates
Bay Associates	Supporta plc (in 2006)
Black & Veatch	Gleeson
Blyth and Blyth	Cowan & Linn
Building Research Establishment (BRE)	Building Performance Group
Capita Symonds	Church Lukas and Ruddle Wilkinson Architects
George Hutchinson Associates	Livingston Gunn Projects
Gwynedd Consultancy	Gwynedd Council consulting and maintenance services (2006)
Hyder	Bettridge Turner, Munich Project, Cresswells Associates and ACLA
Hill International	Knowles (2006)
McAdam Design	Geodelft Environmental
Mott MacDonald	Pettit
Mouchel Parkman	Ewan Group, Honagold & Hills and Traffic Support
Nolan Associates	Erinaceous Group
RPS Group	Burks Green, Ecos Consulting, Harper Somers O'Sullivan and Thonger Safety Associates
Scott Wilson	Roscoe Postle Associates, Ferguson McIlveen, Cameron Taylor Grant DGP
Strainstall Group	Soil Dynamics (Malaysia) and The Railway Engineering Group
TPS	Carillion's consultancy business
White Young Green	Adams Kara Taylor, JC Warnock, Tweeds, Nolan Ryan, Trench Farrow and Farningham McCreadle

Source: *New Civil Engineer*, 2007.

share. At the time of writing a series of these acquisitions is in train, particularly characterised by large US conglomerate consultant groups acquiring large national and international practices in other locations.

Management over the economic cycle – booms and slumps

One of the keys to sound financial management of professional practices is the management of resources against the boom–slump cycle – see Figure 1.2. Professional practices are not typically asset-rich organisations; they are typically cash generators. Cashflow management is therefore the key discipline, which includes the creation and management of cash reserves. The experience during the growth phase of the economic cycle is one of the most difficult phases to manage because success here will largely determine the ability to survive the downturn and to grow market share emerging from the slump. This growth phase is characterised by very healthy cashflows. The minimum requirement is to divide the cash into three: (i) replenish the working capital for the current workload, (ii) invest in continuing expansion, and (iii) take

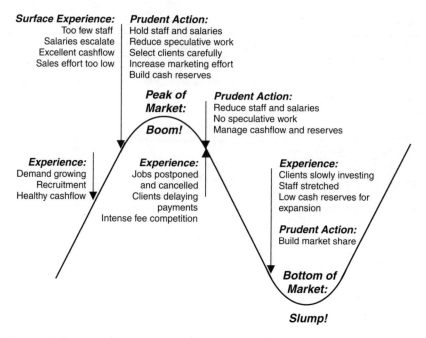

Surface Experience:
Too few staff
Salaries escalate
Excellent cashflow
Sales effort too low

Prudent Action:
Hold staff and salaries
Reduce speculative work
Select clients carefully
Increase marketing effort
Build cash reserves

**Peak of
Market:**

Boom!

Prudent Action:
Reduce staff and salaries
No speculative work
Manage cashflow and reserves

Experience:
Demand growing
Recruitment
Healthy cashflow

Experience:
Jobs postponed
and cancelled
Clients delaying
payments
Intense fee competition

Experience:
Clients slowly investing
Staff stretched
Low cash reserves for
expansion

Prudent Action:
Build market share

**Bottom of
Market:**

Slump!

Figure 1.2 Practice management over the economic cycle

profits (or pay the owners high salaries and declare less profit). A fourth consideration is an important requirement for long-term success, namely the creating of sizeable cash reserves in the forthcoming period and setting up of a sinking fund to survive the inevitable slump. This will require moderating the profit-taking. It will also have an impact upon the ability to expand. Both are good things, especially moderating expansion because this becomes more expensive and efficiency drops simply because staff become more expensive, and hiring new recruits often means taking on people who are less productive or less skilled, owing to pressures in the labour market (cf. Bayer and Gann, 2006). It also has the consequence of being more critical as to which clients and which projects to take on, but as many practices take on clients that are overextending themselves towards the peak of the cycle, this can lead to fewer bad debts or underpayments.

Just before the peak of the cycle, when competitors are expanding, it is hard to rein in expenditure by freezing expansion of staff numbers, to hold staff salaries at reasonable rates and to withdraw from or substantially reduce speculative work (or demand payment at cost). The significance of this is prudent action that is arguably a matter of integrity and definitely a matter of ease of management. When the downturn comes, it is easier to manage reductions in staff numbers, pay freezes and cuts, and morale of those still in employment if the practice is not perceived as having been cavalier at the peak of the boom. It is also less expensive so less of a drain on the cash reserves as cashflow will be in a better position than that of peer practices.

If it is hard to rein in expenditure just before the peak, then it is even more difficult to know when the peak is coming – 97% of the top UK consultants were recruiting in 2007 (Building, 2007). The answer to this usually lies outside the built environment sectors. Although they are usually involved in the downturn in some central way, the signs of a pending downturn can usually be seen elsewhere. There are normally economic indicators and commentators that highlight emergent problems in some other markets; for example, there were problems with some financial markets in the recent downturn a year before the sub-prime market induced the 'credit crunch', and some commentators were worried about the hedge fund markets even though they did not end up being part of the substantive problem.

It is essentially better to slightly misjudge the peak and hold costs too early than to leave it later. The practice may lose some profit but this will normally be less than the bad debts and costs incurred by expanding too much and then retreating. There is considerable evidence that down-sizing does less in reducing costs and increasing productivity than expected, and harms morale extensively (McKinley *et al.*, 1995). The practice will have good cash reserves and in the depths of recession some of the core staff you do not wish to lose can be kept. This is not philanthropy but keeps capacity comparatively intact to respond as clients slowly begin to invest and the practice can build market share at the expense of competitors. This is where prudent action towards the peak really pays off towards the end of the slump and into the upturn.

It pays off in two ways. First, there is some capacity to innovate and develop new ways of doing things for the emergent markets. Second and most importantly there is capacity to build market share, which will largely determine success in the coming growth market. Practices struggling financially at this stage will not have this opportunity. And hence, the cycle is complete, but note that positive cashflow will be experienced ahead of the competitors that are not as well managed, and this gives opportunity not only to continue to expand, but also to build up new reserves for the next cycle before others feel the benefits of growth.

Size also affects the ability to manage the boom and slumps. Large firms have more historical experience generally and should be more secure financially. Small firms are more agile. It is the medium-sized professional practice that has less room for manoeuvre (BD Practices, 2009), whose founders may be most tempted to extract too much income in the growth market and have least experience of managing the period near the peak and into the downturn.

Growth can be organic or through acquisition as cited earlier. Whatever path or combination, a matrix describes the options (Figure 1.3), setting out the investment and risk. To this needs to be added the management risk associated with geographical diversification, although this is not such a

	Market penetration	Service diversification
Existing markets	***Market penetration*** Low risk Low investment	***Service diversification*** Medium risk Medium Investment
New markets	***Market diversification*** Medium risk Medium Investment	***Pioneer*** High risk High investment
	Existing service	**New services**

Figure 1.3 Ansoff matrix for growth

problem for many practices where branch offices are given high degrees of relative autonomy compared to many sectors. However, some of the international multidisciplinary practices, growing through acquisitions, such as AECOM or Atkins, face more intense challenges about quality and consistency of service, reputation and branding.

Structures and management

Growth and transition

Growth is seldom smooth. This is not simply a function of market conditions and market management, but also a function of internal management. Most practices undergo growth, a plateau period and subsequent growth. This is due to barriers of management whereby the span of control reaches its limits and new capacity has to be built. Capacity can be built vertically so a new tier of management can coordinate the lower levels or a new team has to be added horizontally with space consequences too. There seem to be plateaus experienced at around 12 people, 30–50 people, 100 staff and 300 staff. It varies according to discipline and the particular span of management control.

   The creative professional practices tend to adopt the studio model of organisation with a shallow hierarchy to allocate resources and a horizontal team beneath to facilitate interaction for creativity and problem-solving. The more routinised the profession the more hierarchy with a larger span of management control there tends to be, so the barriers to expansion tend to be experienced later. All, however, will tend to experience each growth stage similarly – see Table 1.2. At the limits of each stage a crisis is experienced and nascent practices need to emerge as

Table 1.2 Typical experiences of growth

Growth stage	Barrier to growth	Overcoming the barrier
Stage I	Crisis of leadership	Growth through team working
Stage II	Crisis of autonomy	Growth through strategic direction
Stage III	Crisis of control	Growth through delegation
Stage IV	Crisis of bureaucracy	Growth through coordination
Stage V	Crisis of independence	Growth through collaboration

more dominant. While formal structures, systems and procedures support and facilitate transition, in every case it starts with informally asserting new dominant norms and informal routines (cf. Nelson and Winter, 1982).

Structure and coordination

Within the different types of professional practice – flat structures of intense interaction and knowledge sharing to generate high-quality creative inputs and lever tacit knowledge amongst many architects, more routinised activities of accountancy firms with departments operating under large spans of management control, the more independent, cellular activities of legal firms undertaking higher levels of self-regulated work – there are some common elements that are reflected in the way these firms are structured and coordinated. Mintzberg (1979) identified six types of structure with corresponding coordinating mechanisms of management, which has been developed an extended (see Table 1.3), of which the professional bureaucracy is one, but not usually the only one reflected in a professional practice and not always the dominant one. Added to Mintzberg's original conception is the virtual organisation, which recognised the formal rise of virtual organisations through the internet, but also the increasing recognition of informal

Table 1.3 Organisations, structures and management coordination

Organisational type	Structure	Prime coordinating mechanism
Machine organisation	Machine bureaucracy	Standardisation of work processes
Diversified organisation	Divisionalised	Standardisation of outputs
Innovative organisation	Adhocracy	Mutual adjustment
Missionary organisation	Value-based and/or franchise	Standardisation of norms
Entrepreneurial organisation	Simple structure	Direct supervision
Professional organisation	Professional bureaucracy	Standardisation of skills
Virtual organisation	Networks and project teams	Pooling competencies and standardisation of systems

Source: adapted and developed from Mintzberg, 1979.

associations through, for example, industrial networks, communities of practice and temporary multi-organisational teams – see Table 1.3.

Figure 1.4 depicts these structures and mechanisms, based upon an ideal type presented in an organic form: the strategic apex at the top, a middle line of management coordinating technical and discipline related matters (technostructure) and administrative (support staff) inputs, which are then linked to the operational core and underpinned by core values or ideology. Mintzberg (1979) argued in practice firms departed from the idealised type, proposing the first six of the seven types presented in Tables 1.3 and 1.4, and Figure 1.4.

The professional organisational will probably dominate most professional firms, but this is not automatic. Any organisation may therefore exhibit several types to produce certain configurations of coordination that are subject to change and amendments as firms change their plans and react to emerging situations from internal and external factors. The professional firm is one of the types – see Figure 1.4 – where education, training and standards of practice are largely developed outside of the firm through educational as well as professional institutional requirements. Regulation of standards is typically external too:

> *All that training is geared to one goal, the internalization of the set of procedures, which is what makes the structure technically bureaucratic ... But the professional bureaucracy differs markedly from the machine bureaucracy. Whereas the latter generates its own standards – through the technostructure, enforced by its line managers – many of the standards of the professional bureaucracy originate outside its own structure, in the self-governing associations its professionals belong to ... (Mintzberg et al., 1979: 373)*

This induces the standardisation of inputs required for professional competence (knowledge and skills), with the consequence that practice management can be conducted with a 'light touch' compared to many organisations for controlling and coordinating operational activities. Most organisations are characterised by more than one organisational type, one dominant, with another in tandem to provide a combination, which lends some of the unique characteristics to the practice that render it distinctive in the market, so what sorts of combinations are complementary? Many practices start with an entrepreneurial organisation in tandem with the coordinating mechanism of the professional organisation. The entrepreneurial organisation requires direct supervision as a coordinating mechanism made possible because the practice is very small with the entrepreneurial founder not just supervising but deeply involved with the team and tasks – see Figure 1.4 and Table 1.4.

As practices grow, the founder entrepreneur cannot be so deeply involved in most tasks (Stage I, Table 1.2), yet will retain stronger supervisory oversight, assigning day-to-day activities to people

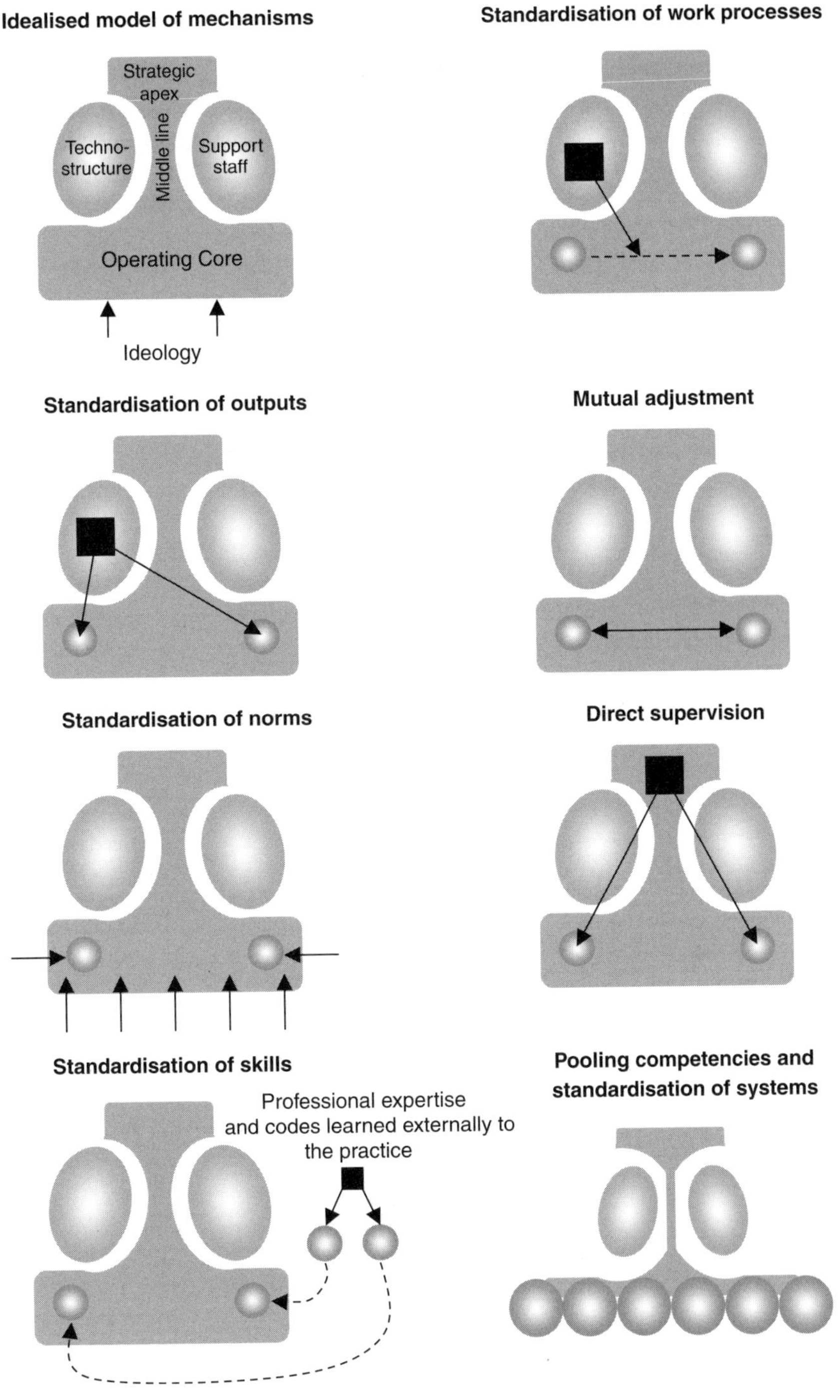

Idealised model of mechanisms

Strategic apex

Middle line

Techno-structure

Support staff

Operating Core

Ideology

Standardisation of work processes

Standardisation of outputs

Mutual adjustment

Standardisation of norms

Direct supervision

Standardisation of skills

Professional expertise and codes learned externally to the practice

Pooling competencies and standardisation of systems

Figure 1.4 Models of organisational structure and coordination

Table 1.4 Organisations, management coordination and decision-making

Organisational type	Prime coordinating mechanism	Decision-making
Machine organisation *Efficiency drivers*	**Standardisation of work processes:** Suitable only for the most routinised markets where tried and tested solutions are required. This is essential to conduct the high-volume, low-margin typical in these markets.	**Procedural:** Flow-line processes are ideal, including the way in which decisions are taken. Control rather than flexibility is important. Compliance to the systems and procedures is seen as essential.
Diversified organisation *Accountability drivers*	**Standardisation of outputs:** Quality and consistency of services across diverse disciplinary areas and across geographical locations.	**Reputation based:** Peer reputation as well as client reputation important in maintenance of brand. Tends towards being risk averse which can stifle the creativity and problem-solving valued in the marketplace and can lead to high levels of self-interest at the expense of clients, stakeholders and society. Compliance and internalisation of values is expected.
Innovative organisation *Learning drivers*	**Mutual adjustment:** Inventiveness and problem-solving by thinking outside of the box is central. Flexible working with listening and sharing knowledge is an important means to make progress.	**Merit based:** Learning sometimes requires rejection of group norms necessary at times, and ruthless pursuit of potential is sometimes necessary, although strong leadership is also needed to keep activities and costs within bounds. Respect and merit are used to resolve tensions between these different courses of action.
Missionary organisation *Drivers for attraction*	**Standardisation of norms:** Conviction that the service is needed is held onto and thus the aim is to line activity to the mission and then attract those who demand the service. Franchises, ethically orientated and evangelical businesses are suited to this mode of operation.	**Belief based:** Decisions are evaluated against a set of core values and beliefs in general and then subjected to evaluation at a more detailed level of compliance.
Entrepreneurial organisation *Drivers giving direction*	**Direct supervision:** All activity must be aligned to the vision and requirements of the entrepreneur, and this is conveyed directly or absorbed through relationships by osmosis.	**Autocratic:** Decisions are top-down. Compliance to the vision and direction is seen as important.

Table 1.4 (*Continued*)

Organisational type	Prime coordinating mechanism	Decision-making
Professional organisation *Proficiency drivers*	Standardisation of skills: Acquired externally from professional institutions, training and continuing professional development. This covers expertise associated with the discipline, any wider body of knowledge, ethics and codes of practice.	Expertise based: Expertise enhanced through experience and professional requirements. Internalisation is key, in order to proficiently contend with societal and client politics in relation to the brief and broader requirements for the service.
Virtual organisation *Delivery drivers*	Pooling competencies and standardisation of systems: Task-driven activity, with pooled competency and system resources.	Negotiated: Decisions are seldom taken without consultation: within teams, across functions and organisations and through short-distance hierarchical negotiations.

responsible for particular projects. A project form of organisation now emerges and will tend to supersede the entrepreneurial coordination in time, which is 'virtual' in that the project form is frequently temporary within each professional practice and the temporary form comes together with other disciplines to create a temporary multi-organisation design team (cf. Cherns and Bryant, 1984).

The founder retains the overall span of management control, resources especially knowledge and imagination being pooled at project level to generate the quality of service amongst the most creative professions (Figure 1.4 and Table 1.4). Architects and some of the most creative and innovative engineers tend to adopt the studio model of working to maximise creative – a particular expression of the professional organisation with both a virtual project character and elements of adhocracy for innovation via mutual adjustment – see Figure 1.4 and Table 1.4.

The more creative professional practices may also exhibit features of the adhocracy structure for the innovative organisations. Whilst the studio model encourages sharing knowledge and facilitating team creativity, some personal and sometimes small group 'space' is needed to pursue and develop new ideas – along the lines of a laboratory of the imagination – where the inventive and innovative is initially formulated and then iteratively tested and refined in the studio involving the architecture or engineering team. This process is arguably less relevant to cost consultant and accountancy practices, but is relevant to some management consultants, especially at the upper end of the hierarchy and to certain legal activities where is structurally hidden due to the preference for more cellular working.

The missionary organisation's standardised norms may be present and particularly relevant under two organisational configurations. First, highly creative practices, which are also called the strong idea practices (Coxe *et al.*, 1987; Winch and Schneider, 1993), especially the signature architects or 'archistars' (see Chapter 6 by Beatrice Manzoni), that have a high profile and strong brand in the market (see Chapter 7 by Hedley Smyth and Sofia Kioussi; cf. Chapter 15 by Kate McGhie) can generate that profile and brand by the values and norms of the founding individual being tacitly imposed on other employees. This is not the case for all strong idea firms as creative design diversity is valued as part of its cultural norms (see Chapter 10 by Ken Shuttleworth). Second, where practices are setting up new branch offices, there may be a desire in the early stages to embed the values of the practice, especially where (many of) the management have not come from one of the existing offices. As with the entrepreneurial structure, this ideological thrust may prove temporary, yet some practices may retain or seek to maintain such structures and coordinating mechanisms in the longer term.

The growing and emergent trends of conglomerate multidisciplinary practices, such as AECOM and Atkins, may place emphasis on the consistency of service quality delivered. One solution to this is the adoption of the divisionalised practice into departments of business units that can be monitored and held to central account for quality. This can induce so-called 'silo thinking' and thus is at the opposite end of the spectrum to the studio model, but if carefully managed and structured, it can be utilised for overall coordination with other structures and processes working within business units and for particular disciplines. The built environment professions are probably somewhat 'behind the learning curve' for establishing these structures yet managing cross-pollination and learning through inter-business unit networking compared to the advertising and media professions, for example WPP (Grabher, 2002; see also Chapter 2 by Graham Winch).

The machine bureaucracy is the least relevant structure to the professional organisation. Whilst there may be elements present, especially amongst the most routinised practices undertaking standardised work, the built environment professions undertaking project work are amongst the least able to follow this form because projects are inherently dealing with high levels of uncertainty (Winch, 2002) and ambiguity (Daft and Lengel, 1986).

Managing imagination and value generation

Returning to the studio model because of its distinctiveness, further exploration is warranted. The studio model has its origin in the artists' studio or 'atelier' (the attic quarters of vertically segregated Parisian housing). The studio or atelier has a short hierarchy to maintain the supervision, which is sometimes partly negotiated socially or informally rather than by appointment, along the lines of the artists' studio or collective. Some hierarchy is needed to manage matters in any studio and this always has a formal element in commercial practice, even if it is self-appointment by the founder. The short or shallow hierarchical management control tends to be direct (cf. entrepreneurial) for each studio to flexibly allocate resources between the several projects typically allocated to each studio in the practice. Bayer and Gann (2006) have analysed bidding strategies suggesting that allocating under-employed staff is more efficient than having a separate bidding function. Management coordination may grow as studios grow to coordinate quality across the studios, which will become more important as practices grow, diversify geographically through setting up branch offices and offer a range of services and disciplines. It becomes dominant for international multi-disciplinary practices.

The studio model is particularly important for strong idea architecture and engineering practices (Coxe *et al.*, 1987; Winch and Schneider, 1993; see Chapter 2 by Graham Winch). Most professional practices will share similar values partly for professional reasons and partly because of the culture of the firm (cf. professional bureaucracy and missionary organisation). Studio managers within the practice will model and impart these practice values, yet there is typically room for individual expression and negotiation of a studio 'flavour' to the culture, except where a strong idea architect (cf. innovative adhocracy) or 'archistar' ruthlessly imposes their design values across the whole practice (cf. missionary organisation). In terms of cultural theory, the studio model adheres closest to the clan and adhocracy cultural positions of Cameron and Quinn (2006) and the competitive individualism and egalitarian enclave of the cultural theory model of Douglas (1999), whereas the more routinised or strong delivery practices adhere to the other positions in the cultural models of hierarchy and market, and hierarchy and competitive individualism respectively – see Figure 1.5.

Ainamo (2007) considered these differences in terms of (i) *resourced-based coordination mechanisms* in creative development work where participative and organic design teams or design centres are the loci of resources, and (ii) *structure-based coordination mechanisms* in creative development work where function and product management are the two loci for focusing resources in more hierarchical and mechanistic structures (see also Chapter 3 by Antti Ainamo).

The studio model has survived and developed as it is most effective in generating creativity and problem-solving. The values inform this process, but it is this type of experiential learning and knowledge sharing which is characteristic of design practices generally and strong idea firms in particular. Kraut *et al.* (1976) stressed the importance of informal

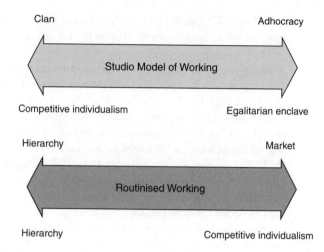

Figure 1.5 Organisational culture and coordinating mechanisms

communication within group interactions, finding that 85% of all communication was informal, of which 50% was the product of people working in close proximity (cf. Stanton *et al.*, 2003), underlining the importance of tacit knowledge sharing (cf. Polanyi, 1958; Nonaka and Takeuchi, 1995) and reflective practice (Schön, 1983).

Learning in professional practice tends towards the experiential or affective rather than the cognitive per se in alignment with the Kolb learning cycle (Figure 1.6).

This has been further developed to account for the creative industries (Figure 1.7), whereby the creative tension is maintained between assimilating/accommodating on the one hand and diverging/converging on the other hand, converging and divergence also being in tension and conflict at times (Beckman and Barry, 2007). These tensions can generate creative excitement and challenges for employees as horizontal processes

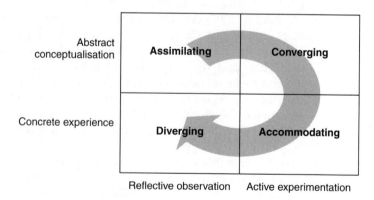

Figure 1.6 The Kolb learning cycle

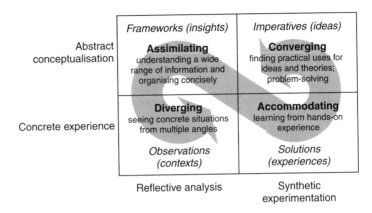

Figure 1.7 The creative learning process

tend to be managed informally 'amongst equals'. The project designer and studio manager frequently participate as equals, yet intervene in hierarchical mode to 'call time' and freeze the process as part of the management of resources and to control quality of output. Heads of projects and studios may play these dual roles – horizontal creativity and hierarchical control – the skill being to know which role is being acted upon at any time and communicate this to other studio members so as not to inhibit the creative flow.

Relationships and management

Relationships and value

Mintzberg said that professions *gather around expertise*, not values – see the professional and innovative organisations in Table 1.4 (Mintzberg, 1979; cf. Mintzberg *et al.*, 1988). Dunn and Baker (2003) said that the old model of revenue calculated as *people power × efficiency × hourly rate* is being superseded by a new model of profitability derived from *intellectual capital × price × effectiveness*, which places greater emphasis on people, their knowledge and how they work together. Practice managers regularly say, *'people are our greatest asset'*, especially when they pitch for work. As noted, investment does not always match the assertion albeit for some understandable reasons. However, it is a different and more profound point that is developed in this section: the importance of relationships.

It is right that the professions gather around expertise (Mintzberg, 1979), but that does not mean that they need to remain primarily gathered around expertise, and the successful practices cannot do so to secure success in the future. The expertise and competence (knowledge and skills developed individually and organisationally in theory and practice) are the tools. As Pryke and Smyth (2006) drew attention to in project management the medium-term historical fetish for tools and techniques has, until recently, overlooked the fact that they are only as good as the hands they are in individually and in teams – it is people who add value working together. In the professions the 'tools and techniques' are embedded in the people. Whilst certain theoretical and practical aspects can be codified as explicit knowledge, much remains implicit knowledge, especially the knowledge and skills that are experiential or affective and are derived from psychomotor learning (such as riding a bike) which are applied by habit. Indeed, the intangibility of these attributes is sometimes hard to express and articulate to oneself, leave alone to others. Yet it is these attributes that constitute the expertise and competence of the professions, and which are mobilised through working relationships.

There remains a lack of awareness amongst the built environment professions of the importance of relationships. Consequently, relationships are typically poorly managed amongst the professions. Although there has been improvement over the past quarter century or so, the full scope remains unappreciated and under-managed. Yet, there are many practices, from the large professional ones with global reach to small local ones, that are perfectly capable of delivering excellent cost control, high-quality design and engineering in their markets and for their chosen segments – what economists call the delivery of *value added* or more colloquially meeting the professional requirements of the discipline. This is insufficient in competitive markets for complex projects for demanding and sophisticated clients. Therefore, it is the professional practices that lever the expertise and competencies from their people with greatest effect that will go beyond those minimal requirements – what is conceptually termed social capital that will deliver *added value*. This social capital is embedded in people and is mobilised through relationships. *Relationship management* will therefore become a key driver of future competitive advantage (e.g. Grönroos, 2000; Gummesson, 2001; Christopher *et al.*, 2006; for the built environment see Smyth, 2000; Pryke and Smyth, 2006).

Relationship management

Relationship management started with relationship marketing, which the professions have intuitively followed for decades in business development, and more systematic approaches have emerged amongst practices – which is not to be confused with customer relationship management (CRM) software, which is a tool that can be an aid to relationship marketing and management. There are essentially two ways in which relationship management facilitates added value creation and delivery:

1. *Internal relationship management* is used to facilitate the mobilisation of social capital embedded within individuals so that this is captured in the service, and the management of the service, so that both the content and its delivery are more effective for the client. This is building upon existing mechanisms, for example the studio model which provides a fertile context for both the development and sharing of social capital, whereby relationships are actively managed to enhance the process – 'investing' in people so they feel more valued, investing and facilitating competency development, providing systems and procedures to further enhance working together especially at critical stages of projects. This is not especially demanding in investment costs and in some cases may only be enhancing what is already achieved. In some cases, this may cut across efficiency drivers, which will need to be addressed by distinguishing between efficiencies that help the client and client budget, and efficiencies that help practice profitability. All the evidence is that enhancing relationship management adds to short-term costs but enhances repeat business and profitability, service effectiveness that looks beyond the short term is preferable to short-term efficiency gains (e.g. Reichheld, 1996; for the built environment see Smyth, 2000).

2. *External relationship management* is used to secure business at the crudest level, which most practices recognise. Significantly, it is used to understand the client requirements that go beyond the request for proposal and briefing documentation towards understanding their business and project strategies, the underpinning and largely unarticulated expectations, and what motivates the key decision makers personally and for the organisation. Working with the client during the business development stages and beyond creates opportunities to reflect upon their needs and inject these into the solutions, which is part of the co-created value process (Prahalad and Ramaswamy, 2004). The practices that arguably have most opportunity to do this are the weakest at it, for example strong idea architects that see the design as an artefact to be accepted on its creative merit – see Chapter 7 by Hedley Smyth and Sofia Kioussi.

What this highlights – especially the second point – is that value delivered by the professions is not ultimately the product of inputs, which is the old model for generating revenue (Dunn and Baker, 2003), but value is the product of market need, in other words what clients want implicitly or explicitly beyond the minimum expected requirements of a competent professional. This is the arena of competitive contest for the next growth market. It will be the practices that are most effective in these ways, incrementally improving over the cycle, that will build market share and be profitable.

What other issues does the management of relationships raise? Some of the systems that can be applied are outlined elsewhere – see Figure 1.8 (from Pryke and Smyth 2006) and Figure 7.1, (Chapter 7 by Hedley Smyth and Sofia Kioussi) that are developed from established work by Storbacka *et al.* (1994) in a project setting. A few of the most obvious and general are set out below, but there are many issues, and practices need to select the 'turf' on which they compete that matches the added value expectations in their market segments and for their (potential) clients.

Project teams are frequently temporary and reconfigured for new and different projects. This can mean that knowledge and skill profiles are selected at a general level and the relevance at a detailed level of creativity, problem solving and decision-making is left to accident or coincidence to a degree. Projects teams and studios or departments are not watertight structures and so organisational networking can solicit valuable inputs, knowledge management systems (based more, or as much, on relationships as IT solutions can help). Studios provide an interface between the project team and the practice as a whole, representing a form of programme management structure, but many practices could benefit from enhanced programme management, particularly if this is relationship based.

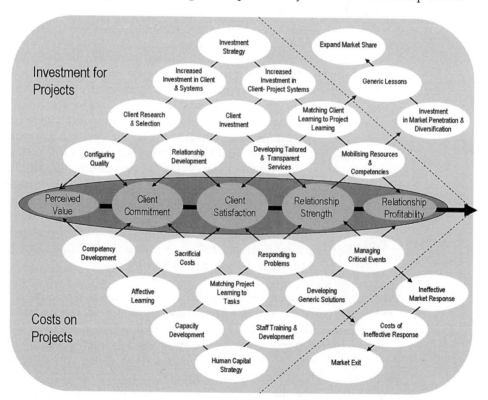

Figure 1.8 The investment and cost dynamics of relationship management for project working

Expertise-driven practices tend to conform to the traditional norms of working in projects which, perceiving project work in terms of tasks (Handy, 1997), is task-orientation (Pryke and Smyth, 2006) at an operational level. A senior management role involves encouraging staff to raise their heads and widen their horizons, and helps them not only to look beyond the immediate tasks but more significantly shifts their vision from the task orientation per se (which is equivalent to the production orientation in other sectors) to a complementary client orientation (equivalent to the customer orientated shift made in many other sectors a long time ago). This helps to change the inward focus, indeed the individualism, in many practices, especially small and medium-sized ones. The problem with individualism, no matter how determined and efficient the working, is individuals who:

- require quick and repeated feedback, the solution being to be tolerant of and work with (rather than ignore) impatience;
- get bored quickly, the solution being to provide broader yet clear goals;
- hate repetitive tasks, the solution being to provide rewards including job satisfaction, be encouraging and facilitate internal and external networking;
- seek new challenges, the solution being to give authority to build and manage external relationships using practice systems and procedures;
- require personal growth, the solution flowing from the above;
- need trust and respect, the solution being to show (by demonstration) commitment to staff.

The solutions to individualism are labour-intensive and time-consuming, and may be challenging for entrepreneurial managers as this implies more of a servant–leader role – forms of facilitation and empowerment from management. However, the direct investment cost is low in terms of the balance sheet, and it may prove decisive in terms of the bottom line over an economic cycle.

Over time, market strengths become mainstay activities – from added value to value added – because competitors copy, staff leave and transfer knowledge and capabilities, and clients come to expect such services as standard. Even the strong idea firms become strong service and delivery firms in time, through this process and as management increasingly apply the innovative generically, and eventually in a routine way (cf. Coxe *et al.*, 1987; Winch and Schneider, 1993; Chapter 2 by Graham Winch). Relationship management is something that can refresh the service and can be developed and enhanced long term. It has been argued that relationship management is a fertile and necessary area for competitive positioning, yet there are internal as well as market reasons for so doing. As professional practices grow, the individual

employees find themselves further away from the centre both structurally and physically. Even managers can feel psychologically further
from the heart of things as the practice grows – see Table 1.2. One
reaction can be to become more individualistic. The same thing can
happen to the firm: that is, as it grows large, the practice can ebb and
flow away from its values and the professional ethos. This can create
conditions in which the employee(s) can identify more with the client
than the employer or discipline. This is fertile ground for the non-
decision-making and mobilisation of bias that yields to corruption
(Bachrach and Baratz, 1970), for example the Enron scandal in which
accountants Arthur Anderson were caught up. As the practice grows,
opening branch offices, becoming multidisciplinary and acquiring competitors, the organisation gains power and prestige, and perhaps the
professional institutions are of less interest in any one country. Thus,
organisational self-interest grows at the possible expense of professional
values and playing an independent role (cf. Chapter 2 by Graham
Winch).

Whilst size matters because local and regional market characteristics
determine the scope for service firms to internationalise (Javalgi
et al., 2003), maintenance of professional standards does too and a
focus upon relationship management can assist with countering these
tendencies.

Relationship management and trust

One of the core values for all professions and a foundation of any
effective relationship is trust. And therefore, this section will conclude
with a look at trust in the built environment professions.

It has been found that trust amongst the design team and with the
client is far higher than with other inter-organisational relationships in
the built environment (e.g. Smyth, 2005; cf. Smyth, 2006; Smyth and
Edkins, 2007). Trust can be inward focused or self-interested, but it
would seem that the larger the number of team members – design team
members, real estate and planning consultants and client – the greater the
social orientation of outward focus tends to be and trust levels broadly
increase in line with that (Smyth, 2005), which could be seen as somewhat
counterintuitive. However, Thompson (1998) found the quantity surveyor role tended to erode the conditions of trust in the client–contractor
relationship. Smyth (2005) found that the quantity surveyor/cost consultant has a considerable drag effect on developing *socially orientated
trust*. This evidence is inter-organisational, yet the most recent evidence
shows that the quantity surveyor/cost consultant tends to undermine
trust between disciplines within their own organisation, namely with
project managers (Ayres and Smyth, 2010). Whilst this is partly a function
of the role of challenging other team members, especially on grounds of

cost, it is partly a function of focusing on expertise and task rather than relationships:

> *The quantity surveyor/cost consultant has a professional role that inherently creates tensions in the relationships, giving rise to a need for them to develop a broader set of competencies beyond immediate professional requirements. (Smyth, 2005: 211)*

It has also been found across many built environment organisations (e.g. Smyth and Edkins, 2007) and in the professions (Smyth, 2005) that management have left relationship management generally and trust specifically to individual responsibility rather than proactive management. Yet trust, and hence relationships, are at the heart of the professions. Therefore, for internal and market reasons the survival of the professions and the competitiveness of individual professional practices is dependent upon how management address these issues.

Summary and conclusion

The chapter has addressed a range of issues, particularly challenges to the professions, the increasing global reach and consolidation of large practices in the marketplace, the structures and management implications of different organisational structures, and the importance of relationships in capturing and delivering value.

Relationship management has been highlighted as an important and arguably neglected area. Evidence to support this neglect points to the scope for practices to secure competitive advantage on this basis. Many of the other chapters describe and analyse issues that are conducted and are addressed through people working together in effective ways.

The demands upon the professions are going to increase from project specific complexities, including sustainability issues, which includes greater consideration beyond the project and service lifecycle, to a range of other factors from regulatory requirements to corporate social responsibility. Coordination within and between organisations is central to effective delivery and in many cases the professional practice plays a key role as a systems integrator. Such systems are human as much as mechanical or procedural, if not more so. Social capital, therefore, is not only the input into projects and services in the shape of expertise and knowledge, it is the very thing that helps people to work together in relationships. This is not purely a function of individual responsibility but is a also a function of strategies, systems and procedures that comprise relationship management of the professional practice.

References

Ainamo, A. (2007) Coordination mechanisms in cross-functional teams: a product design perspective, *Journal of Marketing Management*, 23, 841–860.

Ayres, D. and Smyth, H. J. (2010) Trust between clients and consultants in retail construction, *Proceedings of Cobra 2010*, RICS Foundation, 2–3 September, Dauphine University, Paris.

Bachrach, P. and Baratz, M. S. (1970) *Power and Poverty*, OUP, Oxford.

Bayer, S. and Gann, D. (2006) Balancing work: bidding strategies and workload dynamics in a project-based professional service organisation, *System Dynamics Review*, 22, 185–211.

BD Practices (2009) How to achieve a happy medium, *Survival Strategies, Building Design*, London, pp. 4–7.

Beckman, S. L. and Barry, M. (2007) Innovation as a learning process: embedding design thinking, *California Management Review*, 50, 25–56.

Brook, K. (2008) Developments in measuring the UK service industries, 1990–2006, *Economic and Labour Market Review*, 2(1), 18–29.

Building (2007) Top 250 consultants put on growth spurt, http://www.building.co.uk/story.asp?sectioncode + 32&storycode=3124677&c=1, accessed 16 Aug 2009.

Cameron, K. S. and Quinn, R. E. (2006) *Diagnosing and Changing Organizational Culture*, San Francisco: Jossey-Bass.

Cherns, A. B. and Bryant, D. T. (1984) Studying the client's role in project management, *Construction Management and Economics*, 1, 177–184.

Coxe, W., Hartung, N., Hochberg, H., Lewis, B., Maister, D., Mattox, R. and Piven, P. (1987) *Success Strategies for Design Professionals*, McGraw Hill, New York.

Christopher, M., Payne, A. and Ballantyne, D. (2006) *Relationship Marketing: creating stakeholder value*, Butterworth-Heinemann, Oxford.

Daft, R. L. and Lengel, R. H. (1986) Organizational information requirements, media richness and structural design, *Management Science*, 32, 554–571.

Douglas, M. (1999) Four cultures: the evolution of a parsimonious model, *GeoJournal*, 47, 411–415.

Dunn, P. and Baker, R. (2003) *The Firm of the Future: a guide for accountants, lawyers, and other professional services*, John Wiley & Sons, Hoboken.

ENR (1999) *Top 200 Global Design Firms for 1998*.

Grabher, G. (2002) The project ecology of advertising: tasks, talents and teams, *Regional Studies*, 36, 245–262.

Grönroos, C. (2000) *Service Management and Marketing*, John Wiley & Sons, London.

Gummesson, E. (2001) *Total Relationship Marketing*, Butterworth-Heinemann, Oxford.

Hamel, G. and Prahalad, C. K. (1996), *Competing for the Future*, Harvard Business School Press, Boston.

Handy, C. B. (1997) *Understanding Organizations*, Penguin, London.

Hetherington, W. A. (2008) *The Internationalisation of UK Construction Service Firms: a study of 21st century corporate strategy,* MSc Dissertation in Built Environment Studies, University of the West of England, Bristol.

Ive, G.(c. 2001) *Clusters Proposal,* unpublished, UCL.

Ive, G. and Winch, G. (1999) *Clusters in the Global Construction Industry: a national competitive advantage?* Paper presented to the Dti, unpublished, UCL, London.

Javalgi, R. G., Griffith, D. A. and White, D. S. (2003) An empirical examination of factors influencing the internationalization of service firms, *The Journal of Services Marketing,* 17(3), 185–201.

Jewel, C., Flanagan, R. and Anaç, C. (2010) Understanding UK construction professional services exports: definitions and characteristics, *Construction Management and Economics,* 28, 231–239.

Kolb, D. A. (1984) *Experiential Learning: experience as the source of learning and development,* Prentice-Hall, Englewood-Cliffs.

Knox P. L. and Taylor, P. J. (2005) Toward a geography of the globalization of architecture office networks, *Journal of Architectural Education,* 58(3), 23–32.

Kraut, R. E., Egeth, H. E. and Bevan, W. (1976) The face as a data display, *Human Factors,* 18, 189–200.

McKinley, W., Sanchez, C. and Schick, A. (1995). Organizational downsizing: constraining, cloning, learning, *Academy of Management Executive,* 9, 32–42.

Mintzberg, H. (1979) *The Structuring of Organizations,* Prentice-Hall, Englewood Cliffs.

Mintzberg, H., Otis, S., Shamsie, J. and Waters, J. A. (1988) Strategy of design: A study of 'architects in co-partnership', *Strategic Management Frontiers,* Grant, J. (ed.), Greenwich, JAI Press, pp. 311–359.

Nelson, R. R. and Winter, S. G. (1982) *An Evolutionary Theory of Economic Change,* Harvard University Press, Boston.

New Civil Engineer (2007) March.

Nonaka, I. and Takeuchi, H. (1995) *The Knowledge Creating Company,* Oxford University Press, New York.

OECD (2005) Growth in services: fostering employment, productivity and innovation, Meeting of the OECD Council at Ministerial Level, 2005, www.oecd.org/dataoecd/58/52/34749412.pdf.

O'Neill, O. (2002a) Lecture 1: Spreading Suspicion, *A Question of Trust,* Reith Lectures, BBC Radio 4, London, http://www.bbc.co.uk/radio4/reith2002/ accessed 18 Feb 2010.

O'Neill, O. (2002b) Lecture 3: Called to Account, *A Question of Trust,* Reith Lectures BBC 4, London, http://www.bbc.co.uk/radio4/reith2002/ accessed 18 Feb 2010.

Ormrod Committee (1971), *Report of the Committee on Legal Education,* HMSO, Cmnd 4595, London.

Page, M., Pearson, S. and Pryke, S. (2003) *A Study of Innovation in the UK's Top Quantity Surveying Firms,* RICS Research Paper Series, 4, 26, RICS, London.

Polanyi, M. (1958) *Personal Knowledge,* Routledge, London.

Prahalad, C. K. and Ramaswamy, V. (2004) Co-creating unique value with customers, *Strategy & Leadership,* 32(3), 4–9.

Pryke, S. D. and Smyth, H. J. (2006) Scoping a Relationship Approach to the Management of Projects, *Management of Complex Projects: A Relationship Approach*, Pryke, S. D. and Smyth, H. J. (eds.), Blackwell Publishing Ltd., Oxford, pp. 21–46.

Reichheld, F. (1996) *The Loyalty Effect*. Harvard Business School Press, Boston.

Schön, D. A. (1983) *The Reflective Practitioner: how professionals think in action*, Basic Books.

Smyth, H. J. (2000) *Marketing and Selling Construction Services*, Blackwell Publishing Ltd., Oxford.

Smyth, H. J. (2005) Trust in the design team, *Architectural Engineering and Design Management*, 1(3), 193–205.

Smyth, H. J. (2006) Measuring, developing and managing trust in the relationship, *Management of Complex Projects: A Relationship Approach*, Pryke, S. D. and Smyth, H. J. (eds.), Blackwell Publishing Ltd., Oxford, 97–120.

Smyth, H. J. and Edkins, A. J. (2007) Relationship management in the management of PFI/PPP projects in the UK, *International Journal of Project Management*, 25(3), 232–240.

Stanton, N. A., Ashleigh, M. J., Roberts, A. D. and Xu, F. (2003) Virtuality in human supervisory control: assessing the effects of psychological and social remoteness, *Ergonomics*, 43, 1190–1209.

Storbacka, K., Strandvik, T. and Grönroos, C. (1994) Managing customer relationships for profit: the dynamics of relationship quality, *International Journal of Service Industry Management*, 5(5), 21–38.

Teece, D. J., Pisano, G. and Shuen, A (1997) Dynamic capabilities and strategic management, *Strategic Management Journal*, 18, 7, 509–533.

Thompson, N. J. (1998) Can Clients Trust Contractors? Conditional, Attiduninal and Normative Influences on Clients' Behaviour, *Proceedings of the 3rd National Construction Marketing Conference*, 9 July, Centre for Construction Marketing in association with the Chartered Institute of Marketing Construction Industry Group, Oxford, Oxford Brookes University.

Tombesi, P. A. (2001) True south for design? The new international division of labour in architecture, *Architectural Research Quarterly*, 5, 171–180.

Tombesi, P., Dave, B. and Scriver, P. (2003) Routine production or symbolic analysis? India and the globalisation of architectural services, *Journal of Architecture*, 8, 63–94.

Wenger, E. (1998) *Communities of Practice: learning, meaning, and identity*, Cambridge University Press, Cambridge.

Winch, G. M. (2002) *Managing the Construction Project: an information processing approach*, Blackwell Publishing Ltd., Oxford.

Winch, G. M. and Schneider, E. (1993) The strategic management of architectural practice, *Construction Management and Economics*, 11, 467–473.

2 Strategic management of professional practice

The case of architecture

Graham Winch

Introduction

Much of the construction sector, properly defined, consists of firms organised as professional service firms (PSFs). Whether constituted as partnerships or incorporated, the management of PSFs poses some distinctive challenges, and the unthinking borrowing of managerial approaches from other types of firms can be counterproductive. The aim of this chapter is to explore issues in the strategic management of PSFs by deploying relevant management theory and research adapted to meet the needs of managing those PSFs that provide architectural services.

The ideas presented in this section were first developed as a response to the challenge of teaching strategic management to students on the MSc Construction Economics and Management at the Bartlett School, UCL, during in the early 1990s. They represent the outcomes of a dialogue with those students through both class discussions and dissertation research blended with the research by Eric Schneider for the *RIBA Strategic Study of the Profession* (Winch and Schneider, 1993). The concepts were subsequently developed empirically through a research project on internationalisation by British and French architectural practices, which both demonstrated the robustness of the original approach and also allowed it to be extended to the international context (Carr *et al.*, 1999; Winch *et al.*, 2002; Winch, 2008). This research was funded by Plan Construction et Architecture and conducted in collaboration with Denis Grèzes and Brìd Carr.

The chapter will first present the basic PSF business model derived from the work of Maister (1982; 1993). The argument will then show how architectural PSFs articulate distinctive *operational capabilities* to generate *competitive advantage* using the Winch/Schneider model of the strategic

Managing the Professional Practice: in the built environment, First Edition. Edited by Hedley Smyth.
© 2011 by Blackwell Publishing Ltd. Published 2011 by Blackwell Publishing Ltd.

management of architectural practice (cf. Chapter 3 by Antii Ainamo). However, competitive advantage is only sustainable if operational capabilities are complemented by appropriate *dynamic capabilities* (Helfat *et al.*, 2007), which allow the firm to sustain and grow. We will therefore explore how architectural PSFs articulate dynamic capabilities in the context of the globalisation of architectural practice. For this we draw conceptually on the work of Jones and her colleagues (1998) on *strategic collaboration* modes and Grabher (2002) on *project ecologies*. It is not appropriate in a chapter such as this to conduct a systematic review of the available literature, but reference will be made as appropriate to the growing body of research in the area over the past 10 years. Statements of world rankings in the chapter are taken from the *Building Design World Architecture 100* for 2010.

What is a professional service firm?

Fairly obviously, a PSF is both a service firm and a professional practice, but it is worth examining what each of these labels means in managerial terms. Services play a growing role in advanced economies yet, just as there is considerable variety in types of manufacturing, there is similar variety in types of services, and the combination of customisation and the relatively high skills required for delivery creates a distinctive niche for 'intellectual or professional services' (Gallouj, 2002). It is through the deployment of high skills to create customised solutions for clients that the service firm interacts with the labour market governed by a professional institution to create the PSF.

A distinctive feature of service transactions compared to manufacturing is the relatively high level of interaction with the purchaser – indeed this is arguably their defining characteristic. Thus it is helpful to focus on the transaction to understand more deeply how service firms work. When buying a melon or a car, there is no interaction between producer and purchaser, the retail service provider (shop) being a mere intermediary; when procuring construction services, the interaction is intense. Buying a melon is a timeless spot contract; buying construction services is a process through time (Winch, 2010). Transaction uncertainty in this situation is reduced not by offering on the market a clearly predefined service or product but by offering the intangibility of a capacity to produce, supported by standardisation of the skills that will do the production (Larson, 1977). While the particular modalities vary between countries – see Campagnac and Winch (1997) for a comparison of engineers in the UK and France – the standardisation process involves some form of accreditation by the state or state-approved agencies such as the UK professional institution. This process creates a distinctive *labour market*, structured around who is and who is not eligible to be accredited as a professional in a particular discipline.

The PSF is not the only way of organising the supply of services based on standardised intangibility. In many countries the state provides the services, thereby creating the professional bureaucracy (Mintzberg, 1979). For instance, in China many architectural services are provided by state-owned design institutes such as the China Architecture Design & Research Group, while the in-house architectural services of AdP (Paris airports) and SNCF (French railways) compete internationally as suppliers of architectural services. However, the PSF has become the dominant organisational form for the supply of architectural services, has been particularly important in the globalisation of the supply of those services and is the focus of this chapter.

The PSF business model

Maister (1982; 1993) was the pioneer of the analysis of the management of PSFs. Although his work drew principally on legal practice, he did collaborate with architectural experts (Coxe *et al.*, 1987) to apply his approach to architectural practice. Maister's first contribution is to aid our understanding of the underlying business model of the PSF – and a very simple one it is. Taking a managerial perspective, he focuses on the profitability of professional practice as the key performance indicator defined as the rate of profit per principal (i.e. owner) of the firm. It should be noted that this perspective does not imply a claim that PSF does or should profit-maximise; it is merely a statement of the obvious point that unless a PSF makes a surplus – usually in the form of a profit – it cannot survive and grow in the longer term (Blau, 1984). The greater that profit, the greater is the amount that the principals who jointly own the PSF can choose to invest in developing the firm, such as by entering architectural competitions.

The basic formula adapted slightly from Maister (1993) is:

$$\frac{\text{Profits}}{\text{Principals}} = \frac{\text{Profits}}{\text{Fees}} \times \frac{\text{Fees}}{\text{Staff}} \times \frac{\text{Staff}}{\text{Principals}}$$

Where: Fees are the average fee income per unit of output; Staff is the total payroll cost; Principal is the number of partners or directors (Maister refers only to partners).

What are the managerial levers to increase *profits per principal*? This is the equivalent of return on equity (the capital provided by the owners) for a publicly traded company and is a more appropriate measure because few PSFs are publicly traded. The first lever is *margin*, or the ratio of profits to fee income (profits as a percentage of sales). This in turn is a function of the costs per unit of output and the fee charged per unit of output. All three elements of costs – salaries, other variable costs, fixed costs – can be managed, but only within a limited scope. The largest element of costs is *salaries*, but these are largely set by the labour market and therefore difficult to manage. Turning to fixed overheads, PSFs typically have very few capital assets and even if the firm owns the building it works in, it is likely to be owned by the principals' pension fund rather than the PSF itself. Their only assets really are their people. Other fixed costs such as office overheads, and other variable costs such as travel, are what Maister calls hygiene factors – waste should be avoided, but paring them back is unlikely to make much of a difference to performance and if staff are inadequately resourced performance can be undermined. For instance poor IT systems can reduce staff effectiveness. Clearly the fee charged per unit of output is crucial to margin.

Productivity is the relationship between inputs (staff) and outputs (fee income). The latter is typically measured in terms of billable hours in a cost-plus contract or earned value in terms of a fee-based or fixed-price contract. Careful organisation of work can get the best out of staff so that they are spending the maximum amount of time on fee-earning work such as by using appropriate IT tools and providing back-office support for more mundane tasks. However, there is relatively little opportunity to compete in this area, and pushing up fee earning hours above the normal working week is rarely sustainable in the longer term. Again, the most effective route to profitability is to increase the fee per unit of output.

Leverage is the ratio between the number of salaried staff and the number of principals. The typical organisational structure of a PSF – and indeed many other organisations such as universities – is the triangular one of principals who find the work, associates who oversee the work, and junior professionals who actually do the work. Leverage measures the ratios of staff at each of these three levels. Clearly, for a constant fee level, the greater the ratio of juniors to principals, the more profitable the PSF will be for the principals that own it. The problem for PSFs – and it is this that most clearly distinguishes them from many other organisations including construction contractors – is that there is no systematic difference in educational and other desirable labour market attributes apart from experience between the juniors and the principals. As Maister (1993) puts it, juniors join PSFs not just for jobs, but for careers. Juniors also bring in fresh ideas which can enhance the innovativeness of the PSF. Their lack of experience is compensated through the oversight of the associates and principals who can then charge out the juniors to clients at many multiples of their salary costs.

Managing the trade-offs between margin, productivity and leverage in the context of the market in which the firm competes is called 'balancing the professional service firm' by Maister (1982). Different market positioning through providing different kinds of service can affect the trade-offs between these levers. For instance, more challenging work will tend to reduce leverage because juniors will need greater supervision, but should also allow the attainment of a higher fee level and provide relatively more senior positions giving more promotion opportunities. Growth is another way of providing promotion opportunities while retaining the leverage ratio, but the growth rates required typically outpace the overall rate of growth in market, and so not all can succeed in this strategy. Some PSFs – particularly in management consulting – have explicit up or out policies so as to control growth while retaining the ability to recruit fresh juniors, and some architectural practices will give an associate a job that is too small for the office to get them started on their own. Others take the hint and leave.

Our interview with the Paris office of Renzo Piano Building Workshop indicates how this process works in architectural practice. They hire large numbers of staff from around the world who spend 2–3 years with them before returning to their country of origin with a much enhanced CV. Thus, the considerable turnover of junior staff, which appears inherently exploitative, can also be seen as beneficial for both parties by providing a continuous stream of new ideas for the employer, and accelerated development of CVs for the young architect. Research on the careers of 'star' architects supports this – Williamson (1991) has shown that having worked for or been taught by a star of the previous generation is a necessary, although hardly sufficient, requirement for becoming a star in the next.

Competitive advantage in architectural practice

Maister's PSF business model indicates that there are a number of trade-offs to be made in achieving balance, and so we will now analyse the sources of competitive advantage for PSFs and then indicate how they shape these trade-offs. The success of any financially autonomous (as opposed to subsidised) commercial organisation is a function of its capability to provide some service matched to the need for that service. Capability is a function of the resources available and the routines used to deploy those resources. Capabilities can be operational, that is, supporting present competitive advantage or dynamic, that is supporting the development of future operational capabilities thereby making competitive advantage sustainable. (Helfat *et al.*, 2007).

For an architectural practice, we can think of *operational capability* as consisting of its *resources* which are made up almost entirely of the skills of the professionals it employs, and its *routines* which are its internal processes for generating appropriate solutions to clients' problems and the delivery of solutions in the form of specifications and drawings for approval by clients, development by other professionals and execution by contractors. We can think of *dynamic capability* as consisting of its sustained ability to win new work, which is largely a function of its reputation and its ability to acquire new resources to support that reputation as it grows. In this section we will explore the different configurations of operational capability for architectural practice; a discussion of dynamic capability will follow.

The overall *market* for architectural services generates projects to bid for, some of which will be appropriate for the practice's operational capabilities and organisational structure. Such opportunities for work may come through invitation, marketing initiatives, formal bidding, entering architectural competitions or serendipity. The maximum fee level that the practice can charge for the work is a function of the market it is serving; the minimum level is – assuming hygiene factors are under control – a function of the leverage in its organisational structure and its operational capability. Operational capability also determines the range of types of projects that the practice can bid for, and is a function of the resources available to the practice in terms of the skills of the motivated professionals it deploys and the routines it uses to develop to ensure delivery to the client. These are mainly design development and project management routines. Leverage, as defined above, drives the cost base of the practice. If a firm becomes under-leveraged in relation to its market, it will be unable to cover its costs with fees; if a firm becomes over-leveraged it is likely to suffer deterioration in its operational capabilities and hence fail to deliver to clients, thereby damaging its reputation.

One way of understanding the different configurations of competitive advantage (i.e. balance points between market, operational capability and organisational structure) for architectural practice derives from the work of Winch and Schneider (1993), which builds on the work by Maister and his colleagues on the culture of practice (Coxe *et al.*, 1987; Maister, 1993), the RIBA's *Strategic Study of the Profession* (2002), and Porter (1980) on competitive strategy. The Winch/Schneider framework distinguishes two market dimensions – *project complexity* and *quality preference*, which generate four distinctive configurations of architectural practice. Project complexity captures the challenge of the brief – is it merely a question of adapting known solutions to the particular problem at hand, or are there considerable complexities in terms of stakeholder management, technical requirements, iconic status or whatever to be addressed? The bulk of architectural work is of the lower complexity kind and is the kind of work that most architects do most of the time. Many of the firms tackling less challenging projects are small or are sole practitioners working regionally on small building and refurbishment projects (RIBA, 2003; Larson *et al.*, 1983). Firms doing the more challenging kinds of work tend to be larger, may have multiple offices to attain national or international coverage, and may also be part of larger construction services groups.

The second dimension is quality preference in terms of whether the client wishes to assess the quality of the completed facility in its own terms, or whether the client wishes to bask in the reflected glory of critical acclaim from the architectural establishment – our informant at Ateliers Jean Nouvel expressed this as the difference between 'constructeurs de bâtiments' and 'création architecturale'. This dimension is well illustrated by the differing approaches to the main stadium for the Beijing and London Olympics. In Beijing, the 2008 Olympics were seen as evincing the arrival of China on the international stage as a mature nation and as an opportunity for one-upmanship over Shanghai. Modernising national elites therefore wanted an iconic internationally designed stadium that expressed this new status (Ren, 2008). London, which, in 2012, will be the first city to hold the Olympics for the third time, is more confident of its position as a leading global city and has no serious national contender. It therefore chose to use the Olympics as part of its urban regeneration strategy and opted for a much more functional design that can be downsized following the games. The two local organising committees therefore chose two very different kinds of practices in order to achieve these objectives: the strong idea Herzog and de Meuron in the first case and the strong experience HOK Sport (now Populous) in the second.

The four different configurations that this typology generates can now be illustrated by four vignettes where the interviewee has identified their practice within this typology. It should be stressed that all four configurations are equally viable financially, with the exception of strong ambition, where start-up firms need to evolve into one of the other three configurations to achieve sustained viability.

The practice Tooley and Foster was founded in 1892; clearly it is successful and has deliberately remained relatively small. Shown the Winch/Schneider matrix, the practice defined themselves thus: 'I would say if you talked to our clients they would say we were strong on delivery but also delivering a significant design, something worthwhile.' We can therefore define it as a *strong delivery* practice. Although the ratio of juniors to partners is not high, leverage is increased because there are relatively few associates, and partners pride themselves on personal involvement in all jobs. The practice defines itself very much as a regional generalist:

> *Because we are not a signature practice, one wouldn't expect that there would be one [key project].*
> *Probably quite a good analogy is that it is a bit like a doctor's general practice, not that it is local, because although we are here, our work covers the whole of East Anglia but in the sense that we will take on all kinds*

of jobs. The philosophy is to do with the service we give and responding to each job on an individual basis.

And operationally it defines itself as a '... very *lean* organisation, there [are] no office managers, finance directors, all that is shared between the partners; so there isn't any waste in that respect.' Practice publicity also stresses its CAD capabilities and ability to work for contractors on design-build projects.

Nantois and Meadows are the principals of a loose association called Archi-Media founded in 1992 following periods with leading French and British strong experience practices. It is constituted as a not-for-profit under the 'association loi 1901' provision in French law and is very much a *strong ambition* practice. They have chosen not to open an office so as to maintain their dynamic and flexible structure. If they were to be commissioned to do a building they feel it would be more advantageous to associate with a previously existing office rather than commit themselves to starting up their own. Archi-Media have entered a large number of architectural and ideas competitions, and had their work curated at a number of exhibitions. Although the built object is one of Archi-Media's objectives they do not intend to 'stop architecture' if they cannot build:

> *... architecture could also be realised by other things so conferences are part of our architecture ... a CD ROM, if the purpose is architecture, could be considered to be an architectural project.*

Meadows currently teaches part-time at a Paris architecture school and they continue to work together on various cultural projects.

Andrée Putman is a French designer who has established an international reputation through her interior design projects such the French pavilion for Expo '92 in Seville and was responsible for the stage set in the Peter Greenaway film *The Pillow Book*. Agence Andrée Putman is clearly a *strong ideas* practice, and recent projects include Parisian boutiques and a spa in Germany. It participates in competitions from time to time but client contact remains the single most important factor in winning contracts:

> *... when people come to see us they are coming for a signature project by Andrée Putman. It is this notion of selling a mark or label which is the nature of the 'product' offered by the firm.*

Service to the client is of utmost importance to the practice and clients are guaranteed to get a product that is 'tailored' for them. The strength of the practice is its 'conceptual approach to the design process'; they do not focus on being 'site people' and would often subcontract this part of a project to those more specialised in this area. Andrée Putman is interested in the *total* project and in all types of projects; the firm does not want to limit its range of activities through specialisation. The thing that is most important in every project, whatever its nature, is the strong idea brought by the designers.

Chapman Taylor was founded in 1959; all three original partners have since retired. As it is an internationally successful *strong experience* practice, their clients generally have particular requirements whose main objective is that the development be commercially successful. Their work ranges across retail, leisure and master planning; giving the client a quality service and the product they desire as the firm's main goal. Investors in large mixed commercial developments, for instance, are concerned with the design of the retail elements and require the design skills of specialists such as Chapman Taylor to ensure that it will function smoothly and successfully. Thirty years' experience in the building of shopping developments has given the firm great expertise in the retail area; it was ranked at fourth in world in the sector in 2010. A lot of research is done into the particular nature of the area sited for the development in order to understand what kind of design solution will work best. Chapman Taylor won the Queen's Award for Enterprise in 2009.

The four different market positions of these practices imply different configurations of how competitive advantage is achieved. Firms such as Tooley and Foster are the backbone of architectural practice, providing the buildings in which many of us spend our working and leisure hours. However, they face continual pressures on costs and have difficulty in charging premium fees. In meeting the low complexity/ low peer review quality market for architectural services they empha- sise high leverage and lean organisational capability that ensures the effective delivery of design to clients and contractors. Strong delivery practices tend to use a high proportion of architectural technicians. For instance another long-established strong delivery practice – Ansell and Bailey founded in 1900 – had a ratio of nearly 1:1 architects to technicians when interviewed.

Nantois and Meadows are typical of many strong ambition practices with high architectural ideals but who have yet to connect with a market demand for buildings inspired by those ideals. They sustain themselves through teaching and associated activities, entering reimbursed archi- tectural competitions, and driving taxis. Many star architects get their breaks by finding a patron or winning a competition. For instance, Zaha Hadid had difficulty in finding clients for her ideas after leaving the Office for Metropolitan Architecture in 1980, but became very influential as a professor in a number of leading architectural schools. Her first break came from the patrons Vitra in the early 1990s, but it was not until the early 2000s that she had a significant body of completed work (www. pritzker.com, accessed 26 Feb 2010 – now at www.pritzkerprize.com, accessed 8 Nov 2010). Others fail to get that break and, over time, seek alternative ways of earning a living.

Many strong experience firms are known for their competence in distinctive building types (Winch *et al.*, 2002) and Chapman Taylor enjoys a global reputation for their work on large retail developments. For this reason they obtained the commission for the refurbishment of the iconic *Les Halles* forum in the centre of Paris. Similarly HOK Sport, in what is now a management buy-out, Populous, has built a global reputation in stadia and other sporting facilities. The reputation of such firms for solving clients' difficult problems allows them to charge a higher fee, but competitive pressures reign back what can be achieved. The return on the client's investment in a higher fee is that the new facility will have functional superiority over those that might have been designed by practices perceived by clients as having less experience and competence in that particular building type. The kinds of complex projects that strong experience practices excel in require strong project management by associates, supported by effective information systems to handle the volume of design data. Routines need to be robust, and resources need to have the right levels of skill and experience. This type of firm is probably closest to the classic leverage structure.

The world of the *strong ideas* architectural practice is an intensely competitive one, but competitive in the market for ideas rather than price. Strong ideas practices such as Eva Jiricna Architects are typically named after their star designer, although in reality are often run by a more anonymous managing partner. This is the world of the star system (Larson, 1993; cf. Chapter 6 by Beatrice Manzoni): the architects who become knights and peers in the UK and win the Pritzker Prize internationally. They do much to shape the public perception of architecture, although they are responsible for a very small proportion of architectural output. Such practices rarely compete in the open market like the strong experience and delivery firms; more frequently they are simply invited to do the work, or to enter restricted competitions. Fee levels reflect the lack of price competition. The higher fees compensate for the lack of leverage which is inevitable as the principal design partner has to have some sort of oversight, and operational capabilities are much more organic and continually refreshed by churning amongst junior architects.

These four types of practices are ideal-types, which are empirically robust in capturing a range of practices (Winch, 2008) – any particular practice is closer to one or the other. Over time, practices move through different types as they evolve as organisations – a typical trajectory is from strong ambition to strong ideas, after winning a competition, to strong experience as the founding partners retire (Mintzberg *et al.*, 1985). Strong experience practices can achieve the highest repute in architecture. Gordon Bunshaft spent much of his career with SOM and was awarded the Pritzker Prize in 1988, yet SOM prefers to stress the anonymity of its designers (McNeill, 2009) and is clearly a strong experience practice. Similarly, strong ideas practices such as Agence Andrée Putman and Eva Jiricna Architects can build up considerable expertise in specialist buildings types such as retail boutiques. It could be suggested that Foster and Partners, which is part-owned by private equity and ranked sixth in the world in 2010, is steadily moving towards a strong experience practice configuration with its global network of offices and six design groups.

Sustainable competitive advantage in global architectural practice

Architecture is becoming a global business (McNeill, 2009) and poses particular challenges for practices as they work internationally (Winch, 2008; see also Chapter 1 by Hedley Smyth). There are many drivers of globalisation. One is that clients are becoming more global, and they take their preferred suppliers of architectural services with them as they globalise (Knox and Taylor, 2005). Thus Les Architectes CVZ has worked all over the world for its two principal clients – Carrefour and Club Med. Another is the global branding that buildings by star architects offer aspiring cities (McNeill, 2009; see also Chapter 7 by Hedley Smyth and Sofia Kioussi). Often dubbed the 'Bilbao effect', the *Urprojekt* here is surely Utzon's Sydney Opera House which, although vilified at the time, has become symbolic of both Sydney's and Australia's new-found urban sophistication (Murray, 2004). A third is sometimes overlooked and revolves around the development of sophisticated expertise in specific building types (Winch *et al.*, 2002), which is rapidly communicated around the world. Thus Populous 'encompasses every expertise required to design the greatest gathering places and events worldwide' (http://www.populous.com, accessed 26 Feb 2010), while Chapman Taylor have built shopping centres throughout Europe and the Middle East.

Our concerns here focus on how architectural PSFs gain the dynamic capability (Helfat *et al.*, 2007) to extend the resource base of the organisation. Broadly, there are two ways of accessing the necessary human resources. The first is to collaborate with practices overseas (Winch, 2008); the second is to draw on the home 'project ecology' (Grabher, 2002). Thus we are moving in the argument from treating the architectural PSF as a single organic organisation – what Maister (1985) calls the 'one-firm firm' – to architectural PSFs as both embedded in particular urban environments and as parts of much larger project coalitions. In other words, we are moving to viewing architectural practices as nodes in the networks that deliver facilities to clients.

Jones and her colleagues (1998) draw on social network theory to identify the different ways in which architectural practices collaborate within the larger market for architectural services. Somewhat provocatively, they distinguish between *promiscuous* and *polygamous* network collaboration strategies. Practices deploying promiscuous collaboration strategies collaborate as and when required with no longer-term commitment in the relationship, while practices deploying polygamous collaboration strategies develop multiple continuing relationships in a more strategic manner through time. Later research (Winch, 2007) has shown that there is a correlation between the use of promiscuous strategies by strong ideas practices, and polygamous strategies by strong experience practices.

Again, we can illustrate these collaboration strategies with two vignettes from our Anglo-French research. Our informant at Ateliers Jean Nouvel explained how the practice has a well-rehearsed approach to working outside France. The scheme and concept design work is developed in France and as the project moves towards design definition, Nouvel enters into an association with a local practice which will be responsible for the later stages of the design work. Ideally, the associated practice is identified early and involved during the initial concept stages, while Nouvel will also send architects to work in the offices of the associate practice if needs be. Other strong ideas practices prefer to be independent of local collaborators. As our informant at what is now Rogers Stirk Harbour + Partners told us:

> We don't have any problems about recognising limitations and working with good people outside but generally I think we don't like the idea of taking a building and separating it out and saying, which we are forced to do sometimes, you do interiors ... Basically in France unless it's imposed by the client we don't feel we would need [to associate with a French practice]. We have enough French speakers here.

Strong idea practices tend also to reject the idea of setting up permanent foreign offices as opposed to temporary project-related offices. Rogers Stirk Harbour + Partners stated:

> ... it's design control at the end of the day; unless you have partners who are willing to live permanently in a place, partners who have a very strong connection with the office and can operate with that... but it's almost impossible to control.

Strong experience practices tend to take a very different approach. For instance, John R. Harris was a partnership of architects, planners and designers founded in London with associated offices in Australia, Dubai, France, Hong Kong, Kuwait, Qatar, Shanghai, Taiwan and Thailand all with the late John R. Harris as a partner. The practice has built 34 general hospitals around the world since it won an open RIBA competition for the Doha State Hospital, Qatar in 1952; it was also the original master planner for Dubai. It was recently restructured into JRHP International to strengthen this international profile.

This approach is very much a centralised polygamy, also adopted by practices such as BDP with associated offices in the Netherlands, Ireland and France making it Europe's largest architectural practice by fee income in 2010. A more decentralised, egalitarian approach is to use looser associations of practices, sometimes under the auspices of a European Economic Interest Group (EEIG) (Prost, 1997). For instance, EPR formed an EEIG called Architecturo with Daviel in Paris, Architectes Mahieu in Brussels and Arqui III in Lisbon. As Prost shows, such liaisons are difficult to sustain although Architecturo did complete a project in Portugal for Expo 98. However, the formation of Aedas as a multi-centred practice through global branding and franchising across 40 offices would appear to be taking the internationalisation of strong experience practice to a higher level (McNeill, 2009; cf. Chapter 15 by Kate McGhie) and is challenging the centralised global practices such as RMJM and Gensler with a global ranking of second in 2010.

If practices working globally are unwilling to open offices abroad or enter into a network (centralised or decentralised), how can they assure the dynamic capabilities required for global practice? Knox and Taylor (2005) have analysed how architectural practices are clustered in a few global centres, with London pre-eminent. There are a number of reasons for these clusters of architectural activity including closeness to clients and their sources of funding, and closeness to complementary professional services such as law, finance and engineering which reinforce each other. However, research by Grabher (2002) on the London advertising industry suggests that there is another reason – easy access to a mobile population of professionals who move from practice to practice as their fortunes vary. For professionals, the *project ecology* reduces the impact of the implicit up or out policies of practices as many alternative employers are available locally; for practices they have access to a deeper pool of talent into which they can dip as needs be (Kloosterman, 2008).

The project ecology of architectural practice in a global city such as New York or London means that young architects from many countries cycle through the leading strong ideas practices and can be deployed to support foreign projects as needs be. For instance, our informant at Foster and Partners told us, 'these are not German architects, these are "Foster Germans", which is not the same thing at all', working on their German projects. The importance of the project ecology as a source of multilingual human resources is, perhaps, indicated by Renzo Piano Building Workshop. It is based in Genoa, Italy (with an office in Paris), and it lacks a deep project ecology. The Fondazione Renzo Piano collaborates with 12 architectural schools around the world to attract young architects for six-month periods with the foundation, as 'apprentices' in architectural practice. This arrangement has the potential to supply significant numbers of international architects steeped in the design culture of RPBW, thereby creating its own project ecology.

The prospects for managing architectural practice

In this concluding section, we would like to briefly address, in no particular order, a number of challenges facing architectural practice in the early 21st century.

The recession

Recessions, such as the current one, tend to have major restructuring effects on business sectors. Blau and Lieben's (1983) panel study of New York architectural practice through the 1970s recession suggests that it is the small firms and large firms that will survive, particularly if they are innovative, with many medium-sized firms ceasing to practise (see also Chapter 1 by Hedley Smyth). Small firms tend to enter the recession with low overheads, and can often survive long periods of under-employment while in quantitative terms many do fail. Large firms can cut costs and trade down market, while medium-sized firms can find themselves caught between these two dynamics. Medium-sized firms also appear to be particularly prone to losing the leverage triangle of practice and become more diamond shaped with too few juniors to support the middle ranks of associates (RIBA, 2003). The current recession is likely to see intense competition amongst the strong ambition firms as new entrants to the labour market arrive from the architectural schools and the chances of winning a competition as the first step to strong ideas firm diminishes and job opportunities in the larger firms dry up as they downsize (see also Chapter 6 by Beatrice Manzoni). It will also likely see the disappearance of some familiar names in the market in the middle ranks.

Outsourcing

The rapid developments in ICT over the past 10 years have opened the possibility of outsourcing elements of the architectural design process to low-cost countries (Tombesi, 2001), with India placed strongly to benefit due to its language of education and the modelling of that education on UK practice (Tombesi *et al.*, 2003). Firms such as Architecture Outsourcing in New Delhi (www.architectureoutsourcing.com) provide a number of CAD-based detail design services for architectural practices in the UK, the USA and elsewhere. However, it is unclear how important this development is – Tombesi and his colleagues provide no case studies of outsourcing, and certain features of architectural practice suggest the impact might be limited. First, the dynamics of the project ecology mean that staff costs might be less in the major centres of architectural production than straight cost comparisons would suggest – for instance, Kloosterman (2008; see also Miller, 2006) argues that many junior architects in the Randstaat area work for the minimum wage. Second, the services provided by outsourcing firms are in those areas that will become increasingly automated with the development of parametric design.

Developments in ICT

Clearly the further development of information and communication technologies (ICT) will have a major impact on architectural practice. In particular, parametric design seems likely to transform the design process – it is already being heralded as the foundation of a new architectural language dubbed 'parametricism' (Schumacher, 2009). More modestly, the potential for parametric-based design on a building information model (BIM) platform to transform the architectural process is significant (Eastman *et al.*, 2008). From a management of practice point of view there are likely two aspects to this. First, the economics of practice are changing because significant investment is required in information systems and their support – IT is no longer a hygiene factor in Maister's terms and there are economies of scale in such systems. Smaller practices could find it more difficult to access high-end IT skills and be obliged to use specialist outsourcing suppliers, but if parametrics are as important as some think, then such firms will effectively be outsourcing an important aspect of the core competence of design. Second, many of the entry-level jobs associated with tasks such as door scheduling will disappear, thereby upsetting the customary leverage ratios.

The future of partnership

Current developments threaten the 120-year-old definition of partnership as a 'firm' as:

> ... *the relation which subsists between persons carrying on a business in common with a view of profit* ... *[and] every partner in a firm is liable jointly with the partners, and in Scotland severally also, for all debts and obligations of the firm incurred while he is a partner; and after his death his estate is also severally liable. (Partnership Act, 1890).*

In architecture as elsewhere, as practices grow in size, litigation rises and capital is required for sophisticated IT systems new forms of governance are being sought, and the limited liability partnership (LLP) is finding favour in many jurisdictions – in the UK with effect from 2001. Research on legal practice and the rapid growth of the global 'magic circle' firms (Empson, 2007) suggests that the precise governance form is less important than the maintenance of the 'professional ethos' through the culture of the PSF as a 'practice-centred business' rather than a 'business-centred practice' to use Maister's (1993) distinction. Thus, in contrast to the argument of Pinnington and Morris (2002), growing incorporation in architectural practice does not necessarily connote a growing business orientation (Winch, 2007).

The rise of the mega-consultant

Recent years have seen significant centralisation in engineering consultancy, a trend that has accelerated with the recession. The ninth largest practice in the world by number of architects in 2010 is a subsidiary of the US engineering giant HDR, while the UK engineering consultancy Atkins stands at 13. US-based engineering consultancies such as AECOM are presently growing aggressively through acquisition and are also likely to appear as major players in the architectural market in the near future. Architecturally led multidisciplinary practices such as BDP and RTKL cannot compete in the civil engineering (as opposed to building engineering) disciplines and there is the potential for a growing threat to *strong experience* architectural practices as the scale of projects rises and clients look to transfer more risk to the supply chain.

Sustainability

The challenges of designing for sustainability in general, and to counteract global warming in particular, are particularly difficult given the pivotal role of the built stock. In essence, this is an innovation problem for the supply side, as clients and regulators demand superior performance. The building will likely become a much more tightly engineered 'machine for living in'. Parametrics will play a fundamental role in this tighter engineering; architects are presently the systems integrators of the building design process (Winch, 1998), but they will probably need to redefine this role more clearly in the future if they are to retain that role. This will likely require closer working with the entire project coalitions of specialist designers and contractors as well as the construction managers. Ethical debates around working on contested building types such as airports may also become more intense (McNeill, 2009).

The challenge of globalisation

Construction as a proportion of economic activity falls with economic development, and the western countries appear to be entering a long period of low growth with inevitable consequences for construction activity. The centre of gravity of the global construction industry is clearly moving east – to both the Middle and Far East. Western architectural practices, particularly those based in the UK and Australia, have benefited greatly from the strong demand in those markets, but it is likely that this shift in demand will lead to new clusters of architectural practice emerging. Kloosterman (2008) shows how rapidly the Randstaat architectural cluster emerged around the Office of Metropolitan Architecture, and Grabher (2001) shows how rapidly the London advertising industry moved from being an outpost of Madison Avenue to owning much of it. Beijing, Mumbai, and perhaps Beirut and Kuala Lumpur, would appear to have the potential to develop into new clusters in the global architectural sector complementing the more established strength of Tokyo, Hong Kong and Singapore (Knox and Taylor 2005; Tombesi *et al.*, 2003) and perhaps even challenging London (see also Chapter 1 by Hedley Smyth).

Hypermobility and stamina

As Illich shrewdly remarked, 'speed is one of the means by which an efficiency-orientated society is stratified' (1975: 51); hypermobility through jet travel is surely a major feature of modern architecture. Lord Foster flies his own jet, and Koolhaus spends around 300 nights of the year in hotels (McNeill, 2009). Being a star architect is punishing: for Renzo Piano, 'il n'y a pas un seul projet qui lui échappe à l'agence; on ne peut pas prendre plus de "jobs" que ce que lui il peut suivre.' (there is not a single project that escapes him at the office; one cannot take on more jobs than he can follow) In order to achieve this he spends 10 days of the month in Genoa, 10 in Paris, and 10 visiting sites. The development of ICT seems only to have reinforced the necessity of presence by star architects to ensure that clients perceive that they are getting the design and design control that they are paying for. To be a star architect requires not only creative flair and intellectual rigor but also physical stamina.

The new daedalian risk

Blau (1984) articulates the Daedalian risk at the centre of contemporary architectural practice – see my postscript comment on *make architects*, Chapter 10. The current recession has brought more sharply into focus what might be called the new Daedalian risk of being an architect – the paradox of personal investment in long years of training in the light of poor returns on that investment in through-life income. Other professions, which require similarly high investment, such as medicine, promise superior returns compared to the average graduate; for architects the returns are inferior. While the case of Parrit Leng's scandalous offer (McMeeken, 2010) is probably an outlier, it is a symptom of a more worrying trend. The returns to those at the pinnacle of the profession are great; for most architects, the profession provides relatively poor income and job security through life. Exhortations that five years of education *should* be rewarded with commensurate income are futile; what is needed is a much more thorough-going analysis of how architects can design buildings that add value for clients (Spencer and Winch, 2002) and how that value-adding process is reflected in the architectural syllabus.

Concluding thoughts

Managing architectural practices is challenging, and it become even more so in the years ahead as the western economies recover slowly from the recession. Growth is likely to be fastest in the so-called BRIC countries (Brazil, Russia, India and China); this will open up new opportunities as these countries aspire to a built stock of western standards, but it also represents challenges as architectural service providers from these countries – whether or not they are organised as PSFs – develop the capabilities to compete with the strong idea and strong experience architects based in the west. The latter group is also likely to be increasingly challenged by the aggressive expansion of full-scope engineering consultancies. As the recession in construction deepens, many medium-sized practices that have not paid attention to what Maister calls their balance – particularly by being under-leveraged – will flounder. The number of frustrated strong ambition practices will also grow, augmented annually by graduates from architectural schools who cannot find work with downsized established practices.

While moving from strong ambition to strong ideas through winning an architectural competition or finding a patron is the dream of many young architects, only a few will succeed, and they are likely to be the graduates of the handful of architectural schools where the present generation of stars teach, and to have served their time as a junior in a successful strong ideas practice. For most aspiring architects, gaining competence in specific, innovative, building types – the various aspects of sustainable design are an obvious option here – is the route to competing on the basis of strong experience and being more likely to yield success in the longer term.

Moving successfully from strong ambition to one of the other categories implies acquiring dynamic capabilities. This can be done by forming alliances on either a promiscuous or polygamous basis with complementary practices or, perhaps more easily, drawing on the local project ecology. As the practice grows, enormous demands are placed on the principal, particularly in strong ideas practices, and success requires stamina as well as talent. Whatever the ambition, careful attention needs to be paid to balancing the architectural PSF in terms of the relationship between organisational structure, operational capabilities and the market for architectural services.

Organisationally, architectural practices stand at a three-way intersection between the creative industries, professional services and the construction industry. For this reason they are fascinating to scholars of organisation. Their creativity also plays a crucial role in shaping the built environment in which we live, work and play. For this reason they are fascinating to scholars of the spatial environment. This chapter has drawn on both these literatures to provide insights to the challenges of their management which, I hope, will be of value to those who actually earn their living through architectural practice.

References

Blau, J. R. (1984) *Architects and Firms: A Sociological Perspective on Architectural Practice*, MIT Press, Cambridge.

Blau, J. R. and Lieben, K. L. (1983) Growth, decline and death: a panel study of architectural firms, *Professionals and Urban Form*, Blau, J. R. La Gory, M. E. and Pipkin, J. S. (eds.), State University of New York Press, Albany.

Campagnac, E. and Winch, G. M. (1997) The social regulation of technical expertise: the corps and profession in Britain and France, *Governance at Work: The social regulation of economic relations in Europe*, Whitley, R. and Kristensen, P. H. (eds.), OUP, Oxford.

Carr, B. C. Grèzes, D. and Winch, G. M. (1999) *Export Strategies of Architectural Practices: an Anglo-French Comparison*, Bartlett Research Paper 5, UCL, London.

Coxe, W., Hartung, N. F., Hochburg, H. H., Lewis, B. J., Maister, D. H., Mattox, R. F. and Piven, P. A. (1987) *Success Strategies for Design Professionals*, John Wiley & Sons, New York.

Eastman, C., Teicholz, P., Sacks, R. and Liston, K. (2008) *BIM Handbook: A Guide to Building Information Modeling*, John Wiley & Sons, Hoboken NJ.

Empson, L. (ed.) (2007) *Managing the Modern Law Firm: new challenges, new perspectives*, OUP, Oxford.

Gallouj, F. (2002) *Innovation in the Service Economy: the new wealth of nations*, Edward Elgar, Cheltenham.

Grabher, G. (2001) Ecologies of creativity: the village, the group, and the heterarchic organization of the British advertising industry, *Environment and Planning A*, 33, 351–374.

Grabher, G. (2002) The project ecology of advertising: tasks, talents and teams, *Regional Studies*, 36, 245–262.

Helfat, C. E., Finkelstein, S., Mitchell, W., Peteraf, M. A., Singh, H., Teece, D. J. and Winter, S. G. (2007) *Dynamic Capabilities: understanding strategic change in organizations*, Blackwell Publishing Ltd., Malden MA.

Illich, I. (1975) *Tools for Conviviality*, Fontana/Collins, Glasgow.

Jones, C., Hesterly, W. S., Fladmoe-Lindquist, K. and Borgatti, S. P. (1998) Professional service constellations: how strategies and capabilities influence collaborative stability and change, *Organization Science*, 9, 396–410.

Kloosterman, R. C. (2008) Walls and bridges: knowledge spillover between 'superdutch' architectural firms, *Journal of Economic Geography*, 8, 545–563.

Knox, P. L. and Taylor, P. J. (2005) Toward a geography of the globalization of architecture office networks, *Journal of Architectural Education*, 58, 23–32.

Larson, M. S. (1977) *The Rise of Professionalism*, University of California Press, Berkeley.

Larson, M. S. (1993) *Behind the Post-modern Façade: architectural change in late twentieth century America*, University of California Press, Berkeley.

Larson, M. S., Leon, G. and Bolick, J. (1983) The professional supply of design: a descriptive study of architectural firms, *Professionals and Urban Form*, Blau, J. R. La Gory, M. E. and Pipkin, J. S. (eds.), State University of New York Press, Albany.

Maister, D. H. (1982) Balancing the professional service firm, *Sloan Management Review*, Fall, 15–29.

Maister, D. H. (1985) The one-firm firm: what makes it so successful, *Sloan Management Review, Fall*, 3–13.

Maister, D. H. (1993) *Managing the Professional Service Firm*, The Free Press, New York.

McMeeken, R. (2010) An Offer You Can Refuse, *Building* 19 March.

McNeill, D. (2009) *The Global Architect: firms, fame and urban form*, Routledge, New York.

Miller, V. (2006) Exploited Youth, *Building*, 10 March.

Mintzberg, H. (1979) *The Structuring of Organizations* Prentice-Hall, Englewood Cliffs.

Mintzberg, H., Otis, S., Shamsie, J. and Waters, J. A. (1988) Strategy of design: A study of 'architects in co-partnership', *Strategic Management Frontiers*, Grant, J. H. (ed.), JAI Press, Greenwich.

Murray, P. (2004) *The Saga of the Sydney Opera House*, Spon, London.

Pinnington, A. and Morris, T. (2002) Transforming the architect: ownership form and archetype change, *Organization Studies*, 23, 189–210.

Porter, M.E. (1980) *Competitive Strategy*. Free Press, New York.

Prost, R. (1997) *Pratiquer l'Architecture à l'Echelle Européenne: Un Défi?* CSTB, Paris.

Ren, X. (2008) Architecture and nation building in the age of globalization: construction of the national stadium of Beijing for the 2008 Olympic Games, *Journal of Urban Affairs*, 30, 175–190.

Royal Institute of British Architects (2002) *Strategic Study of the Profession Phase 2: Strategic Overview*, RIBA, London.

Royal Institute of British Architects (2003) *Strategic Study of the Profession Phase 3: Clients and Architects*, RIBA, London.

Schumacher, P. (2009) Parametricism: a new global style for architecture and urban design, *Architectural Design*, 79, 14–23.

Spencer, N. C. and Winch, G. M. (2002) *How Buildings Add Value for Clients*, Thomas Telford, London.

Tombesi, P. A. (2001) True south for design? The new international division of labour in architecture, *Architectural Research Quarterly*, 5, 171–180.

Tombesi, P., Dave, B. and Scriver, P. (2003) Routine production or symbolic analysis? India and the globalisation of architectural services, *Journal of Architecture*, 8, 63–94.

Williamson, R. K. (1991) *American Architects and the Mechanics of Fame*, University of Texas Press, Austin.

Winch G. M. (1998) Zephyrs of creative destruction: understanding the management of innovation in construction, *Building Research and Innovation*, 26, 268–279.

Winch, G. M. (2007) *Business and Network Positioning in Professional Service Firms: the case of architectural practice in international markets*, Presented at Academy of Management, Philadelphia.

Winch, G. M. (2008) Internationalisation strategies in business-to-business services: the case of architectural practice, *Service Industries Journal*, 28, 1–13.

Winch, G. M. (2010) *Managing Construction Projects: an information processing approach*, (2nd ed.), Blackwell Publishing Ltd., Oxford.

Winch, G. M. Grèzes, D. and Carr, B. (2002) Exporting architectural services: the English and French experiences, *Journal of Architectural and Planning Research*, 19, 165–175.

Winch, G. M. and Schneider, E. (1993) Managing the knowledge-based organisation; the case of architectural practice, *Journal of Management Studies*, 30, 923–937.

3 Cross-functional coordination

Conceptual model and its application in professional design practice

Antti Ainamo

Introduction

Firms in the current highly competitive business of the built environment are under constant pressure to have new services to offer that are both timely and responsive to customer needs. To cope with this pressure, these firms have personnel that are specialised in the design and marketing or sales functions. Frequently, they call on these personnel to collaborate, to work on developing new offerings together, even with specialists from other functional areas, such as those from construction engineering or facility management. What can these firms do to make such cross-functional collaboration even more effective? Given the pressures for a built environment that is timely not only to business concerns but responsive to multiple societal, cultural and ecological needs, this question is clearly of fundamental importance.

Many researchers across the design disciplines have shown that the mere existence of cross-functional team structures is not a panacea for making design and project cycles as compact as possible or for improving success rates and quality design. The offerings of each service provider must genuinely appeal to customers, and not only meet minimum requirements identified by market-orientated team structures. The offer should also fit customers' systems and technologies from other service offers to the same group of customers.

Olson and his colleagues have been among the many who have argued that there is more than one kind of effective cross-functional team structure to cope with the diverse requirements imposed on a firm. As such, the work of Olsson and others adds to earlier contingency theory and resource dependency theory, which has long argued that the appropriate kinds of structures range from bureaucratic approaches to more decentralised participatory mechanisms. The new twist to earlier

Managing the Professional Practice: in the built environment, First Edition. Edited by Hedley Smyth.
© 2011 by Blackwell Publishing Ltd. Published 2011 by Blackwell Publishing Ltd.

research, however, has been the proposition that marketing-led structures are generally more participative, more efficient and more effective
than are more traditional bureaucratic structures for projects (e.g. Olson
et al., 1995; 2001). The evidence that Olson and the others provide for their
argument is derived from their study of 45 projects by 12 firms in widely
varying product-based industries (Olson *et al.*, 1995). In their study,
they specified mechanisms that differentiate participatory structures
from bureaucratic ones and marketing-led structures from, say, sales-
or design-led ones. The generalisation made by them on the basis of their
study is that marketing-led or participative structures are more effective
than are bureaucratic structures when there is a focus on: (i) subjective or
objective *measures* of product and team performance, as opposed to other
measures of performance, (ii) *attitudes* of team members toward the
process, whether these attitudes be negative or positive and (iii) the
timeliness or efficiency of the new product development process, rather
than other criteria for success. Worth noting is that Olson and his
colleagues do not mention the many societal, cultural and ecological
needs that have recently arisen as success criteria to the front-end.

Pursuing the path opened of Olsen and his colleagues, Ainamo (2007)
has focused on design as the 'product' and thus how to organise cross-
functional design teams, which also brings services into the picture.
Ainamo compared three firms in different industries: information and
telecommunications technology-based products; engineering and consulting services; and retail and fashion services and products, finding
that marketing (marketing communications, delivery and pricing)
should be in the leading role when the industry offering is a product
and both the product concept and product components have reached
'closure', that is, have stabilised. In contrast, when the product components evolve rapidly, the sales function should be in the lead of communications, delivery and pricing. Product and/or service design ought
to be in the lead in comparison to both marketing and sales when not only
the product components but also the product concept evolves rapidly
(Ainamo, 2007). The task of design in such instances is to cope with
creative tension – even outright clash of interests – that goes with the
differences in the various tasks of these three functions. The relevant
newness of the Ainamo (2007) study, together with its triadic focus on
engineering and consulting services, a cultural industry like textile and
fashion and a socially transformative industry like information and
communication, sheds at least seminal attention on the kinds of societal,
cultural and ecological needs that go with the modern built environment.
Yet, Ainamo (2007) does not focus on challenges that are particular to
services for the built environment. There is a need for further illumination
of how do such challenges may appear, and how to address the challenges.

In contrast to the many researchers who have focused on differences in
the tasks and orientations of different functions, above, an equally
numerous group of researchers has focused on issues that result from

the differences in professional specialisation and cultural disposition of participants in cross-functional design work. This second group of researchers has argued that underlying technical tasks and differences of opinion between professional specialisms go 'naturally with the territory' (Hutt, 1995). Such tensions of disposition can lead to very serious differences in opinion and even to cultural clash, especially in situations where professional differences are amplified by national or other cultural or institutional differences (Orr and Scott, 2008). Researchers in this third group have sought to genuinely appreciate the 'human dimension' related to differences in task, profession, culture and so on, and how professional colleagues are sometimes, in practice, able to reach out across to the 'other' field of task specialisation or professional or cultural disposition – or all of the above – even when the differences in principle are significant (Meyer, 2002; Pryke and Smyth, 2006; Orr and Scott, 2008; Ainamo, 2009).

Still other researchers have focused on how the phases of a design and project cycle differ from one another, rather than focus on the differences in task orientation, professional opinion or cultural disposition between the participants. According to this third main group of researchers, the peculiar characteristic of the built environment is that many of the most complex systems take on the shape of an immobile construction such as a high tower, office block or housing area only when they are 'frozen' (Weick, 2003; Boland and Collopy, 2004). Going back to the time before this 'freezing' happens, at first there are only ideas – often architectural concepts – in a 'fluid' or design phase. Besides the frozen–fluid dichotomy that is characteristic of the built environment, another characteristic of this environment is that the process of building seldom begins from scratch. Rather, the design phase involves processes of discovery and exploration of what is 'good' in earlier buildings or other such artefact-structures. While the differences are thus highly significant in theory, the frozen and the fluid phases may in professional practice be joined together both by a process of exploitation of what is directly useful and by a process of reinvention of what is not directly useful even if (aesthetically) interesting.

With these starting points established, the key questions addressed in this chapter are as follows:

1. How do the foregoing kinds of research findings about how to organise cross-functional teams in various industries apply in the built environment?
2. How do they apply in the various forms of professional practice for this sector, which can be considered to comprise an industry in their own right?

To address these two questions, this chapter selectively draws upon research on the built environment, building mainly on the literatures of organisational structure, management and marketing research to extend in new directions our conceptual and applied thinking on the effective management of cross-functional teams, their management and professional practice.

Overview of the key theoretical ideas

Development of conceptual models or frameworks and the application of such models into effective and efficient modes of operation follow a two-step process that has worked in countless industries and also in various forms of business services and professional practice related to such industries. This chapter continues by developing a conceptual model for describing, studying and comparing various mechanisms for coordinating activities involved in the design and project cycle of the built environment, to usefully describe and provide guidance on:

- how different types of organisational structures influence inter-functional interactions and interdependencies in different ways;
- why different coordination structures are better suited to managing the functional interdependencies involved in the different types of work related to the design and project cycle that is characteristic of the built environment;
- how the interaction between the type of work and the type of coordination mechanism employed affects such outcomes as the speed of the development process, the attitudes of the people involved in that process and the building's ultimate success in its context of use.

Within research on cross-functional coordination, the research on cross-functional product development has progressed furthest. We start out in that research literature and work our way through to the design and project cycle in the industry so that, in the final section, we discuss implications for professional practice in the built environment.

Olson *et al.* (1995), Ainamo (2007) as well as others (e.g. Scott and Davis, 2007; Mintzberg, 1979; Galbraith and Nathanson, 1978) have identified several kinds of lateral linkage mechanisms that organisations use to coordinate functional interactions across the full spectrum of organisational activities, including offering design, or what they call the new product development process. On one hand, structures that are more bureaucratic tend to produce better outcomes on less innovative projects, such as those involving routine services, product and service line extensions or improvements; functional structures often produce specific efficiencies based on the advantages of specialisation, and each speciality, in turn, gives rise to a need for cross-functional interaction and coordination between them. On the other hand, participative structures focus on facilitation of cross-functional knowledge and activity flows. Participatory structures are likely to improve the effectiveness and timeliness of the development process when the product or service being developed is truly new and innovative (Astley and Zajac, 1991). All in all, the two kinds of structures identified by the above four groups of researchers cluster into two distinct sets of mechanisms:

1. Traditional structure-based coordination mechanisms.
2. New resource-based coordination mechanisms.

Traditional structure-based coordination mechanisms

Organisations have long had a variety of structural forms from which to choose when implementing a strategy. Within the research tradition focusing on 'organisation design' (Galbraith and Nathanson, 1978), 'structure' is an agglomeration of formal organisation configuration of roles and administrative mechanisms that control and integrate knowledge and information, work activities and other resource flows. The formal organisational structure in most contemporary business firms reflects this kind of functional division of work according to specialities such as design, marketing, finance and cost control, production and delivery and research and development (R&D). To manage coordination between specialities, organisations typically rely on a range of coordination mechanisms and lateral linkage devices to structure and to connect relatively autonomous functional units (Scott and Davis, 2007):

■ *Bureaucratic control/hierarchical directives*: The most formalised and centralised – and the least participative – mechanism relies on standard operating procedures and the oversight of a high-level general manager to coordinate activities across functions. Each function is organised as a department that operates with relative autonomy within the constraints imposed by hierarchical directives, and therefore most communication flows vertically within each department. The general manager serves as the primary communication link and arbiter of conflicts among the various functions. When applied to the built environment, such mechanisms will result in the classic project-based organisation, where business is organised with each project in turn broken down into tasks, which are sometimes bundled into sub-projects. Functional activities occur sequentially. The output of each task and sub-project in the overall development project is thrown over the wall from one functional department or organisation to the next, with the emphasis being on optimisation and efficiency (Ainamo, 2005). The attitude will be task-oriented, yet there will be an atmosphere of 'no blame' on consultants and their staff because of professional and organisational codes

and project procedures (Provera *et al.*, 2009), which together necessarily constrain complete freedom to creatively design genuinely
new solutions.

■ *Individual liaisons*: In this coordination structure, individuals
within one or more functional department or organisation are
assigned to communicate directly with their counterparts in other
departments, thus supplementing some of the vertical communication found in bureaucracies. Through such liaison, individuals carry
no formal authority to make decisions and resolve inter-functional
conflicts, as they often wield informal influence by virtue of their
centrality within communication networks that cross functional
boundaries (e.g. Druskat and Druskat, 2006). In the organisation
of Kone, the world's fourth largest elevator contractor, for example,
individual liaisons play an important role in negotiating technology
and design for challenging projects where world-class architects are
involved; the first project is establishing personal relations and
common practices, and this is when 'the largest value' is created
(Kiukkonen *et al.*, 2007).

■ *Temporary taskforces*: The temporary taskforce represents the institutionalisation of repetitive interaction patterns amongst liaising individuals in the context of a specific project. Because taskforce members
represent various functions and they interact directly rather via rules
and procedures, this is a more participative and less formalised
mechanism than those above. On the other hand, the temporary
taskforces remain more a bureaucratic than a participative structure
in that higher-level managers typically retain their authority to govern
taskforces by assigning them their central tasks, imposing directives
for, and across, taskforces, and mediating disagreements among
taskforce members (e.g. Gersick and Davis-Sacks, 1990).

■ *Integrating managers*: Under this coordination structure, an
additional management position or role is superimposed on the
functional structure. The manager assigned to this coordinating
position within any particular organisational hierarchy (e.g. an
account manager or a design manager in an architectural practice,
a project manager in a cost consultant practice) has the challenge to
penetrate and operate across organisational boundaries. Professional
organisations can benefit from enhancements having integrating
managers who know how to achieve successful results through
personalised forms of influence, persuasion, encouraging and facilitating group decision-making, sometimes even at compromise
(e.g. Druskat and Druskat, 2006; Kioussi and Smyth, 2009).

■ *Matrix structures*: Whereas the two previous mechanisms maintain
the primacy of the functional–departmental structure, a matrix
organisation structures activities according to multiple foci:
a focus on the services or products, a focus on some other kinds

of offerings, a focus on markets, by function, or any kind of combination of the above. In a matrix organisation an employee can thus be a member of a functional department and a service- or customer-focused business unit simultaneously (e.g. Loosemore, 2006; Morris, 2006; Smyth, 2006). As an example of a matrix structure of an interesting kind, Gehry has notoriously been found to integrate two elements in his architectural design: creative ideas, and their translation into material reality (Weick, 2003). This works because the creative ideas revolve around Gehry, the person, whereas their translation involves Gehry Partners, his firm as a whole. The creative design studio within a practice may perform the same role, whereas fruition requires a broader set of resources within the firm and the multi-organisational design team. Seen differently, Gehry Partners is really about a formulation–implementation dichotomy and its resolution through integration, whereas in many other professional practice firms an integration–implementation dichotomy is more common; there is struggle first to integrate disparate ideas and then a struggle for effective implementation or delivery. Gehry as an architect is more interested in creativity and formulation than in integration and the translation of his ideas for others. According to Weick (2003), Gehry feels sometimes that when his ideas are translated in the interest of coordination, this threatens the integrity of these designs. Yet, as long as Gehry himself is the major partner of the firm, his views will always hold sway. In striving for a 'fully optimal solution' (Boland and Collopy, 2004), Gehry and Gehry Partners amount to an essentially one-man-firm strategy for transgressing compromise and mediocrity that sometimes go with the matrix structure, which seldom has a built-in bureaucratic decision-making rule or procedure. In more complex matrices iterative negotiation endeavours to resolve such tensions and agreed compromise may result at times.

New resource-based coordination mechanisms

The recent studies of Gehry and his firm fit the findings of resource-dependency research, which has an extensive history within research on management and organisational structures (cf. Pfeffer and Salancik, 1978). Resource dependency is a research approach that has been used to explain interactions across personnel from different functional units in a firm (Gupta *et al.*, 1986; Ruekert and Walker, 1987a). This kind of research has found that two new structural forms have gained popularity as organisations have searched for ways to improve the timeliness and effectiveness of their product development efforts within ever-more-rapidly changing environments (Olson *et al.*, 1995):

1. ***Design centres***: Like temporary taskforces and matrix structures, a design centre is a coordinating unit. It is a permanent or at least semi-permanent addition to an organisational structure. Members of the centre may engage in multiple development projects over time (Nonaka and Takeuchi, 1995). Design centres are seldom an alternative to a bureaucratic organisational structure. Rather, they are structures that are usually superimposed on an existing structure. Thus, a consultant in an independent contractor of professional engineering services can work in a project in addition to being a member of the industrial research department and being attached to a particular business unit (Ainamo, 2005). When applied to new service development, a complex authority structure is created: individuals are responsible to both a functional manager and a project manager, for example. Within this context, in a way similar to how Gehry and his firm work, the senior or founding partner/director will typically look after the quality of inputs in a range of teams in the design centre or studio, which role he or she does not necessarily carry out in a fashion that would be authoritarian or hierarchical in an obvious way.

2. ***Design teams***: Like matrix structures and design centres, design teams bring together a set of functional specialists to work on a specific new service or product development project. Unlike these the matrices and centres, however, a design team is not a permanent structure. Teams form to carry out a given mission, brainstorm, self-organise to develop norms of their own, find identity in what they do, and disband or reconfigure when the mission is accomplished. As long as they exist, teams tend to be largely self-governing and may choose their own creative leader(s) under a shallow management leadership or structure, establish their own operating procedures and resolve conflicts through consensual group processes (Gersick and Davis-Sacks, 1990; Sutton and Hargadon, 1996; Ainamo, 2005). Because they are not frozen structures but constantly evolving and thus fluid, they are free to chase radically new kinds of creative ideas (Boland and Collopy, 2004). The design team is often that part of the organisation that does the most creative part of a project (Sutton and Hargadon, 1996; Weick, 2003; Cova and Salle, 2006; Ainamo, 2007; 2009).

Determinants of an appropriate set of coordination mechanisms

Given the endogenous creativity of teams, why are they not the dominant organisational structure – after all, participants in design teams share information across functional boundaries on a frequent and informal basis and undertake interdependent tasks concurrently rather than sequentially? Individuals within such structures tend to adopt a customer or project focus rather than a functional orientation. At the design-team level of analysis, increased autonomy, lower centralisation of authority and fewer rules and regulations appear to lead to collaborative and highly successful decision-making and consensual conflict resolution (Olson *et al.*, 1995; Boland and Collopy, 2004; Weick, 2003; Ainamo, 2007).

Participative decision-making, consensual conflict resolution and open communication processes in such organic structures reduce barriers between individuals and functional groups. The result is an atmosphere where creative ideas and innovations are proposed, critiqued and refined with a minimum of financial or social risk. Design teams, at the participative extreme of coordination mechanisms, have clear advantages for coordinating service and product development. By facilitating the open exchange of creative ideas and analytical perspectives across multiple functions, the odds of producing innovative offerings that successfully address market desires as well as aesthetic, technical or operational requirements are increased (Sutton and Hargadon, 1996). One result is a high retention rate of vital information that may otherwise be lost or altered with other mechanisms and an increase in the likelihood that decisions made early in the process will also make sense in later work stages.

The reasons why design teams are not the dominant organisational structure is that design teams, as well as participative organisational structures, have both advantages and disadvantages. Control and reward mechanisms in organic and participative structures focus on the outcomes of the particular project or the local market, rather than on corporate goals or global responsibilities. Creating and supporting multiple team structures – each incorporating a full complement of functional specialists and dedicated resources – often amounts to inefficient use of personnel and facilities when analysed by any set of conventional economic measures. This explains why different disciplines are conducted through different organisations or subsidiary departments in large multidisciplinary firms. Project teams within the design studios of architecture and engineering firms are typically small and have flat structures and short chains of command. This facilitates complex and informal communication patterns, participative decision-making and consensual conflict resolution, which otherwise would be much more time-consuming and much less efficient processes than are structures tightly coupled with bureaucratic control, yet they are less creative and therefore less effective.

Design teams are the easiest target for spelling out how these disadvantages play out. Design teams come and go as there are few formal systems for transferring personnel from one project to the next. Thus, the design team dynamics are typical complex (cf. Gehry, 2004), and so increasing the likelihood across the roles and functions will facilitate creative design and problem solving (Ainamo, 2007). While the most creative ideas for design or problem solving often arise from the multi-organisational design teams and project teams involved with the built environment, delivering these ideas into the project are normally conducted in a vertically integrated organisation that includes project execution (cf. Ainamo, 2009; Fynes and Ainamo, 1998). Design teams may be ideal for a creative architectural firm (e.g. Gehry 2004), but many creative architectural firms do not have – and historically relinquished – the capabilities necessary for the implementation and delivery phase of a large and complex engineering project (Kamara *et al.*, 2002). For implementation, the customer requires other consultants and contractors with delivery capabilities (Kiukkonen *et al.*, 2007; Ainamo, 2005; Skaates *et al.*, 2002).

Given the need to balance these tensions of (organisationally internal and external) design teams, we propose that architecture, engineering or contracting firms in the built environment can benefit from research on contingency and resource-based coordination mechanisms across industries. This range of literature suggests the various coordination mechanisms be positioned along a continuum ranging from relatively hierarchical, mechanistic and tightly coupled structures such as various kinds of bureaucratic control, on the one hand, to participative, organic and loosely coupled structures such as design centres and (internal and multi-organisational) teams, on the other. Points along the continuum reflect differences in underlying technical tasks that the different functions such as marketing and architectural design have, as well as differences in professional opinion, cultural disposition and phase in the design-and-build cycle. Some functional activities, departments and firms ought to have autonomy to develop their own methods and make their own decisions, while other activities, departments and firms must be engendered to develop capabilities to deliver creativity, problem solving and, where appropriate, standard solutions that professionals have developed. Rules and operating procedures in bureaucratic structures are by definition more formalised and much more rigidly enforced than they are in the participative structures. Authority is centralised. It is decentralised in participative structures.

Earlier studies in other industries than those in the built environment have found the need for integration between marketing and project delivery, on the one hand, and design and the other parts of R&D, on the other hand. The need for integration increases as a function of (i) the aggressiveness of organisational strategy for developing and entering new offering markets and/or geographical markets, and (ii) perceived uncertainty in the task environment. For architects the integration takes the form of structuring relations between design-formulation inside the design studio and marketing or selling creativity and track record outside the studio to new clients and in new segments.

A firm's ability to achieve the desired degree of integration between the two sides of the particular dichotomy that is faced tends to be a function of (i) the structural and operating characteristics of the mechanism used to coordinate the functions (e.g. centralisation, formalisation and participative decision-making) and (ii) personnel factors, such as socio-cultural differences between managers for different activities, departments and across design team firms (and contractors in design-and-build procurement markets). A firm's creative success is contingent on how well the degree of inter-functional integration achieved matches the ideally required level of integration (cf. Gupta, Raj and Wilemon, 1986) for each market segment and the firm's place within it. In innovation studies, it is common to analyse two dimensions of newness: (i) the developing firm and (ii) the marketplace. As defined by the Booz, Allen, & Hamilton (1982) typology, innovations span new-to-the-world innovative projects, me-too projects, line extensions and product modifications. In built environment markets, this does not always mean the uniqueness of design, but the degree of standardised processes in achieving generic design solutions.

Translating the findings of the review to apply in the built environment

In sum, studies of cross-functional coordination outside the built environment suggest that it is advisable to differentiate between the more bureaucratic and the more participative structures, on the one hand, and between the client focus of marketing and the project focus in design, on the other hand. Interactions between functional specialities should be structured differently when the strategic and environmental circumstances change. Performance levels of the firm in the built environment in this view are contingent on how well the coordinating mechanism used to structure a function or cross-functional project fits the demands of the task to be performed and pressures of the extra-organisational domain (cf. Ruekert *et al.*, 1985). However, there is a lack of marketing focus in many of these studies. While some of the findings in the foregoing literature may be understandable for industrial and contracting engineers, there is a need to explain the findings for architects and civil engineers, in particular. The research literature on marketing is interesting, but the peculiar challenge in the built environment is that few architectural firms, for example, have dedicated and prominent marketing functions, aside from exceptions that are almost all to be found in the USA.

When Olson *et al.* (1995) and Ainamo (2007; cf. Hall 1987; Ruekert and Walker 1987a; 1987b) studied projects and generated and tested propositions concerning contingent relationships between functional coordination mechanisms and performance outcomes, they found that employees are more willing to work closely with other functional specialists in participative structures where they perceive that need.

How do the findings from outside the built environment apply in the context of the built environment? Architects and design engineers do not create products in the traditional sense, but usually produce fully developed design concepts only after they have been contracted or have successfully marketed their generic capabilities of creativity and track record. Organic and participative coordination structures are required to facilitate resource flows and resolve conflicts effectively because professionals in the built environments charged with discipline-related tasks work in a state of interdependence. This is straightforward, and multidisciplinary boundaries tend to keep different disciplines in their own departments, sometimes structured as divisional subsidiaries. What is less straightforward is the marketing function which is frequently less well understood and coordinated. Coordination is higher where it is developed amongst those in the professional discipline, but typically awareness of the function is weak and the reverse is also true. This largely remains an unresolved tension in the coordination mechanisms.

The work of architects and design engineers tends always to terminate at the fluid or design phase, well before the frozen or delivery phase. This can lead to a lack of quality throughout the design and project cycle and a lack of relationship management of, and feedback into, marketing from the client (see Chapter 7 by Smyth and Kioussi). Informal cross-functional coordination and intra-organisational networking outside the constraints of contract procedures prevails, with marketing and formal business development a secondary consideration. Sutton and Hargadon (1996) and Pryke and Smyth (2006) extend this idea of networking to inter-organisational networking, which works informally and effectively.

Reasons why interactions among functions such as marketing and design differ under different circumstances – and therefore why different coordination mechanisms might be more effective (Ruekert and Walker, 1987a) – include a number of situational factors, such as a complex and turbulent external environment or aggressive and risk averse contract strategies, inward focus and self-interest of disciplines and departmental, information-processing skills, competences, or combinations of these.

Spanning the external boundaries of the organisation in design projects in the built environment is needed to access critical expertise, information and other resources that can be found only outside disciplines – and hence organisations – and sometimes outside the project. Ainamo (2007, 2009) sums up that the most participative structure will not only span functional boundaries inside the organisation, but also span the external boundaries of the organisation. For ideas to travel in one modern organisation, this sometimes happens so that professional participants share information in multi-organisational design team meetings and within broader networks for transfer to happen between people within one organisation, which is more likely where hierarchies and internal horizontal functional boundaries are strong (Meyer, 2002; Ainamo, 2005).

The relationship between functional interactions and coordination mechanisms

Converting the abstract or concept into a tangible offering, delivering it to potential customers when and where they want it, providing it at a price that they are willing to pay, and earning at least a reasonable profit, requires the application of many different skills and the solution to a variety of functional problems. Specialisation of activity creates a need for coordination across interdependencies since one function can seldom carry out the total integrated service. In the built environment, by contrast to most other sectors, the service is sold prior to its production. As a result the service is being sold as expectations based upon hope derived from track record on a B2B model. It is this that underpins the lack of awareness concerning the marketing function, particularly where the traditional view of the professions prevails, that is, the service sells itself on merit, which remains typical of many strong idea practices and signature architects (Coxe *et al.*, 1987).

Hence, the functional interdependence and the flow of information and other resources across functional departments is typically ill-defined, complex and difficult especially because of the 'lumpiness' of order books and the paradox that marketing effort needs to be maximised when workloads are highest because of lead times (cf. Aldrich and Pfeffer, 1976; Pfeffer and Salancik, 1978; Olson *et al.*, 1995). As projects are secured, design studios and professional teams are allocated resources to facilitate design and professional service development in participative structures (Olson *et al.*, 1995) with short hierarchies to facilitate ideas generation and knowledge sharing (see also Chapter 7 by Smyth and Kioussi). Specialists become more dependent on one another at this stage, yet this can lead to an internal rather than client focus.

In the built environment, therefore, communication and resource flows are primarily horizontal across studios and teams, and bottom-up within teams. Short, and thus secondary, vertical flows occur from the board to studio and team structure and also from the director or partner in allocating resources in the team. This is typically carried out through weekly review meetings. Such weekly reviews will include some reflective bottom-up assessment of needs in some practices, especially those working within innovative and creative firms such as signature, 'archistar' or guru architects (Coxe *et al.*, 1987; see also Chapter 2 by Graham Winch and Chapter 6 by Beatrice Manzoni). In general, individual preferences have relatively little influence over integrating various functional activities (cf. Galbraith and Nathanson, 1978; Mintzberg, 1979), yet iterative reassessment and negotiation is part of being a reflective practitioner where costs cannot be totally known in advance (cf. Ainamo, 2005; 2007). Thus, management in the firms in the built environment may be more likely to employ more organic and participative mechanisms than in other industries.

Service development – a reflection of firm and marketplace

Cutting-edge designs are realised using marketing and management principles of strong idea practices (Coxe *et al.*, 1987) and 'archistars' (see Chapters 2 and 6) with which clients identify (Chapter 7). In such practices service modifications can be frequent, whilst at the other end of the spectrum more routinised practices are found in firms emphasising strong delivery (Coxe *et al.*, 1987). Between these two extremes are service developments, typically developed internally, that are subsequently introduced to the marketplace and me-too services and to products that are new to the firm but not the market. A range of relevant competencies is needed across the marketplace. Firms are not always as shrewd at promoting their service track record during the sales process as they are at promoting their track record by building and procurement type. This is one way of helping firms improve the integration of aspects of the marketing function as well as promoting firm resource management and client management more effectively.

Other competencies are related to inspiring and imagining design concepts, others to developing and detailing the design, and still others to implementing the processes and delivering the outcomes of construction (cf. Henderson and Clark, 1990). Gehry and other similar creative 'archistar' strong ideas practices specialise in creative competences. Design engineers and strong service practices tend to be specialise to a greater degree in the development and detailed design competencies (Ainamo, 2005). Practices strong on delivery focus upon application of standard solutions, whilst implementation or execution largely is externalised to contractor organisations (Kamara *et al.*, 2002). Experience is one of the principal ways of synthesising knowledge that has been accumulated within a firm for a particular market position (Ainamo, 2005; Madhavan and Grover, 1998; Hoch and Deighton, 1989; Newell and Rosenbloom, 1981).

Discussion and conclusions

A flexible, studio and project-by-project contingency approach is likely to produce better outcomes on a variety of performance dimensions than adopting a one-size-fits-all approach to organising and managing product development efforts. There are degrees to which firms can be flexible, hence the division of firms by discipline and into occupying different market positions and segments within each discipline. Within firms, organic, decentralised, participative coordination mechanisms are associated with better design development performance. These kinds of mechanisms result in design and services perceived by customers and other stakeholders to be of higher quality. The key problem area is balancing design and service quality elements in structuring and coordinating the management mechanisms, especially the role and form of marketing that feeds the service. Success in this area facilitates design development (see also Chapter 7 by Smyth and Kioussi and Chapter 11 by Larry Malcic) and makes break-even times are shorter, as well as making stakeholders more satisfied. Management should adopt more bureaucratic and formal coordination mechanisms to manage projects involving relatively familiar and routinised design, yet develop more participative, self-governing structures for projects involving more innovative and creative design concepts (cf. Coxe *et al.*, 1987; Chapter 2 by Graham Winch, Chapter 9 by Stephen Pryke and Chapter 12 by Jeremy Watson). Design centres, studios and design teams are not a panacea but contingent artefacts for managerial decisions and design. Clearly, they are organisational structures that warrant managerial attention because of their advantages in nurturing creativity and problem solving, yet they cannot be treated as mechanistic solutions for managing professional practice.

Architects have tended to stress the importance of a founding or chief architect in managing firms. Marketing has touted self-governing, cross-functional team structures for business management, especially as a tool for improving the speed and effectiveness of the design development efforts of firms. This chapter strengthens this realistic approach as a more evaluative and subtle one for determining and refining team structures and coordination – it all depends on the context and resources managed via iterative assessment, typically weekly. Yet far more work is needed at the detailed level of operation to establish the nature of experience and competencies suited to different disciplines and for different market segments. Further work including prescriptive research is specifically needed regarding the marketing function. Current management approaches have therefore evolved and are sometimes assumed to be appropriate, yet the structuring and coordinating of roles will become even more critical in the future as the complexity of work increases around additional sustainability requirements and whole life cost expertise, hence the justification for further examination through research.

References

Ainamo, A. (2005) Coevolution of knowledge management processes: drawing on project experience in a global engineering consulting firm, *Research in Management Consulting*, 5, 107–129.

Ainamo, A. (2007) Coordination mechanisms in cross-functional teams: a product design perspective. *Journal of Marketing Management*, 23, (9–10), 841–860.

Ainamo, A. (2009) Building working relationships with 'others', *Building Research & Information*, 27, (1), 222–225.

Aldrich, H. E. and Pfeffer, J. (1976) Environments of organizations, *Annual Review of Sociology*, 2.

Astley, W. G. and Zajac, E. J. (1991) Intraorganizational power and organizational design: reconciling rational and coalitional models of organization, *Organization Science*, 2, 399–411.

Boland, R. J. and Collopy, F. (2004) Design matters for management, *Managing as Designing*, Boland, R. J.and Collopy, F. (eds.) Stanford University Press, Stanford, pp. 3–18.

Booz, Allen & Hamilton, Inc., (1982) *New Product Management for the 1980s*, Booz, Allen & Hamilton, Inc., New York.

Cova, B. and Salle, R. (2006) Communications and stakeholders, *The Management of Complex Projects: a relationship approach*, Pryke, S. D. and Smyth, H. J. (eds.), Blackwell Publishing Ltd., Oxford.

Coxe, W., Hartung, N., Hochberg, H., Lewis, B., Maister, D., Mattox, R. and Piven, P. (1987) *Success Strategies for Design Professionals*. McGraw Hill, New York.

Druskat, V. U. and Druskat, P. (2006) Applying emotional intelligence in project working, *The Management of Complex Projects: a relationship approach*, Pryke, S. D. and Smyth, H. J. (eds.), Blackwell Publishing Ltd., Oxford.

Fynes, B. and Ainamo, A. (1998) Organisational learning and lean supply relationships: the case of Apple Ireland and its local suppliers, *Supply Chain Management*, 3, (2), 96–107.

Galbraith, J. R. and Nathanson, D. A. (1978) *Strategy Implementation: the role of structure and process*, West Publishing Company, St Paul.

Gehry, F. O. (2004) Reflections on designing and architectural practice. In: *Managing as Designing*, Boland, R. J. Collopy, F. (eds.), Stanford University Press, Stanford, CA, pp. 19–35.

Gersick, C. J. G. and Davis-Sacks, M. L. (1990) Summary: task forces, in *Groups That Work (And Those That Don't): creating conditions for effective teamwork*, Hackman, R. (ed.), Jossey-Bass, Inc., San Francisco.

Gupta, A. K., Raj, S. P. and Wilemon, D. (1986) A model for studying R&D: marketing interface in the product innovation process, *Journal of Marketing*, 50, 7–17.

Hall, R. H. (1987) *Organizations: structures, processes & outcomes*, Prentice-Hall, Englewood Cliffs.

Henderson, R. and Clark, K. (1990) Architectural innovation: the reconfiguration of existing product technologies and the failure of established firms, *Administrative Science Quarterly*, 35, 9–31.

Hoch, S. J. and Deighton, J. (1989) Managing what consumers learn from experience, *Journal of Marketing*, 53, 1–20.

Hutt, M. (1995) Cross-functional working relationships in marketing, *Journal of the Academy of Marketing Science*, 351–357.

Kamara, J. M., Augenbroe, G., Anumba, C. and Carrillo, P. (2002) Knowledge management in the architecture, engineering and construction industry, *Construction Innovation: Information, Process, Management*, 2(1), 53–67.

Kioussi, S. and Smyth, H. J. (2009) Brand Management in Design-led Firms: the case of architecture practices in the design-construction-development market

5th Thought Leaders International Conference on Brand Management, The Athens Institute of Education and Research (ATINER), 6–7 April, Athens.

Kiukkonen, J., Happonen, E., Ollila, I., Valkama, P. and Vepsäläinen, T. (2007) Assessing and prioritizing major projects, Mat-2.177 Seminar on case studies in operation research, Helsinki: Helsinki University of Technology, 9 May, 2007.

Loosemore, M. (2006) Managing project risks, *The Management of Complex Projects: a relationship approach*, Pryke, S. D. and Smyth, H. J. (eds.), Blackwell Publishing Ltd., Oxford.

Madhavan, R. and Grover, R (1998) From embedded knowledge to embodied knowledge: new product development as knowledge management, *Journal of Marketing*, 62, (4), 1–12.

Meyer, J. (2002) Globalization and the expansion and standardization of management knowledge, in Engwall, L.and Sevón G. (eds.), *The Expansion of Management Knowledge: carriers, flows and sources*, Stanford University Press, Stanford, 33–44.

Mintzberg, H. (1979) *The Structuring of Organizations*, Prentice-Hall, Englewood Cliffs.

Morris, P. W. G. (2006) How do we learn to manage projects better? *The Management of Complex Projects: a relationship approach*, Pryke, S. D. and Smyth, H. J. (eds.), Blackwell Publishing Ltd., Oxford.

Newell, A. and Rosenbloom, P. S. (1981) Mechanisms of skill acquisition and the law of practice, in *Cognitive Skills and Their Acquisition*, Anderson, J. (ed.), Lawrence Earlbaum, Hillsdale, 1–56.

Nonaka, I. and Takeuchi, H. (1995) *The Knowledge Creating Company*, Oxford University Press, New York.

Olson, E. M., Walker Jr., O. C. and Ruekert, R. W. (1995) Organizing for effective new product development: the moderating role of product innovativeness, *Journal of Marketing*, 59, (1), 48–62.

Olson, E. M., Orville, WalkerJr., C. O., Ruekerf, R. W. and Bonner, J. M. (2001) Patterns of cooperation during new product development among marketing, operations and R&D: implications for project performance, *Journal of Product Innovation Management*, 18, (4), 258–271.

Orr, R. J. and Scott, W. R. (2008) Institutional exceptions on global projects: a process model, *Journal of International Business Studies*, 39, (4), 562–588.

Pfeffer, J. and Salancik, G. R. (1978) *The External Control of Organizations: a resource dependence perspective*, Harper and Row, New York.

Provera, B., Montefusco, A. and Canato, A. (2009) A 'no blame' approach to organizational learning, *British Journal of Management*, DOI: 10.1111/ j.1467–8551.2008.00599.x.

Pryke, S. D. and Smyth, H. J. (2006) *The Management of Complex Projects: A Relationship Approach*, Blackwell Publishing Ltd., Oxford.

Ruekert, R. W., WalkerJr., O. C. and Roering, K. J. (1985) The organization of marketing activities: a contingency theory of structure and performance, *Journal of Marketing*, 49, 13–25.

Ruekert, R. W. and Walker Jr., O. C. (1987a) Marketing's interaction with other functional units: a conceptual framework and empirical evidence, *Journal of Marketing*, 51, 1–19.

Ruekert, R. W. and Walker Jr., O. C. (1987b) Interactions between marketing and R&D departments in implementing different strategies, *Strategic Management Journal*, 8, 233–48.

Scott, W. R. and Davis G. (2007) *Organizations and Institutions*, Sage, New York.

Skaates, M. A., Tikkanen, H. and Alajoutsijärvi, K. (2002) Social and cultural capital in project marketing service firms: Danish architectural firms on the German market, *Scandinavian Journal of Management*, 18(4), 589–609.

Smyth, H. J. (2006) Measuring, developing and managing trust in relationships, in *The Management of Complex Projects: a relationship approach*, Pryke, S. D.and Smyth, H. J. (eds.), Blackwell Publishing Ltd., Oxford.

Sutton, R. and Hargadon, A. (1996) Brainstorming groups in context: effectiveness in a product design firm, *Administrative Science Quarterly*, 41, 685–718.

Weick, K. (2003) Organizational design and the Gehry experience, *Journal of Management Inquiry*, 12, 93–97.

4   Challenges of growth in a medium-sized engineering design consultancy

Andrew Edkins, James Barrett and Hedley Smyth

Growth in small to medium-sized project-based organisations is a challenge, and firms are likely to experience a number of 'growing pains' as systems and structures adapt (Flamholtz and Hua, 2002). The challenge takes distinctive forms. Workload and resource planning are examined within this chapter, including how workload and resource planning affect other policies. Structures, systems, processes and tasks must change and adapt through organic evolution and conscious change management and restructuring (Kreitl *et al.*, 2002; cf. Penrose, 1995). Major organisational changes are led by alterations in communication and management attitudes (Drucker, 1955). The issues associated with growth in the professional services sectors is relatively unexplored in the literature (Løwendahl, 2000; Cooper *et al.*, 2000; Scott, 2001; Kreitl *et al.*, 2002). A contribution to this area is therefore to be made by reviewing the case of an engineering design consultancy firm in the building services sector of the UK. The case is analysed, and recommendations explore the means to overcome the challenges that similar firms face.

Professional services firms differ from other business enterprises in two distinct ways: first, the services provided are highly customised and second, the majority of the staff employed are highly skilled professionals (Maister, 2003). However, Løwendahl (1997) states that the work of professional service firms requires a significant amount of client interaction and discretionary effort with other firms and indeed its staff guided by professional norms of conduct to facilitate external interaction as well as service quality.

The chapter is divided into three sections, the first of which discusses the key challenges that project-based professional service firms face during periods of growth. The second discusses the case company, particularly workload and resource planning, and the final section discusses possible methods of achieving growth objectives.

Managing the Professional Practice: in the built environment, First Edition. Edited by Hedley Smyth.
© 2011 by Blackwell Publishing Ltd. Published 2011 by Blackwell Publishing Ltd.

The challenges facing firms during growth

Professional service firms are facing complex and sometimes ambiguous challenges in client and personnel markets, induced through increasingly sophisticated social and technical demands. Stumpf *et al.* (2002) comment that professional service firms operate through labour-intensive practices in order to satisfy such demands. Maister (2003) suggests that survival is based upon the trinity of service, satisfaction and success; thus, pursuing ambitions or a strategic mission is dependent upon meeting demands of clients and staff.

Firms undergoing growth nonetheless experience uneven workloads, continuously targeting potential clients, identifying future potential pipelines even though there may be a steady bedrock of work, including repeat business clients (cf. Løwendahl, 1997; Smyth, 2000; Kreitl *et al.*, 2002). This renders it difficult to tell how sustained the medium-term growth is, as well as managing the uneven pattern of high volumes of short-term work and the consequential stretched resource base and conversely short-term overcapacity. In periods of boom, short-term under-capacity of resource can lead to some projects being allocated resources in ways that lead to other projects in the portfolio experiencing missed deadlines and stressed working (Bayer and Gann, 2006). Such pressures can lead to mistakes being made, which may then lead to work having to be redone and the potential for reputational damage. Redesign and rework of calculations and documentation exacerbates demands on resources, as staff from other project teams are drafted in to assist or alleviate a crisis. Externally, the activities of other design team members and the iterative nature of design work in general may further affect internal workload.

Planning the use of resources on design tasks is one of the most important activities that management are required to undertake (Maister, 2003: Miles *et al.*, 1993). Scheduling work is a management function. Planning and scheduling do not overcome or eradicate the problems of periods of too much work for the resource base available, but engender a state of greater preparedness and provide a basis for contingency planning. Yet this resource-based planning function can be somewhat neglected during periods of growth, where the emphasis can turn too much to getting the immediate tasks done. Maister (2003) argues that most professional service firms reward the volume of work won, rather than any projects' ability to add to profits. The senior management of professional service firms would typically seek comfort in the volume of work secured in future periods, rather than the specific profitability composition of that pipeline. A possible result is that in uncritically securing work there can be situations that tend to the highly resource-intensive and ultimately low-profit-making. The focus on short-term selling of services to secure a volume of work can come at the expense of medium-term business development and marketing that might have helped to smooth short-term fluctuations in workload. In summary, workload increases can lead to focusing upon short-term thinking when long-term issues need current attention and resources, so that they do not become critical problems for the future.

A recent but pre-credit-crisis UK survey indicated that building services engineering firms were the hardest hit by skills shortages in the industry (Building Services Journal Online, 2008). Dainty *et al.* (2005 p. 387) add that, for the construction industry, 'continued growth in output, coupled with its unpopularity as a career choice, has led to extreme pressure on its labour market capacity'. Therefore, changes in the personnel market will also be a specific challenge for firms to face during growth. Without the staff and skills to respond to clients' needs, service quality can be compromised. This affects projects in hand and indirectly feeds into market reputation, which may eventually impact on the ability to obtain future work.

During a recession, firms may have to (and in fact typically do) let go of staff who were hired in more prosperous times as either permanent staff or on a contract basis (see case epilogue in this chapter for further evidence of this). This reduction in physical numbers can reflect the downturn in the volume of work, but may not always resolve the skills gap; work requiring high levels of expertise (specialist technical knowledge and/or high levels of experience) can fall to those left who are now coping with a greater variety of work (albeit a reduced volume), and so can be found to be working under considerable stress in order to minimise working capital and improve cashflow. The focus is on retaining solid engineering competence and the function associated with 'middle management' is forsaken. This may result in an organisational model of maximised resource efficiency rather than resource effectiveness.

Drilling down to a finer grain of analysis, management of professional service firms may not have the necessary experience or skills required to manage the next growth phase (Hitt *et al.*, 2001), especially as growth tends to go through step changes rather than following a steady or incremental trajectory. Drucker (1963 p. 219) says, 'as the company grew, the job grew. But the man did not grow with the job.' Partners, directors, and senior managers frequently say, when pitching for work, 'people are our most valuable asset'. Human resources are often quoted as being of most importance (Canals, 2001; Løwendahl *et al.*, 2001; Maister, 2003; Bordoloi, 2006), yet actions do not always align with this type of statement. Consultants in financial terms tend to be cash generators or cashflow managers rather than investors in human resource development and social capital generation (see Chapter 1 by Hedley Smyth). In firms growing from smaller to medium or larger the real danger is that what appear to be great people are recruited for their technical and professional skills who, in management terms, create systems and micro-cultures that end up causing more and larger management problems in the future.

The ability to have qualified staff with the right skills at the right time and the right quantity is therefore critical but is an area of tension between financial management in market boom and slump, and for firm growth and contraction. Broadly, the emphasis should be to build market share in times of recession and then focus on growth of profit margin during boom. Towards the peak of the boom and towards the end of step changes of firm growth, staff expansion should be frozen. Coming out of the trough of recession and preparing to make the next growth step, staff expansion should be made ahead of the competition to secure the most competent staff (see Chapter 1). Increasing staff capacity to cover workload increases, firms are then faced with a decision on whether they hire graduates or trainees and develop them internally, or acquire experienced trained staff from other practices (Kor and Leblebici, 2005), or some combination of both. The strategy adopted may depend on the stage in the market and firm growth cycle, plus the specific strategy towards human resources.

Firms growing quickly may focus on lateral recruitment from other firms, as this resource brings immediate explicit experience and carries tacit knowledge. This also applies for staff recruited via short-term contracts. Such staff, or contracting agencies, are typically aware of their bargaining power (except when possibly coming out of a trough in the market) and so can add significant costs to the business and therefore individual projects. This increases demands for working capital, is demanding on cashflow and can squeeze long-term profits. In boom times, any staff overtime payments can further squeeze profits in the short term. Regular overtime in the short run should ideally be borne by the least expensive, but still capable staff. Ideally, experienced staff should only be expected to work overtime to meet deadlines for critical elements of high value projects in order not to expend goodwill and in order to protect the resource base where relevant (the more senior and therefore highly paid staff do not typically receive overtime payments as they have an established place in the firm and are valued accordingly, ultimately achieving part-owner status and a share of the residual profits).

The resource-based view of the firm focuses upon the conscious and unconscious development of competencies over and above those needed for the rationale of the firm, such as engineering in this case, to which resources are allocated to sustain and develop the competencies to levels of competitive advantage (e.g. Wernerfelt, 1984; Rumelt, 1984). Such competencies are valuable because they tend to be intangible, inimitable and can be spread and embedded in the firm (Prahalad and Hamel, 1990; Barney, 1991). For consultants they typically arise out of combinations of specialist professional knowledge and creativity, organisational culture and norms, and reflective people and a learning organisation (e.g. Schön, 1983; Dunn and Baker, 2003). Human resources are central, yet the paradox is the willingness to invest in people, who then become attractive to competitors and leave, coupled with the difficulty of embedding the competencies in the culture, systems and procedures. This is particularly difficult for the medium-sized practice seeking to make a step change to a larger one. The commitment and resources necessary are considerable and tend to stretch the capabilities to the full with the attendant risks of diluting quality and scuppering expansion. Yet stretch is also a necessary feature of successful competency development (Prahalad and Hamel, 1990).

Founders of firms tend to set the culture and develop procedures, which can have long-term implications for growth. It is not always just the merit of the professional capability that leads to success. Creating and replicating the organisational and management success is critical, thus having a culture and systems that can accommodate growth is very important. Transitioning from small to medium or medium to large size requires internal coherence, and one means of providing this is prior recruitment of trainees and graduates, as they are easiest to mould to the firm. This needs to occur some while before transition, because induction, adaptation and adoption of the culture, plus working experience takes time (Malos and Campion, 1995; cf. Maister, 2003). During the step change, recruitment from very similar practices, typically immediate competitors, is desirable.

Competitors will also be seeking to acquire good staff so looking after staff – including when they are stretched – through development and identifying career paths is important (Thompson, 2001). Retention strategies are critical (Coff, 1997; Steffy and Maurer, 1988). This is not merely a matter of having people to conduct projects but includes reproduction of the culture and retention of core knowledge (Lepak and Snell, 1999) – cognitive, experiential and habitual. At almost all times people are stretched to meet client requirements, but sometimes more than others. Stress is a major factor and relates to resource allocation. High stress levels challenge physical and psychological health, affecting reliability of output and time-keeping, retention and the culture in the long term (Gray, 2001).

The issues raised in growth of the firm would appear to be the domain for the human mind, given the subtleties of issues, but the world of IT has for some time recognised that the problems of allocating and managing human resource is one that can aided by computer software. Firms seeking such IT-based support can go to the market where it will find many modern systems that can be bought as off-the-shelf software packages. Once it is bought, however, the remedy is not immediate or assured. The software can be considered as deaf to the firm's unique set of characteristics and can take time to become useful. For example, enterprise resource planning (ERP) systems, which integrate business information and processes into a single database that collects and stores data from a number of departments and functions, may take three years for benefits to be maximised (Abdinnour-Helm *et al.*, 2003). These packages typically can accommodate growth without impacting upon other systems, except where they are tailored to the firm's needs in ways that prove constraining for the long run.

There are, however, two distinct disadvantages. First, most professional service firms adopt a range of software tools, to cope with both the general issues of running a business, and the specific IT tools that they will need. To the extent that the same standard tools are used, greater importance is put on what the key staff do because they represent the intangible assets and social capital of firms for competitiveness, along with specialist technical capabilities. Second, many ERP packages are expensive investments, particularly for small to medium-sized firms. For a smaller firm it is not just the cost of the software, but the need for training, ongoing support, and the cost of collecting the data, that needs to be considered for a whole-life cost to be estimated. This can be orders of magnitude higher than the 'ticket price' quoted. It is therefore not surprising that some claim that software packages have comprehensively failed to deliver (Bailey, 1999; Scott and Vessey, 2000; Hitt *et al.*, 2002; Huin, 2004).

Therefore, how resources are allocated to capital expenditure and human resources is important for growth, particularly in the short- and medium-term, but sometimes with long-term implications that need careful consideration as part of firm strategy and in tactical implementation and operation. Workload and resource planning are key issues for firms to tackle during organisational growth. These aspects are examined in a case study firm, a small to medium-sized engineering consultancy that underwent a sustained period of growth, particularly during the early part of the 21st century – 2000–2007.

Case company

Silcock Dawson & Partners (SDP) is an established player in the delivery of mechanical and electrical services on both commercial and governmental projects.

At the time of the study, SDP had grown to be a medium-sized engineering design consultancy with a head office in the counties north of London (northern home counties) in the UK. SDP has a successful track record in delivering a range of building-related services principally for UK-based clients. Its range of work spans many areas of building services and its projects are drawn from all aspects of the private and public sectors. Critically, the firm has a number of repeat client organisations that elect to have an ongoing serial relationship with the firm because SDP delivers building-service-related design and associated services on their large portfolio of properties. This private sector partnering ethos coexists with SDP's ability to respond to public sector competitive tendering for projects that are large enough to be above the European Union's limit that triggers full EU procurement rules. These larger public sector projects are therefore expected to be managed under the terms relating to the primary contract, which could lead to significantly different requirements from SDP.

The case study examines the processes and systems that both enabled and restricted strategic growth objectives.

SDP describes its vision and mission as involving the aspiration to become the first-choice consultant for a client seeking its kind of service and to achieve sustainable and profitable growth.

SDP was set up in the mid 1980s, being founded on the talents of a small core ownership team from which it had grown. According to the managing director the pattern of growth was 'organic and somewhat haphazardly, up until about 10 years ago' (this being the end of the 1990s). At its peak (the relevant time for this case) it employed over 120 professionals in four regional offices in the UK. Early organisational growth from the single office was primarily through expansion into a number of market sectors and geographic regions, with the acquisition of two firms and the opening of three additional offices (one subsequently closed and one merged with an acquired firm).

During this early period the make-up of the staff was predominantly senior engineers and associates, reflecting a need to have experienced engineers with the skills to lead projects and interface with clients. Management overhead was minimal, but recognised as essential. As SDP grew, so junior engineers were increasingly employed, but in relatively small numbers throughout the four offices to supplement existing staff, thus not significantly adding to the cost base but providing a resource to expand once assimilated into the firm.

At the end of the 1990s, SDP hired management consultants to advise the business on how it should manage its growth. A primary result was an acknowledgement of the importance of its people, plus recommendations for some structural changes necessary to run a growing company. The senior management team, as owners, were allocated specific functions to oversee in the future operations based upon the vision statement and informed by a business plan. More stringent management and financial controls were introduced covering each functional department – finance, HR and operations. A regional director was also appointed for each of the four offices with a significant attendant increase in overhead cost as this additional management layer was created. The sales turnover continued to increase year-on-year yet profits had fallen despite (and in some cases due to) some of the changes made to the management control systems and procedures. The dramatic increase in turnover, staff numbers and workload was clear evidence that the firm was experiencing growing pains, particularly concerning the control of its workload and resource planning across the firm. These issues had risen to become priority concerns by 2005–6.

The firm invested in an IT package that was orientated towards the management of the project commissions on which engineers were allocated. This system, comprising a customised commercial off-the-shelf (CCOTS) product, was used for a variety of purposes, but was mainly linked to the commercial activities within the firm, particularly the information on which projects were live and on what activity basis the invoices were to be generated.

The strategic business plan for SDP set annual turnover targets in order to achieve net profit objectives of the owners. The projected profit for 2010, set before the 'credit crunch', informed the action to examine opportunities and constraints for growth within the firm. Each regional director was given a sales target, agreed amongst the senior management team. There was an underlying assumption established from the previous history of the firm that certain turnover levels would consistently generate certain profit margins and yield the 'pot' from which bonuses could be distributed on top of the basic salaries to directors. But, as the literature review has shown, this link, even if all things are carried out as before, does not necessarily equate to the same profit margins due both to the increase in managerial investment levels, and to operational efficiency and effectiveness levels changing through periods of growth. Yet there was an immediate feeling that more is better, and so directors focused their attention on securing more work with the concern being that too little work causes cashflow problems. Directors used phrases such as:

- *We were trying to keep a lot of balls in the air at the same time.*
- *We became 'jacks of all trades and masters of none'.*
- *The emphasis is on getting the work in.*
- *The office has more work than can be accommodated.*

As Maister (2003) points out, meeting sales targets can result in directors paying insufficient attention to the strategic desirability of the client and project to the portfolio of work and to the profitability of the work once secured. To counteract this, although sales targets are set, the firm astutely recognised that the gross profit margin ultimately influences the individual bonuses received, with the result that, for any bonus to be given, both the sales and gross margin targets have to be achieved. The combined effect, however, remains the risk of securing volumes of what transpire to be less profitable work that is (increasingly) conducted with overstretched resources, or with rapidly escalating recruitment and retention costs resulting in further profits squeeze.

The identification of this ongoing problem led the senior management of SDP to recognise that the workload of staff was a key area where improvements were required. It was argued that a better system would allow management to see where resources were already fully utilised, which would warn directors of impending workload problems.

The senior management team therefore invested in a two-year knowledge transfer partnership (KTP) to look at developing an enterprise resource planning (ERP) system to overcome this. Nadler (1993 p. 92) suggests that 'the greater the pain and dissatisfaction with the current state of the organisation, the greater the motivation to change and the less resistance'. Due to the problems that resourcing was having on the operations of the firm, and the associated potential benefits from improvements, there was a desire to change the way in which the firm approached resourcing. Resource planning had been conducted by the directors through observation of staff and their teams, informal discussions with staff, and through projecting invoicing (billing) over the upcoming period. One key problem with projecting invoicing as the basis for resource planning is that workload and fee income do not necessarily match, particularly where the company had explicitly or implicitly accepted the risk of completing the design for a fixed or capped fee. Any such problems in profit erosion were then exacerbated by the cashflow problem caused by any lag in settlement of client invoices. The engineering-dominated paradigm present in SDP became increasingly concerned that their accounting reports were showing debtor days increasing as invoices issued by SDP were not being paid in a timely way. This led to a separate endeavour by SDP's accounts team to harry overdue payments. It became increasingly clear that a significant contributor for fee and resource planning is to accurately monitor the level of work in progress and fees invoiced in advance against individual projects through their life.

As a result of the senior management discussions around these areas, an in-house resource planning and monitoring system (RPMS) was developed to meet the specific needs of the company. The challenge was to understand how the engineers (the firm's key resources) were progressing the projects to which they were allocated so as to allow those planning future workloads to understanding how each office/sector/team/individual engineer was 'loaded' and therefore what the free capacity was and where it was located. Senior management were involved in discussions regarding the type of system output that was required, how this was to be presented and the data requirements implicated.

The actual calculations and algorithms used to determine workload were developed through extensive testing and refinement over a period of 4–6 months, with additional output and methods of data entry being introduced. Users provided feedback about how the system achieved its objectives and suggested improvements that made the system a powerful management tool.

The lower levels of management within the firm understood the reasoning behind the changes, were convinced of the potential benefits, and acted accordingly (Abdinnour-Helm *et al.*, 2003). Through the data entry and reporting, the RPMS indicated that some engineers had excessive workload given the deadlines. The resultant action is to focus these engineers on fewer projects to reduce the workload.

There was some scepticism amongst directors whose groups and offices were currently performing to the previously required level of operational performance (cf. Nelson and Winter, 1982). These engineers and managers in SDP felt that they understood the situation 'on the ground' and that more 'head-office measurement' and involvement was unnecessary. This is explained because people tend to follow the same routines as long as performance is above a reasonable level, therefore heuristics or judgements were made as they had been previously (Oster, 1982), so the reporting from the new system did not automatically change practices until the system demonstrated that it could assist managers. The benefits of the system began to manifest when decisions were aligned with the new information. The system proved its usefulness as previously overloaded engineers commented that they had noticed a fall in their workload – a positive and visible effect with the group director having available information on individual workloads and apportioning and reallocating where necessary. This exercise of effective resource levelling, although potentially giving the impression of reducing workflow and therefore potential profit, is about workload being spread across the entire resource base in a more informed way. This is to be contrasted with the approach that relies on 'gut-feel', reliance on the 'usual suspects', and 'the way we've always managed'.

The system's value was intrinsically linked to the need to populate the various databases with accurate and timely information, requiring either self-reporting or management time to collect and/or complete. This is a burden or cost that, in small firms, is not made explicit because informal communication and tacit knowledge is to the fore and, in small professional service firms, management is not what anyone wants to do – they are there to practise their professional skills and 'get on with the job'. However, the evolution from a small/medium firm to a fully fledged medium – nay possibly large – firm involves the formalised need to collect, collate, report and act on such information, and this need was communicated well. The problems created by avoiding this 'distracting and time-wasting' set of activities eventually becomes sufficient to require the design and deployment of more sophisticated approaches, resulting in this case in not only the implementation of the resource management system, but also the clearly articulated need for quality data to feed into the system. This pressure from senior management resulted in the growing response towards providing the necessary data.

Processing the resulting information produced a number of insights into what the engineering base personnel were working on. One line of investigation showed that around 45% of the time spent by staff was on work that was below their perceived level of expertise. In examining the cause of this large possible area of reduced value-added it was found that part of the problem was the historically perceived need for senior engineers to take an initial prominent and client-seen role on projects. On larger and more complex projects this highly visible 'front-end' commitment then drew the engineers in, and although there was a range of responses to this, the cumulative effect was to engage the experienced engineers deeply in their projects and largely overlook the training and development of existing staff or the hiring of graduates and trainees to undertake the more routine tasks on projects. This oversight or failure was justified on the basis that such activities diverted efforts from the core set of actions that needed to be addressed as work continually arrived on everyone's in-tray. This focus on simply getting on with the job in hand was compounded by the difficulty of finding the right staff. Recruitment consultants were being commissioned to search for the skilled staff to undertake the increase in workload, with the agencies charging 15–20% of the starting salary of the staff recruited who, as noted earlier in this chapter, knew they could command high levels of remuneration, this raising the firm's cost base significantly. In addition to permanent recruitment there was also a requirement to take on more temporary contract personnel.

The resultant imbalance between senior and junior engineers had the consequence of increasing the inability or unwillingness to delegate work to lower-cost staff, with results of both inefficient utilisation and the possible 'burnout' of some senior engineers. In this loop of greater work, greater pay and greater stress, there was an inevitable increase in engineers leaving, and an increasing vacancy rate through staff attrition. With poaching of good staff prevalent as the market heated up, this attrition rate could rapidly expand. This then only further exacerbates the costs and challenges of recruitment.

As noted, stressful work squeezes time for engineers to adequately brief juniors, leading to systematic under-delegation (Maister, 2003) with too many juniors/trainees working ineffectively through being left to their own devices. Whilst juniors and trainees had been recruited in small numbers throughout the firm's four offices, which was an entirely sensible development, it was realised that the firm, according to the managing director, had 'not been good at training historically', requiring a change of attitude on behalf of the owners who founded the firm and who were not used to this type of formal investment. An anecdotal example was where the firm provided funds for one of its staff to pursue a Master's degree, but once the degree was completed, this engineer subsequently left for another firm. Whilst there may be various employment-contract 'lock-ins', such investment in key staff always carries a risk, and to mitigate the detrimental consequences involves the consideration of clearly managing the recipient's career path. Whilst there always remains the possibility that the recipient will still choose to leave, such a planned management approach should reduce the likelihood of such incidents and prove the investment in such qualification acquisition to be worthwhile. The firm's response to this person's walking away (and the firm's investment) could have led to a rescinding of all such offers, but the firm's response was indeed to continue to develop a policy of staff investment, with the introduction of allocated and managed training budgets and staff being encouraged to submit a business case for them to be given places on training or educational courses. Whilst this may have been a painful lesson for the company, the result was a more wise and mature approach towards future staff development.

The two-year KTP itself charted the evolution and maturity of the firm's approach as it grappled with its own growth. This can be recast because the initial driver was to seek an answer to the obvious problems of 'why do we never seem to make as much money as we first think we will?' to the ultimate – if now rather obvious – recognition that the firm's highly complex and autonomous asset base was effectively being under-managed. This issue of under-management in this case, as no doubt in many others, was due to the founders of the company being motivated by the area of their professional skill.

As the firm grew, so more likeminded people joined, and whilst there was an obvious need for some degree of management, it was never going to be as rewarding for a qualified engineer to get involved in management as it would be to have the thrill of bringing exciting new work in, or relishing the difficult technical challenges that were there to be solved and results dispatched. When firms are small, such light-touch management styles work and not only is work done, but the firm manages to manage. However, as firms grow, so they will each come to a point at which the 'old ways' are simply no longer fit for purpose. This may be when the firm grows as measured by people employed, diversity of work delivered, number of offices run, or range of clients serviced. Whatever triggers the 'tipping point', it will be the case that professional services firms have to accept that they need professional management approaches and that there will be many prices to pay, be they measured in money needed, time spent or former flexibilities now foregone. Whilst growth may be a pleasant problem for these types of firm to have to deal with, it is still a problem.

Towards implementing growth strategies

Growth is the consequence of historical and current decisions where client-specific and market opportunities permit (cf. Kreitl *et al.*, 2002). Strategic organisational development requires a mindset with long-term vision (Flamholtz, 1995) to inform and develop detailed management policies and systems, help encourage positive attitudes towards change and staff support (Thompson, 2001), and which has to start with owners and senior management in the case of professional service firms (Maister, 2003; cf. Drucker, 1955). In the light of the case evidence, the suggestion of Maister (2003) that directors should primarily focus upon the amount of profit, then the profit margin, rather than sales target is applicable.

Future success cannot be simply based upon past practice (Canals, 2001). Emergent structures, systems and procedures can face resistance, even at senior management level as the case shows. Whilst past success may be based upon the firm being good at what they do (Drucker, 1955; Maister, 2003), especially for small to medium-sized firms, growth in medium-sized firms will require more than technical capability and require management that is operating at the level of competitive excellence. Firms require an appreciation of their capabilities and resources, and need to develop systems and procedures that are themselves – or that support other – core competencies (Prahalad and Hamel, 1990), which become part of the human assets or social capital of the firm. This may arise from the knowledge and experience of staff, which is embedded into supportive structures and processes that are spread across teams, divisions and offices to improve efficiency and effectiveness of services delivered to clients. Therefore, a second key management measure is added service value (Canals, 2001). The two are linked in that added value increases repeat business – and hence the amount of profit – and increases the ability to charge premium profit. This has parallels with the distinction between hygiene profit and healthy profit levels (Maister, 2003).

Leverage can be used to match skills against project requirements (e.g. Kor and Leblebici, 2005), that is, delegation down the organisational structure to the point where work can be undertaken effectively at the lowest cost. When resources are scarce, for example in a booming building services market, effective leveraging is a creative response to HR scarcity. Routine work can be more easily delegated further down the organisational structure to low-cost staff, even where some of the value content is high. Therefore, repetitive work should ultimately involve a higher proportion of juniors and trainees than specialised projects with high levels of engineering creativity, problem solving (e.g. Bruce and Daly, 2007) and management of uncertainty (e.g. Winch, 2002) or ambiguity (Daft and Lengel, 1986). Leverage can also create opportunities to develop less-experienced staff (Kor and Leblebici, 2005) and thus forms part of organisational stretch for growth.

Hitt *et al.* (2001) comment that leveraging can positively affect performance through efficiencies, in addition to the transfer of knowledge with supportive mentoring and oversight for the transfer of knowledge and experience. Leverage is effective where it is part of conscious strategy implementation and is conducted in a considered way in relation to staff capacity and capabilities rather than on a purely reactive or in a 'common sense' way. Delegation systems help monitor and control the leverage process. Without monitoring, the junior staff may develop their own approaches, culture and work patterns, which can affect the quality of the work as well as induce a sense of being undervalued. Without adequate management, these staff may become demoralised and this may lead to them leaving just as they become of greater use and start to significantly contribute to the organisational culture, which only serves to indirectly increase firm costs. A mentoring process could cover this, which will also act as a basis for knowledge transfer from the experienced employee to the junior. The cries of concern about the time-cost of such endeavours, from the existing middle to senior staff members, should therefore be countered with the expected cost of *not* taking any such action.

As this chapter has continually emphasised, people are the most important assets of a professional service firm. The management of such firms needs to change the balance of recruitment at different times. Two factors need to be taken into account: the growth of the firm through (i) its client base and repeat business, and (ii) a more general growth in the market. In the first case there are immediate needs, yet anticipation of a step change requires advance recruitment of junior staff. In the second case there are more observable trends, anticipation being needed to recruit experienced staff ahead of the competition. This may sound both easy and obvious, but when the market generally is becoming highly buoyant, all intelligent firms are aware of this and the summed consequence is that achieving this is, in practice, is far harder than when described on the pages of a book.

Continuously developing the human resource base involves experiential development, mentoring, training and education. Direct costs increase with each option, but indirect costs increase in reverse order. Experiential development appears cost-effective, yet insufficient support and overstretching these resources result in poor quality work, rework, and loss of good staff with the consequential loss of knowledge, recruitment costs and the costs associated with induction and growing into the new roles and organisational culture.

Continued investment in staff is more tangible than the more passive modes of development, and it shows commitment to staff. It is claimed to generate greater benefits (Hitt *et al.*, 2001) than carrying the hidden and indirect costs of experiential learning and mentoring. Training and development that is firm-specific may also limit the amount of staff turnover. When employees are satisfied with the challenging nature of the work, have the opportunity to advance their skills and knowledge, and are given a career plan, they may be less likely to move firm as their sunk costs (those for which they could not get recompensed if they were to leave) would be growing.

All these measures are components of creating opportunities for effective resource planning and for undertaking effective resource planning within a growing firm. Resource planning tools aid operational decision-making. Effective resource planning is also important during peaks in growth. Once workload in the market tails off, it is too late to focus again on business development and other sales activity. The paradox of marketing is to maximise sales efforts at the height of market growth, especially diversifying the type of work and client base. Fruits from such efforts typically take at least 12–18 months to come through. Effective resource planning is needed for senior management at the height of the market to permit increased selling, guided by profitability criteria, for the downturn. Therefore, the common emphasis upon growth by increasing sales, as typified in the case study, is succeeded by prioritising and selecting (i) profitable work (rather than volume), which is resourced in balanced ways to add value and realise the profit, and (ii) selling with a longer time horizon to manage both the growth phases of the firm and mitigate the potential for a downturn in the market. To do this there is a need to both recognise and learn in real time (Schön, 1983). Forward planning of resources becomes 'super-critical'.

Epilogue to the case study

The epilogue to this case study is that SDP's challenges of dealing with growth were then replaced with the problems created by the global financial crisis. The impact on the construction sector was swift and heavy. With both funds and confidence low, capital investment in construction works either ceased or was throttled back, with designers and other professional services firms in construction feeling the effect very quickly.

SDP then moved from a situation of trying to cope with too much work, to trying to survive with much lower levels of work. The impact on the company's headcount is indicated by the following statistics. The growth in staff headcount in 2006 and 2007 was 24% and 21% per annum respectively (following similar high annual growth rates in the previous years of the millennium). From the peak in 2008 the decline in headcount was then 15% and then 32%. In 2006 SDP had 82 staff. By 2008 this had risen to 123 staff, but by 2010 it was down to 71, as shown in Figure 4.1.

At the time of writing it is hoped that the reduction in staff numbers is bottoming out, but the post-credit-crunch economic situation is not one that has been faced before, so SDP and many other firms like them are not able to feel the return of confidence and growth of the pre 2008 era.

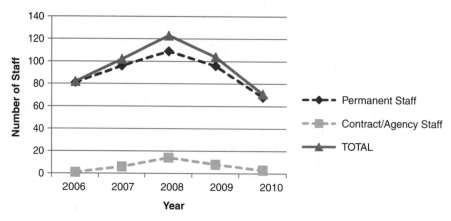

Figure 4.1 SDP staff profile 2006–2010

Conclusions and areas for further research

This chapter has examined some of the challenges that professional service firms face with respect to growth, using an engineering design consultancy as a case study. One of the key challenges faced during growth is controlling workload and having the ability to plan its resources in advance and effectively managing the resources in the present.

Staff resources, their personal development and recruitment, provided a particular focus on the basis that consultancies are essentially a people-business, and the asset value embodied in staff and managed through the culture, systems and procedures of the firm constitute both the human and social capital that increasingly represents a decisive element of competitive positioning. In other words, being excellent in the chosen discipline is a 'given' and the added value comes through the combination of specialist technical expertise, a customer-centric service delivery approach and total management effectiveness. This presents a particular challenge for small and medium-sized practices undergoing step changes of growth.

The chapter has demonstrated conceptually and through case analysis that managing such step changes requires changes in attitude, culture, systems and procedures from the senior to junior levels of the firm.

Two areas for further research are (i) a more detailed case analysis of the effects of recession (as illustrated by the case epilogue), and (ii) a detailed analysis of career paths and whether their provision yields medium and long run advantages for the firm overall and whether criteria can be established between specialist managers and practitioners who are promoted into management positions.

Acknowledgement

The authors are very grateful to Chris Smart from SDP for his valuable contribution and comments on this chapter.

This research was conducted as part of a two-year UK government funded knowledge transfer partnership.

References

Abdinnour-Helm, S., Lengnick-Hall, M. L. and Lengnick-Hall, C. A. (2003) Pre-implementation attitudes and organisational readiness for implementing an Enterprise Resource Planning System, *European Journal of Operational Research*, 146(2), 258–273.

Bailey, J. (1999) Trash haulers are taking fancy software to the dump, *Wall Street Journal*, 9 June.

Barney, J. B. (1991) Firm resources and sustained competitive advantage, *Journal of Management*, 17(1), 99–129.

Bayer, S. and Gann, D. (2006) Balancing work: bidding strategies and workload dynamics in a project-based professional service organisation, *System Dynamics Review*, 22(3), 185–211.

Bordoloi, S. K. (2006) A control rule for recruitment planning in engineering consultancy, *Journal of Production Analysis*, 26(2), 147–163.

Building Services Journal Online (2008) *Skills shortage deepens; services hit hard*, 22nd June, http://www.bsjonline.co.uk/story.asp?sectioncode=730&storycode=3103785.

Bruce, M. and Daly, L. (2007) Design and marketing connections: creating added value, *Journal of Marketing Management*, 23(9–10), 929–953.

Canals, J. (2001) How to think about corporate growth, *European Management Journal*, 19(6), 587–598.

Coff, R. W. (1997) Human assets and management dilemmas: coping with hazards on the road to resource-based theory, *The Academy of Management Review*, 22(2), 374–402.

Cooper, D. J., Rose, T., Greenwood, R. and Hinings, B. (2000) History and contingency in international accounting firms, *Globalisation of Services: Some implications for theory and practice*, Aharoni, Y. and Nachum, L. (eds.), Routledge, London.

Daft, R. L. and Lengel, R. H. (1986) Information richness: a new approach to managerial behaviour and organization design, *Research in Organizational Behavior*, Staw, B. M. and Cummings, L. L. (eds.), JAI, Greenwich, pp. 91–233.

Dainty, A. R. J., Ison, S. G. and Briscoe, G. H. (2005) The construction labour market skills crisis: the perspective of small-medium-sized firms, *Construction Management and Economics*, 23(4), 387–398.

Drucker, P. F. (1955) *The Practice of Management*, Elsevier, Oxford.

Dunn, P. and Baker, R. (2003) *The Firm of the Future: a guide for accountants, lawyers, and other professional services*, John Wiley & Sons, Hoboken.

Flamholtz, E. (1995) Managing organizational transitions: implications for corporate and human resource management, *European Management Journal*, 13(1), 39–51.

Flamholtz, E. and Hua, W. (2002) Strategic organizational development, growing pains and corporate financial performance: an empirical test, *European Management Journal*, 20(5), 527–536.

Gray, R. J. (2001) Organisational climate and project success, *International Journal of Project Management*, 19(2), 103–109.

Hitt, M. A., Bierman, L., Shimizu, K. and Kochhar, R. (2001) Direct and moderating effects of human capital on strategy and performance in professional service firms: a resource-based perspective, *The Academy of Management Journal*, 44(1), 13–28.

Hitt, L. M., Wu, D. J. and Zhou, X. (2002) Investment in Enterprise Resource Planning: business impact and productivity measures, *Journal of Management Information Systems*, 19(1), 71–98.

Huin, S. F. (2004) Managing deployment of ERP systems in SMEs using multi-agents, *International Journal of Project Management*, 22(6), 511–517.

Kor, Y. and Leblebici, H. (2005) How do interdependencies among human capital deployment, development, and diversification strategies affect firms' financial performance? *Strategic Management Journal*, 26(10), 967–985.

Kreitl, G., Urschitz, G. and Oberdorfer, W. J. (2002) Corporate growth of engineering consulting firms: a European review, *Construction Management and Economics*, 20(5), 437–448.

Lepak, D. P. and Snell, S. A. (1999) The human resource architecture: toward a theory of human capital allocation and development, *The Academy of Management Review*, 24(1), 31–48.

Løwendahl, B. R. (1997) *Strategic Management of Professional Service Firms*, Handelshøjskolens Forlag, Copenhagen.

Løwendahl, B. R. (2000) The globalisation of professional business service firms: fad or genuine source of competitive advantage? *Globalisation of Services: Some implications for theory and practice*, Aharoni, Y. and Nachum, L. (eds.), Routledge, London.

Løwendahl, B. R., Revang, O. and Fosstenløkken, S. M. (2001) Knowledge and Value Creation in Professional Service Firms: A Framework for Analysis, *Human Relations*, 54(7), 911–931.

Maister, D. (2003) *Managing the Professional Service Firm*, Simon & Schuster. London.

Malos, S. B. and Campion, M. A. (1995) An option based model of career mobility in professional service firms, *The Academy of Management Review*, 20(3), 611–644.

Miles, G., Snow, C. C. and Sharfman, M. P. (1993) Industry Variety and Performance, *Strategic Management Journal* 14(3), 163–177.

Nadler, D. A. (1993) Concepts for the management of organizational change. In: *Managing Change*, Mabey, C. and Mayon-White, B. (eds.), Sage, London, pp. 85–98.

Nelson, R. R. and Winter, S. G. (1982) *An Evolutionary Theory of Economic Change*, Harvard University Press, Boston.

Oster, S. (1982) Intraindustrial structure and the ease of strategic change, *Review of Economics and Statistics*, 64(3), 376–383.

Penrose, E. (1995) *The Theory of the Growth of the Firm*, Oxford University Press, Oxford.

Prahalad, C. and Hamel, G. (1990) The core competencies of the organization, *Harvard Business Review*, 63(3), 79–91.

Rumelt, R. P. (1984) Towards a strategic theory of the firm, *Competitive Strategic Management*, Lamb, R. B. (ed.), Prentice-Hall, Englewood Cliffs.

Schön, D. A. (1983) *The Reflective Practitioner: how professionals think in action*, Basic Books.

Scott, J. E. and Vessey, I. (2000) Implementing Enterprise Resource Planning Systems: the role of learning from failure, *Information Systems Frontiers*, 2(2), 213–232.

Scott, M. C. (2001) *The Professional Service Firm: the manager's guide to maximising profit and value*. John Wiley & Sons, Chichester.

Smyth, H. J. (2000) *Marketing and Selling Construction Service*, Blackwell Publishing Ltd., Oxford.

Steffy, B. D. and Maurer, S. D. (1988) Conceptualizing the economic effectiveness of human resource activities, *Academy of Management Review*, 13(2), 271–286.

Stumpf, S. A., Doh, J. P. and Clark, K. D. (2002) Professional service firms in transition: challenges and opportunities for improving performance, *Organisation Dynamics*, 31(3), 259–279.

Thompson, J. L. (2001) *Strategic Management*, Thomson, London.

Wernerfelt, B. (1984) A resource-based view of the firm, *Strategic Management Journal*, 5(2), 171–180.

Winch, G. (2002) *Managing the Construction Project*, Blackwell Publishing Ltd., Oxford.

5   Sustainability into practice

How the sustainable development agenda has impacted on the surveying profession

David Shiers, Tim Dixon and Miles Keeping

Introduction

This chapter explains the ways in which the sustainability agenda has impacted on the day-to-day practice of chartered surveyors. Globally, the majority of surveying firms now accept that land and buildings must be managed in a more environmentally responsible way and that this principle is key in developing and delivering successful and appropriate business strategies for themselves and their clients.

As a profession, chartered surveyors provide guidance and expertise to a wide variety of property-owning and user organisations ranging in size and type from small, local businesses to international pension funds and other investment fund management organisations whose property assets may be worth many millions of pounds. For these larger clients, the surveyor will often manage vast portfolios of commercial, industrial and residential property and advise the owners on the disposal, purchase, management, maintenance and refurbishment of buildings and on the development of land for new construction. Consequently, surveying firms can help to determine the success of climate-change and environment agendas across many countries, and, in the UK, play a vital role in helping the government meet many of its environmental commitments.

The introduction of a raft of new property-related environmental legislation (see below) is clearly a major driver of the changes that have occurred within all property professions in recent years. Although ensuring that a client's properties are legally compliant is arguably the most important duty that chartered surveyors undertake, a number of the more progressive practitioners have used these new laws not as a simple endpoint but rather as a way to help clients review and improve their entire business model. The notion of businesses becoming more socially and environmentally responsible is increasingly accepted as making good

Managing the Professional Practice: in the built environment, First Edition. Edited by Hedley Smyth.
© 2011 by Blackwell Publishing Ltd. Published 2011 by Blackwell Publishing Ltd.

long-term financial sense, adding value and differentiating themselves from their competitors. Moreover, a company's commitment to corporate social responsibility (CSR) or the adoption of an environmental management system such as ISO14001 can also introduce a feel-good factor among staff, customers and clients as the organisation is seen to be 'doing the right thing' for society and the planet. Finally, given the role that chartered surveyors play in advising a range of clients on land- and property-based sustainability issues it is of paramount importance for them, and indeed other professionals in similar advisory roles, to be seen to 'walk the talk'.

Changes that reflect a more sustainable approach within surveying companies have included the appointment of directors of sustainability and new staff with environmental expertise in order to provide better 'green' advice to clients, the introduction of in-house energy efficiency programmes, improved waste management and transport policies, and, in education, the teaching of environmental principles on many property degree and CPD programmes. Though much has been achieved, more progress is sought in number of key areas by both the professional body (the Royal Institution of Chartered Surveyors – RICS), and by many of its members.

In a report published by the RICS in 2007, a number of recommendations were made to further improve member's access to guidance and knowledge on sustainability, to enhance training and skills and to help raise awareness among clients of the importance of the sustainability agenda (Dixon *et al.*, 2007).

Examples of recent or pending environmental legislation in the UK

A raft of new regulation has come from the EU and through the UK Parliament and will continue to do so. Some of the significant measures which impact on the surveying profession and their property-owning clients are shown in Table 5.1.

The surveying profession

The educational, professional and ethical standards of chartered surveyors are set by the Royal Institution of Chartered Surveyors, which is the pre-eminent organisation of its kind in the world, with members operating from 146 countries. As a profession, chartered surveyors are involved in:

- the valuation of residential and commercial property in terms of both capital and rental value;
- giving advice on forms of tenancy agreement;

Table 5.1 Examples of important environmental legislation in the UK

The Energy White Paper (2007) and the Micro-generation Strategy (2006)	*'The Code for Sustainable Homes'*: the government announcement that all new homes in England are to be zero carbon by 2016
'The Code for Sustainable Buildings': the government proposal that all new non-residential in England are to be zero carbon by 2019	*Building Regulation* upgrades – due 2010, with even more rigorous carbon emission targets
Site Waste Management Plans Regulations (2008)	*'Decent Homes'* standard, tackling fuel poverty and general levels of condition and amenity of social housing
The requirement for Section 106 agreements, often demanding measures to encourage sustainability and bio-diversity	The growing adoption by planning authorities of the *'Merton Rule'*, a requirement for all new developments to incorporate a percentage of renewable energy technologies in the overall energy supply provision
The Carbon Reduction Commitment	*The Energy Building Performance Directive – Recast 2010*
The Eco-Design Directive – the scope of which will be extended to cover all energy-related products and cover minimum requirements for products with significant environmental impacts	*The Renewable Energy Directive* requiring adoption of national targets for renewables that are consistent with achieving the Commission's target of reaching 20% agreed in the '20-20-20' initiative
Construction Products Directive (89/106/EEC): the intention is to replace existing national standards and technical approvals with a single set of Europe-wide technical specifications for construction products; under the Directive, a product bearing the CE marking will be presumed to meet the requirements of these specifications; energy economy and heat retention is an essential requirement	

- identifying and managing property investment opportunities;
- agency work, involving the marketing, letting and sales of commercial and residential property;
- giving technical advice on building defects, maintenance and repair;
- property development and project management;
- quantity surveying;
- land and building surveying;
- property management and facilities management.

Surveyors can provide these professional services across the entire range of size and type of property from small-scale residential buildings to large, complex commercial buildings and development projects in the office, industrial, leisure and retail sectors.

The RICS monitors and manages the activities of its membership through a 'professional group' structure, whereby surveyors must satisfy the Institution that they are competent to practise in one or more of specified key skills areas. Following completion of an RICS-recognised undergraduate or postgraduate degree (usually a BSc or MSc from a higher education institution) prospective members are required to pass

Table 5.2 RICS professional groups

Building Control	Building Surveying
Commercial Property	Dispute Resolution
Environment	Facilities Management
Geomatics	Management Consultancy
Minerals and Waste Management	Planning and Development
Project Management	Property Finance and Investment
Quantity Surveying and Construction	Residential Property
Rural	Valuation

an assessment of professional competence (APC) test, and thereafter to maintain a record of continuing professional development (CPD) throughout their career. To be a practising member of the RICS, surveyors are also normally required to carry appropriate professional indemnity (PI) insurance. The main building-related RICS professional groups are shown in Table 5.2.

Although the surveying profession is not widely acknowledged as one of 'early adopters' of sustainable development (in common with many others in the construction and property sectors), the RICS now has a list of mandatory *sustainability competencies* for membership and are required to be included in all of the above specialist areas of expertise. These competencies are as follows:

- At *level one* (for all pathways and professional groups), members must demonstrate knowledge and understanding of why and how sustainability seeks to balance economic, environmental and social objectives at global, national and local levels, in the context of land, property and the built environment.
- At *level two*, members must provide evidence of practical application of sustainability appropriate to their area of practice, and of awareness of the circumstances in which specialist advice is necessary.
- At *level three*, members must provide evidence of reasoned advice given to clients and others on the policy, law and best practice of sustainability in their area of practice.

In 2005, the RICS also put forward a sustainability policy (developed by the UK Government's Sustainability Commission) to be adopted by members.

RICS sustainability policy principles

'At global, national and local level, RICS and its members are committed to creating and maintaining a healthy environment...' (RICS, 2010b). Requirements are to:

- promote community development and social inclusion;
- promote social and environmental equality;
- encourage the sustainable use of resources;
- reduce waste generation and dispose of waste responsibly;
- protect and enhance the natural environment;
- strive to reduce energy consumption;
- promote sustainable design, development and construction;
- promote sustainable land use and transportation;
- (when pursuing economic goals) seek to enhance or at least minimise negative social or environmental impacts.

In recent years, many of the leading surveying practices have developed the necessary sustainability skill sets to offer a wide range of professional services across the entire property lifecycle (Figure 5.1). Whilst this in-house expertise would not normally extend to the more complex environmental auditing aspects of say, lifecycle assessment or full carbon or energy auditing, most large surveying firms would have access to environmental consultancies through whom they could provide this information to clients.

A survey of some 15 leaders of RICS professional groups in 2006 (carried out by Forum for the Future) suggested sustainability impacted across three potential dimensions for surveyors:

1. Strategy and management – for example, front-end planning and investment, rural development, procurement.
2. Application and assessment – for example, whole-life costing, environmental impact assessment, remediation.
3. Promotion and education – for example, advising and briefing clients and building users, and promoting principles to other professions.

Figure 5.1 The Sustainable Property Lifecycle incorporating the range of professional services offered by many surveying practices (Source: adapted from GVA Grimley, 2009)

In simple terms, the building lifecycle operates over the stages outlined in Table 5.1 with the built environment professions involved at various stages. To underpin its key professional focus on sustainability, the RICS has also produced a number of guidance documents which are designed to inform practitioners:

■ *Sustainability and the RICS property lifecycle* (RICS 2009c)
■ *Surveying sustainability* (RICS 2008c)
■ *Carbon management of real estate: A guide to best practice* (RICS 2008a)
■ *Breaking the vicious circle of blame – making the business case for sustainable buildings* (RICS 2008b)
■ *Sustainable property investment and management* (RICS 2008d)
■ *Towards a low carbon built environment: A roadmap for action* (RICS 2009a).

These documents seek to engage members of the surveying profession in two ways. First they appeal to surveyors to take a more active strategic role in determining environmental policy at both the governmental and professional body level. For example, in *Towards a low carbon built environment: A roadmap for action*, the authors encourage...

> ...*organisations like the RICS to lobby and support an effective policy framework of carbon targets. Currently, the Government is setting policies for zero carbon new housing. However, insufficient attention is being paid to the existing housing stock. This is largely because it is not clear who should pay for the improvement measures' (RICS, 2009a).*

The report goes on,

> ...*the RICS has the expertise to assess the costs of action versus the risks of inaction for the property sector and is well placed to undertake this assessment. If the results of this assessment are in line with the findings of the Stern Review, then this work would be a way to demonstrate to RICS members that it is better to bear the cost of action now to avoid the far higher cost of adaptation ... The RICS can play a role in raising the level of awareness and promoting the development of skills relating to carbon savings in the property and construction sectors. This is particularly important for its own membership, but there is scope to work with related professions to improve' (Ibid.)*

Second, these reports seek to encourage surveyors to step up their own environmental commitment because they can then offer a better service to clients and hopefully provide expertise that other firms may not be able to provide. For example, in the *Carbon management of real estate – a guide to best practice* (RICS 2008a), information is provided for those businesses '...looking to build on their environmental credentials whilst also improving their financial bottom line.' The guide includes information on:

- baseline or benchmark assessment (carbon footprinting);
- carbon emission reduction techniques;
- taxes and incentives;
- forecasting an organisation's future carbon footprint;
- financial and carbon emissions appraisals.

This guide also uses relevant research findings to help support the case to clients for greater commitment to sustainability. For example:

> *The financial case for greater energy efficient property in the UK is growing with CBI/GVA Grimley's recent Corporate Real Estate Survey reporting that on balance 61% of companies would pay more rent for a 'green' building although only 81% of these would pay marginally more. In addition, two studies carried out on the US market by the New Building Institute (NBI) and CoStar indicate that buildings with high LEED or ENERGY STAR ratings perform better in terms of energy use and have been commanding higher rents and improved occupancy.*
> *(RICS, 2008)*

Current issues in surveying practice

Chartered surveyors are of course just one member of the property team providing a very wide range of expertise and advice to clients. The team includes architects, engineers and planners, all of whom must share a common vision of project objectives and the nature of the service being provided to the client throughout the property lifecycle.

Similarly, the three pillars of sustainability – *environmental, economic* and *social* – mean that property professionals are being required to incorporate greener principles across a wide range of their activities. These common principles can be difficult for the specialist within a surveying practice to incorporate into their day-to-day practice. It is partly for this reason that the appointment of the 'Director of Sustainability' has proved an increasingly popular idea among surveying firms and it is their responsibility to co-ordinate sustainability policy, and inform, explain and update the practitioner on the environmental implications of their professional activities.

It is also important to recognise that a fourth dimension – that of 'culture and governance' has a vital part to play in the policy and societal factors which influence sustainable outcomes in the built environment.

As mentioned previously, bringing the sustainable development agenda into the mainstream amongst chartered surveyors and other property professions has been largely driven by a number of external factors. Whilst this change is most clearly seen in the larger practices, it is likely that as these factors will continue to exert pressure on organisations to do business in a more sustainable way. Even relatively small firms of surveyors have to adapt to new business models and to reconfigured, redefined statements.

Client demand to manage and occupy buildings in a more sustainable way in order to meet their own customer and user expectations is now common, and there are ongoing PR and marketing pressures to be more seen to be environmentally responsible. These issues have now moved into mainstream businesses, with many companies recognising the business benefits of sustainable business practices and processes. This change is seen as a response to (i) government mandates aimed at reducing carbon footprints; (ii) public pressure; (iii) new business opportunities; and (iv) the shift towards greater corporate accountability, as companies recognise the benefits of 'going green'.

We have also seen the rise of socially responsible investment (SRI) strategies (which includes socially responsible property investment), where 'social, environmental and/or ethical considerations are taken into account in the selection, retention and realisation of investments and the responsible use of rights (such as voting rights) attached to investments' (Insight Investment, 2008: 2 based on Mansley, 2000).

For example, in the UK, 'this has been driven by changes in legislation (e.g. Pensions Act, 1995 and Trustees Act, 2000) as well as the moves of large insurance companies to engage on SRI criteria across all their equity funds. Today almost £200bn of UK equity holdings are subject to SRI engagement activities as part of SRI or corporate governance policy/guidelines.' (Dixon *et al.*, 2007: 5).

Recent work by the United Nations Environment Programme (Finance Initiative) (UNEPFI, 2008) presents 10 principles for responsible property investment (including a focus on sustainable buildings), each demonstrated by a collection of international case studies, which explain the financial and environmental value of responsible property investment.

Environmental legislation has also focused the business community's attention on reducing carbon emissions. In 2008, for example, the Climate Change Act called for an 80% reduction on 1990 UK carbon emission levels by 2050, a target which is now legally binding. The Act also introduced an interim target of a 21–31% reduction by 2020 (below 2005 levels), as well as five-year 'carbon budgets', and the Climate Change Committee has recently set specific targets for non-domestic buildings in the expectation that there is technical potential to reduce emissions by 11 $MtCO_2$ through zero- or negative-cost energy improvements. Any government department failing to operate within the five-year budgets will have to report to the UK Parliament to explain shortfalls and could be subject to judicial review. This forms a triumvirate of new legislation (alongside the Energy Act 2008 and Planning Act 2008), which is also designed to strengthen the drive towards renewables in the UK (Dixon *et al.*, 2009).

Shareholders too are now more aware of the need to be environmentally risk averse in the design and management of the buildings in which they invest, and are increasingly concerned about possible future financial loss arising from environmental litigation from building occupiers, cases of contamination, pollution or profligate use of resources including energy. This is turn has put pressure on the surveyors who manage these buildings or who are involved in developing the brief for new-build development projects to ensure that the best sustainable techniques and materials are specified.

The principles of sustainable development have been adopted by many property-owning organisations as part of their corporate social responsibility (CSR, or what is increasingly referred to as broader corporate responsibility – CR) initiatives. The ways in which buildings are designed, constructed and managed are important elements in any CSR policy. Buildings have also increasingly been seen as valuable investment assets, which must be carefully and responsibly managed. The International Business Leaders Forum defines CSR as:

> *Corporate behaviour that demonstrates open and transparent business practices based on ethical values and respect for employees, communities and the environment (IBLF, 2010)*

However, even against this background of increasing legislation and increasing levels of awareness of the many business case advantages for more environmentally responsible property practices, change has been slower than might have been expected in the property professions. As the RICS 'Green Profession' report stated in 2007:

> *The potential contribution of the built environment to sustainable development objectives is well-documented, and is becoming increasingly well-recognised within the property community ... Development location, the re-use of land, the nature and design of 'green buildings' and the practices, methods and materials employed during construction are all areas with obvious sustainability implications for both commercial and residential developments ... However, this lack of progress has been characterised as a 'circle of blame' where investors claim they would fund more sustainable development if the market asked for them and developers would provide them, but investors in their view would not pay for them. (Dixon et al., 2007: 5)*

This circle of blame has proved difficult to break, but it is possible that the landscape is about to radically change as the choice as to whether or not to build or manage buildings in a green way is taken out of the hands of property owners.

The prospect of radical new legislation such as the introduction of the mandatory Code for Sustainable Homes (all new residential property to be 'green' after 2016) and the Carbon Reduction Commitment (in effect, a tax on energy (in)efficiency in existing non-residential buildings) will be powerful 'sticks', superseding the 'carrot' of voluntary 'green badging' schemes and enhanced CSR credentials.

At the same time, leading property-owning businesses increasingly will not be prepared to have energy inefficient, unhealthy buildings as part of their stock. Price Waterhouse Coopers has gone on record as saying that it will only occupy 'green' space, and the UK government have stated that all their new buildings and large refurbishment projects must achieve high BREEAM ratings.

Prudential Property Investment Managers (PruPIM) have over £11 billion of property under management (primarily office, industrial and retail property) and have pursued an environmentally responsible strategy to buildings for some years and demand the highest possible green standards of all their professional advisers including the chartered surveyors with whom they work.

Other UK property companies and developers such as British Land, Stanhope and Land Securities are adopting BREEAM standards for new projects. For example, Land Securities set a target for the years 2005–06 for all their major office developments to possess a BREEAM standard of 'very good', with an ideal of 'excellent', and British Land committed to being carbon neutral from 2008/09. In the retail sector, there has been considerable activity towards promoting sustainable practices, Marks & Spencer for example introducing 'Plan A', a five-year 'eco' plan which strives to provide a continuous assessment of environmental performance in its buildings.

Most surveyors are very aware of the ongoing changes to the world of property, and whilst in the past, some may have seemed slow to engage with the sustainability agenda, significant changes in practice have occurred within many firms and the beginnings of this have been captured by recent research for RICS.

In 2006, the RICS commissioned Oxford Brookes University (UK), University of Melbourne (Australia), Georgia State University (USA), and King Sturge LLP (UK) to undertake a research project to examine how RICS registered surveyors were engaging with the sustainability agenda and to identify the 'green tools', techniques and sources of information that they were using when providing professional advice and services. A survey of 47,000 RICS members was carried out across three main global regions (UK and Europe, the Americas and Rest of the World) from June 2006 to March 2007. A response rate of 10% was achieved for the main online survey and 14% for a follow-up survey. The report found that the most significant drivers for surveying practices to adopt more sustainable practices within the office were legal compliance; responsibility to protect the environment; and ethical and moral reasons (Dixon *et al.*, 2007). The report also found that although 40% of the respondents had not used any 'green tools' or techniques (e.g. BREEAM, Envest, The Green Guide to Specification in the UK, and LEED, Green Star in the USA and Australia) in the previous year, some 21% had used them four or more times.

Following on from this work, in July 2009, the RICS and Oxford Brookes University completed the first stage of an ongoing monitoring survey of RICS members and their engagement with sustainability, called *RICS Green Gauge* (RICS 2009b). The main findings are based on responses from approximately 1500 RICS members collected via an online survey. The study found that:

- more than 40% of all respondents have used sustainability tools, techniques and information four or more times during the last year, which is double the 2006/07 survey total;
- more than half of respondents are using such tools more frequently than one year ago;
- more than two-fifths believed the tools were very useful or useful;
- building control, management consultancy and environment also had higher levels of 'very useful' responses than other groups.

This report also concluded that sustainability is an increasingly significant issue in surveying practices with nearly three-quarters of those surveyed considering it to be 'highly relevant' to their work, an increase of 13% on the 2006/07 survey – see Figure 5.2.

The survey revealed that the most important sustainability issues for surveyors were energy (73%), waste management (43%), natural resource consumption (33%), transport issues and land contamination (30%). It is these issues therefore that have tended to drive the most

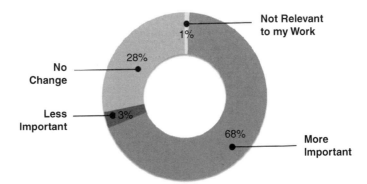

Figure 5.2 Perceived importance of sustainability compared with 1 year ago (Source: adapted and developed from RICS 2009b)

significant recent changes in practice and which can be seen in a range of initiatives.

Regular in-house sustainability updates, usually via company intranet systems, and raising awareness of new environmental legislation is one type of initiative: for example, information on energy performance certificates (EPCs) and display energy certificates (DECs) and the likely impacts and liabilities for clients under the carbon reduction commitment (CRC). Intranet updates are also typically used to explain the obligations of property owning clients and their professional advisers under new or upcoming EU and UK government law and policy.

'Green' in-house protocols and procurement policies are also used. For example, a number of surveying practices have attained ISO14001 accreditation, under the terms of which they are required to manage office waste more responsibly, consider green travel plans for their staff, reduce energy consumption through awareness-raising initiatives such as 'turn off the lights' campaigns and the installation of movement sensors for offices in order to reduce energy use. Some firms have also promoted greater use of video and telephone conferencing rather than travelling to meetings in regional offices.

As part of their ISO14001 schemes, some firms have introduced mandatory online sustainability quizzes and tests, to be completed by all professional staff on an annual basis.

In-house green procurement policies – covering the purchase or rental of goods and services including office space, stationery, cleaning products – and the vetting of the environmental credentials of subcontractors and suppliers have been applied widely. Whilst insisting on environmentally responsible practices being adopted by larger suppliers has been found to be successful (PruPIM 2009), smaller suppliers can find it difficult to allocate the necessary time and resources to changing their procedures. Some surveying firms have proceeded incrementally in such circumstances, favouring 'engagement' over 'screening', by trying to get the supplier or subcontractor to move incrementally in a more sustainable direction.

Companies such as GVA Grimley, DTZ, Drivas Jonas, CB Richard Ellis and Gleeds, as well as the RICS itself, have appointed in-house directors of sustainability or 'sustainability champions' who are charged with disseminating and managing sustainability information and professional skills within the organisation. Often, it is the director of sustainability who will take responsibility for managing the environmental legislation intranet updates and in-house CPD and training programmes. Finally, changes to external CPD programmes and take-up of sustainability-related training is undertaken. This provides staff with advice and expertise in key areas such as the use of energy-saving technologies, the specification of lower-impact construction materials, enhanced knowledge of environmental legislation and environment assessment schemes such as BREEAM, capability to carry out carbon auditing schemes, and understanding of green leases.

Possible future developments

Factors such as new building legislation affecting energy efficiency and the UK government's stated policy of only commissioning green buildings for the government estate, have meant that for many the argument to enhance standards for new-build is largely 'won'. There is, of course, always more that can be done, and the issue of less-polluting energy sources and the use of renewables is still a huge challenge for engineers and technologists. However, many property professionals and environmentalists believe that it is the management of existing building stock, which now requires urgent attention.

The introduction of EPCs, DECs and the CRC will no doubt focus the attention of property owners on energy inefficient buildings as these will increasingly attract additional energy costs and energy tax costs as well as the stigma of poor energy ratings.

The carbon reduction commitment (CRC) is a new mandatory carbon emissions cap-and-trade scheme developed by the Department of Energy and Climate Change, Scottish Government and Welsh Assembly, and which is intended to reduce the carbon emissions of non-energy-intensive organisations in the UK. The scheme places legal obligations on an estimated 5000 or so 'participant' organisations to disclose their energy usage, efficiency and/or carbon footprint, and buy or trade carbon credits through the scheme. Target participants are companies large enough in their operations to use half-hourly metering for recording their electricity use. They qualify for participation if their usage in 2008 was over 6000 MWh. The CRC is likely to include such organisations as supermarkets, water companies, banks, local authorities (including state-funded schools) and all central government departments. Although some details of the CRC have still to be finalised, in simple terms, each organisation involved will need to forecast its energy consumption and buy enough allowances to cover emissions. Those organisations that perform best will receive 'recycled revenue' and high rankings in the publicly available performance league table. The first year of trading in the scheme is from April 2010 to March 2011 – see www.defra.gov.uk/carbonreduction for further details.

It is highly likely that as the owners of large property portfolios become more aware of this legislation, surveying practices will receive many new instructions to carry out energy appraisals and audits of older buildings. It is also likely that as their liability for the most poorly performing properties becomes apparent to clients, surveyors will also be asked to either prepare proposals for retrofitting or else to organise their immediate disposal as poor assets. Indeed, to some extent, this process has already begun as many buildings must now display EPCs, which show the building energy efficiency performance.

There has been concern among property investors that poor EPCs may stigmatise buildings and that a low score becomes synonymous with poor quality and high running costs, thus adversely affecting both rental and capital value. Some owners have been reported as having carried out initial energy rating appraisals of commercial buildings to identify those properties that seemed likely to be at the lower end of the EPC scale of A–F. Where the necessary improvements to the building fabric and environmental systems were not deemed to be cost effective, the properties have, apparently, been considered for disposal.

It seems highly likely that, in the future, lifecycle performance, energy efficiency and carbon emissions will be a relevant factor in many more property decisions than has been the case previously. In response, surveyors are becoming more proactive in raising client awareness, identifying potential future problems and providing appropriate solutions. To this end, many practices will continue to provide educative presentations to clients and help them in preparing environmental strategies for their properties.

A case from practice

GVA Grimley is a multidisciplinary property consultancy, providing expert guidance at all stages of the property lifecycle, including planning, development and regeneration; building and project management; property agency; and investment and valuation.

Their management feels that sustainability is highly relevant to all aspects of property and that it has become increasingly so in recent years. GVA Grimley began to offer sustainability consultancy services in 2006 and there were a number of reasons behind this move. Unsurprisingly, given the nature of the business, the chief reason was that the firm considered that there was a market need – i.e. that clients would pay the firm to provide advice on a range of sustainability issues.

Drivers

For GVA Grimley, the principal drivers in developing the necessary skills-sets in-house were originally twofold and responsive to market conditions. First was client demand both for sustainability services and in expecting their supply chain to be evidently on the path to sustainability. Second was the regulatory context affecting both the GVA Grimley's business and client businesses. Being a progressive organisation, GVA Grimley also foresaw business opportunities to cross-sell sustainability and other services, and to enhance their offer as a business in recruiting new, progressively minded staff.

Process management

As the business case for developing their sustainability capabilities evolved, the process of managing this development rested in 2006 with a steering group of senior individuals from different aspects of the business. These individuals represented different client-facing constituencies within the business and were led by the managing director. The function of this group was to identify opportunities for providing services to clients and decide what the business needed to do to address its own environmental issues. During both of these activities, the steering group made use of the business's research team to assess the market demand for sustainability services and the changing regulatory environment. Communicating the results of the research involved the marketing and PR team presenting the research findings to clients and also to the internal audience, the latter activity being seen as essential to ensure broad buy-in within the company to the aims of the steering group.

All of this activity required the business to recognise that an increasing amount of resource was required to undertake it. Business development budgets were used to finance the various activities initially but it soon became apparent that in order to meet its aspirations, training, marketing and recruitment budgets would also need to be used. It was also clear that expertise would need to be acquired which could provide leadership within this field. GVA Grimley recruited a head of sustainability in 2008. The business had, prior to this, also 'bought' (through internal purchasing) the expertise of an existing staff member to manage the attainment of the ISO14001 standard (environmental management systems – EMS).

The head of sustainability led GVA Grimley to acknowledge that their focus in achieving better levels of sustainability should always be on maintaining a top-quality service offer whilst achieving environmental impact reduction. In order to maintain this focus, close working relationships between the head of sustainability, the firm's managing director, its training team, the ISO14001 coordinator and the head of the marketing and communications team was essential.

GVA Grimley has used its commitment to sustainability to enhance its training initiatives. The intention was to view these from a management perspective in terms of a whole-systems, holistic, property lifecycle approach. For example, although it was the first property adviser to provide training to its teams to become BREEAM Assessors, the aim was not to provide a team of personnel who would undertake BREEAM Assessments but rather to ensure that teams had suitable knowledge and understanding of pertinent sustainability issues. The dedicated 'green team' was drawn from across all areas of its business, GVA Grimley actively seeking to manage positive change that helps the environment and creates sustainable places through its planning, building, investment and project management teams.

The early commitment to the environment was reinforced through 'housekeeping'. The business therefore drew up a policy, which pledged to make reductions in CO_2 emissions and increase waste recycling. The firm was awarded ISO14001 certification in 2008 for the environmental management that it began to incorporate into its business activities in 2006. In order to increase buy-in to the concept of sustainability, it was important to manage communication internally about the benefits that issues like ISO14001 accreditation have realised; staff would then see that being actively encouraged to be more environmentally aware and to help by actively taking part in the new schemes was not 'just another initiative' nor something divorced from their client-facing activities. The EMS has resulted in lower costs with the implementation of energy-saving devices, new waste management systems and encouraging more recycling. Take-up has been exceptional with teams putting into place their own procedures to support the EMS.

Further evidence of 'walking the walk' came in January 2009, when GVA Grimley moved to new premises in Glasgow that were certified as BREEAM excellent. The company also moved its offices in Bristol in June 2009 to another BREEAM excellent building. These were further demonstrations of commitment to environmental matters, as well as demonstrations of the firm's understanding of the importance of such matters to clients.

Management time spent in achieving ISO14001 was considerable: this included a proportion of the time of the managing director and other directors who oversaw parts of the process and sat on a steering group, an associate who ran much of the process with support from an external consultant, the head of facilities and his team of regional administrators who were chiefly involved in on-the-ground implementation of the EMS in the 12 UK offices, plus the head of communications, and some time of the in-house designers was used in devising a communications strategy and newsletters. For example, the director who was charged with overseeing some of policy development and pilot study in the initial stages of the firm's implementation of its travel plan was required at one stage to devote at least a day per week to these non-fee-paying activities. This required the establishment of practice protocols to enable the firm to value the attainment and enhancement of its ISO14001 accreditation including shadow pricing of the director's time commitment in internal charging mechanisms.

Effects on practice management of adopting ISO14001

The implementation of ISO14001 accreditation resulted in a number of changes to the way in which the business was managed, some of the principal ones being:

- Running cost reductions: having established targets to reduce resource consumption, including energy and consumables as well as travelling between offices and, where practicable, to clients, GVA Grimley has seen associated cost reductions, such as 5% of the electricity bill in the first year. This required specific management focus on individually small areas of cost reduction, which may otherwise have fallen below the radar in terms of cost-cutting priorities.
- Encouraging less travelling and ability to target funding towards cheaper travel: the achievement of ISO14001 gave added impetus to invest in and use video-conferencing systems and to develop an agreed policy on whether to fund private travel, and to encourage greater use of public transport. Driving this change was challenging and involved changing established behaviours.
- Simplification of the approach to business systems: implementation of ISO14001 led to a streamlined approach to other ISO-related management systems such as those for ISO9001 (quality assurance), ISO18001 (health and safety) and ISO27001 (security). This has enabled the business to adopt a management approach that does not 'silo' these important practice management functions but integrates them.
- Communicating with staff: sustainability is a matter which many staff consider to be personally important to them and worthwhile for the business to be undertaking. Responses to staff surveys often highlight the importance of 'green' issues to staff and, importantly, to potential staff. Presenting new environmental initiatives, explaining why new policies are being adopted and commending good practice all represent added reasons for the firm's leadership to communicate with staff.

Barriers

There are several barriers to note:

- Fears were expressed prior to the attainment and implementation of some sustainable practices that the cost of implementing them would be disproportionate to their benefits. Reference to existing and prospective client requirements for GVA Grimley to have achieved ISO14001 before any work could be successfully won, soon overcame such fears. For example, the firm became able to maintain its position on various public sector consultancy frameworks, which require such accreditation. Internally communicating this message – and that approximately one third of its £100m annual turnover is attributed to public sector contracts – has allayed these fears.

■ There was some wariness about implementing a travel plan across the business: possibilities included reducing funded staff car parking, reducing car allowances and increasing the expectation that staff would use public transport. These concerns were addressed through careful consultation, which included undertaking surveys to elicit support for the concept of a travel plan and to identify the reasons for the wariness that existed. For example, some fears about personal security and the availability of buses when travelling at night were addressed by use of local authority and local police data and communications pieces. Data on existing travel impacts were derived from staff surveys. As an incentive to complete these, respondents to surveys were offered the opportunity to forego anonymity in return for the opportunity to receive retail vouchers.

■ Instances where the firm had insufficient expertise to address particular environmental issues were quickly identified. The firm worked with experts to achieve suitable solutions: for example, suppliers of paper and printers to improve environmental efficiency, and buying in suitable expertise to help identify solutions concerning the GVA Grimley travel plan.

Outcomes

There have been a number of very positive results and business benefits, which have included:

■ client retention and winning work;
■ better visibility in the marketplace;
■ more joined-up business.

Client retention and winning work

It is increasingly evident that many organisations have a 'green mandate' or at least aspirations to achieve higher levels of environmental sustainability than was previously the case. This is particularly so with public sector clients, which represent 30% of GVA Grimley turnover. Private sector clients increasingly have green intentions and thus requirements for advice too, across sub-sectors such as investment, development and occupation of space.

In order to capitalise on this need, GVA Grimley analytically identified where opportunities lay by using business planning activities. This has been achieved through coordination by the chief executive of business development activities by client relationship management champions, who have themselves coordinated working groups to identify where the opportunities lie and how best to exploit them in respective markets. As well as this market analysis, business planning has necessitated a stock-take of the firm's capacity to perform the necessary functions to maximise opportunities, the result of which has involved buying in resources and developing existing talent. At times, the business has identified that new or amended service lines exist whereas at other times, some services can be described as added-value offers, which can mean that clients may not pay for the service but will appreciate its delivery and be more likely to retain GVA Grimley. Provision of carbon auditing services is an example of a new service line, while an example of an amended service line with a 'green' angle is property management services, where a range of approaches can be adopted, including ones that emphasise the importance of environmental sustainability at appropriate points of intervention by property managers in the management of a building. An added-value service is exemplified by the offering of delivering CPD sessions to client teams on particular issues.

One area where many businesses are keen to develop performance is that of cross-selling services. Sustainability services lend themselves to cross-selling because sustainability issues feature throughout the property lifecycle. Those personnel who are acting for clients as an agent, a planning consultant or valuer raise relevant sustainability issues to the client and may lead to advice being offered. Likewise, sustainability advisors are also encouraged to cross-sell other services. GVA Grimley utilises a 'cross-selling league table' to identify how well business units perform referring work to other teams. This process has enabled managers to identify two linked and key management tools that have led to further improvement in this area: internal sustainability education and better communication of existing and developing sustainability capabilities within the business. The former is aimed at ensuring that key service capabilities and experience are widely understood, supported by expert seminars, while developing communications has meant that teams delivering sustainability services have worked closely with the communications and marketing teams to develop a range of messages, for example via capability sheets and case study materials.

Better visibility in the marketplace

The requirement for 'green' property advice and services has been growing at a fast rate. Developing capabilities means better visibility in the marketplace, promoted via CSR information and case study publicity materials, and by developing a range of communications media for external audiences including redesigning its web presence. Managers within the business have had to ensure that other elements of the marketing and communications functions of the business have refocused their attentions to include this area from internal PR activities, external PR agencies as to in-house events teams.

More joined-up business

One of the chief spin-off business benefits has been the increased amount of multidisciplinary team working. It is not uncommon for sustainability issues to require the attention of people from disciplines such as property management, building consultancy and agency to solve them appropriately. However, it must be noted that this approach took considerable management time to facilitate; many B2B companies provide services by teams operating in discrete sections of the business. In seeking to provide cross-cutting, multidisciplinary team working, GVA Grimley had to undertake business planning to analyse market opportunities as well as to determine how internal processes, such as internal accounting and business development support, could fit this different approach.

Achieving higher levels of environmental sustainability has also meant that the regional office network worked closely together, for example in the attainment of ISO14001, which has generally improved intra-office communication. Business operations have been streamlined by bringing environmental management, quality management, health and safety management and security management within one operating system. When, for example, qualifying a supplier, this can be carried out simultaneously from four perspectives. Evidence of sound environmental management is sought in terms of energy, waste and procurement KPIs.

Conclusions and recommendations

In a report written by the Oxford Institute for Sustainable Development at Oxford Brookes in 2007 and updated in 2009, a number of conclusions were reached, and recommendations made, identifying possible ways forward in terms of policy and strategy for the RICS and for individual practices and practitioners. Given the current recession the 2009 'green gauge' report (RICS, 2009b) also suggested not only that the RICS, its members and other key stakeholders should continue to work together and place a strong emphasis on education and training to raise awareness of sustainability globally, but also that the RICS itself should provide an integrated sustainability information service (based around a consolidated RICS 'microsite') which draws together professional groups and global regions.

At a more strategic level, however, both reports made key suggestions for the main stakeholders involved, the summary points being as follows:

- **The RICS**
  - Further strengthening its leadership role and helping to coordinate CPD and training and education initiatives as well as engaging with those faculties where sustainability is considered less important. To take two ongoing examples, providing cogent arguments for relevance in the residential and valuation faculties would be a positive response to the emerging sustainability agenda as further legislation takes hold both in the UK and overseas. The publication of VIP 13 and changes to the Red Book have helped considerably in this regard.
  - RICS members continue to need better guidance on sustainability tools and best practice examples of sustainable development. The institution needs to provide this through improved information and 'global awards schemes', which target such developments and best practice.
- **RICS members**
  - High-quality education and training are at the heart of mainstreaming sustainability within the built environment professions. With an increasing emphasis on client-led instructions and as new legislation starts to bite, it is imperative that RICS members and their organisations ensure that employees are up to date with the latest thinking on sustainability and the tools that underpin this, including encouragement of members to engage with the UKGBC's STEP Programme.
  - High-quality continuing professional development allied with emerging core competencies in professional development for RICS membership will need increasingly to include the sustainability agenda.
  - Many younger professionals are insufficiently engaged in sustainability work, so more senior professionals undertake substantial areas of this work.
- **Education and training institutions**
  - Providing relevant education and training in sustainability, as this is required by employees and their organisations. This means sustainability explicitly featuring in all built environment courses, including showing how its impact can be measured in financial, environmental and economic terms.
  - Higher education institutions partnering with RICS and its members to ensure that surveyors are fully engaged and skilled to the highest level to meet the challenges that climate change and other factors will present to the built and natural environments.

Ultimately RICS members have a key role to play in educating clients, including the moral and ethical issues. Only in this way can the 'circle of blame' be broken and a 'virtuous circle' of sustainability in the built environment be created (RICS, 2007). As one respondent from the commercial sector in the UK put it (RICS, 2007 p. 36):

> *Becoming aware of environmental issues is a moral imperative for all property professionals. It probably never was, and certainly no longer is, a minority issue.*
> *We must change along with the rest of society.*

References

Grimley (2009) *Our Approach to Sustainability*, GVA Grimley, London.

Dixon, T., Colantonio, A., Shiers, D., Gallimore, P., Reed, R. and Wilkinson, S. (2007) *A Green Profession? RICS members and the sustainability agenda*, RICS, London.

IBLF (2010) International Business Leaders Forum definition, www.iblf.org/csr.

Insight Investment (2008) *Eurosif SRI Transparency Guidelines*, Insight, London.

Mansley, M. (2000) *Socially responsible investment: a guide for pension funds and institutional investors*, Monitor Press, Sudbury.

PruPIM Prudential Sustainability Report (2008), Published 2009, p 7.

RICS (2007) *A Green Profession? RICS Members and the Sustainability Agenda*, Royal Institution of Chartered Surveyors, London.

RICS (2008a) *A guide to best practice: carbon management of real estate*, RICS Guidance Note, RICS, London.

RICS (2008b) *Breaking the vicious circle of blame – Making the business case for sustainable buildings*, RICS, London.

RICS (2008c) *Surveying sustainability*, RICS, London.

RICS (2008d) *Sustainable property investment and management*, RICS, London.

RICS (2009a) Executive Summary, *Towards a low carbon economy: a roadmap for action*, RICS, London. pp. 8–9.

RICS (2009b) *RICS green gauge survey*, RICS, London.

RICS (2009c) *Sustainability and the RICS property lifecycle*, RICS, London.

RICS (2010a) Professional groups structure: www.rics.org/professionalgroups.

RICS (2010b) Sustainability Policy Statement: www.rics.org/sustainability.

UNEPFI (United Nations Environmental Programme Initiative) (2008) *Responsible Property Investing: What the Leaders are Doing*, UNEPFI, Geneva.

Section II

Managing Specific Issues in the Professional Practice

6 Equipping project teams for competitions

Architecture practices in the Italian market

Beatrice Manzoni

In recent decades architecture has been exposed to changes influencing the complex nature of architectural services and the profession. Under these circumstances project-based organisations are not only a typical configuration of the industry (Gunnarson and Levitt, 1982), but also a way to cope with increasing complexity and rapid changes (Hobday, 2000).

Therefore, while projects are the organisational outputs, teams are the mechanism that these temporary organisations rely on to be more effective (Ancona and Caldwell, 1992). Existing literature, apart from considering individual performance inside the team, has investigated how team performance, affected by its composition, impacts on project success (Guzzo and Dickson, 1996). However, management research says that 'results from empirical studies have been inconsistent regarding which composition variables are predictive of team performance' (Bell, 2007: 596).

The aim of this chapter is to explore the relationship between team composition and performance in project and ideas competitions in Italy. We aim to present an overview of the architectural competitions scenario and specify what team composition, if any, leads to superior performance. Performance is not always recognised at the competition phase: positive performance is linked to an award or a mention, negative performance to no awards.

The chapter is organised as follows. First, we review existing literature on project-based organisations as a way to cope with a dilemma typical of architectural firms that are caught between creativity and efficiency. Owing to these coexisting drivers, architecture often needs and relies on heterogeneous features, also typical of the actors involved, that help

Managing the Professional Practice: in the built environment, First Edition. Edited by Hedley Smyth.
© 2011 by Blackwell Publishing Ltd. Published 2011 by Blackwell Publishing Ltd.

pursue innovation and manage complexity and cross-functional expertise. Furthermore architectural products result from projects, and architecture relies on project-based structures, despite the difficulties that the architecture profession seems sometimes to have in forming effective teams (Evbuomwan and Anumba, 1998). Second, we investigate team composition for competitions from a multiple perspective in the Italian setting. We focus on the following variables: age, nationality and reputation of the architects or practices involved. We analyse whether and how these dimensions influence project performance, in terms of award outcome, looking at some recent Italian architecture competitions. Finally, we present some reflections and suggestions for architectural practices, together with directions for future research.

Theoretical framework

Architecture firms are service, professional and creative organisations (Winch and Schneider, 1993b; Jones and Livne-Tarandach, 2008). As service organisations, they are characterised by intangible and heterogeneous products, especially at the competition phase where the output that these firms provide is made up of concepts, drawings and feasibility plans, as the design has still to be fully developed and built. Architecture firms are also professional organisations, as access to the labour market and professional practice are institutionally regulated in Italy. Finally, they are creative organisations, because private and public clients hire architects to provide novel solutions to spatial problems (Thornton *et al.*, 2005).

This search for novel solutions or originality explains why creative acclaim, rather than business success, is often the major stimulus to practice, to the point that some architectural practice strategies are driven by the interest in competitions and awards for design rather than by financial reward and growth (Mintzberg *et al.*, 1988; Michlewski, 2008). According to Thornton *et al.* (2005), two drivers coexist in the profession: a creative logic and an efficiency one. A synthesis between these two vocations is rare, together with an agreement about the profession's core or specialised domain. Architecture resists a definition of its boundaries and internal specialisation, maintaining eclectic and interdisciplinary features in relation to strategy, logic, market orientation and actor responsibilities and roles (Blau, 1984).

Therefore, inter-organisational temporary organisations are used in architecture to pursue innovation, manage product complexity and cross-functional business expertise, reduce risk and deal with complexity and changing markets (Hobday, 2000). Moreover architecture has been traditionally characterised by project group structures (Gunnarson and

Levitt, 1982), and projects are its main organisational output before the buildings are built (Flanagan *et al.*, 2005). This is the reason why Blau (1984) describes the industry as involving specialised and interrelated tasks, regularly directed towards single projects.

However, notwithstanding this project-based configuration, architecture has also been traditionally regarded as an intrinsically individualistic activity. Recently a relevant relational dimension has been recognised, originating from collaborative networks among multiple actors (Yoo *et al.*, 2006). Among big companies, the absence, for example, of pure architectural actors emerges clearly at the European level (STD, 2009), in favour of interdisciplinary/inter-organisational groups. Projects can be generally associated with a temporary team on the one hand consisting of architects, designers, engineers, quantity surveyors and other specialists, preparing designs, specifications and contractual documents (design group); and on the other hand contractors, subcontractors and suppliers, constructing and financing parties (constructing group) (Yoo *et al.*, 2006; Winch, 2008), even if the precise configuration of project coalitions varies from project to project and depends on the client and the requirements of the particular project.

However, even where the composition, the relationships and the interactions inside a team are clear, 'selection processes in this sector have frequently focused on organisations' individual professional capabilities rather than on their collective ability to integrate and work together effectively' (Baiden *et al.*, 2006: 14). Moreover the industry has shown in the past a limitation in forming effective teams, but when winning teams have been created they tend to be replicated over the years (Evbuomwan and Anumba, 1998).

In sum, architecture exhibits an unsubstantiated link between team composition and performance and also the ability of the industry to form and maintain effective teams. How can this be examined further? Existing literature and interviews with industry experts suggest that team composition in architecture competitions can be looked at from different perspectives: age, nationality and reputation of members. We investigate whether and how these three dimensions, which have yet to be systematically examined, influence the team development and overall performance in competitions, measured in terms of award outcome and matching award criteria.

Age: old hands vs newcomers

In temporary and project-based settings, a relevant distinction when deciding how to form team configurations is the one among old hands and newcomers (Chen, 2005). Combinations of former members who have worked together in teams, old hands' are more experienced, familiar, routinised and can speed up task execution (Ilgen *et al.*, 2005), while new combinations, 'newcomers', are less experienced but sometimes offer novel prospects for creativity and experimentation, together with higher internal and market risks (Jackson and Joshi, 2004).

Architecture presents on the one side old hands where members have worked together in various combinations within proven firms that have a strong track record, and, on the other side, young or untried architects who have limited experience of working with each other in the firm and sometimes with other firms. Proven firms are old hands for the industry, standing at the core of their social field (Cattani and Ferriani, 2008) – architecture – and having greater exposure and access to sources of legitimacy, intended as a mix of acceptance and reputation. They are either 'strong experience' practices or 'strong ideas' ones, according to Winch and Schneider (1993a). They generally undertake and are preferred for limited competitions for expensive projects and ally with other old hands among property developers and building contractors. In contrast, young or untried architects, frequently newcomers in the industry, stand at the borders of the field with fewer opportunities to get exposure, trying to invest more in distinctiveness to gain further credibility (Jones and Livne-Tarandach, 2008). They are 'strong ambition practices' (Winch and Schneider 1993a), but they are typically formed recently and often awaiting a first major commission. They generally go for open ideas competitions for a twofold reason: first, open contexts admit everyone, and second, ideas competitions often ask for a design concept only, a few boards and no significant work experience needed. However, there are some exceptions: limited contexts sometimes accept and ask for newcomers, first because newcomers – especially when they are 'strong ideas' firms – potentially produce more innovation and originality compared with old hands (Larson, 1994) and second because there are some policies requiring that newcomers be given opportunities to enter the market, paired with old hands.

From these considerations, we expect differences in team composition when looking at open or limited competitions. However, in general we expect the newness of the firm and their teams to the industry, notwithstanding their potential originality, to have a negative impact on the competition performance (intended as being awarded), owing to a lack of substantial experience in doing competitions. It is possible that *the age of the architectural practice (or architect) positively influences competition performance: the more the experience of a practice, the higher the probability of winning a competition.*

Nationality: national vs international

There are mixed results from management literature as to how international diversity impacts on team performance. According to some studies (e.g. Earley and Mosakowski, 2000) the effects on performance are positive, but according to some others they are negative in the long run (e.g. Watson *et al.*, 1998).

In architecture until recently most practices have been organised around a local, regional or national framework, but globalisation changed this (Knox and Taylor, 2005). The architecture industry has nowadays the choice between different market strategies: regional, national, international, multinational, global and transnational (Girmscheid and Brockmann, 2008). Many European countries are dominated by international practices, due to policies of international architectural competitions and selection (Marinoni, 2007). Winning a *concourse* is, in fact, according to Winch (2008), one of the four strategies for entry into foreign markets, together with following a client, marketing and via network partners. Some architecture practices have therefore recently developed a multi-city presence to serve an international clientele. An RIBA survey in 2008 on 46 of the UK's largest practices, for example, show that architectural companies work more and more abroad, 20% of work on average is located overseas, with the Middle East, western and eastern Europe being the most popular overseas markets. More than 30% said that winning international work is 'not a problem', while 36% said winning foreign work only occasionally creates problems (Henley, 2008).

What we therefore expect is that international teams, whether they have one overseas member, a local branch office or perhaps employees with an international education and professional experience, have greater possibilities to win competitions, as 'clients aspire to gain status for their project through the involvement of an internationally renowned architect' (Winch, 2008: 10). It is possible that *the degree of internationalisation in a team positively influences competition performance: the more international the practice, the higher the probability of winning a competition.*

Reputation: archistars vs common professionals

Reputation has proved critical at organisational and individual level, being a reflection of past performance and consequently a predictor of future performance (Kilduff and Krackardt, 1994).

In architecture a strong reputation is typical of so-called 'glamorous signature architects' or 'archistars' (Larson, 1994; Lo Ricco and Micheli, 2003). They are architects who have, individually, built leadership and brands and are able to balance credibility and creativity, where credibility is labelled as legitimacy, and creativity as distinctiveness (Jones and Livne-Tarandach, 2008 – see also Chapters 7 and 15). Moreover, they seem to be able to positively influence the competition performance, due to the high symbolic connotation of their work. However, the archistars' effects on project performance have not been clearly qualified or quantified. There is also no full agreement on their role in influencing the outcome of competitions, and moreover on how much value a 'big-name' architect actually adds to a project and specifically to what performance dimensions (Rybczynski, 2006). In addition, few studies have been conducted to investigate how the success or failure of a project can impact on a firm's competitiveness (Flanagan *et al.*, 2005), which means that it is not clear that previous successes can influence future performance in competitions. Existing literature shows that the mechanism for how an architect's reputation can foster bidding competitiveness has not been fully explored (see also Chapter 7). In addition, management studies investigating the role of team diversity on performance have usually ignored the status dimension (Jackson and Joshi, 2004) and Perretti and Negro (2006) suggest that research is needed to compare the impacts of status with those of established measures of team diversity.

From these considerations, it is relevant to investigate whether and how archistars can make the difference on project performance. It is possible that *the presence of well-reputed members (or even archistars) in the team positively influences competition performance: the higher the status of the architect, the higher the probability of winning a competition.*

Methods and results

Research setting: Italian architecture competitions

Understanding the structure and the dynamics of the architectural and planning services offer is a complex issue, due to the difficulties encountered, especially in Europe, in collecting and assessing data. Data is not always available and comparable across markets.

Moreover systematic studies on design competitions are rare, as Van Wezemael (2008) observes most research takes the form of individual case studies. At the end of the 1980s, Nasar (1998), reviewing literature on competitions, observed that most of the existing studies provide description of single competitions and projects, not really aiming at offering suggestions to run competitions (e.g. De Haan and Haagsma, 1988; Spreiregen, 1979; Strong, 1996; Taschen, 1994; Wynne, 1981). Later on Tostrup (1999, 2009) examined again specific competitions exploring the rhetoric of proposals while Collier (2004) provides accounts for international competitions comparing different countries. With Kreiner (2006, 2009) we see a new stream aiming at understanding competitions' strategic and organisational implications for firms.

Therefore, competitions are an interesting research setting for multiple reasons. First, they are currently debated in the EU (Adamczyk, 2004) due to the changes in policies requiring an element of competition in the public procurement of buildings and infrastructure (Sudjic, 2005). While competitions have a long history in Germany, the Netherlands and Spain, in Italy they are quite new mechanisms, trying to become legitimate as transparent and efficient mechanisms.

Second, they are a 'highly institutionalised interaction ritual' (Jones and Livne-Tarandach, 2008: 1082), which architectural firms and developers use to secure projects, and a key strategy for building architectural firms' reputations (Mintzberg *et al.*, 1988). 'Built or unbuilt, the projects ranked in an important competition are published, diffused, examined, discussed, and entered as credits in their authors' résumés' (Larson, 1994: 472). Open competitions are in fact a way to make a name for oneself and, later on, a 'name' gets one invited to compete in restricted contexts. According to the architect Cesar Pelli, 'they open up opportunities to talented architects that may be young and unrecognised to become recognised' (Anthony, 1991: 207). Moreover they have always attracted architects, but even more so in recessionary times, and this should depend therefore, at least partially, on something other than the economy (Larson, 1994).

Third, competitions are the favourite way for developers and clients to sample styles, produce variety in the pool of alternative built environments from which solutions can be drawn and an architect selected (Kreiner, 2009). According to Gutman (1988), with their ritual aspects, architectural competitions best illustrate the diversity of the architectural field, of the teams participating and of the jurys' reading of emergent architectural trends, doing a lot to 'make people conscious of architecture and talk about it' (Michael Feinknopf, local partner of Erickson, in Nasar, 1998).

Finally, Volker and Prins (2006) state that design competitions open up great possibilities for understanding the link between the process of designing and managing the design and the added value of the design product.

What also makes competitions so interesting and controversial is the opposite side of the coin. Many architects are generally critical of competitions for different reasons. They may not get the best solution; they impede the dialogue and the interaction with the client; they often end up with un-built projects; and therefore they exploit architects who invest enormous amount of resources to play a game which has always just one winner (Anthony, 1991; Nasar, 1998).

The focus of this study is on project and ideas competitions in which architecture practices submit design proposals required by public or private clients. A jury or a panel is appointed by the client to decide on the winning design, whose architect is sometimes awarded the commission for the work in the case of project competitions.

Italy, chosen as the research setting, is one of the most particular in Europe. It is in fact the country with the largest number of architects registered in its professional association: at the end of 2008 they were 136,186, while in 2006 they were 123,000: one architect registered for every 470 inhabitants against a European average of 996 inhabitants. Notwithstanding the large number, the average age is high, with 44% 46 or more years old and 37% between 35 and 45: only 19% are under

35 years old, explaining the difficulty for young professionals to enter the professional association. Moreover with up to 253,000 companies working in the field of planning and technical activities, this corresponded to 33.6% of the European total in 2005. It presented the largest number of operating units but the lowest average size of company in terms of employees (1.4), being a nation with many small entrepreneurs. Finally, preceded by Spain, Italy held eighth place in the business of planning services with 17 billion US dollars, compared to the 529 of the entire world. But, due to the large number of architects, 'the average income per practice is reducing, apart from the one of some few archistars or well recognised professionals whose work is often rewarded by a legislation system which is not encouraging the architectural quality and the protection of the profession' as the vice-president of the Italian National Council of Architects, Planners, Landscapers and Curators reports (CNAPPC, 2009). In addition, Italy does not 'export' much of these services (STD 2009), yet it 'imports' a considerable amount, as many Italian municipalities pursue policies of architectural competitions that are open to international firms (Marinoni, 2007).

If we want to have a closer look at numbers related to competitions in Italy, unfortunately there are no aggregated statistics depicting the Italian competitions context in recent years, apart from the data provided by Oice/Informatel presented in the following table (Table 6.1).

Another source generally used by practices to search for competition announcements and results is Europaconcorsi, which is one of the most complete and used databases on competitions. Offers to compete and outcomes provide information on architectural competitions since 2000. Data from Europaconcorsi are triangulated with Archiworld which is the competitions archive by Italian National Council of Architects, Planners, Landscapers and Curators. Starting from this database, the design competitions held in Italy in 2008 were recently mapped (Manzoni, 2010), reporting on 196 competitions whose results were published in 2008 (132 were announced in 2008, 62 in 2007 and just one in 2006). Of these, 67 were project competitions, while 129 were ideas ones; 76% of them had a public client while the 24% a private one. In terms of the target of the competition, 42% were addressed to architects registered to the profession in Italy, while the 58% were addressed at European and international professionals. Even when the target is extra-national, the language

Table 6.1 Project and ideas competitions announced in Italy from 2000 to 2009

	2000	2001	2002	2003	2004	2005	2006	2007	2008	2009
Project competitions	58	94	85	77	58	95	74	89	77	61
Ideas competitions	50	79	116	126	106	131	120	186	179	126
Total	108	173	201	203	164	226	194	275	256	187

Source; *Oice/Informatel.*

to compete remains Italian (this is the case for all of the national and regional competitions and for the 82% of the extra-national ones). Regarding the format of the competition, 93% were open. Interesting data that characterises the Italian market relates to the location of the competitions and to the type of projects required. Competitions are evenly distributed geographically in the north, centre, south and isles, mostly in cities that have less than 100,000 inhabitants. Projects were mostly urban design and regeneration interventions (36%), but also buildings for culture and education (15%) and transport and facilities (14%). Moreover, 88 competition announcements declared a budget for the works which averaging €14 million, but varying from €10,000 to more than €350 million. Considering the total budget of the prizes, in most of the cases (66%) it was under €30,000 while just 6% were over 150,000.

Research sample and variables

Within this scenario, the research was conducted on 179 architecture projects submitted to 10 projects and 10 ideas competitions in 2008 opened to both Italian and international professionals. These are some characteristics of the samples: 12 competitions were open, 8 were limited; 11 anonymous in one stage, 9 in two stages (named in the first and anonymous in the second); 14 had public clients and 6 private ones; 10 competitions were held in cities with 20,000–150,000 inhabitants, and 7 with over 300,000. Types of projects are different, varying from education and cultural buildings to residential ones and urban regeneration and design interventions. For each submitted project, data was collected concerning its performance (ranking) and the characteristics of the team designing it.

The competition result is seen as a performance criterion, ignoring building realisation effectiveness and efficiency as competitiveness dimensions, because the project at the competition phase had not then been realised. We assume that the competition result can be considered a measure of the value of the project and that it comprises the 'diversity, inclusivity and complexity of the concept' of performance (Flanagan *et al.*, 2005: 990), which is multi-defined, multi-measured, multi-layered and dynamic. Several studies focus on the factors leading to project success. The aim is to satisfy the client's needs, related to function, aesthetics, business goals and image (Volker and Prins 2006). In competitions, clients express their needs by providing an assignment, including the judgement criteria, to which firms react by sending in a concept design. Both parties are willing to create the best match possible.

Generally speaking project performance, depending on a team, can be defined as the 'extent to which a team is able to meet established objectives' (Hoegl and Weinkauf, 2005: 1290), and this is the reason why team composition becomes relevant in assessing its performance.

Different measures for team composition have been proposed in the past (e.g. Moreland and Levine, 1992), but we decided to preliminarily focus on the following ones, based on the literature review and on initial interviews in the field:

- *Team age*, computed considering the number of years of professional practice, both for firms and individual architects.
- *Team nationality*, measured considering the practice's location in relation to the competition and client location, and the previous experience of the practice abroad in the case of Italian architects: we distinguish between local or Italian teams with no international experience, Italian ones with international experience and foreign ones.
- *Team reputation*, computed according to the number of citations in two Italian specialised architecture journals from 1996 to 2008.

The results

Regarding team characteristics, from descriptive statistics, we observe that the average age of the architecture professionals is 20 years old for ideas competitions and 27 for project ones. In fact, if we look at the distribution across intervals of years, in ideas competitions architects with less than 15 years of work experience represent 37% against 25% of the project competitions.

However, when we go to see the characteristics of those winning professionals compared to the 'losers' we do not see relevant differences across performance in terms of age distribution (Table 6.2), when looking at very young professionals (less than 5 years' experience) only 2 of them were ranked in the first four positions. Does age not really matter in a

Table 6.2 Performance of the teams according to age

			Age of the practice/professional			
			0–15 years	16–30 years	Over 30 years	Total
Ranking position	11th and more	#	17	29	20	66
		%	25.8%	43.9%	30.3%	100.0%
	5th to 10th	#	14	14	8	36
		%	38.9%	38.9%	22.2%	100.0%
	1st to 4th	#	22	12	20	54
		%	40.7%	22.2%	37.0%	100.0%
Total		#	53	55	48	156
		%	34.0%	35.3%	30.8%	100.0%

Table 6.3 Performance of the teams according to nationality

			Local teams	National teams with no experience abroad	National teams with experience abroad	Non-Italian teams	Total
Ranking position	11th and more	#	7	17	13	32	69
		%	10.1%	24.6%	18.8%	46.4%	100.0%
	5th to 10th	#	15	12	8	5	40
		%	37.5%	30.0%	20.0%	12.5%	100.0%
	1st to 4th	#	32	25	7	4	68
		%	47.1%	36.8%	10.3%	5.9%	100.0%
Total		#	54	54	28	41	177
		%	30.5%	30.5%	15.8%	23.2%	100.0%

country with one of the highest average ages for the profession? Or are competitions becoming a real opportunity for newcomers?

Looking at the location of the practice, some interesting observations come from the comparison between ideas and project competitions: ideas competitions see most local teams (48%) and almost no foreign teams (7%), while moving to project competitions the percentage of local architects decreases (19%) at the expense of the foreign ones (34%). This might suggest that practices with experience abroad or international ones are more willing to go for project competitions.

Looking at the relationship between nationality and performance on our sampled projects (Table 6.3), local teams with no experience outside the region of the competition win more than international or national teams with experience abroad. Foreign teams are found in the top four positions in 6% of the cases, while the 46% of them rank lower than tenth. Almost the opposite is true for local teams: 47% are in the first four positions and 10% in the last ones. Does being locally specific really matter then, notwithstanding the increasing tendency towards internationalisation?

Finally, reputation provides some interesting results contradicting the hypothesis of competitions looking for and rewarding 'big' names. In ideas competitions the average number of citations in specialised journals is less than 1.0, rising to 4.3 for project competitions, even if in both types of competitions the most frequent number of citations is zero. Moreover, the vast majority of architects competing for ideas competitions have never been published before (90%), while 42% participating to project competitions had been published before.

But are 'published' architects more easily winning competitions? Actually not (see Table 6.4), as the percentage of architects with citations in our sampled projects decreases when going to the top ranking positions: 86% of winning architects have no citations, while 46% of those getting the lowest rankings in competitions have already been published.

Table 6.4 Performance of the teams according to their reputation

			No citations	At least one citation	Total
Ranking position	11th and more	#	37	32	69
		%	53.6%	46.4%	100.0%
	5th to 10th	#	32	9	41
		%	78.0%	22.0%	100.0%
	1st to 4th	#	59	10	69
		%	85.5%	14.5%	100.0%
Total		#	128	51	179
		%	71.5%	28.5%	100.0%

Does it mean that being published is not a predictor of performance in competitions at all? Or perhaps reputation is (also) measured in a different way?

Conclusions: implications for the architectural practices and directions for future research

The role of team composition for project performance has been recently studied in different creative industries (Perretti and Negro, 2006; Soda *et al.*, 2004), yet it has not been systematically explored in architecture. The industry, has in fact, lacked an adequate theoretical background or empirical test for this issue.

A first contribution of this chapter was, therefore, to try to understand whether there were some team composition variables in architecture able to explaining competition performance. Managerial implications could have derived for architectural practices, equipping teams for competitions and understanding which could be the best composition depending on the type of competition. Architectural competitions are sometimes considered as a pure gamble (Kreiner, 2006), but this also happens because it is not easy to discover the key to winning. But does this key to winning really exist? The analyses of a sample of Italian competitions would say that the 'black box' about team design in architectural competitions has still to be opened. At least for some variables that are debated topics in Italy and are proven to be significant in other sectors, although no significant results emerge apart from the fact that being local is still, contrary to any internationalisation strategy, a winning characteristic. This might confirm the connate scepticism architects have towards competitions, driving them to say, for example, that 'considering the low success rate of competitions entries, it is not worth the effort' (Anthony, 1991: 176).

A second contribution was to provide an insight into the Italian architecture industry, integrating existing but dispersed data about competition results. Despite the recent availability of data about competitions in Italy, this setting has not been systematically studied yet. The competition approach has, in fact, only recently become well structured with availability of information, also due to the changing policies at the European level. The research provided a general picture of the recent competition market for architecture firms and their project teams. It contributed some useful insights about the architect labour market and the dynamics and operations within the firms.

The research has developed a stream of analysis on architectural competitions and contributed to a fruitful debate on practice management, especially as most of the studies on competitions have analysed single architectural competitions. Kreiner (2009) started looking at competitions from the management viewpoint, but again focusing on case studies. Future research starting from this contribution could first enlarge the sample, also extending the analyses to longitudinal comparisons; second they could include other variables, such as the ones related to the composition of the jury, which decides who wins and such as those related to team working processes; and third compute advanced statistical analyses. Moreover multiple case studies could be selected to investigate the link between specific characteristics of team composition and team working processes and their contributions to different project success and award dimensions. Finally our study does not examine the content of competition announcements concerning specific requirements from the client that might influence team composition – an extremely important point as Kreiner (2006 and 2009) observes for the process of selecting a winner is dominated by sense-making which involves a process of reasonable interpretation that is intertwined with, but not solely determined by, the definition of selection criteria.

Acknowledgement

Some of this research was conducted with support from the ASK Research Centre, Bocconi University.

References

Adamczyk, G. (2004) *Architectural competitions and new reflexive practices*, Presentation for the joint ARCC–AEEA Conference, Dublin.

Ancona, D. G. and Caldwell, D. F. (1992) Bridging the boundary: external activity in performance in organizational teams, *Administrative Science Quarterly*, 37(6), 34–65.

Anthony, K. H. (1991) *Design juries on trial: the renaissance of the design studio.* New York: Van Nostrand Reinhold.

Baiden, B. K., Price, A. D. F. and Dainty, A. R. J. (2006) The extent of team integration within construction projects, *International Journal of Project Management*, 24, 13–23.

Blau, J. R. (1984) *Architects and Firms*, MIT Press, Boston.

Bell, S. T. (2007) Deep-level composition variables as predictors of team performance: a meta-analysis, *Journal of Applied Psychology*, 92(3), 595–615.

Cattani G. and Ferriani S. (2008) A Core/Periphery Perspective on Individual Creative Performance: Social Networks and Cinematic Achievements in the Hollywood Film Industry, *Organization Science*, 19(6), 824–844.

Chen, G. (2005) Newcomer adaptation in teams: multilevel antecedents and outcomes, *Academy of Management Journal*, 33, 334–65.

Collyer, G. S. (2004) *Competing globally in architecture competitions*, John Wiley & Sons, London.

CNAPPC (2009) *La crescita degli iscritti agli albi e la crisi profonda del mercato*, 1.

De Haan, H., Haagsma, I. (1988) *Architects in competition. International architectural competitions of the last 200 years*, London: Thames and Hudson.

Earley, P. C. and Mosakowski, E. M. (2000) Creating hybrid team cultures: an empirical test of international team functioning, *Academy of Management Journal*, 43: 26–49.

Evbuomwan, N. F. O. and Anumba, C. J. (1998) An integrated framework for concurrent lifecycle design and construction, *Advanced Engineering Software*, 29 (7–9), 587–97.

Flanagan, R., Jewell, C., Ericsson, S. and Henricsson, P. (2005) *Measuring Construction Competitiveness in Selected Countries Final Report*, University of Reading, http://n.1asphost.com/competitiveness/.

Flanagan, R., Lu, W., Shen, L. and Jewell, C. (2007) Competitiveness in construction: a critical review of research, *Construction Management and Economics*, 25(9), 989–1000.

Girmscheid, G. and Brockmann, C. (2008) *Global Players in the World's Construction Market*, Working paper, ETH Zürich.

Gunnarson, S. and Levitt, R. E. (1982) *Is a Building Construction Project a Hierarchy or a Market?* In:Riis, J. O. (ed.) Proceedings of the 7th World Congress on Project Management. Internet Congress, Copenhagen.

Gunnarson, S. and Levitt, R. E. (1982) *Is a Construction Project a Hierarchy or a Market?*, 7th Internet Congress on Project Management.

Gutman, R. (1988) *Architectural Practice: a critical view*, Princeton Architectural Press, New York.

Guzzo, R. A. and Dickson, M. W. (1996) Teams in organizations: research on performance and effectiveness, *Annual Review of Psychology*, 47, 307–38.

Henley, W. (2008) Hiring foreign architects set to become harder, *Building Design*, 12 September, 3.

Hobday, M. (2000) The project-based organization: an ideal form for managing complex products and systems? *Research Policy*, 29, 871–93.

Hoegl, M. and Weinkauf, K. (2005) Managing task interdependencies in multi-team projects: a longitudinal study, *Journal of Management Studies*, 42(6), 1287–1308.

Ilgen, D. R., Hollenbeck, J. R., Johnson, M. and Jundt, D. (2005) Teams in Organizations, *Annual Review of Psychology*, 56, 517–43, Fiske, S., Schachter, D. and Kasdin, A. (eds.).

Jackson, S. E., Joshi, A. (2004) Diversity in social context: a multi-attribute, multi-level analysis of team diversity and performance in a sales organization, *Journal of Organizational Behavior*, 25, 675–702.

Jones, C. and Livne-Tarandach, R. (2008) Designing a frame: rhetorical strategies of architects, *Journal of Organizational Behavior*, 29, 1075–99.

Kilduff, M. and Krackhardt, D. (1994) Bringing the individual back in: a structural analysis of the internal market for reputation in organizations, *Academy of Management Journal*, 37, 87–108.

Knox P. L. and Taylor, P. J. (2005) Toward a geography of the globalization of architecture office networks, *Journal of Architectural Education*, 58(3), 23–32.

Kreiner K. (2006) *Architectural Competitions: a Case-study*, Working Paper, Center for Management Studies of the Building Process, CBS ed., Copenhagen.

Kreiner K. (2009) Architectural Competitions – Empirical Observations and Strategic Implications for Architectural Firms, *Nordic Journal of Architectural Research*, 2, 3, 37–51.

Larson M.S. (1994) Architectural competitions as discursive events, *Theory and Society*, 23(4), 469–504.

Lo Ricco, G. and Micheli, S. (2003) *Lo spettacolo dell'architettura, Profilo dell'archistar©*, Mondadori, Milano.

Manzoni B. (2010) Le PBE nell'architettura: team di progetto e concorsi, in Biffi A. (eds.) Project based enterprise. Pensare ed agire per i progetti, Milano: Egea, 325–48.

Marinoni, G. (2007) Milan: an evolving city, *Milano Boom, 'Lotus International'* 131.

Michlewski, K. (2008) Uncovering design attitude: inside the culture of designers, *Organization Studies*, 29, 373–92.

Mintzberg, H., Otis, S., Shamsie, J. and Waters, J. A. (1988) Strategy of design: a study of 'architects in co-partnership', *Strategic Management Frontiers*, Grant, J. (ed.), JAI Press, Greenwich, 311–59.

Moreland, R. L. and Levine, J. M. (1992) The composition of small groups, *Advances in Group Processes*, 9, 237–280, Lawler, E., Markovsky, B., Ridgeway, C. and Walker, H. (eds.), JAI Press, Greenwich.

Nasar, J. L. (1998) *Design by competition: making design competition work*, Cambridge University Press.

Perretti, F. and Negro, G. (2006) Filling empty seats: how status and organizational hierarchies affect exploration versus exploitation in team design, *Academy of Management Journal*, 49(4), 759–77.

Rybczynski, W. (2006) Architectural branding, *The Wharton Real Estate Review*, Fall issue.

Soda, G., Usai, A. and Zaheer, A. (2004) Network memory: the influence of past and current networks on performance, *Academy of Management Journal*, 47(6), 893–906.

Spreiregen, P. D. (1979) *Design competitions*, New York: McGraw-Hill.

STD, (Swedish Federation of Consulting Engineers and Architects) 2009, Sector Review. The Consulting Engineering and Architectural Groups. A Swedish and International survey: http://www.std.se/MediaBinaryLoader.axd?

MediaArchive_FileID=3cc1d6c7-b31f-40d4-b55d-0a01bbd7a55d&MediaArchive_
ForceDownload=true (accessed 20 Sept, 2010)

Strong, J. (1996) *Winning by design: architectural competitions*, Oxford: Butterworth-
Heineman Architecture.

Sudjic, D. (2005) *Competitions: the Pitfalls and the Potential*, The Politics of Design:
Competitions for Public Projects Conference.

Taschen, B. (1994) *Architectural competitions (Volume 1: 1792–1949 and 2: 1950-
today)*, Naarden, The Netherlands: Cees de Jong.

Thornton, P. H., Jones, C. and Kury, K. (2005) Institutional logics and institutional
change in organizations: transformations in accounting, architecture and
publishing, *Research in the Sociology of Organizations*, 23, 127–72.

Tostrup, E. (1999) *Architecture and Rhetoric: Text and Design in Architectural
Competitions, Oslo 1939–1996*, Andreas Papadakis Publisher.

Tostrup E. (2009), Tracing Competition Rhetoric, *Nordic Journal of Architectural
Research*, 2(3), 23–36.

Van Wezemael, J. E. (2008) *The Complexity of Competitions – the quest for an adequate
research design*, Paper presented at the Conference on Architectural Competitions, Stockholm.

Volker, L. and Prins, M. (2006) Measuring the Effect of Steering Techniques
on Value Creation in Architectural Design, *Proceedings of COBRA 2006*, the
Annual Research Conference of the Royal Institution of Chartered Surveyors,
September, London.

Watson, W. E., Johnson, L., Merritt, D. (1998) Team orientation, self-orientation,
and diversity in task groups: their connection to team performance over time,
Group & Organization Management, 23, 161–189.

Winch, G. and Schneider, E. (1993a) The strategic management of architectural
practice, Construction Management and Economics, 11, 467–73.

Winch, G. and Schneider, E. (1993b) Managing the knowledge-based organization: the case of architectural practice, *Journal of Management Studies*, 30(6),
923–37.

Winch, G. (2008) Internationalisation strategies in business-to-business services:
the case of architectural practice, *The Service Industries Journal*, 28(1), 1–13.

Wynne, G. G. (Ed.) (1981) *Winning designs: the competitions renaissance*, New
Brunswick, NJ: Transaction Books.

Yoo, Y., Boland, R. J. and Lyytinen Jr., K. (2006) From organization design to
organization designing, *Organization Science*, 17(2), 215–29.

7 Client management and identification

Hedley Smyth and Sofia Kioussi

An overview of client management

Professional practices in the built environment have tended to be intuitive managers of their clients. Client management is theoretically part of marketing. Professional status and certification has restricted the adoption of explicit marketing practices in many countries and for many disciplines. This has been changing, and many practices have increasingly embraced marketing (Smyth, 2000). Others remain reticent, believing marketing to be based upon manipulation rather than merit of expertise and service output. This is more the case for architecture practices, where there has been a professional disdain for the commercialism of marketing (Kotler and Connor, 1977). Designers generally and architects in particular, passionate about their work, believe it should speaks for itself, and thus marketing is an anathema. This chapter shows the picture as more subtle – design helps to build relationships, and relationships build the design reputation and market profile of the practice. Relationship building and reputation is also part of brand development, which together facilitate client identification.

Client management and marketing have multiple dimensions. This chapter will focus upon three levels: relationship marketing, brand management and especially honing down to an important yet little understood issue of client identification. These three levels will be considered for architecture design practices. The analysis will have general lessons for all professional practices in the built environment, with greater resonance for those engaged in design, yet with a particular focus upon architecture because of the visual aspect of their design work.

It is the visual mode of design training and thinking that can seem at odds with commercial and marketing management, hence a disdain for these disciplines occurs. Yet both design and marketing share considerable cerebral input of creative ideas. Advertising, branding and other promotion involve considerable creativity, design and inventiveness.

Managing the Professional Practice: in the built environment, First Edition. Edited by Hedley Smyth.
© 2011 by Blackwell Publishing Ltd. Published 2011 by Blackwell Publishing Ltd.

Architects, it is hoped, will find this chapter user-friendly as the theoretical analysis engages with visual imagery, providing a conducive language to provide a more adequate bridge between architecture design and marketing than has hitherto been the case.

The chapter proceeds by introducing the background to relationship marketing, brand management and client identification. A deeper look is then taken at client identification. Client identification is then considered where design is the core business and how design invokes and stimulates clients to identify with the design and the practices. This analysis is supported by field research of strong idea architecture practices. This analysis is used as a foundation for developing further conceptual understanding of the means by which architects can more effectively manage client identification using design and relationship management.

Background in theory and for practice

Many practices think of marketing as mainly transactional – the so-called 4Ps of price, product, place and promotion – which has minimal relevance for tailored services (Smyth, 2000; Kioussi and Smyth, 2009a). Relationship marketing (e.g. Christopher *et al.*, 2006), on the other hand, is a systematic way of more consciously developing practice–client interaction that tries to restore the sole proprietor–local-customer link that tends to be lost in large firms and global and corporate businesses. Nurtured relationships provide opportunities to add service value and improve repeat business. Professional practices and architects have greater appreciation of these connections. Thus many practices implicitly employ relationship marketing and an increasing number have explicitly adopted relationship marketing and management over the past decade. Figure 7.1 shows a practice management process model for guiding explicit relationship marketing and management – see Storbacka *et al.* (1994) for the origins of this model.

The model requires strategic investment and tactical management with attendant cost (the top and bottom ellipses in the figure) in order to manage the relationships over the lifetime of work for the client. Client commitment is a key transitional step (Figure 7.1), which involves building loyalty, trust and empathy that is pivotal for client identification. Loyalty and trust are already strong relationship elements in most client–architect relations (e.g. Smyth, 2005). Empathy is most closely linked to engendering client identification, hence can be further enhanced by relationship marketing. Practices benefit from focusing on relationship building where there is scope for improvement. For example, gap analysis using the SERVQUAL model identifies differences in service perception between supplier (consultant) and customer (client)

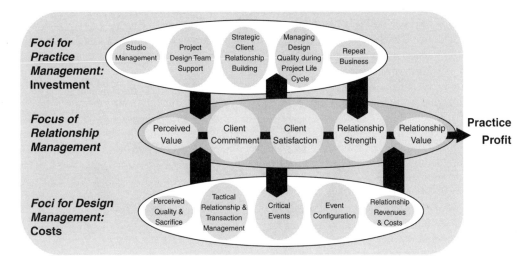

Figure 7.1 A simplified model of relationship project management. Source: adapted and developed from Pryke and Smyth, 2006

using the dimensions of reliability, assurance, tangibles, empathy and responsiveness (Parasuraman *et al.*, 1985; 1994). Another example is provided by the conditions of trust inventory by creating fertile conditions for trust around integrity, receptivity, loyalty, discretion and openness as behavioural intent (inputs) and consistency, promise fulfilment, fairness, competence and availability as behavioural ability (outputs) (Smyth, 2005; cf. Butler, 1991). A practice may focus on related behaviours that require improvement, such as receptivity, responsiveness and availability by developing specific guidelines and codes of conduct to improve these related areas.

Branding and client identification relate to design, yet are part of marketing. Client identification provides a bridge between design and relationship management, which in turn flows from relationship marketing (Figure 7.2). Branding and customer identification have largely been analysed from the corporate perspective (Ahearne *et al.*, 2005), the client perspective being somewhat neglected. Conceptualising visual imagery for branding provides an important bridge between the design process and the development of client identification. Design initiates the process, with relationship marketing deepening client identification further.

Design follows the brand in most industries. Design quality gives rise to the most visible and tangible image of the firm. Design becomes a tangible element of marketing (Olins, 1990). It facilitates marketing (Bruce and Daly, 2007) and brand development in particular for both the product and the promotion of the product. Design can be decisive in facilitating customer and client identification. This is not replicated in the same way where design is the core business (Kioussi and

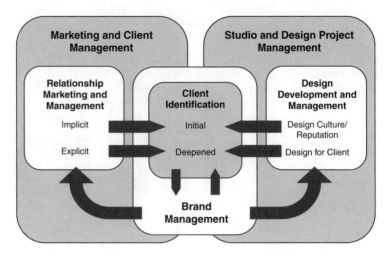

Figure 7.2 Client identification and brand management in relation to design and marketing

Smyth, 2009a). Where design is the core business, brand follows design. The design culture or 'design attitude' (Boland and Collopy, 2004; Michlewski, 2008) drives the practice and permeates all activities: organisational culture, structure and processes. This design attitude gives rise to the brand, is projected into the market through the design output and is reinforced through relationship marketing (Kioussi and Smyth, 2009a).

Whilst architectural and urban identity has been explored physically and sociologically (e.g. Davis, 1990), less attention has been paid to how the clients and users identify with buildings and facilities. There is an absence of research on how these clients and end-users identify with the design, the firms and their employees. End-users fall into two categories. There are end-users who occupy the buildings and those who use the facilities as visitors. There is also the general public who are onlookers, experiencing the visual image of the external design in the built environment or seeing photographic images in the media. Onlookers include peer assessment through the architecture press, which plays an important part of establishing architectural brands, setting trends that influence public opinion along similar lines to haut couture in the fashion industry. In these ways, buildings act as sculptural 'billboards' for prominent design practices, and may act as 'billboards' for corporate clients where design image forms part of the corporate brand.

Research into brand management within architecture firms demonstrated a significant yet previously unarticulated link between the design, design process and client identification (Kioussi and Smyth, 2009a). How client identification comes about remains insufficiently understood. Jones and Livne-Tarandach (2008) explored rhetoric and language. They found architects used client vocabulary and business logic alongside their own rhetorical language as a means to legitimise practice competencies around design and spatial analysis – a 'one-way street' but in the opposite direction to client identification. There is a lack of conceptual parameters at the brand-client interface. This chapter builds upon work developing in this area (Kioussi and Smyth, 2009b) by scoping our understanding of client identification arising from design, marketing and branding. Three visual concepts are used from the work of Schroeder (2007) to help this process. The three concepts are visual, which provides a familiar and useful bridge for architects to engage more rigorously with marketing and branding. The conceptual categories are *the visual language of architecture, snapshot aesthetics* and *the transformational mirror of consumption*. The visual language of architecture is formal and explicitly used in design imagery, including architecture. The concept of transformational mirror of consumption is implicitly prevalent in design-led markets, including architecture. This concept facilitates understanding co-created value as part of client identification in and engaging with the design process. Such co-created value accrues as personal capital to individuals, as social capital to the corporate client and as social capital to the architecture firm too. This visual category can be applied within marketing and brand management with the concepts of snapshot aesthetics and the visual language of architecture for different functions and in different design markets.

Client identification

There are three related areas: personal identity, social identity and identification. How identity arises provides a context for appreciating identification, particularly client identification. Identity arises from a sense of self, defined in terms of feeling accepted, secure and significant (Anderson, 1990). This sense of identity is an overall condition, although associated feelings vary according to context and prevailing circumstances. Significance is particularly linked to the marketplace; for example, many people get a strong sense of significance from what they achieve at work (McGee, 1998). Significance is related to equity, for example status and market standing, whilst acceptance and security are more related to equality.

Brands primarily connect to significance; for example, wearing clothing of an upscale brand may lend a sense of significance to someone, which in turn may reinforce perceptions of acceptance and security. Particular brands convey messages about the nature of a person's identity; for example it may be 'cool' to wear Nike compared to another major brand. The 1996 movie, *You Got Mail*, encapsulates the brand-identity link when Tom Hanks is commenting,

> *The whole purpose of places like Starbucks is for people with no decision-making ability whatsoever to make six decisions just to buy a cup of coffee. Short, tall, light, dark, caf, decaf, low fat, non-fat, etcetera. So, people who don't know what the hell they are doing, or who on earth they are, can for two-ninety-five get not just a cup of coffee, but an absolutely defining sense of self. Tall! Decaf! Cappuccino!'*

The movie promotion of Starbucks aided brand globalisation. More importantly, if brands can develop markets where unsophisticated decision-making prevails, then how much more critical is identification in markets requiring highly complex and sophisticated decision-making, such as design and project markets? It becomes important where complexity leads to strong client identification through design and relationship management.

Personal identity theory (Stryker, 1980) states that roles help people to define their identity. Roles particularly lend significance, the derived sense of self becoming an 'active creator of social behaviour' (Stryker, 1980: 385). Stryker (1968) therefore linked role identities to experiential outcomes, recognising that some identities have greater impact on outcomes than others. Commitment, for example long-term commitment, is based on relationships and their strength (see Figure 7.1), and has the ability to reinforce roles and hence identity. Long-term commitment, frequently defined within specific roles, can come out of brands and client identification in terms of the product and people delivering a service.

Social identity theory involves perceived alignment or oneness with a group of people. Social identification arises from the types of individuals, the salience and prestige of the group. Social identification leads to activities that are congruent with, and provide support for, institutions that embody the identity (Ashforth *et al.*, 1989). Idealised and stereotypical perceptions of self and others tend to inform identification with others and groups as seen in organisational socialisation, roles and intergroup relations.

Personal and social identity theories are linked (Hogg *et al.*, 1995). Personal identity theory particularly analyses experience and internalisation, which is important for client identification. Social identity theory robustly addresses cognitive factors because these have important confirming and reinforcing functions in client identification. Social identity in a role and within groups helps individuals maintain a sense of self and self-worth as well as giving a forum for projecting a positive and aspired sense of self (Tajfel, 1982).

Identification develops out of personal and social identity. Identification invokes empathy from one person or group to another. For example, personal suffering of one kind can help someone identify with the same or a similar sort of suffering experienced by another. In other words, we can 'put ourselves in your shoes'. A brand soliciting a positive emotional response gives a sense of well-being through the quality or label with which we wish to be associated – we want to 'put ourselves in their shoes'. Identification therefore works at two levels. It starts with the product or service being supplied along with the corporate brand, the organisation and the individuals behind the product or service. The first level of response is empathy based upon past experience, which invokes a sense of well-being, often but not always linked to significance. For example, Volvo cars as a brand had a reputation for safety and solidity, invoking from our past experience the need for these factors, and its brand reputation supplies that sense of reassurance, in this case working as much with security as significance. The second level is empathy directly informed by our aspirations for future experience – a sense of getting closer to aspired levels of well-being. Apple products have a reputation for quality design and 'cool' image, linking a sense of current peer acceptance and our aspirations as to how we wish to project ourselves to others and what we wish to become. Aspirations are based in personal significance. Both Volvo and Apple value design, and are examples of design following the brand. In design-led companies, such as architects, brand follows the design. What difference does this make?

Client identification in design-led firms

For a prominent area of marketing, there are few models of brand development in general (de Chernatony *et al.*, 2003). There is even less on client identification, and a dearth on firms where design is the core business.

Clients identify with the design approach – design attitude and track record – then identify with the specific design solution for their facility. The strength of the design approach governs the potential for identification through the design. Therefore, in architecture 'strong idea' firms (Coxe *et al.*, 1987; Winch and Schneider, 1993) and archistars (e.g. Manzoni *et al.*, 2009; see also Chapter 6) have the strongest design approach, embodied in the reputation from past work and the completed designs seen by the (potential) client. The strength of design is a product of a creative culture, the 'design attitude' (Boland and Collopy, 2004; Michlewski, 2008), manifested in a studio model of organisational structure (Kioussi and Smyth, 2009a). Once the practice is appointed, the client and users become involved with the design process as the design for their facility is iteratively conceived and developed. Client identification increases during this process as a result of the specific design to the extent that the emergent design is an expression of themselves, that is, embodying self-image of who they are, who they think they are and who they aspire to be. The way in which this occurs in detail has only started to be explored in architecture (Kioussi and Smyth, 2009b).

Architects have historically focused primarily on the design. They assign the service to a secondary, albeit important, role. The responsive engagement of the client is generally recognised and welcomed within this secondary role, yet active client management is typically implicit or absent. The quality of engagement with the client tends to be perceived as the product of (i) design reputation and how good the specific design for the client is, (ii) how good the client is and the extent to which they value design, (iii) how good the relationships are between the parties as a result of 'personal chemistry'. In summary, the perception can be summarised as the product of design merit and social coincidence. It is not typically seen as something more complex, specifically the iterative interaction between the design and developing strength of relationships. In partic- ular, relationships are not seen as something to be proactively managed in the same way that creativity is facilitated and managed through the practice structure and routines. Nor is it appreciated that doing so will improve design quality for a project and over time be reflected through reputation (especially referral and influencer markets – see Christopher *et al.*, 2006; Kioussi, 2008) and in the brand (Kioussi and Smyth, 2009a).

An investigation into five architecture practices confirmed the primacy of design over such service considerations (Kioussi, 2008). This was a reflection of management issues being lower priority, sometimes to the detriment of design quality and reputation. The professional disdain for marketing was in evidence amongst the architecture practices (cf. Kotler and Connor, 1977). Yet there was a high concern for service quality through elements of proactive corporate management as all five practices were also directly engaged with construction and development. The motivation was to deliver the design quality throughout the project lifecycle to clients. Consequently, the link between the client and the practice was more intense over the whole project lifecycle, although it was weaker at the early stages where the development function meant that conceptual design was carried out prior to client involvement and sometimes in order to generate client interest (cf. Kioussi, 2008).

Several pertinent findings from this study inform the analysis here. The first finding was confirmation of design 'speaking for itself' – pure merit. Thus, when clients approached these practices it was viewed as 'automatic' and devoid of relationships or the need to explicitly develop these. Yet it was also found that a considerable amount of relationship marketing was implicitly conducted by all the practices. A further finding was that this unrecognised relationship marketing was a key element of building the brand through client identification (Kioussi and Smyth, 2009a). Whilst client identification commenced with an emotional response to the design approach of the firm, it deepened as the relationships developed. This occurred in two ways, the first being the sense of identification amongst those with whom the clients had direct contact, that is, the people implicitly acting in key account management (KAM) roles (cf. McDonald *et al.*, 1997; Kempeners and van der Hart 1999). The second is the identification with the practice as an organisation, that is, reflected through the design attitude and through others with whom the clients had some contact or indirect knowledge beyond those in KAM roles (Kioussi and Smyth, 2009a).

It is suspected that relationship building is important for most architecture practices, although awareness may be weaker amongst strong idea practices compared to strong service and delivery practices (cf. Coxe *et al.*, 1987). The strong idea and service firms operating in the quality design-construction-development markets covered in the study maintained constant and regular client links throughout the project (Kioussi, 2008). Traditional commission-based practices sometimes have greater early involvement of the client, which provides relationship development opportunities through design iteration during the concept design stage, although the involvement may be less in the latter stages of the project lifecycle. The design development and associated relationship may potentially induce deepening client identification through both the specific design and relationship building with key people and the organisation.

This process of identification has been poorly articulated for two reasons, one practice-based and one conceptual. The practice-based reason resides with the professional disdain for marketing, especially amongst strong idea firms. The conceptual reason rests with the corporate focus rather than a customer and client focus on branding and identification (Ahearne *et al.*, 2005), and hence the recommendation from the study for 'a more thorough analysis as to the way in which branding engenders customer identification' (Kioussi and Smyth, 2009a: 9). This neglect of the process of client identification is not merely a matter of tracing the psychology of identification, perhaps aided by personal and social identity theory. It also has to do with inadequate conceptual language to articulate such an exploration, particularly at the client–architecture interface. This is where the recent theoretical developments around images of brand culture can contribute.

Scoping and understanding customer identification

This analysis provides a language for scoping and understanding client identification at the client–architecture practice interface. Particular emphasis is placed upon how the communication from the architecture practice affects clients. Verbal language and rhetoric has the opposite effect and may act as a barrier to identification (cf. Jones and Livne-Tarandach, 2008). Visual communication has the means to build identification, and directly and indirectly affects design. This visual language is important in order to provide (i) an understanding as to how identification begins to take hold in the hearts and minds of clients and users, and (ii) a bridge between design and relationship building for the architecture practice.

The work of Schroeder (2007) provides a conceptual typology for beginning to articulate and categorise these design outputs. Schroeder addresses visual advertising and brand management, focusing upon the visual representation of the product through advertising. Architecture, where brand follows the design, is visualised directly through the product rather than represented in advertisements. It is also indirectly represented through the important process of media peer review (cf. Winch and Schneider, 1993). Thus, design is manifested in the final artefact or product as an advertisement in itself – the sculptural billboard. Many buildings, particularly from eminent strong idea practices (Coxe *et al.*, 1987) and archistars (Manzoni *et al.*, 2009), are like large urban billboards. These billboards are primarily facilities in use that also promote the architecture practice, promote the client where the building reinforces the corporate brand (cf. Kioussi and Smyth 2009b), and the city or urban area in the city (Smyth, 1994). Schroeder (2007) provides three conceptual categories of cultural, ideological and rhetorical images that create value. Visual imagery, including design, is a powerful form of communication because it invokes and resonates with both personal experience and aspirations that are open to individual interpretation and perception (cf. Bargh, 2002).

The visual language of architecture is the first and most obvious of the three categories as it employs the term 'architecture', albeit in a generic sense, which Schroeder frequently applies directly to buildings. This term echoes formal and classical aesthetics. Schroeder uses the examples of banks that present classical or solid and formal representations of their institution, often buildings or their facades, in their publicity (Schroeder, 2003). The image communicates professionalism and institutional longevity, even though such stability, strength and security have been complemented by speed of operations (Schroeder, 2007) that are frequently housed in semi-transparent glass cathedrals of corporate power. This is also the traditional language of the architecture practice in brochures, peer media and coffee table publications. This type of image projection connects with social identity theory concerning architecture peer groups. It also facilitates client identification through the design of buildings, supporting and developing client corporate branding. The strong idea architects and archistars may allocate most promotional resources to this visual language, as they appreciate that design quality sells their services. Visual imagery is implicitly the doorway to stimulating client identification, initially on design merit, yet subsequently through relationship development. The strong idea practice has more to gain than the strong service practice (cf. Coxe et al., 1987). The strong service practice stands to gain largely by portraying the solid professional image through this language in brand management.

Snapshot aesthetics is the mostly recently popularised visual language. Small digital handheld cameras and mobile phone cameras produce instant images, reflecting the time, place and sentiment of the moment. This immediacy provides the source of interest in the pictures rather than formal compositions and aesthetic principles. Such images appear accessible, realistic and authentic, casual reflections of everyday life. Well-known brands use this approach in their advertising, Schroeder citing leading upscale fashion brands, including Yves Saint Laurent and Apple using this visual language (Schroeder, 2007; 2008). Snapshot aesthetics appear far from staged, although they are clearly thought through and sometimes highly contrived too. For an architectural image or photo to be consider as a snapshot, it needs a sense of spontaneous imperfectness showing real things, for example lights and window blinds as they would be used with the presence of people depicted in real-life positions and functioning movement. Light can be used to give a sense of movement and informal geometry.

Snapshot aesthetics is the least used language of architects, although some practices, Make Architects (Make Architects, 2009), depict creativity in action in this way (rather than the buildings) on their website. There is scope for greater use to provide clients with an accessible visual doorway to identification plus engaging end-users by depicting buildings in use. Thus snapshot aesthetics provides supplementary support to the language of architecture, encouraging identification through the human dimensions of personal and social identity of clients and end-users.

The transformative mirror of consumption is the most important language for design-led branding. It is based upon the emotional response of the perceiver to the visual image. Schroeder (2007) considers this in advertising as both literal and symbolic. He uses advertisements where mirrors or reflections are used to reveal and reinforce attributes of the onlooker. There are precedents in art. *The Rokeby Venus* by Velazquez has the women in self-reflected vanity, and the viewer is drawn into the picture as the pose presents vanity as a sensual depiction for them. Yves Saint Laurent has parodied this and other works of art. They add a clothed man on the floor, also holding the mirror of self-reflection, the juxtaposition of the two figures inviting the viewer to see the product as transforming and aspirational. This device is frequently used in the adverts, for example Coloma Coffee adverts of the late 1990s (Schroeder and Zwick, 2004) and MOTO KRZR in 2006 (Schroeder, 2007) are cited as seminal examples, which are echoed in other adverts by Yves Saint Laurent, who even combine the transformational mirror with snapshot aesthetics on occasions.

The more frequent application is symbolic – an indirect invitation to the viewer. The viewer starts as onlooker, the emotional response engaging the viewer who interprets the image according to their perceptions and meanings. The language of architecture and snapshot aesthetics can provide images that also act as doorways to this type of response, so an image can be in a dual category with a dual function. This transformational mirror category involves both parties actively creating something – the architect the design and the client an emotional response, which is part of their socially constructed reality based upon both the concrete and the symbolic (cf. Berger and Luckman, 1984; Bourdieu, 1984). Such emotional response creates a value for the artefact in the marketplace of consumption.

Strong architecture potentially stimulates a strong emotional response, hence provides a mirror of transformation. Where client perceptions and meanings strongly resonate and align with the architecture and the design intentions of the architects, personal identification is reinforced and social identification amongst those representing the client organisation and end-users is also reinforced. Resonation and alignment are reflections of (i) the self-image of the client in terms of their current requirements and their aspirations concerning their personal lifestyle (Kioussi and Smyth, 2009a), and (ii) corporate ambitions, which may also be reflected through building design to reinforce the corporate brand. This is co-created value (Prahalad and Ramaswamy, 2004a): 'Points of interaction provide opportunities for collaboration and negotiation, explicit or implicit, between the consumer and the company – as well as opportunities for those processes to break down' (Prahalad and Ramaswamy, 2004b: 9).

Although architects have some disdain for marketing, relationship marketing is trying to manage interactions, and brand management couples 'design attitude' with the relationship strength to encourage identification and develop practice profile (Kioussi and Smyth, 2009a). This co-created value is set out in Figure 7.3. This figure primarily addresses the architecture practice, client and end-user in relation to the building and its design. The architecture practice is portrayed as a project organisation (see Chapter 1), which may be a dominant client perception, except perhaps concerning strong idea practices. The wider context is important as the public, called the 'onlooker' in Figure 7.3, is part of the social identification process and indirectly the reputational profile of the architecture practice. The onlooker is included as part of the broader co-creation of social capital. Figure 7.3 identifies eight stages and these are explored in more detail in Table 7.1, linking the stage to the type of promotion and relationship building that practices might consider in changing their roles as more active marketers and brand managers. Indicative links to Schroeder's categories – the language of architecture, snapshot aesthetics and design as transformational mirrors of consumption – are also provided.

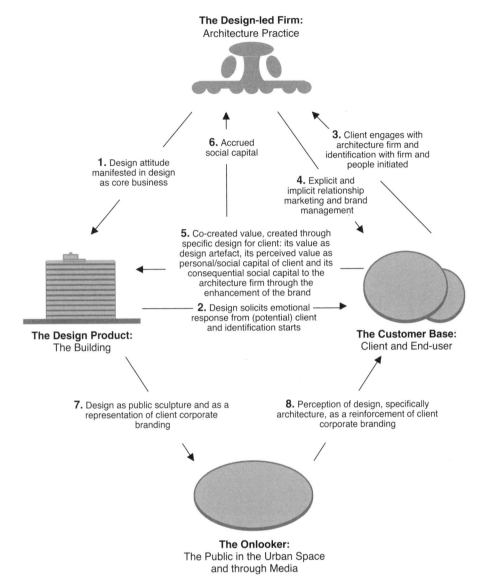

The Design-led Firm:
Architecture Practice

1. Design attitude manifested in design as core business

6. Accrued social capital

3. Client engages with architecture firm and identification with firm and people initiated

4. Explicit and implicit relationship marketing and brand management

5. Co-created value, created through specific design for client: its value as design artefact, its perceived value as personal/social capital of client and its consequential social capital to the architecture firm through the enhancement of the brand

2. Design solicits emotional response from (potential) client and identification starts

The Design Product:
The Building

The Customer Base:
Client and End-user

7. Design as public sculpture and as a representation of client corporate branding

8. Perception of design, specifically architecture, as a reinforcement of client corporate branding

The Onlooker:
The Public in the Urban Space and through Media

Figure 7.3 Value creation co-value creation, identification and social capital. Source: Kioussi and Smyth, 2009b

Creative management

An overarching message of this chapter is that the founders and senior people in architecture practices have nothing to fear from management, marketing and branding. Their disposition to shun management

Table 7.1 Co-created value, relationship marketing and brand management

Stage	Forms of engagement
1. Design attitude manifested in design as core business	Product: visual language of architecture Promotion: visual language of architecture (photographic) and snapshot aesthetics amongst some younger practices
2. Design solicits emotional response from (potential) client and identification starts	Product: transformational mirror of consumption Response: client identification initiates desire for further engagement with the practice
3. Client engages with architecture firm and identification with firm and people initiated	Architect typically sees this as a response on design merit Client wants to develop relationship to reinforce identification Architects may implicitly build relationship management to reinforce design as a transformational mirror for the client
4. Explicit and implicit relationship marketing and brand management	Promotion: explicit relationship marketing and brand management to reinforce client identification and enhance market profile using combinations of the visual language of architecture, snapshot aesthetics and recognising the power of design as a transformational mirror, which is guided and facilitated through relationship management

5. Co-value creation through specific design for client: its value as design artefact, its perceived value as personal/social capital of client and its consequential social capital to the architecture firm through the enhancement of the brand	Product: specific design developed soliciting:
	(i) a return to stage 1, plus
	(ii) transformational mirror of consumption, the process being reinforced by:
	   a. client feedback soliciting development of concept design with architects
	   b. relationship deepened with architects through the process
	Client identification reinforced through this co-created value process

6. Accrued social capital	Co-created value adds product value for the client More significantly, in the long-term co-creation adds brand value to the architecture firm in the market and status to the client, which is manifested as corporate brand value if the client is an organisation The transformational mirror dominates at this stage, increasingly developed through the relationship rather than design per se
7. Design as public sculpture and as a representation of Client corporate branding	Product: visual language of architecture Promotion: visual language of architecture (photographic) and snapshot aesthetics (photographic)
8. Perception of design, specifically architecture, as a reinforcement of client corporate branding	The visual language of architecture as dominant

relies heavily on the expertise and codes of professional conduct to regulate activities with a light touch (Mintzberg *et al.*, 1986). Carefully implemented, management can enhance creativity. The chapter has argued:

1. Designs invoke emotional responses from potential clients, starting the identification process.
2. A relationship is established through the commission.
3. Specific design for the new client further develops client identification – practices to develop formal routines between the responsible designer for the project lifecycle and the client; to discuss in what ways identification is in evidence and what actions can be taken to enhance this; then, review them during each design stage as part of design reviews and as part of regular (weekly) studio team meetings.
4. Subsequent deepening of client identification depends not on design per se, but also on how well the relationships are developed. Practices of relationship marketing and management provide the means to actively enhance client identification – practices to develop formal and informal routines that link the above review processes to relationship management principles that set out processes guided by particular behaviours, for example:
    - keeping a record of 'soft' commitments and promises against which delivery is measured;
    - stipulating minimum response times from responsible designer to client, design team consultants and contractors (including honesty about availability and holding responses from other staff when responsible designer is indisposed);
    - having norms to create an outward focus to overcome opportunism and excessive business self-interest;
    - maintaining regular contact between commissions.
5. The process of deepening client identification through relationship management is more likely to solicit the richest feedback on design content and thus improve design development for the client and for reputation in the market.

These processes of relationship marketing are reasonably pragmatic and variable between firms, yet they may appear uncomfortable for some founders and senior management. The visual imagery of branding used by Schroeder (2007) provides a language to bridge marketing and design. It will not cover all the dimensions of effective relationship marketing to improve design quality, brand and profile presence, but it will provide a means to overcome the disdain, sharing a visual vocabulary that is about design, and will improve client identification through literal and symbolic application.

Conclusions and recommendations

Previous research has found that client identification has yet to be fully understood (Kioussi and Smyth, 2009a). This chapter has explored the process of client identification. It is conceptually part of marketing and, specifically, branding. It also links with issues of personal and social identity. Furthermore it is embedded in design, and utilises a visual language. Three categories of visual branding were used – the language of architecture, snapshot aesthetics and design as transformational mirrors of consumption – to help conceptualise creating design in the market in relation to the psychological response of clients and end-users.

Two principal recommendations flow from the analysis for practice and research:

1. Architecture practices should be more active in brand management and client identification – the visual language is more conducive to the design community than management language per se.
2. Further research is required as to how clients and end-users identify with design and designers – the psychological and social processes whereby identification develops at a detailed level.

References

Ahearne, M., Bhattacharya, C. B. and Gruen, T. (2005) Antecedents and consequences of customer-company identification: expanding the role of relationship marketing. *Journal of Applied Psychology*, 90(3), 574–585.

Anderson, N. T. (1990) *Victory over Darkness*, Regal Books, Ventura.

Ashforth, B. E. and Mael, F. (1989) Social identity theory and the organization, *Academy of Management Review*, 14(1), 20–39.

Bargh, J. A. (2002) Losing consciousness: automatic influences on consumer judgement, behavior and motivation. *Journal of Consumer Research*, 29, 280–285.

Berger, P. L. and Luckmann, T. (1984) *The Social Construction of Reality: a treatise in the sociology of knowledge.* Penguin, London.

Boland, R. J. and Collopy, F. (2004) Design matters for management, *Managing as Designing*, Boland, R. J. and Collopy, F. (eds.) Stanford University Press, Stanford, pp. 3–18.

Bourdieu, P. (1984) *Distinction: a social critique of the judgment of taste.* Harvard University Press, Cambridge.

Bruce, M. and Daly, L. (2007) Design and marketing connections: creating added value. *Journal of Marketing Management*, 23(9–10), 929–953.

Butler J. K. (1991) Toward understanding and measuring conditions of trust: evolution of conditions of trust inventory. *Journal of Management*, 17, 643–663.

de Chernatony, L., Drury, S. and Segal-Horn S. (2003) Building a services brand: stages, people and orientations. *The Services Industry Journal*, 23(3), 1–21.

Christopher, M., Payne, A. and Ballantyne, D. (2006) *Relationship Marketing: creating stakeholder value.* Butterworth-Heinemann, Oxford.

Coxe, W., Hartung, N., Hochberg, H., Lewis, B., Maister, D., Mattox, R. and Piven, P. (1987) *Success Strategies for Design Professionals.* McGraw Hill, New York.

Davis, M. (1990) *City of Quartz: excavating the future in Los Angeles.* Verso, London.

Hogg, M. A., Terry, D. J. and White, K. M. (1995) Tale of two theories: a critical comparison of identity theory with social identity theory, *Social Psychology Quarterly*, 58(4), 255–269.

Jones, C. and Livne-Tarandach, R. (2008) Designing a frame: rhetorical strategies of architects, *Journal of Organizational Behavior*, 29, 1075–1099.

Kempeners, M. and van der Hart, H. (1999) Designing account management organisations. *Journal of Business and Industrial Marketing*, 14, 310–327.

Kioussi, S. (2008) *Quality Design, Construction and Development Enterprises: exploring the model and marketing strategies for integration. Report*, UCL, London.

Kioussi, S. and Smyth, H. J. (2009a) Brand management in design-led firms: the case of architecture practices in the design-construction-development market, *Proceedings of the 5th Thought Leaders International Conference on Brand Management* 6–7 April, Atiner, Athens.

Kioussi, S. and Smyth, H. J. (2009b) Client identification with design and the architecture firm: scoping identification through design-led visualisation, Proceedings of Changing Roles: new roles; new challenges 5–9 October, Delft University of Technology, Rotterdam.

Kotler P. and Connor R. A. (1977) Marketing professional services. *Journal of Marketing*, 41(1), 71–76.

Make Architects (2009) Webpage, http://www.makearchitects.com/#/practice/profile/, accessed 12th May

Manzoni, B., Morris, P. W. G. and Smyth, H. J. (2009) Equipping project teams to win tenders: an insight into Italian architecture projects, *ARCOM*, 7–9 September, Nottingham.

McDonald, M., Millman, T. and Rogers, B. (1997) Key account management: theory practice and challenges. *Journal of Marketing Management*, 13, 737–757.

McGee, R. (1998) *The Search for Significance.* Word Publishing, Nashville.

Michlewski, K. (2008) Uncovering design attitude: inside the culture of designers. *Organization Studies*, 29(3), 373–392.

Mintzberg, H., Otis, S., Shamsie, J. and Waters, J.A. (1986) Strategy of design: a study of 'architects in co-partnership'. In: Grant, J. (ed.) *Strategic Management Frontiers.* JAI Press, Greenwich.

Olins, W. (1990) *Corporate Identity*, Thames and Hudson, London.

Parasuraman, A. Zeithaml, V. and Berry, L. L. (1985) A conceptual model of service quality and its implications for future research. *Journal of Marketing*, 49, 41–50.

Parasuraman, A. Zeithaml, V. and Berry, L. L. (1994) Reassessment of expectations as a comparison standard in measuring service quality. *Journal of Marketing*, 58, 111–124.

Prahalad, C. K. and Ramaswamy, V. (2004a) Co-creating experiences: the next practice in value creation, *Journal of Interactive Marketing*, 18(3), 5–14.

Prahalad, C. K. and Ramaswamy, V. (2004b) Co-creating unique value with customers, *Strategy & Leadership*, 32(3), 4–9.

Pryke, S. D. and Smyth, H. J. (2006) Scoping a relationship approach to the management of projects, *Management of Complex Projects: A Relationship Approach*, Blackwell Publishing Ltd., Oxford, pp. 21–46.

Schroeder, J. (2003) Building brands: architectural expression in the electronic age, *Persuasive Imagery: a consumer response perspective*, LM Scottand R Batra (eds.), Lawrence Erlbaum Associates, Mahwah.

Schroeder, J. (2007) Visual analysis of images in brand culture, *Go Figure! New directions in advertising rhetoric*, BJ Phillips and E McQuarrie (eds.), W. E. Sharpe, Armonk.

Schroeder J. E. (2008) Snapshot aesthetics in brand culture, *International Network of Visual Studies in Organizations*, The Photographers Gallery, University of Exeter.

Schroeder J. E. and Zwick, D. (2004) Mirrors of masculinity: representation and identity in advertising images, *Consumption, Markets and Culture*, 7(1), 21–51.

Smyth, H. J. (1994) *Marketing the City*, E & FN Spon, London.

Smyth, H. J. (2000) *Marketing and Selling Construction Services*, Blackwell Publishing Ltd., Oxford.

Smyth, H. J. (2005) Trust in the design team. *Architectural Engineering and Design Management*, 1(3), 193–205.

Storbacka, K., Strandvik, T. and Grönroos, C. (1994) Managing customer relationships for profit: the dynamics of relationship quality. *International Journal of Service Industry Management*, 5(5), 21–38.

Stryker, S. (1968) Identity salience and role performance: the importance of symbolic interaction theory for family research. *Journal of Marriage and the Family*, 30, 558–564.

Stryker, S. (1980) *Social Interactionism: a social structural version*, Benjamin/ Cummings, Palo Alto.

Tajfel, H. (1982) Social psychology of intergroup relations, *Annual Review of Psychology*, 33, 1–39.

Winch, G. M. and Schneider, E. (1993) The strategic management of architectural practice. *Construction Management and Economics*, 11, 467–473.

How thin to win

FM service provision issues

Kathy Roper

Managing professional practice in facility management requires an unusually broad balance of activities. Balance of sales, with technical expertise, human resource management, and also the important component of relationship, makes the professional practice of facility management one of the most precarious, yet rewarding, practices.

Facility management, as defined by numerous associations and experts, includes a broad scope of services to benefit an organisation's workforce, and supports the primary objectives of the organisation. These services normally range from strategic planning for workspace needs, real-estate transactions, operational maintenance of workspaces, mail, reprographic and other administrative services, as well as constant updates to the organisation's workspaces to keep them organisationally appropriate and functional as rapidly changing organisations transform and innovate. The International Facility Management Association (IFMA) defines facility management as, 'a profession that encompasses multiple disciplines to ensure functionality of the built environment by integrating people, place, process and technology' (IFMA, 2009). This broad range of potential services is one area of primary importance and potential failure for facility management practices.

Historically, facility management professional practices sprang from one primary area of expertise. As the acceptance of outsourcing expanded and corporate users sought single-source or all-in-one providers, many professional service providers expanded their offerings and services. Ikon, a copier and printing organisation, provided expertise in outsourced reprographic services. Their expansion into mail, shipping and other document services led to their current business as 'document management strategists', addressing a full range of document planning and services. Jones, Lang, LaSalle began business as a Chicago real estate brokerage company and is now a global property, investment, energy

Managing the Professional Practice: in the built environment, First Edition. Edited by Hedley Smyth. © 2011 by Blackwell Publishing Ltd. Published 2011 by Blackwell Publishing Ltd.

planning and project management service organisation. Johnson Controls, which began business as a room thermostat manufacturer, now provides services in automotive interiors, building efficiency and power solutions.

The desire to be everything to everyone is a tempting, yet an impossible, business model. Thoughtful professional practices recognise their limitations, and many have focused on limited services in which they can provide true expertise and value. The way in which firms choose to limit their scope, as indicated by the examples of Ikon, Johnson Controls and Jones, Lang LaSalle, differentiate the offers and appeal to particular customers and market segments. Even considering the maturation of outsourcing practices over the past decade, there remains primary business issues that are difficult and recurring in today's facility management professional practice. Three of these are addressed in the remainder of this chapter:

1. Client/contractor relationships.
2. Minimising costs while maximising value or 'how thin to win' the bid.
3. Managing scope creep while maintaining a customer service orientation.

Client-contractor relationships

Essential to any good contractual relationship is the 'fit' of the parties in the relationship. As shown in Figure 8.1 professional practice framework, the relationship between the client-user and the professional service provider is the most critical and essential consideration of any contract for professional facility management services. The scope and key performance indicators (KPIs) of every contract are important, but most procurement processes have developed these to fine detail. Price is, of course, an important consideration, but even outside the boundaries of the legal contract, the relationship of the client and the contractor has major impacts. Before procurement processes begin, the reputation, image and recognition, as well as financial stability of the professional facility management practice is paramount. Many requests for proposals (RFPs) will be sent to only the well-known organisations, requiring successful bidders to have a background and track record of quality. For this reason, it is often difficult for start-up organisations to gain clients without a privileged opening or market entry to provide the first client introduction or experience. Start-ups in facility management, as shown in historical experience, start small and grow their business over time, gaining credibility and recognition as they expand.

The importance of the client–contractor relationship is often underevaluated or even overlooked in traditional procurement practices.

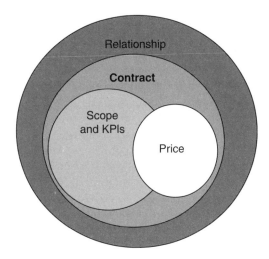

Figure 8.1 Professional practice framework

Especially in public sector organisations, with procurement regulations emphasising low price competitive bidding, the value of positive relationships is not easily quantified. Unfortunately, these people issues have been known to overshadow even otherwise good contracts, often resulting in legal wrangling to dissolve or renegotiate unhappy relationships.

It is often difficult to even get in front of the busy facility management executive to discuss the potential offered by professional facility management practices. They often view the opportunity as 'another thing to manage' – another thing under which they are 'drowning' and yet for this reason they particularly need the help and expertise offered. The most reliable method is to build trust in their busy environment. Sending a short article related to their specific organisational need might be a step to demonstrate expertise and goodwill. The article may not relate directly to your service but demonstrates that you take the time and trouble to understand clients and have their improvement in mind. Often internal facility managers are penalised by their management for not doing a good enough job, and these managers face the fear of losing their position, when in fact the ability to turn over (parts of) the service via a contract to an expert who can provide the best job may save this manager's reputation and job within the organisation. Helping the client to reach this understanding without another office visit or time away from their schedule may be possible with a good reputation, appropriate advertising and timely low-key contact as provided in the example of the article. The goal of the professional provider is to establish trust, and build on this during business development, in order that the potential client participates positively in specifying portions of the service content, around your service offer, and that the client then goes on to lever a more finely tuned and demanding service out of the contract agreement and throughout the service period. This is a form of co-created value that secures business and competitive advantage directly for the professional practice and indirectly for the client (Prahalad and Ramaswamy, 2004a; b).

While all the influences upon the relationship are not shown in Figure 8.1, there are many that exist and should be considered. The major impact of the relationship and alignment of similar values and expectations is known as 'fit.' This term is also used in traditional human resource hiring, such that the objective of finding the correct attitude and values, as well as experience and expertise are considered when bringing someone new into the organisation. This is even more important when a contract organisation joins with the core organisation to provide services, since numerous personnel typically fulfil the contract and they must all meet similar guidelines for how to work with the customer organisation in order to be successful in this area of aligning attitudes, values and expectations. While employees of the contract provider are required to conform to the professional values and standards of their organisation, they must also be 'client facing', that is, flexible enough to align with the client organisational norms, which should be possible with a reasonable inter-organisational 'fit'.

Inter-organisational relationships, those between two or more separate organisations, have been studied by Ring and Van de Ven (1994) and described as 'socially contrived mechanisms for collective action, which are continually shaped and restructured by actions and symbolic interpretations of the parties involved' (p. 96). When positive relationships can be established, typically additional work, extensions of contracts and successful re-bids are frequent. Negative relationships almost always end in non-renewed and terminated contracts, even when savings are demonstrated. Ring and Van de Ven discuss a concept of 'actions and symbolic interpretations' which can be demonstrated with a positive example of a contractor with values similar to those of the core organisation, and who comes into the client organisation with staff who have cheerful, up-beat attitudes and this positive relationship results in customers who notice the positive attitude and view their delivery of service as more positive in satisfaction surveys. A negative example of the symbolic interpretation would be a new provider who did not live up to the previously provided level of customer service, and was defensive when questioned about it, and this provider's results of customer satisfaction surveys showed poor scores and a decline in the overall satisfaction level from the facilities service organisation.

Obviously, every person is different and exhibits their own personality in each situation, but for service organisations, the leadership expectations and examples set by managers can strongly influence and model the expected behaviours that align with the customer values and expectations. The best providers have a high level of training and expectation for their staff and their own values often may be higher and more positive than required. This is an important area of best value contracting that performance-based contracts can deliver. Giving the provider the ability to innovate and improve service delivery, and incentivising these improvements, provides positive actions and symbolic interpretations of the parties for mutual benefit.

There are multiple settings for inter-organisational relationships that can be developed, from a simple purchase or buy/sell contract, through various equity position ventures or exchanges. Several of these are outlined in Figure 8.2. Types of inter-organisational relationships, which is adapted from work in the mid 1990s by Mockler (1997). This figure, with small or larger, long-term buy/sell contracts to equity partnership and joint ventures, illustrates that many different structures exist for working with outside organisations. For long-term services, some organisations have found that an entirely new entity, formed in partnership with former customers and providers, may provide a more stable, profitable structure for all. An example of such a new entity would be the spin-off of specific service functions, for example, space reconfiguration planning and implementation from an imaginary JCN company's in-house staff, into a joint venture company composed of the employees of JCN who formerly planned and implemented these reconfigurations, now joined with ABC furniture-moving organisation with expertise in cubicle installation and handling, so that both organisations become more expert in their core areas, and the new company has an immediate opening or opportunity with the JCN core company. In the early days of outsourcing, this was not an uncommon type of relationship, rather than the purchase of the services from ABC furniture

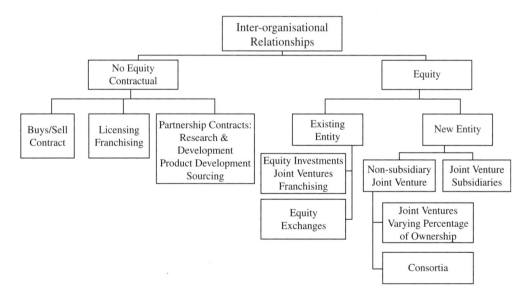

Figure 8.2 Types of inter-organisational relationships. Source: Mockler, 1997

company, and the dilemma of how to handle the in-house staff during and after the new contract. The new entity or company arrangement frees both JCN and ABC to focus on their expertise, and the new entity begins with experienced staff, but sets its own mission and objectives, while retaining the values of employees who moved from JCN merged with the expertise of ABC.

It may be helpful to remember the suggestion of Franklin (1997), that outsourcing requires a double-prong approach, which values both an economic approach and a behavioural approach. The economic approach requires the practice to clearly understand its strategy from the economic basis, as well as equally addressing the behavioural approach including 'commitment, persistence, knowledge, pride and interpersonal qualities of an organization's people' (Franklin, 1997: 373) when determining strategy. A sole focus on either one can result in deficiencies that may not be easily overcome, and which can synergistically reinforce each other when addressed in tandem.

In summary, two popular quotes come to mind as advice for maximising client relationships. Business consultant and academic Michael Porter curtly reminds us, 'It's relationships, stupid!' in his book, *Competitive Advantage* (1985). And advice to help with adjusting our relationship expectations prompted by biologist and evolutionist Charles Darwin, that it is not the strongest of the species that survives, nor the most intelligent, but the one most responsive to change (1996). Despite the range of possible organisational decisions enabling best value service opportunities, and inspiring advice, cost always remains a factor which dominates and frequently dictates how facility management professional practices compete.

Minimising costs while maximising value

The essential charge for any facility management organisation is to maximise value to the client organisation and minimise or eliminate costs where reasonable. With in-house facility management this is always a challenge, but with professional practices, it is a life or death of the organisation balance. In order to cover all business costs, each advisory and service contract must be appropriately bid in order not only to cover all costs, but also to provide for profit so that the organisation can sustain itself. With competition at its toughest during economic crises, one facility management service provider, Gary Merrow (personal communication, August 16, 2009) commented that during the credit crunch, 'It's all about understanding how thin to win you can become'.

As facility management clients become more focused on costs, this thin margin of profitability is often comparable to walking a razor's edge. Not only are facility management providers forced to second-guess competitor bids, they must also maintain their margin and not dip below actual costs, to be able to survive on the one hand and meet customer specifications and expectations on the other. This can become a contentious situation, especially where there is scope creep. During recession, many professional practices look to secure a client with a flat (little or no profit) bid for the first few years, expecting to discover innovations and efficiencies during those years that can enhance profits during the longer range years of the contract. Another strategy is to align services for a client so that shortages in one area can be covered by increased profit in other areas. However, this is somewhat dangerous if clients are required or expect to change allocation of work in multiple areas over the course of the contract, potentially leading to the profitable area shrinking and/or the flat, unprofitable areas expanding.

A similar and more risky strategy has been to organise so that clients with flat profit margins are cross-subsidised from more profitable clients – cover annual overheads first and then seek (premium) profits. But with credit crunch cutbacks, such as seen in banking, housing, automotive and leisure and travel, there have been contentious hence costly relations, contractual disputes, renegotiated contracts and a loss of business for professional practices. Each practice must determine their own risk potential and attempt mitigations to address major risks. Obvious measures for new contracts include avoiding known risky industries, avoiding financially weak clients or clients with adverse reputations, withdrawing bids for potentially unprofitable clients (usually those with high leverage), and not responding to requests which could not become profitable. Such features are not unusual in today's marketplace.

Other strategies that can mitigate potential risks to profits include forming alliances or partnering agreements with existing maintenance providers, especially for specialised equipment, so that both partners share the risk and profit from one client. It may also open up new market segments and potential for bidding for larger consultancy and service provision than would otherwise be the case. Some facility management professional services offer these alliances as a benefit of their service. Clients often view it as an expansion of services and it aids them in reaching the single point of contact (SPOC) that they often seek in order to minimise contract management. For a few types of specialised practice, the economic downturn has provided a growth opportunity. Take for example, the relocation or reconfiguration management sector within a facility management practice. As organisations cut staff and limit real-estate transactions, these organisations are faced with increased move, add and change (MAC) activity. Other organisations are taking advantage of reduced real-estate costs and are relocating to less expensive space, creating growth for project managers, movers and other related specialists. With limited staff, these one-off projects provide opportunities that did not exist at this level in a more stable market.

In the USA where most government contracts favour minority and small-business contracts to meet specific guidelines or quotas, strategic alliances with these smaller practices is a good way to share in gaining access and competitive opportunities with governmental organisations. It also meets the intended purpose in helping to educate and provide experience for these smaller firms as they interact with the larger, more established providers. However, the competitive realities have resulted in many smaller firms being swallowed up in acquisitions by the larger practices, reducing the competition in many locations to only the big, major companies, whose strategies are based around building market share in recession to favourably position themselves for the upturn.

Another current and important issue for any organisation, but one that is hitting the facility management technical practice especially hard, is that of hiring and retaining appropriately skilled workers. In former times the US military services provided valuable training and experience in many of the technical skills required of facility management practice. These well-trained technicians left military service and moved into commercial industries to design, plan, manage and service facilities since shortly after World War II through to the late 1980s. But as military budgets are stretched, this training is no longer the stronghold that produced experienced workers for other industries and now the USA is left with a dwindling cadre of technical experts that technical colleges and programmes are not adequately filling. Therefore, the successful facility management practice in the near term will be the one that successfully locates, hires and retains technicians and technical managers. As it is said, 'It's a dog-eat-dog world out there in facility-land' and only the astute and adaptable organisations will come out on top during this expected dearth of technically trained workers. Whenever an employee leaves an organisation, knowledge as well as profits go with them. The time, energy and financial investment in their training and orientation to the organisation are lost; additionally, time, energy and cost then must be spent to bring a new employee on board and get them adequately trained. New employees typically enter the organisation at the bottom of the quality and productivity curves, which reduces effectiveness and competitiveness of the practice. Skill shortages and training only raise costs, so employee retention, where possible, is a key competitive advantage.

Employee engagement, as described by Roper and Phillips (2007), suggests solutions for the dilemma of a minimised workforce through development of a work culture and the hiring of employees who possess innovative and creative skills. That is those who take personal responsibility and have an authentic motivation for company success as well as their team and personal success, and this includes those who usually have an emotional bond with the company, its mission and values, yet are also flexible enough to work with, and adopt roles to fit, their clients' needs, as noted earlier. These engaged employees are motivated to provide superior customer service and know that this impacts the practice's bottom line profitability as well as inducing high levels of client satisfaction.

The younger generation, often referred to as Generation Y, or Gen-Y, coming into the workforce today has different motivations from previous generations of workers. After watching their parents compete for the few senior positions and suffer burnout and fatigue, Gen-Y desires a more balanced work and life scenario. They may be engaged, but they expect to work in various distributed ways, even as they serve client needs. They have grown up with and are intimately familiar with technological innovations and new ways of working to minimise their required time in the office, yet they are still alert to providing superior customer service in most cases. Not only do these young workers desire a good work–life balance, but they have also been shown to be especially interested in opportunities to develop and advance their careers through training and tend to remain longer with an employer who provides those benefits. A 2004 survey by Fairis (2004) of Gen-Y workers showed that they would wait only an average of ten months for an advancement opportunity to develop before concluding that advancement was blocked and that they should look elsewhere for more rewarding career moves.

Succession plans can help to avoid the illusion of blocked opportunity, and although guarantees of advancement cannot be made in the contract world of facility management practice, the investment in employee training to prepare them for future opportunities is one step toward increased engagement and retention. This is also a requirement if an organisation is to fill the voids of retiring and aging trained workers who are now or who soon will be leaving the workforce. All these workforce issues have a cost associated with them, but without the competitive advantage of skilled, engaged employees, the practice cannot maintain momentum and compete effectively in the current marketplace. Investments that balance the thin margin of profit with competitive advantage can keep facility management practices valuable and essential to their clients.

Managing scope creep while maintaining a customer service orientation

The reality of facility management is that a careful balance between customer service and judicious responsibility is an operational imperative. For the facility management professional practice the balance is made more difficult by the constant pressure from the customer to reduce costs, yet maintain or even increase service levels and value. And nowhere does this balance become more precarious than staying within the contract scope to avoid expansion of service without amendments to the contract. Scope creep is the growth of a contract or project scope by inevitable changes that occur as time, expectations and reality changes. This creep or expansion is a natural result of downward pressure for reduced costs and increased service and value by the customer. Such creep has to be identified and managed, which requires additional payment rather than absorption. It must be managed in a firm, yet tactful manner if the customer is to maintain the perception of quality and positive service from the provider. Preventing any scope creep is almost impossible since rapid change in all types of business is the norm, but minimising the amount and extent of the creep can usually be managed with strategic and thoughtful planning, and the customer will help to minimise it too as they realise such additions do not come free.

The first step to minimising scope creep would be to initially set achievable contract perimeters for the practice. Over-committing to the client to gain the contract can only backfire later when reality and tendencies for scope creep occur. This is a type of risk management. Realistic and achievable scope definition, and discussion of these perimeters on a frequent basis with the client can help to minimise creep during the contract and provide a positive setting for dealing with inevitable changes. This aids identifying creep as it occurs. When everyone understands the limits of the contract and this discussion is part of normal updates and reviews, the opportunity to address contract changes or amendments is much easier and well accepted by the client. This is the management of the creep.

Negotiating contracts that provide a win-win for client and practice provider are the ideal environment in which to deal with scope creep. When a client expects honest interchange with their contractor, the atmosphere is, of course, much more conducive to discussing limitations of the contract than an atmosphere where the client tries to direct and manipulate the contractor into a win-lose position – the client winning and the contractor losing. The contract can even be structured to include language detailing how scope expansion will be handled and lay out specifics as to when and how much each party will handle in each situation.

Scope creep is usually a negative term, but in some instances, the more positive side of contract changes can benefit both the client and facility management provider. These are typically incentive clauses that are becoming common with performance-based contracts. The client specifies expected outcomes rather than detailed specifications, and when the provider beats the outcomes, either in cost, value or satisfaction, there are remuneration rewards, or other shared rewards that benefit the provider as well as the client. Clients who demand all savings are typically those who also do not understand performance-based contracts and do not benefit from good relationships with their providers (or employees in most cases). These organisations are rarely as successful as their enlightened counterparts who tend to have a higher customer loyalty factor, making them more competitive and able to extend the goodwill in all their interactions. Finding the clients with these values is critical to expanding and growing facility management practice. Otherwise, the professional practice is constantly in 'defend and recover' mode with their clients as they manage change in the original scope and definitions of the contract for services.

Managing the scope change process, since it is inevitable, is required in almost all contracts. Some tips for success can be found by developing a formal change process which includes having a simple document to request written changes; contract language which includes authorisation levels for change approvals; a joint review between client and contractor to analyse the impact and costs of proposed changes; and, of course, the final approval and specification of changes must be signed by the appropriate level officer as previously designated in the contract for such changes.

Another type of scope creep can essentially be called client growth. Once a practice demonstrates their expertise and fit with a client, they may have the opportunity to grow the business by either expanding the scope of service or expanding the breadth of facilities covered. Many organisations will limit the first contract with a professional practice as a risk assessment method to ensure good fit and delivery of service. Once it is positively received, the ability to offer and gain expanded services can grow the contract or add new contracts for additional services, enabling the growth of the professional practice.

Conclusion

The future for facility management professional practice is not dissimilar to other businesses. Development of strong human resource management skills, along with ongoing technological updates will be required for service professionals to maintain a profitable practice. Another key skill to aid business development and success of the practice in the future will be the ability to organise efficiently and to develop networks for gaining client access, as well as staying abreast of the many business trends and changes that directly impact how clients expect to receive service, manage their bidding processes and evaluate service in the facility management arena. Staying in contact on a frequent basis with clients, one-on-one, can be a touchstone for superior service delivery.

As discussed in the opening comments, the temptation to be everything to everyone, however, should be avoided. Sticking to areas of expertise or wisely affiliating with partners to expand services is the cautionary and more successful way to manage a professional practice.

As quoted from Herbert Bayard Swope (ThinkExist.com, 2009), journalist and first winner of the Pulitzer Prize for Reporting, 'I cannot give you the formula for success, but I can give you the formula for failure – which is: Try to please everybody.' It may be that professional firms try to increase the range of services and deliver these in a differentiated way as the economy grows. This possibility could be presented as a recommendation for practice, yet the market ultimately drives change such that academic research and recommendations form one influence, leaving managers to weigh up the whole picture.

References

Darwin, C. (1996) *The Origin of Species*, Oxford World's Classics, Oxford University Press, Oxford.

Fairis, D. (2004) Internal labor markets and worker quits, *Industrial Relations*, 43(3), 573–94.

Franklin, P. (1997) Competitive advantage and core competencies, *Strategic Change*, 6, 371–375.

IFMA (2009) http://www.ifma.org/what_is_fm/index.cfm, accessed 28 August

Mockler, R. J. (1997) Multi-national strategic alliances: a manager's perspective, *Strategic Change*, 6, 391–405.

Porter, M. (1985) *Competitive Advantage*, Free Press, New York.

Roper, K. O. and Phillips, D. R. (2007) Integrating self-managed work teams into project management, *Journal of Facilities Management*, 5(1), 22–36.

Prahalad, C. K. and Ramaswamy, V. (2004a) Co-creating experiences: the next practice in value creation, *Journal of Interactive Marketing*, 18(3), 5–14.

Prahalad, C. K. and Ramaswamy, V. (2004b) Co-creating unique value with customers, *Strategy & Leadership*, 32(3), 4–9.

Ring, P. S. and Van de Ven, A. (1994) Developmental Processes of Cooperative Interorganizational Relationships', *Academy of Management Review*, 19(1), 90–118.

ThinkExist.com (2009) Herbert Bayard Swope quotation attribution from www.ThinkExist.com, accessed 24 September.

9 Innovation in professional service providers

UK quantity surveying practices

Stephen Pryke

Introduction

Motivations and inspirations

Life under the regime of the time sheet is tough – every 15 minutes of time to be allocated to a particular and appropriate client account; some allowance for administration, downtime and desk tidying, the odd networking lunch, but no more than 10% of the total. As a young and highly ambitious quantity surveyor (QS) in a growing practice, the culture and lifestyle seemed natural, not to say desirable – being recognised for achieving tasks in less than the target hours deduced from the fee bid was honourable and ultimately contributed to the prospects of promotion to partnership status for some. Years later, in more reflective mood, and trying to make sense of this increasingly complex industry of ours, I wonder whether the plethora of management texts are right, for example:

> *A business does not exist to be efficient; it exists to create wealth for its customers. . . . An obsessive compulsion to increase efficiency (doing things right) reduces firms' effectiveness at doing the right things. (Dunn and Baker, 2003:12–13)*

Doing *the right things* requires the existence of strategy and innovation; doing *things right* implies a lack of both. So it is that the financial management service providers, typically but not essentially, the chartered quantity surveying practices and cost consultants (implied in the acronym QS henceforth), are tarred with the 'efficient but ultimately uninnovative' brush. This chapter seeks to explore the proposition that QS practices in the UK have failed to innovate. The chapter provides

Managing the Professional Practice: in the built environment, First Edition. Edited by Hedley Smyth.
© 2011 by Blackwell Publishing Ltd. Published 2011 by Blackwell Publishing Ltd.

some context for the discussion and then presents a definition of innovation by way of a brief literature review. The chapter then reviews
some previous work carried out by the author with others (Page,
et al., 1999; 2004), before attention is turned to some very recent evidence
that looks at innovation in QS practices in the face of difficult trading
conditions encountered during 2009–10.

Background

The QS practice forms part of the growing UK knowledge economy, the
Construction Industry Council (CIC) pointing to a rise in the employment within professional services firms as a whole from approximately
180,000 in 1996 to 270,000 in 2005 (CIC, 2008:27, cited in Lu & Sexton, 2009). In the professional services sector of construction there is
a predominance of small practices – 98% of firms employ less than
50 people (CIC, 2008:i).

   Service providers working with some of the UK's largest clients such
as British Airports Authorities (BAA), Defence Estates and Slough
Estates have had the benefit of understanding the needs of the innovative
client. Indeed, innovation has been seen as an important activity in
improving the performance of the UK construction industry (Tavistock
Institute, 1997). Yet even the QS's principal professional body, the Royal
Institution of Chartered Surveyors (RICS) has conceded that the existence and prevalence of the professional practice (as a model for a firm),
has stifled innovation in QS firms (Thompson, 1968). Winch (1998) has
argued that the specialisation that the professional bodies have pursued
constitutes a fragmentation. Certainly the plethora of bodies representing the various trades and professions seems excessive when compared
to the role of the British Medical Association in medicine. The emphasis,
where innovation has occurred in construction, has tended to be in the
area of product (building materials and components) rather than process
(Gann, 1997; 2000). Innovation has predominantly involved contractors
and material and component suppliers. The problem has also been that
the professional bodies in construction have not seen their role as brokers
for innovation in the way that exists in other sectors (Winch, 1998).
Contrast this with the work of Miller *et al.* (1995) on the flight simulation
industry where the professional body plays an active role as an actor in
the *innovation superstructure*, alongside clients and regulatory bodies. The
specialist component and systems suppliers and the aircraft assemblers,
with the professional body, provide the *innovation infrastructure*, and
the interface between the *superstructure* and *infrastructure* is managed by
a systems integrator. It is the systems integrator firm that supplies
complete flight simulators to airlines.

   Page *et al.* (2004) argued that a number of reports dealing with
construction have called for radical changes to the way in which

construction is procured (e.g. Latham, 1994; Egan, 1998) and yet, arguably, these innovations do not necessarily act as a catalyst, or indeed driver, for innovation in the QS practice. Research carried out by Pryke (2001) used social network analysis to look at communication and incentive structures associated with reforms in procurement strategies. The research revealed that, although the prominence of individual actors is significantly altered by the procurement approach and that incentives frequently do *not* reinforce roles and relationships dictated by network positions, QSs are typically quite isolated in their roles. There are incentives for other project actors to avoid establishing relationships and the QSs are minimising linkages with other actors to reduce the cost of providing a profitable service to their clients.

The British Property Federation survey carried out in 1997 and cited in Egan (1998) pointed towards dissatisfaction with QS services amongst 30% of construction clients. The QS Think Tank report (RICS, 1998), in response to the survey, suggested that changes in procurement methods, better application of IT, and competition might provide impetus for change and innovation. Since that time there has certainly been a high level of diversification amongst what were previously traditional QS practices, and we return to this point later.

We have looked at the case made against the QS and at some of the reasons for the assertion that QSs do not innovate. Let's now consider the position of the QS practice in the UK construction industry and perhaps assemble a defence to these criticisms. In the face of criticism from clients about a lack of innovation from QS practices, a partner from one of the top 20 UK QS practices replied with, 'If clients want innovation we can give them innovation; they need to instruct us accordingly and they must expect to pay for the innovation – we are trying to run a business!'

Making money from service provision requires a clear framework within which relatively young and inexperienced junior staff can operate. The use of relatively low-cost staff in the provision of professional services is important to the profitability of providing such services. The provision of professional services, the process and nature of the 'product' or service provided has to be viewed within the legal context of duty of care principle for professional services and the requirements of professional indemnity insurance. Little wonder that the average QS practice manages its risk through the use of well established routines, what Spender (1989) would have referred to as standard 'industry recipes'. Radically new approaches to service provision and the way in which services are delivered, introduce risk in an environment where practices are wanting to have their staff interface with clients, rather than just the partners who might traditionally have constituted the face of the practice.

If QSs are accused by their clients of lacking in the innovation department, their defence might be that the supply chain and project environments place limitations upon the potential for innovation, and their main professional body has not supported or facilitated innovation.

Before we move on to discuss the evidence in support of innovative behaviour in QS practices, we need to define innovation.

So what is innovation?

Some argue that the rate of innovation in construction is lagging behind other sectors (e.g. Gann, 2000; Winch, 1998). At the same time, there is a powerful argument that construction is not one industry at all; indeed, there are many examples where firms have product or services that they sell to construction offered alongside non-construction products and services. Much of what has been written about innovation in construction has focused upon *product innovation* rather than process.

Freeman (1989, cited in Page *et al.*, 2004) describes innovation as a nontrivial change and improvement in process, product or system that is novel to the institution developing the change. Sexton and Barrett (2003) acknowledged that the innovation needs to be new to the firm but not necessarily to the world as a whole. Winch (1998) adopts Van de Ven's (1986) definition that it is the management of new ideas into good currency, which pays homage to Schumpeter's contention that innovation is essentially the *application* of invention, rather than invention itself (Schumpeter, 1976, cited in Winch, 1998) Clearly, Freeman's definition does not seek to exclude invention, evolution or discovery which are essential prerequisites of any innovation in practice. This definition is therefore preferred for the purposes of the discussion in this chapter. Page *et al.* (2004) adapted the Schumpeter (1934) classification of innovation, for the purposes of studying innovation in professional service firms. These classifications are:

- *Service product innovation*: the development of a completely new service product or a significant improvement of an existing service product.
- *Process innovation*: the introduction of completely new or significantly improved methods of producing or delivering services including new information and communication technologies.
- *Market innovation*: the activity of the firm in entering new markets or developing a new niche within an existing market or developing new opportunities for business.
- *Organisational innovation*: the introduction of a new or significantly improved organisational structure, management system or work practice within the firm.
- *Resource innovation*: the acquisition, organisation and management of new resources, that is, people, knowledge and information (Page *et al.*, 2004).

These innovations within professional service firms are devised and implemented within the context of increasingly complex projects (Pryke and Smyth, 2006). The complexity of these projects (and, increasingly, the *programmes* within which these projects sit) influence significantly the manner in which innovation takes place; the complexity also has an effect on the manner in which innovations are implemented and their ultimate effectiveness or usefulness. Project, programme and supply chain environments very frequently have characteristics that relate to complex product systems (Miller *et al.*, 1995), which have the following characteristics:

- many interconnected and customised elements organised in a hierarchical way;
- non-linear and continuously emerging properties where small changes to one element of the system can lead to large changes elsewhere in the system;
- a high degree of user involvement in the innovation process (Winch, 1998).

Whereas the first two points resonate very clearly with construction project, programme and supply chain environments (cf. Bresnen, 2009; also discussed below), the user involvement varies considerably depending on the procurement route and the particular client involved – for a detailed discussion of the involvement by clients in their supply chains see Pryke (2001; 2009). Large developers, working within a principal contractor or construction management procurement structure, tend to demand and provide very high levels of user involvement – the client engages quite intensively with the service providers.

There are issues of definition and classification of innovation, as well as a question about the extent to which novelty constitutes innovation within any given project, programme or supply chain context. Accepting some necessary compromise in these areas we move to a discussion of the reasons why firms in construction innovate.

Why do firms in construction innovate?

Egan (1998) pointed out that improvements and profitability could, potentially, be realised through innovations. Innovations might achieve (inter alia) improved customer focus, integrated processes and teams, improved quality of product and process (presumably) and commitment to people. The majority of QS practices in the UK are small. Sexton and Barrett (2003) argue that small firms in construction innovate for survival, stability and development. Increasingly customers are making more sophisticated demands on firms in construction and expecting *service* solutions (Davies, 2001) in an environment where technical solutions relating to products and components are beyond the interest of many clients, and innovation in these areas is expected to form part of the process of design.

Gann and Salter (2000) argue that innovation is driven by information and communication technology (ICT) and the diffusion of information, and also by the desire of the owner-operator type of client to improve management of projects. They also draw attention to the importance for professional service providers of reputation. Reputation is an important factor in gaining work particularly where new markets are to be penetrated. Those fortunate practices with high profile reputations very often have the resources to invest heavily in innovation, which, if the implementation is successful, enhances reputation and success in winning new work. Gann and Salter (2000) refer to the ability of Ove Arup, now Arup, to have successfully achieved and maintained a high profile reputation, the design for the Sydney Opera House being regarded as a pinnacle. This has been despite potentially damaging publicity in the case of the design for London's Millennium (pedestrian) bridge.

QS professional service providers innovate for a variety of reasons. Small and medium practices innovate to keep up with the larger practices in the hope that clients will recognise and identify with the characteristics of the larger practices displayed and have the confidence to place increasingly large projects with these smaller firms. All QS practices, regardless of size, will want to exploit technology in a way that improves the level and accuracy of service provided and that enhances or maintains profitability. Finally, all QS practices form part of a project team and/or standing supply chain, and their activities are influenced by the systems and output requirements dictated by the client and other project actors (typically the consultant project manager) within those environments. QSs do not play a dominant enough role to dictate or influence processes and systems employed by other project actors, unless of course they happen to have been appointed project managers as well, in which case they have increased prominence. We have moved some way towards deciding how we define and classify innovation in QS practices; we have also looked at some of the reasons why this happens. Let us now turn our attention to *how* innovation might take place.

How does innovation occur?

Seaden *et al.* (2003) argue that innovation is triggered by key events in the business environment, rather than being initiated by the internal research or innovation programmes of a firm. Each new project presents a new or partially unfamiliar set of circumstances through which, arguably, innovation might be triggered or precipitated in some way. Seaden *et al.* (2003) also argue that innovation behaviour varies with the size of the firm and is often resisted by those working within the firm. Sexton and Barrett (2003) offer a more conceptual framework. They argue that there are two schools of thought in terms of the process of innovation – these are the *rational school* and the *behavioural school*. The rational school is predominant and regards innovation as multi-stage and linear. Maidique (1980) suggests that this linear process might comprise recognition of the need for innovation, invention, development, implementation and diffusion. CERF (2000:3) provides a little more detail, the process of innovation consisting of:

- conceptualisation of the idea and its definition;
- refinement of the idea through research, testing and development to create a new product (or new service product);
- testing and verification of the idea in a real-world setting;
- further refinement using data gathered from the previous stage;
- introduction in the marketplace for widespread use.

Set against this structured rational approach is the behavioural approach – the idea that the creation (though presumably not necessarily the *implementation*) process is quite chaotic – 'controlled chaos' (Sexton and Barrett, 2003).

Page *et al.* (2004) classified the way in which innovation occurs into *incremental* and *radical*. Incremental innovation occurs through the improvement, albeit quite significantly, of existing product or process ideas – 'learning by doing'. This seems to refer to an evolutionary process where the thinking practitioner is able to identify innovations through an intimate knowledge of existing processes and products, coupled with a really well developed understanding of client needs. Radical innovation involves technical breakthroughs, new products and new organisational forms or structures. Page *et al.* (2004) recognise that the knowledge and information necessary for innovation come from internal and external sources. External sources include clients, suppliers, contractors, subcontractors, consultants, universities, government laboratories, other agencies and licensees.

Winch (1998) makes a number of interesting observations about the way in which innovation occurs. He argues that there are two basic processes involved in achieving innovation: *diffusion* and *implementation*, which is in line with the position above. Innovation is thus created through formal research and development programmes, or is transferred from other sectors, from overseas, copied from leading innovators in the relevant field, or some combination. From the viewpoint of the professional service providers, Winch notes that innovation is implemented in the *project* and not the *firm* and has to be negotiated with other project actors. Others have argued (e.g. Pryke, 2009) that much innovation in construction occurs within the context of the *supply chain*, more specifically through standing supply chains involving ongoing collaborative relationships between interdependent firms. However created, once the innovation is established and its feasibility tested, the challenge is to implement successfully across a range of projects, requiring what Winch refers to as 'codification' – organising the idea into a system with its own language and procedures.

Gann (2000) adopts a pragmatic view of innovation that includes the rational and behavioural schools of Sexton and Barrett's (2003). Gann (referring to some earlier work by Dosi, 1982) argues that there are three characteristics of innovative environments:

1. *Evolutionary* – the development of research along particular paths, shaped by social and institutional conditions; evolution occurs along a particular path determined by economic trade-offs.
2. *Irreversible process* – it is unlikely that engineers will ever return to the widespread use of slide rules, to carry out structural calculations, for example.
3. *Self-organising* – order within systems is largely unintentional, emerging through interactions between technological progress, economic activities and institutions governing decisions and expectations.

Gann and Salter (2000) slightly refine the self-organising category, stating:

> *Firms have to manage innovation in multi-technology environments, responding to changes in software, engineering, information and material technologies, rising costs and the need to deal with increasing complexity due to social and political circumstances. (Gann and Salter, 2000:961)*

Gann *et al.* (1996) provided an illustrative case study of how innovation might occur involving RM Parsons, a US engineering firm. The idea was essentially to provide feasibility stage strategic advice, in addition to the more commonly offered design, procurement and construction services. This was achieved by expanding their existing engineering design software packages to include project management and geographic information systems, of relevance to feasibility and planning activities. These changes required changes to procedures within the firm, the development of new relationships with 'clients, design organisations, contractors and suppliers, government agencies, financiers and political groups' (Gann and Salter, 2000: 962).

There are a number of opposing views about how innovation occurs. Do key events drive the need for innovation, perhaps causing a quite dramatic innovation or cluster of innovatory ideas, involving innovation in product and process and structure and resources, perhaps to achieve penetration of a new market or to avoid a catastrophic loss of an existing market or market share? This is a 'big bang' model of innovation. Set against this is an iterative and incremental type of innovation involving relatively small changes but as part of an ongoing programme of continual evolution and innovation. The first is chaotic and dramatic; the second might be much more measured and rational, perhaps led by a champion or team looking, full time, at ways to innovate. Perhaps the answer is both – sometimes the innovation is modest and involves the transfer or assimilation of simple improvement to product, process or structure; on other occasions the business environment demands something far more dramatic. Finally, is innovation a function of project team activity (Winch, 1998) or the supply chain, particularly the standing supply chain (Pryke, 2009)?

Barriers to innovation

Barriers to innovation are problems and constraints affecting implementation. Bresnen (2009) suggests that difficulties might arise in the diffusion of innovations in practice (diffusion across a number of projects). This, he argues, is because any particular innovation is an abstraction from context and the re-embedding of these innovations in future projects requires some *interpretive flexibility*. The idea of interpretive flexibility is a reference to the work of Bijker, *et al.* (1987), cited in Bresnen (2009) and relates to our ability to make sense of new ideas through enactment. Sexton and Barrett (2003) refer to CERF (1998) and argue that construction (albeit referring to the US construction industry) is infamous for the barriers that it places in the way of innovation. They argue that project-based, service-enhanced forms of enterprise are inadequately addressed in the innovation literature generally. They also observe that innovation is not necessarily always good – there is the potential for innovation to jeopardise the viability of the firm. As an example of this we might refer to the instance where Atkins introduced a new invoicing system for client accounts; the system failed and threatened the financial stability of this established and profitable practice.

Many feel that the project environment itself is a barrier to innovation (see for example, Sexton and Barrett, 2003). It is argued that transferring innovation from project to project is difficult, and fragmentation is an inhibiting factor. Similarly, Miozzo and Ivory (1998, cited in Sexton and Barrett, 2003) argue that the structural characteristics of UK construction restrict large-scale innovations, partly because the capacity for small and medium enterprises to innovate is limited by their inability to form long-term project and supply chain relationships.

Salter and Torbett (2003) lament the fact that innovation in (engineering) design is typically measured in financial terms and not with reference to quality or buildability. Winch (1998) alleges that QSs stifle innovation in design actor firms because they *manage the process of appropriation of rewards* for innovation for clients; that is, they identify and measure savings occurring through variations, which includes many (potential) innovations, and this ensures that the client receives this money rather than the innovator – contractor, specialist subcontractor or supplier. In addition, where adversarial relationships exist, the ground for innovation is likely to be infertile.

If the QS's role is to harvest or harness the rewards for innovation on behalf of the client, it is not likely that this actor will volunteer savings made within the QS function itself. Winch (1998) argues that some sort of gain share arrangement is therefore desirable with professional service firms.

Finally, Gann (2000) charted the development of the 19th century specialisations in construction and their institutionalisation into the chartered professions, noting that the role of the professions was to:

- protect good practice;
- control quality for the benefit of clients;
- be knowledge repositories (gathering data about success and failure in projects and the reasons attributed);
- accredit institutional standards;
- publish journals dealing with new methods and technologies.

Gann (2000) reflects that, by the 1990s, the professions were just as likely to cause inertia (resisting innovation) as they were to promote innovation.

The section looked at barriers to innovation and asked whether Bresnen's (2009) claim that the project environment inhibits innovation because of the difficulties in transferring knowledge between projects. We also considered the point that innovation is not always successful; a good innovation might fail in implementation or might be perceived as an undesirable change. So innovation is not all about benefits and returns; there are risks to reputation and revenues. Others have argued that the pressure on innovations to deliver lower costs is undesirable. Financial incentives to innovate in construction have, some have argued, been constrained by perverse financial incentives.

An adversarial environment is less likely to deliver innovation than the collaborative one; competition can be good but it can also be inefficient and constraining. Finally, we also lay blame for a lack of sufficient innovation at the door of the professional body – in the case of the QS in the UK, this is the RICS). The RICS is not alone in adopting a strategy that does not place it in a very central position in terms of instigating or acting as a catalyst for innovation. This is something that we need to reflect upon because it is common in other industries for the professional or trade body to play a much more central role in promoting innovation.

The chapter opened with proposition that QS practices have traditionally not innovated or have innovated insufficiently in the eyes of some of their clients. That proposition is now challenged and some evidence to the contrary presented.

How have QS practices innovated?

A 2004 study involving 27 of the largest UK quantity surveying practices at that time (Page *et al.*, 2004) noted the considerable pressure from client organisations for improvements in satisfaction levels for clients of QS practices (BPF, 1997, survey cited in Egan, 1998). Reports commissioned by the RICS (1991; 1998) noted that clients were critical of traditional QS services and were looking for a more proactive, customer-orientated service with a greater emphasis on client organisational strategy. Page *et al.* (2004) reflected that the QS's longstanding role as information managers placed them potentially at the centre of information and communication technologies. Some might argue that project managers and, more recently, supply chain management consultancies, have also moved comfortably into the role of information managers.

Page *et al.* (2004) looked for evidence of innovation using the Schumpeterian classification of innovation: service product innovation, process innovation, market innovation, organisational innovation and resource innovation (Schumpeter, 1934, cited and adapted in Page *et al.*, 2004).

In terms of service product innovation, Page *et al.* (2004) found that QSs were quite adept at diversifying services, many previously traditional practices moving away from document preparation and post-contract financial management into legal services, planning supervision, taxation and capital allowance advice, building surveying, value management, facilities management, mainstream management consultancy, design and services provided to non-construction sectors (e.g. shipbuilding). Some of the slightly more extreme types of diversification for QSs included production process management, lottery monitoring, energy management and medical planning and equipping.

Under process innovation they identified two forms of innovation that stood out, the first being the move towards collaboration with other professional service firms – either those offering similar services already or those operating in quite different service areas. Second, QSs seemed to be particularly well placed to exploit IT quite rapidly. In the first case, the framework environment put QSs into a position of having to innovate on process in the context of a reduction in the need to compete purely on the basis of fee competition. There was increasing use of 'bodyshopping', where staff from a consultant worked temporarily, but sometimes for long periods, in the offices of the client or a project office. The desire to demonstrate the ability to provide a more integrated service and a broader range of services as a 'one-stop shop', pushed smaller practices into collaborative relationships with others offering complementary services. IT was a very proactive area of process innovation, perhaps partly because successful selection and implementation can so often lead to improvements in efficiency and profitability. The very largest of the practices were able to make substantial investments, developing intranets and extranets to provide access to information for staff and clients. There was also evidence of electronic quality assurance systems, practice manuals and other procedural systems to enhance consistency of service provision for clients (Page *et al.*, 2004).

Market innovation occurred amongst practices entering new markets for their services in, for example, project programming, project management and IT services. Work for the oil and gas industries was achieved in the case of one practice. The study found that most of the practices interviewed had established offices outside of the UK and nine of the 27 firms had more offices outside of the UK than within it. Generally, UK practices expanded into foreign markets through the acquisition of, or partnership with, an established local firm. There were successful niche markets for two QS firms in law and dispute resolution. In some cases Page *et al.* (2004) reported clear evidence of the use of careful management of client relationships, continually adapting the service provision and anticipating the needs of the clients.

Organisational innovation took the form of new structures, systems and work practices arising from changes of ownership structure from partnership to plc. The study found that flatter structures were the order of the day: there was a move away from a top-down hierarchy with partners winning work and heading up each client account towards greater empowerment and responsibility for younger and more junior staff with regular client contact and the responsibility to deliver project services. Some of the firms interviewed expressed a need to develop knowledge management systems and to foster the learning that comes through shorter links with key project actors by a relatively larger group of staff than was the case with traditional hierarchical practice structures. It was recognised that the flattening of the structure and exposure of more junior staff to clients brought the need to provide additional support through information systems and knowledge management, so as to avoid the potential for professional negligence claims. Some firms had gone as far as to appoint individuals with the role of promoting innovation. The use by some of centres of excellence, focus groups and innovation champions was also reported.

Resource innovation showed some really interesting new developments. QS practices were essentially discovering the need to professionalise a number of the functions previously carried out by QSs and administrators. Apart from acquiring specific and appropriate specialist professional staff to meet the demands of changing types of workload – lawyers, planning supervisors, project managers, engineers – increasingly the QS practice was seeking professionals to help run their business, typically in the area of IT, market research, accountancy and human resource management.

How are QSs innovating in changing conditions?

The 2004 study covered buoyant trading conditions, but how are practices innovating in the difficult trading conditions of 2009? A small sample of those practices involved in the 2004 study (Page *et al.*, 2004) were approached to try to identify whether the broad patterns of behaviour relating to innovation in QS practices was continuing or changing over time.

QS practices continued to broaden their service offer, using an increasingly diverse range of staff types to deal with ever more highly specialised sets of services. Examples of this are party wall advice, capital allowance, fire insurance and the creation of bespoke service offers combining cost management, value management, risk and programme management. The need to remain flexible and responsive in the process of service provision was emphasised, the demands of each new project and its client creating a need to demonstrate the ability to provide a bespoke project and client-orientated service as a means of distinguishing from the service offered by other professional service providers. There was evidence that surviving clients over the mid 2008 to 2009 period and beyond had become 'brutal' towards their service providers. Practices were seeking ways of reducing client build costs by, typically, around 30%; one major food retailer had 'negotiated' a 40% reduction in fees for its QS service partners, although 'imposition through market power' may be a more appropriate term. Practices were widely being encouraged to streamline their service provision towards a 'no-frills' minimalist yet still value-adding service: 'The client has said that he only wants the executive summary in future, not a detailed report showing the breakdown of the main recommendations' said the senior partner from one of the UK's largest QS consultancies.

Recession denies the opportunity to penetrate new markets geographically, particularly where the recession is worldwide. These conditions do, however, open up opportunities to provide services to those impacted by the recession. Some of the respondents reported an increase in services provided directly to banks as clients – advice on valuation of partially completed developments, and completion of partially completed projects following insolvency of developers. There was also an increased awareness of the need to monitor property development schemes by funders.

Organisational innovation was more difficult to find evidence for, but clearly de-layering and downsizing have been widespread, perhaps the norm. Redundancy and salary reduction were commonplace. The need to remain and continue to be increasingly efficient had led some organisations to increase peer and bottom-up review as a means of organisational self-analysis. Some practices reported senior staff becoming more accountable to other, perhaps less senior staff, which traditionalists find quite difficult – the days of very tall, almost military, hierarchies of rank and status have largely disappeared.

Human resources have undergone a minor revolution since the 2004 study. This partly reflects the diversification of service offer and the need to employ specialists in the fields of building surveying, project management, risk management and programme management. It also reflects a shift towards non-cognate entry into the profession. Some practitioners reported that the employment of a graduate with a degree outside of construction, coupled with a part-time and in-post study programme at postgraduate level, provided highly flexible, cerebral young staff who commanded the respect of their clients. One practice reported that an important client had adopted the non-cognate entry approach and there was some pressure to reflect this in the recruitment approach of the practice. Practitioners report the need, increasingly, to understand and empathise with the strategic needs of their clients, a continuing evolving move towards the strategic, and away from the technical, aspects of financial management per se. Non-cognates were seen by some to be important in working towards this new emphasis in service provision. Graduate recruitment seemed to have been badly hit, despite the recognition of the value added to the business by these individuals. One large practice reported an 80% reduction in annual graduate recruitment since the downturn in the UK construction industry. Another had to withdraw written job offers, immediately prior to work commencement.

The process of innovation in QS practices is normally implicit and tactical; it is responsive and perhaps opportunist. In recessionary conditions, however, innovation is seen as the single most important factor in the survival of the business. The senior partner in one of the UK's largest practices said, 'It is no longer business as usual', which would normally involve a 'land and expand' approach where a range of services might be cross-sold to clients following the initial appointment for a single type of professional service. The need to maintain the key resources of the business and to ensure some return for risk and investment provide strong incentives for innovation. Clients continue to be important in the occurrence of innovation for QS practices. Contractors, particularly the largest, increasingly emerge as clients in their own right alongside more traditional clients. Some felt that a move towards the evolution of very large construction and property service organisations of the type found in mainland Europe would inevitably change the type of QS client. Universities seemed to be developing their role as catalysts for change and innovation, partly through the provision of research-based and innovative programmes of study, and partly through the use of government Knowledge Transfer Partnerships. The role of construction professional bodies was seen to have been disappointing in their general ability to offer guidance and services of value to professional service providers. There was some reference to the future abandonment of the professional bodies in the context of a widening service provision that increasingly did not reflect the professional practice service classifications.

One large practice had set up a strategic review of the way in which construction was procured on behalf of clients and the related services provided by the practice. This was seen as essential to command the interest of clients and to be competitive in a market where the smaller practice could routinely undercut fee bids. This is a business where there is always a smaller practice with lower overheads posing a potential threat. The large practices have leverage in the marketplace and are able to exploit this leverage through programmes of projects and the use of bulk purchase and standardisation across the programmes. Survival was, increasingly, seen as being based upon the ability to collect innovative ideas and exploit them very quickly, in perhaps 90 days or less.

In summary, the QS practice operating in very tough trading conditions is typically placing increasing emphasis upon the following aspects of its service to clients:

- high-quality and timely communications with clients;
- faster project and programme set-up times, shorter contract periods and lower construction costs, with lower costs being delivered partly by economics and partly through lower specifications;
- good-quality, suitably equipped and trained staff;
- use of supply chain management to identify value and cost opportunities across the whole extended supply chain;
- releasing the benefits of economies and process integration through increasing emphasis upon *programmes* rather than *projects;*
- international sourcing of material and professional services.

Summary and conclusions

QS practices have diversified into a range of new services in response to increasingly sophisticated demands from clients and their increasingly complex projects over the past three decades. Yet this is only one sort of innovation – service product innovation. QS practices in 2009 are fighting hard to survive and are seeing the ability to innovate quickly and in a way that has impact on their clients' businesses as a major factor in this survival. Apart from the diversification mentioned above, until mid 2008, 'doing things right' for their clients was enough to maintain a healthy business (for example, Davis Langdon made a £48.6 m profit on a turnover of £197 m in 2007/8); from mid 2008 onwards QS consultants have entered a very different business environment, where survival has relied on the ability to innovate on process, market, organisational issues and the use of resources.

The main professional body associated with QS activities has failed to broker innovation and is seen by many to stifle potential innovation amongst professional service provider practices. In addition, the professional practice model for business tends to constrain innovation through risk averse, professional negligence avoidance, procedures that emphasise accuracy and safety in services rather than overtly rewarding innovation. Professional service providers make money by employing relatively young and inexperienced entrants to the profession and charging their clients a large mark-up on this basic input cost for the services received. There is nothing wrong with this professional service, but it does mean, in a profession involved with very large sums of money and very high client risk, that innovation might be slightly constrained.

QS practices may allow themselves the luxury of modest levels of organic innovation arising from their business activities during times of boom, but market conditions inevitably become very harsh in a recession and perhaps the good times have not prepared these practices sufficiently to deal with the recessionary onslaught from clients. Innovations that clients notice and respond to are increasingly flowing from longer-term relationships. Improvements in cost and value are derived from working with supply chains associated with programmes of work, rather than individual projects. Although it is acknowledged quite widely that adversarial relationships do not deliver innovation within projects, ironically it is the adversarial relationships developing during recession that have aggressively driven much of the short-term innovative behaviour, particularly by larger practices.

This chapter started with a brief insight into the life of a young trainee QS working for a medium-sized practice in the UK. The anecdote illustrated a culture within QS consultancies, if only traditionally, of doing things right – getting the figures right and the reports on the client's desk on time. The chapter moved on to review some of the views held about QSs by client groups and the statements that reflected these views in some major reports into the construction industry. The picture painted of innovation-averse professionals was not borne out by the research carried out by Page *et al.* (1999 and 2004), which found that QS practices exhibited a wide range of innovative behaviour. More recent research showed that the rate and type of innovation carried forward from more buoyant times was insufficient to ensure the attention of key clients as the construction industry moved into recession. A new type of innovation was needed that resonated more closely with the very pressing strategic needs of clients; this innovation had to be invented and implemented very rapidly to provide competitive advantage for individual QS practices.

Acknowledgements

The author would like to thank the partners in the 27 QS practices that contributed towards the material used in this chapter.

References

Bijker, W. E., Hughes, T. P. and Pinch, T. J. (1987) The Social Construction of Technological Systems: new directions in the sociology and history of technology, MIT Press, Cambridge.

Bresnen, M. (2009) Learning to co-operate and co-operating to learn: knowledge, learning and innovation in construction supply chains, in Pryke, S. D. (ed.) *Construction supply Chain Management: concepts and case studies*, Blackwell Publishing Ltd., Oxford.

CERF (2000) *Guidelines for Moving Innovations into Practice*, Working draft guidelines for the CERF International Symposium and Innovative Technology Trade Show, CERF, Washington.

Construction Industry Council (CIC) (2008) *Survey of UK Construction Professional Services 2005/6*, CIC, London.

Davies, A. C. (2001) *Integrated Solutions: the new economy between manufacturing and services*, SPRU, Brighton.

Dosi, G. (1982) Technological paradigms and technological trajectories, *Research Policy*, 11, 147–162.

Dunn, P. and Baker, R. J. (2003) *The Firm of the Future: A guide for accountants, lawyers and other professional services*, John Wiley & Sons, New Jersey.

Egan Report DETR (1998) *Rethinking Construction*, DETR, London.

Freeman, C. (1989) *The Economics of Industrial Innovation*, MIT Press, Cambridge.

Gann, D. M. (1997) Should government fund construction research? *Building Research and Information*, 25(5), 257–67.

Gann, D. M. (2000) *Building Innovation: complex constructs in a changing world*, Thomas Telford, London.

Gann, D. M., Hansen, K., Bloomfield, D., Blundell, D., Crotty, R., Groák, S. and Jarrett, N. (1996) *Information Technology Decision Support in the Construction Industry: current developments and use in the United States*, Department of Trade and Industry Overseas Science and Technology Expert Mission Visit Report, SPRU, Brighton.

Gann, D. M. and Salter, A. J. (2000) Innovation in project-based, service-enhanced firms: the construction of complex products and systems, *Research Policy*, 29, 955–972.

Latham, Sir Michael (1994) *Constructing the Team*, HMSO, London.

Lu, S-H. and Sexton, M. (2009) *Innovation in Small Professional Practices in the Built Environment*, Blackwell Publishing Ltd., Oxford.

Maidique, M. (1980) Entrepreneurs, champions and technological innovation, *Sloan Management Review*, Winter, 59–76.

Miller, R., Hobday, M., Leroux-Demers, T. and Olleros, X. (1995) Innovation in complex systems industries: the case of the flight simulation, *Industrial and Corporate Change*, 4(2), 363–400.

Miozzo, M. and Ivory, C. (1998) *Innovation in Construction: a case study of small and medium sized construction firms in the North West of England*, Manchester School of Management, UMIST, Manchester.

Page, M., Limeneh, M., Pearson, S. and Pryke, S. D. (1999) Understanding innovation in construction professional services firms; a study of quantity surveying firms, *Proceedings of the 5th COBRA Conference*, September 1999, University of Salford.

Page, M., Pearson, S., Pryke, S. D. (2004) *Innovation and Current Practice in Large UK Quantity Surveying Firms*, RICS Foundation Research Paper Series, 4, 25.

Pryke, S. D. (2001) *UK Construction in Transition: developing a social network approach to the evaluation of new procurement and management strategies*, PhD in Building Management, The Bartlett School, UCL.

Pryke, S. D. (2009) *Construction Supply Chain Management: concepts and case studies*, Blackwell Publishing Ltd., Oxford.

Pryke, S. D. and Smyth, H. J. (2006) *The Management of Complex Projects: a relationship approach*, Blackwell Publishing Ltd., Oxford.

Royal Institution of Chartered Surveyors (1991) *Quantity Surveying 2000: the future role of the chartered quantity surveyor*, RICS, London.

Royal Institution of Chartered Surveyors (1998) *The Challenge of Change, QS Think Tank, 1998: questioning the future of the profession*, RICS, London.

Salter, A. and Torbett, R. (2003) Innovation and performance in engineering design, *Construction Management and Economics*, 21, 573–580.

Schumpeter, J. A. (1934) *The Theory of Economic Development*, Harvard University Press, Cambridge.

Schumpeter, J. A. (1976) *Capitalism, Socialism and Democracy*, (5th ed.) Allen and Unwin, London.

Seaden, G., Michale, G., Doutriaux, J. and Nash, J. (2003) Strategic decisions an innovation in construction firms, *Construction Management and Economics*, 21, 603–612.

Sexton, M. and Barrett, P. (2003) A literature synthesis of innovation in small construction firms: insights, ambiguities and questions, *Construction Economics and Management*, 21, 613–622.

Spender, J-C, (1989) *Industry Recipes: an enquiry into the nature and sources of managerial judgement*, Blackwell Publishing Ltd., Oxford.

Tavistock Institute (1997) *Effective Learning Networks in Construction*, The Tavistock Institute/CIRIA Workshop Briefing Paper, London.

Thompson, F. M. L. (1968) *Chartered Surveyors: The growth of a profession*, Routledge and Kegan Paul, London.

Van de Ven, A. H. (1986) Central problems in the management of innovation, *Management Science*, 32(5), 570–607.

Winch, G. (1998) Zephyrs of creative destruction: understanding the management of innovation in construction, Building Research and Information, 26(4), 268–279.

Section III

Reflections upon Practice

10   The make experience

Ken Shuttleworth

In the beginning – making a start

After 30 years of working in an established architectural firm amongst many talented designers, I knew what I wanted for the future and exactly what kind of design studio I aimed to create. I wanted to set up something that was substantially different from – and better than – what any other architect had done before. So in January 2004 I founded Make Ltd – also known as Make Architects, Make Places, 'those guys who appeared on *The Apprentice*' in 2006, the popular UK TV programme, and, to people who know us well, simply 'Make'.

I wrote a list of all my thoughts and aspirations for the practice, right from the outset. It did not really amount to a mission statement, primarily because something so meandering could never fit on a billboard. It was more like a pledge of ideas – potential founding principles that had accumulated over many years and which might contribute to a philosophy.

They were as follows:

- We are a studio; never an office!
- The kind of studio we strive to be is one that is totally design-led, always producing light, bright and exciting buildings.
- It should be succession-driven, so that the studio will continue indefinitely.
- The office will be in a secure location in London's West End, near tube stations, shops and cafés.
- Make is a workshop environment that is open plan, without cellular offices – and with no exceptions. Everybody should use the same style of desk and chair – again, with no exceptions.
- The building should be dominated by models at the centre of everything and all computers should run state-of-the-art software.

Managing the Professional Practice: in the built environment, First Edition. Edited by Hedley Smyth.
© 2011 by Blackwell Publishing Ltd. Published 2011 by Blackwell Publishing Ltd.

- It should be friendly, never treating anyone unfairly – a place where nobody shouts or gets stroppy. Make should be an environment where we all share the credits, with high visibility in the press for all, forged from a culture of good relationships.
- We will use the tube, bus and Heathrow Express as much as possible. It will be a sociable atmosphere with lots of parties and trips, a place where we treat other architects, consultants and contractors as friends, and our clients and our staff as allies, not obstacles.
- Weekend work, though, shall not be encouraged.
- There will be a career path directly to the top.
- Make will be an environment that stands for design excellence – quality, on time, on budget, searching and researching.
- It will be a culture of listening; there shall be no design by committee. The ethos within will be one of leading by example, never asking anyone to do anything that you are not prepared to do yourself, and where everyone 'mucks in'.

So far, so Utopian. But there was more:

- Make will be led from the front, not pushed from behind, and it should be a studio where every project is a 'wow' – nothing less. It will be a place where work is fun and you can make a difference – a culture that reinvents the way it works, continuously.
- The new practice will focus on the client and the project; it must never compromise its identity, but reinforce it in everything it does. And it should be a place where we make an impact and celebrate every day. It will be a culture that challenges, is inquisitive and exploratory, and which is known for its listening architects.
- It will give clients excellent service and treat them as partners. It will be known for its passion.
- And, lastly, Make will be a place where everything, and anything, is possible.

Trust – making firm foundations

So, how did we get there – to a situation where all of the above pledges are broadly in place? Partially, the answer lies in our decision to go down an unusual path in terms of what has turned out to be our very democratic, fair structure – we are a company owned by a Trust.

It has always been my fundamental belief that a business relies on the loyalty of the people who work there, and that those people should be rewarded by sharing in their own successes. At Make we believe in the extraordinary talents and abilities of our people, and want that belief to be explicitly demonstrated in the business model. So we created Make as a 100 per cent employee-owned company, which is held in trust for the benefit of everyone in the company, without exception. This means that all profits are distributed to everybody. Everyone is equal and all new joiners are greeted on their first day, as partners. The success of this inclusive and self-motivating structure is reflected in a very low employee turnover compared to the rest of the profession and, incidentally but importantly, a notably different atmosphere about the place when compared to other practices. Everyone embraced and developed this atmosphere, quite naturally. Comments along the lines of: 'it's so friendly and supportive' and 'I can't believe how transparent everything is – the accounts can be viewed by everyone' are often heard among recent joiners.

My inspiration for all of this initially came from hearing about the highly successful John Lewis Partnership business model, where as an experiment in industrial democracy, John Spedan Lewis took control of the business on the death of his father John Lewis, and promptly signed away all his personal ownership rights. All the shares were to be held in trust for all the employees – who were also known as 'partners'. Spedan Lewis famously said that if his employees shook the cocktail, they should also be able to drink the drink.

By contrast, the majority of private companies are set up by entrepreneurs. Most founders have a view that they will eventually make their exit via a trade sale or flotation (see Chapter 18). I did not want to go down that route. Many architectural practices have floundered after the founders left, having become too dependent upon a person or key people and his, her or their ideas of creativity and running a studio. I was extremely lucky to have the opportunity to take the Trust idea forward with Make. Why? I wanted the studio to reflect a philosophy of creating an environment where ideas thrive and expectations are challenged to achieve the best possible design. It has been a challenging and highly rewarding experience. Designers are given the freedom to create great work owing to the absence of destructive pressure imposed upon them from a more conventional management structure – see Images.

So, why is the studio not named after the founder, like so many other practices? Well, it's simple, really – succession, sharing and credits. I feel very strongly that no entrepreneur makes money without the creativity and loyalty of the people working for him or her. It follows, then, that those people should be rewarded for such loyalty by sharing in the successful businesses they help to create. Neither is it only a share in the profits; job security is very important, too – perhaps especially so in today's economic climate. So in our structure, the company cannot be sold unless, of course, it is in the best interests of every single employee in the practice. In fact, we have already had approaches from parties wishing to buy Make, and we have turned them all down. My business partner Barry Cooke and I are the first trustees – with one share each – and the trust contains a complex raft of measures, including the appointment of a 'protector'. We put this system in place to ensure that future trustees uphold the vision. Without the consent of this protector, successor trustees cannot act. Like Spedan Lewis, I have irrevocably given away any ownership rights, and the trust was deliberately structured in such a way that I can never get them back. All employees – no matter how senior or junior – are partners in the business and share in the profits.

Each employee is also offered the same package of benefits. Entitled 'Make protects', this package comprises life insurance, a non-contributory personal pension and optional private medical insurance. The benefits are supplemented by an Employee Assistance Programme for anyone with personal or business-related problems. Employees have an annual entitlement of four weeks' holiday, excluding Bank Holidays, rising to five weeks after one year of employment. Everyone is allotted additional holidays between Christmas and New Year, when our studios are closed.

We place a high importance on personal development, too. In order to ensure that we're completely up to date, we invest in training and research. Appropriate internal and external training takes place following in-house CAD assessments. We carry out obligatory CDM training with external consultants. Less common training modules are available too – optional extras include art classes, presentation coaching and classes to develop language and writing skills. A reasonably high proportion of new recruits are students who spend their year out with us between their Part 1 qualification and their diploma course. Making up around 10 per cent of our workforce, these students are given good guidance and encouragement, and we take a great deal of care to ensure that they are allocated the most appropriate projects and given the required technical training. They work alongside everyone else and earn their share of the profits as partners.

This may all sound like the ideal practice – a kind of designers' heaven. However, there are a few challenges to working with such an organic beast. It's difficult to predict how the practice will grow, and in what direction. I always said that we should stop when we hit 60 people, but before Christmas 2008 we had as many as 145 partners. Recessionary pressures have meant we have had to reduce this figure, however – we are now at around 80 – which we did with as little disruption as possible, offering staff 'gap' years, three-day weeks and sabbaticals. But even here the wind-down was far easier – almost a positive thing – because of the Trust structure and because of our openness about figures to all staff. Our Edinburgh office also broke away to set up independently. More broadly, challenges are such that life at Make can be a bit like a white-water ride – the best advice is to hang on tight! You never quite know what is going to happen – planning ahead is difficult, so it is important to constantly readjust any set ideas we may have had.

Designing things – making good

As architects, we believe in starting our designs from first principles and challenging expectations. This means, at the very beginning of a project, challenging our brief and listening. It also requires understanding. What do our clients really want? But our most important goal is in providing a design solution that far exceeds expectations. In other words, some people may come to us with preconceived notions of what they want – we strive to achieve something better than this conception and the goal is that they go away happier. It helps, too, that we do more than one version of a design – which is also more than clients often expect. To achieve this goal, we aim to form a partnership with our clients in order to develop the project together. After all, we cannot design a building on our own. Rather than create a situation of 'us and them', we work with the client, spending time and taking care to achieve an appropriate solution, together. We are passionate about detail, and believe that only the highest level of quality control will produce the standard of design we have set ourselves. Getting the particulars correct is critical. It is not just about getting them right on paper, but about seeing them through to construction and completion. An example of this in action is our work at 55 Baker Street (see Image 10.1), where the

Image 10.1 55 Baker Street, London. Source: © Make Architects, photographer Charlotte Wood, 2010 – reproduced with permission

initial idea to transform the former M&S headquarters building was the best solution for the site from concept to reality – and which was completed in a very short time frame.

Our aesthetic approach is in some ways quite a simple one. We strive to offer design solutions, which are set in the age in which we live, and continue to build upon the modernist tradition. But, in addition, all of our projects have a sustainable dimension to them and contain an example of how we can move the agenda forward in terms of ecology. This is no add-on: all of our work has this sustainability principle embedded within it as a fundamental, with other elements overlaid. In terms of a methodology, we work at every stage directly with models, both physical and virtual. We find that a three-dimensional, hands-on approach is the best method of exploring massing, space and light.

We work with the world's leading consultants, including engineers, quantity surveyors, model-makers, 3D image-makers, graphic designers and artists. Collaborating with artists has been incredibly interesting and rewarding, particularly on the recently completed Grosvenor Waterside residential scheme for client St James Urban Living on the Chelsea Dock (Image 10.2). We included artist Clare

Image 10.2 Grosvenor Waterside, London. Source: © Make Architects, 2010 – reproduced with permission

Image 10.3 City of London information centre. Source: © Make Architects, 2010 – reproduced with permission

Woods from the beginning of the project to create a beautiful artwork etched on the buildings' facade.

Debate and discussion about our design work is always encouraged. Everyone at Make is involved with design debating and brainstorming on every project. Team members on each job contribute to the development of every aspect of their project, and each individual's ideas and contributions are taken seriously. Every person has something unique to offer, so we can all learn from each other. We do not conduct formal design reviews. Instead we rely on the fact that our office is all open plan and that scheme designs are pinned up on the walls for anyone to comment on or come up with new ideas about. Staff often just grab each other for informal chats. Such an environment means that – we hope – Make is seen as an ideal studio for students and young designers to work alongside more experienced architects. For their part, the younger members of our workforce certainly add to the mix. To this end, we actively support all those taking courses and exams, not just those taking their final qualifications. Internal seminars and lectures, and support for external events, are all part of the Make programme of learning. In addition, the way in which our staff learn to enhance their design creativity and its application to projects, alongside how this fits with our office credo, gives us an edge, we believe, with peers and clients.

Personally speaking, after a successful career of managing and being managed, it's always hard to let go of the reins, however slightly. I still sketch up many of the design ideas and maintain strong relationships with all clients on a daily basis. But I do get a small twinge of sadness as well as an overriding sense of pride as I see the project team and client working the designs up and onto site. I still design buildings and draw every day – no-one will stop me doing that – and my role includes a quality control element over the office's creative process. But ours is an egalitarian structure where the best ideas – whether they happen to come from me or from other staff – are those which are taken forward.

What's next – making the future?

So, what's next?

For architecture and the wider world, the biggest challenge is climate change – it is as simple as that. With half of all CO_2 coming from buildings, we need to set examples for other architects to follow. But the extra challenge with climate change recently has been the economy, forcing buildings to be more efficient. As a result I believe that the next generation of buildings will go back to basics – there will be a return to good, rigorous, simpler buildings that avoid the curves and fancy shapes – and just work.

As far as Make is concerned I have set out the aims, structuring and some of the processes that renders ours a distinctive architecture practice. I believe that the provision of a stimulating working environment is fundamental to growth and learning – I tried to lay some foundations for that from the start. To an extent, this working environment has evolved organically, and there is no railroad track on which we have to travel – the practice is free to roam, make changes and improve. Happily, though, I also believe that we are getting some of the basics right: our studio is a vibrant, zesty, challenging place to work. It is a studio that is full of life, with a sense of ownership. And, ultimately, it exemplifies that at Make we are passionate about doing the best we can – where everything is possible.

Postscript Comment to *The make experience* by Ken Shuttleworth

Graham Winch

The challenge of how architectural firms address the Daedalian risk (Blau, 1984) of creative practice is enduring. Daedalus was a highly skilled craftsman (especially as a labyrinth architect, less so as an aeronautical engineer) who embodied the paradox of the creativity of his art and the worldly constraints around him. Blau uses this myth to articulate the risks inherent in architectural practice where the conditions of initial creative success can be suppressed by that very success because of the inherent tension between architecture as art and as business compounded by the tension of these two with social values (Cohen *et al.*, 2005). Blau's research captures this paradox well, and Ken's description of the organisation of Make demonstrates a sophisticated attempt to address it. My aim in this short commentary is to assess the innovative approach taken at Make in the context of existing research on the management of architectural practice and thereby to identify some of the challenges that Make is likely to face as it develops in the future.

The bluntest statement of profession as business is articulated by Maister (1993) who identifies profits per partner as the professional equivalent of return on capital employed with the leverage ratio of juniors to associates to principals as the key performance metric. The essence of leverage is to charge out the juniors who actually do the work at a higher rate than they could obtain on their own account thanks to the oversight provided by seniors. This inherently exploitative relationship – Maister (1982) uses the Marxist term 'surplus value' to capture it – works because juniors have the opportunity for promotion to principal (partner/director) via the associate level, or to use the experience and prestige gained while working for an established firm to set up on their own.

This harsh view of architectural practice is in strong contrast with the essentially collegial view presented by Cuff (1991) in her extended essay on practising architecture. What both perspectives have in common is that architects are driven by high professional values to work long hours in the aspiration of eventually creating a building that makes a difference while remaining solvent. At the same time, Blau (1984) shows that a collegial way of working does produce the most effective environment for creativity. How is this paradox to be resolved? A case study of one strong ideas practice suggests that its resolution involves the 'invisible walls' and 'silent hierarchy' (Brown *et al.*, 2010) of architectural practice within an espoused collegial culture. So, although the rhetoric of practice is democratic and inclusive, the younger architects soon learn that the practice of practice means that it is the principals' definition of the most appropriate solution to the design problem at hand that will hold sway. While more osmotic than explicit, the orientation of the culture of practice around reinforcing the reputation of the principals remains central.

Make clearly has a high awareness of these issues and has attempted to address them in a creative way. The principal innovation is to share ownership of the practice on the model of the John Lewis Partnership in retail. This deserves to be successful in terms of the motivation of the creative process, but Maister's analysis would suggest that there will be some issues in the medium term (Make is six years old at the time of writing). The two main issues would appear to be career development and business development. In career development terms, the current relatively young profile of the practice will be looking for advance through junior to associate then to senior positions. In the absence of high growth – which would appear unlikely in the current climate – people will therefore either tend to be promoted, or they will need to leave in order for Make to retain an appropriately leveraged organisational structure. If they are all promoted, Make faces becoming diamond shaped like Trad-Co in the RIBA research or even an inverted pyramid like Quality-Co (RIBA 2003: 51) with resultant implications for competitiveness. While all architectural practices face this risk, Make's commitment to full employee participation does increase this particular Daedalian risk. It might therefore be worth thinking about a proactive policy of helping associates to set up on their own if they are not likely to make it to senior management level.

The issue in business development is how Make can acquire the human resources required for expansion in new markets. Ken's chapter focuses on the culture of practice in its newly refurbished central London offices, yet Make is entering a number of architectural competitions in East Asia, and is currently (http://www.makearchitects.com, accessed 26/03/10) master planner for a major development in Tianjin, China. One notable feature of the John Lewis Partnership is how limited its geographical scope is for a major retailer, and how slowly it has expanded regionally in the UK. It is unlikely that the globalising pressures in the market for architectural services will allow Make the luxury of slow geographical expansion. Careful thought needs to be given to how the culture of practice in London is replicated for Chinese projects. One way forward might to be to establish something like the Fondazione Renzo Piano working with Chinese architectural schools to ensure a regional flow of talent imbued with the Make culture of practice thereby extending its 'project ecology' – see Chapter 2 for a discussion on this.

Make is a brave attempt to be different in architectural practice, inheriting strong design values from Foster's and already making a distinctive contribution to the built environment. It represents an innovative attempt to address the Daedalian risk of architectural practice. I wish it well, but it would benefit from heeding Maister's analysis of the logic of practice and think creatively about how to address the issues collegially rather than churning exploitatively in the coming years and to create a project ecology that enhances opportunity for young architects in the markets it seeks to enter.

References to Postscript Comment

Blau, J. R. (1984) *Architects and Firms: a sociological perspective on architectural practice*, MIT Press, Cambridge.

Brown, A. D., Kornberger, M., Clegg, S. R. and Carter, C. (2010) 'Invisible walls' and 'silent hierarchies': a case study of power relations in an architectural firm, *Human Relations*, 63, 525–549.

Cohen, L. Wilkinson, A. Arnold, J. and Finn, R. (2005) 'Remember I'm the bloody architect!' Architects, organizations and discourses of profession, *Work Employment and Society*, 19, 775–796.

Cuff, D. (1991) *Architecture: The Story of Practice*, MIT Press, Cambridge.

Maister, D. H. (1982) Balancing the professional service firm, *Sloan Management Review*, Fall, 15–29.

Maister, D. H. (1993) *Managing the Professional Service Firm*, The Free Press, New York.

Royal Institute of British Architects (2003) *Strategic Study of the Profession Phase 2: clients and architects*, RIBA, London.

11 Squaring the circle

Delivering international services locally

Larry Malcic

HOK has long had to balance its global brand with a determination to allow individual offices to pursue their own, unique ways of doing things. It is a classic management problem, which began to arise in the late 20th century – seeking to be more than a dispersed collection of offices with a single name, and less than a monolithic, inflexible global presence directed from above. This chapter explores how HOK has been addressing this problem.

HOK was founded in 1955 in St Louis, USA, and over the past half century the business has grown to encompass 25 offices employing approximately 2200 people. The business, which still locates its financial and operational homes in the USA, splits the world into three typical zones:

1. The Americas
2. Asia
3. Europe, Middle East and Africa

HOK London is the lead office for Europe (see Image 11.1), Middle East and Africa. The borders of these zones are not absolute, and there can be some blurring at the edges; the Washington DC office, for example, has undertaken work in eastern Europe without upsetting the managerial applecart. This is fairly indicative of the way that HOK operates – the business model is clear, robust and well understood, but nobody wants to operate within a straitjacket, and exceptions are made where appropriate. This presents another balancing act: quite apart from ensuring the practice can operate as a convincing global entity from very local centres, we also place a premium on good personal relationships. Internal decisions are often taken through a process of negotiation, which depends, in turn, on a good deal of talking and giving a voice to

Managing the Professional Practice: in the built environment, First Edition. Edited by Hedley Smyth.
© 2011 by Blackwell Publishing Ltd. Published 2011 by Blackwell Publishing Ltd.

Image 11.1 HOK London office

every office in the business. It is almost certainly not the most efficient business model (and it may even be a little top heavy), but it is one that serves to preserve and represent the diversity of the practice. We prefer consensus built from varied points of view, even if it takes time to achieve. The value we place on diversity and collaboration underlies much of our culture. It flows naturally into both our management approach and design ethos. We have no single, identifiable house style in terms of design, nor a single design process; offices are fairly free to conduct their affairs as they see fit as long as they produce quality projects and remain profitable.

The culture of the practice is therefore a little difficult to pin down; we believe we have a system in place, which is tight enough to hold us together, but loose enough to permit flexibility where it is needed. In a very real sense, our values are fixed, but our methods are always fluid; we embrace innovation and change.

The weave

The office network is, in fact, just one part of a two-way weave. In a sense, each office operates as its own practice; no office is subsidised by the others and each location seeks and undertakes its own work. However, offices are encouraged to share staff and expertise. This is especially so across specific sectors, where HOK has decided to offer expertise from the position of an integrated global business. These sectors are: health-care, transport and aviation; science and technology; justice buildings; master-planning; and 'advance strategies', a discipline in which we help clients align business goals and methods with their building require-ments. These sectors operate across the office network, and sector specialists do not necessarily report to the management principal of the office but, rather, to the leader of the sector geographically based anywhere in the world. Generally, these sectors are not profit centres in themselves, as individual offices receive project fees in direct proportion to their share of the work. Master-planning and advance strategies are, however, run as global businesses that are entirely separate from the office network; residing at each office is a master-planning and advance strategies team, but fees are accumulated centrally. This distinction recognises the reality that both of these groups offer a special service to clients, and have a separate relationship often independent of other architectural service offerings of the wider practice.

HOK as a business can, then, be imagined as the warp and weft of a textile; individual offices are encouraged to develop their own client base and direction, whilst the weave across the business matrix is a series of business units, which operate (and are marketed) as global ventures.

The London network

Over the years it has been possible for the London office to emerge as one of HOK's largest teams in its own right, and playing a pivotal role in multi-office collaborations. Our core values of diversity and collaboration are very much in evidence when multiple offices form a single project team. The New Doha International Airport, for example, is being managed through a collaboration with the San Francisco and New York offices, with additional staff in London and Doha; the UK Centre for Medical Research and Innovation, to be built in Kings Cross, was won as a London-led partnership with the Atlanta and St Louis offices, where much of the company's laboratory expertise is located.

Such multi-region collaborations are probably exemplified by the way the company responded to an invitation to submit a design proposal for the King Abdullah University of Science and Technology in Saudi Arabia. Against a very tight deadline, six HOK offices from around the world collaborated in formulating a design by 'chasing the sun': in a single 24-hour period, offices worked on designs, which were handed over to fresh design teams as one working day ended and another began. 'Live' collaborations are also made possible through our 'advanced collaboration room', where BT and Cisco 'Thunder' technology allows teams located on different continents to manipulate digital models simultaneously, relaying the results instantaneously on a large display screen. Around the world this investment in technology has enabled great savings in transport costs and created a platform for collaboration unique to HOK.

Even with technology to bind teams in different locations together, these large, complex projects require especially experienced project management skill. They also require special protocols, agreed by everyone, that strike a balance between clear procedures and flexible working practices. Finally, they have to be infused with a spirit of cooperation, based on a sense of shared purpose by the team and an equitable distribution of the fee among the participants.

HOK operates a highly collaborative business model – stopping short of integration, to allow offices to maintain a strong sense of independence. It is also a model that we have pushed beyond the confines of the practice. The 'European Architecture Network' effectively boosts London's reach by five offices. By forming strategic alliances with practices in Italy, Germany, Spain, France and Belgium, we can offer technical expertise where our partners can offer local knowledge, language and contacts. Originally, the network began as a formal association, with legally binding rules (e.g. projects should be for mutual benefit and no poaching of staff allowed), but it now tends to operate in a looser way built on a foundation of trust and friendship. Through the network HOK has – by joining forces with French firm Arte Charpentier – been appointed to work on a project for Nantes airport – something we could probably not have won alone, and which Arte Charpentier (with little airport expertise) might not have won either.

The goal of this complex organisational structure is to offer a local response quickly, effectively and convincingly while being simultaneously capable of providing real depth in terms of experience and expertise. It is an objective, though, that requires considerable management effort.

Management structure

The London practice is amongst the largest of HOK's global network in terms of staff numbers, but the administrative centre is still located in St Louis, where the practice was founded. The financial and management centre is located in San Francisco; it is here that the chairman and the CEO are based. They are part of a small 'executive committee' which is where the practice's strategic leadership resides. This committee encompasses the following functions/roles:

- chairman;
- president;
- chief executive officer;
- chief financial officer;
- chief talent officer;
- marketing director;
- operations director.

In hierarchical terms, the main board, HOK Inc. board of directors (in which legal responsibility for this private corporation resides) sits below the executive committee. The board encompasses committee members as well as around a dozen others, such as the leaders of global business units and the principal offices. The London office's design director and managing principal are both members of this board, for example. This board meets face-to-face twice a year. Monthly meetings, however, are conducted through video conferencing. These virtual meetings, timed to maximise the number of participants located across the globe's time zones, tend to address financial and resourcing issues, and comparative figures from the office network are analysed and difficult questions often asked. What distinguishes HOK, perhaps, from other multinational practices is that each office has substantial freedom over creative matters, but financial standards are very much set from the centre. Offices are monitored via a complex matrix of measures including profitability, fee structures and margins, staff costs and the ratio of creative-managerial-support staff. Figures provided by each office are compiled centrally, allowing comparisons to be made between different locations. Through these financial performance statements, offices can clearly benchmark themselves against their peers, and good management practice can emerge. Equally, a practice-wide planning and resourcing system (employing computer program Deltek Vision) allows the global business to see where spare capacity is located, and which teams are becoming stretched. This system (which depends, of course, on people entering accurate data in a timely fashion) allows work to be distributed efficiently. Certainly, in times of recession, it allows us to consider redeployment and relocation of staff before resorting to redundancies – and losing skills forever.

HOK also maintains four 'core boards', which is where many of the practical, day-to-day decisions are taken. Covering management, marketing, delivery and design, these four boards are made up of executive committee and main board members, as well as others from offices, global business units and key support functions. Policies made at this level are company-wide, such as the commitment to adopt 3D modelling tool Revit for all new projects, to explore new contracting methods such as the AIA's 'Integrated Project Delivery' mechanism, and agreeing on client relation management (CRM) standards. The entire business model is highly inclusive – it is not exactly a bottom-up business model but rather one which has been designed to keep a conversation going upwards and downwards until a broad consensus can be reached. In truth, it can be a slow and laborious process yet is one that permits few surprises and where many people (within practical limits) are given a voice. It is a method which suits the culture of HOK as a private company with 300 internal shareholders and no institutional investors. We only have to answer to ourselves, and the general feeling, often articulated by the chairman, being if it *feels* right then it probably *is* right.

Managing creativity at HOK london

Project design and management almost echoes the division of labour represented by the four core boards. In keeping with North American practice, projects tend to be managed not by a single project architect, as is often typical in the UK, but by a triumvirate of specialists who each concentrate on one of the three core tasks of management, delivery and design. The idea is that roles be divided according to individual strengths to ensure that every aspect of the design and delivery is well served, while avoiding putting too much responsibility on the shoulders of a single person. One architect will be given responsibility for concept design, liberating them from the tasks of project management (including resourcing and financial control), and technical delivery (involving, for example, coordinating with contractors and co-professionals, and site visits). This is a model which works particularly well for very large projects, such as the St Bartholomew and the Royal London Hospitals or UKCMRI, where the three principal tasks of design, management and delivery are each sufficiently complex to occupy individuals on a full-time basis.

Whilst this division of labour is the norm in London, the practice sometimes chooses to employ a more traditional 'project architect' system on smaller projects – a school or justice buildings, for example, up to a value of £25–30 million. Projects of this scale are, we judge, sufficiently self-contained to warrant more control being given to a single person. Moreover, this does satisfy a particular need for people who do not wish to become confined to specific roles. This is an answer to the challenge posed by the tripartite project management system – although it certainly suits people who wish to concentrate on particular tasks, there are others whose ambitions lie in a more generalist role, seeing projects through from design to delivery. Indeed, the design specialists can sometimes feel remote from the later delivery and construction stages of a project, while management and delivery architects might also crave more input at the design phase. The tripartite system is a model not without potential flaws or pitfalls. It reduces problems associated with overburdening a single individual, avoids a long-hours culture and promotes the idea of teamwork, but it can confuse the client seeking a single point of contact. We have found that giving project architects overall control of smaller projects answers many of these problems, while allowing the practice to develop a healthy mix of specialists and general-ists. We also realise that the division of labour must be carefully considered in terms of promotion; project and delivery specialists some-times tend to be offered high-profile, senior roles within the practice, partly because of the exposure to finance and managerial pressures and partly because of an unspoken assumption that design leaders relish the opportunity to develop creatively without having to assume wider business responsibilities.

The emphasis on architects working to their strengths, namely design, management and delivery, establishes an informal matrix in which, on the one hand, teams work closely together to produce their projects, but on the other hand senior designers, project managers and technical architects confer and consult with one another to discover and share best practices. This is especially true in the arena of design. The senior designers, or design specialists, meet on a weekly basis to review and critique work in the office. In conjunction with the weekly reviews, several days a month are set aside for more formal reviews. These reviews seek not only to comment on and improve the projects being designed, but also to become forums for the broader discussion of architectural philosophy and direction. In recognition of the very public nature of architecture and building, outside reviewers join the internal design specialists to promote honest, critical and vigorous debate. Eminent critic and educator Sir Peter Cook currently participates in these monthly reviews, providing robust commentary and useful comparisons drawn from his encyclopaedic knowledge of contemporary and historic examples. This collegiate culture fosters a spirit of shared endeavour and emphasises the importance of team-work and collaboration that underlies HOK's philosophy of practice, whilst seeking to ensure that every project and design achieves its full potential.

Present challenges

The operational processes described above have served HOK very well and allowed the practice to grow to be one of the largest design-led firms in the world. Size alone, however, is neither our goal nor our focus; rather, it is a useful and necessary tool to ensure the quality and diversity of talent required to produce intelligent and memorable projects and places. Our practice platform, created by our desire to collaborate, and reinforced by technology, has proven itself remarkably resilient and effective despite the cyclical nature of our profession and industry. The mix of local creativity and international accountability, of specialists and generalists, of office-based projects and practice-wide sector teams, combine to create a responsive and flexible professional practice that is able to operate on projects of vastly different complexities and scales. We constantly monitor business processes to assess their effectiveness during a downturn – and we are especially mindful of the ratio between fee-earning staff and those who perform essential mana-gerial roles. Individual offices have to remain profitable if they are to continue practising; the network they create when considered as a whole, woven with the matrix of specialist skills, support one another and provide a competitive edge.

More than 50 years ago HOK pioneered the idea of an integrated service delivery model, bringing together architecture, town planning, interior design, landscape architecture and graphics. We continue to explore how we can expand the way in which we serve client needs and extend the range of our design offerings, so that our design thinking can be applied across the entire lifecycle of buildings and communities. We are seeking to redefine many of the industry practices and processes that currently hamper efforts to achieve higher productivity and better quality in the built environment. For example, the adversarial, even acrimonious, relationships between architect, client and contractor that is assumed and promoted in building contracts offers no opportunity to create better buildings. Rather, it creates a blame culture and inhibits positive innovation. HOK is active in developing new forms of contract that encourage collaboration, often based on the use of a single building information model. The building information model, with embedded intelligence, will mitigate errors and speed up coordination, fabrication and construction. The goal is a partnership of common interest in creating profitable, sustainable projects and communities.

Looking ahead, HOK will continue to evolve, but certain characteristics are likely to continue:

- an emphasis on the creative strength provided by diversity;
- a high value placed on teamwork, cooperation and collaboration;
- a reliance on management principles of consensus and shared values;
- continued investment in leading-edge technology;
- innovation in the definition and delivery of our services.

In order to maintain HOK's position as a global design leader, the current leadership recognises the need to identify and encourage new leaders within the practice. If, as Shakespeare writes, 'Past is prologue', the values and culture that created HOK will continue to guide its future growth. We will seek out professionals with initiative and imagination who value the benefits of collaborative thinking. New leaders may well expand the design service offer of HOK to continue to diversify the practice. Leaders will be expected to recognise new technologies and exploit the improvements in design and delivery that they offer. We will always place our emphasis on intellectual talent, the ability and willingness to listen to others, to engage in informed debate and to join together in common enterprise to solve some of the most complex problems of human habitation and community.

Postscript Comment to *Squaring the circle: Delivering international services locally* by Larry Malcic

Beatrice Manzoni

With 25 offices in The Americas, Asia, Europe, Middle East and Africa, HOK is among the top five global intelligence corps (GIC), using Rimmer's (1991) definition for global architecture firms with a network of offices in multiple countries. However, being global is not only about being glamorous architects (Larson, 1994), designing iconic buildings and branding cities (Jencks, 2006). In fact, the globalisation of architectural practices – a phenomenon emerging in the latter half of the 20th century – poses several challenges in terms of the design and delivery of buildings, both from a strategic and an organisational perspective.

Larry Malcic's chapter specifically gives some hints about two of these challenges, which have been also discussed in recent architecture and management literature. The first challenge deals with embedding a building in its local context, calling for choosing among local, regional and global strategies and coherent organisational structures. The second challenge is related to ways of coordinating work, sustaining organisational creativity across different offices and countries, and balancing between a shared common culture and local offices' flexibility. This postscript comment elaborates on these two challenges, linking together insights from the HOK experience and theory from existing literature.

Considering the first challenge, according to Faulconbridge (2009) global practices have to deal with putting global designs in their place, avoiding a process of cultural homogenisation (Cody, 2003). To do that, 'it is often a mistake to set out to create a worldwide strategy. Better results come from strong regional strategies, brought together into a global whole' (Ghemawat, 2005: 98). Adopting regional strategies, instead of pure local or global ones, calls in fact for creativity, flexibility and adaptation to the changing business context. This is the reason why HOK encourages individual offices to develop their own strategy and client base according to their market's specificities and accepts 'blurring borders' between zones.

Moreover, different strategies exist, according to Winch (2008), for entry into foreign markets (following a client, winning a competition, marketing and via network partners) as well as alternative modes of organisation in relation to these strategies (a temporary liaison with a local architectural practice, a temporary office, a network partner, a joint venture and a subsidiary). HOK adopts many of these, partly from

having subsidiaries around the world. It relies, for example, on collaborative networks and strategic alliances with practices in Italy, Germany,
Spain and Belgium, to whom HOK offers expertise in exchange for local
knowledge and contacts.

Choosing an organisational asset parallels with the business strategy,
being however something different. Coxe *et al.* (1988) distinguish among
strategies related to how a firm does its work (design technology) and to
the philosophy of the firm impacting how it will organise and operate
(organisation values). One of the most renowned management studies
focusing on architectural practices (Mintzberg *et al.*, 1988) traces the
actions of an organisation over a significant period of time to understand
how and why strategies developed and changed. It distinguishes among
job strategies, related to the nature of the architectural work done, and
organisational strategies, related to the manner in which the firm pursued its work. The job strategies in HOK are described as the 'warp and
weft of a textile' and the organisational ones reflect them: for those
business areas offered as special services to clients, for example, business
units are centralised with no duplications at local levels. For many other
sectors, on the contrary, each local office is free to organise itself.

What HOK tries to balance is the global brand with individual offices'
freedom to pursue unique ways of doing things. In the literature this is
recognised as the 'tension between unity and variety in project-based
organisations that pursue unique solutions' (Yoo *et al.*, 2006: 228) and
cross-refers to the second main challenge emerging from the chapter and
reviewed in this postscript comment. How can we foster creativity,
providing general guidelines for creative design project solutions but
allowing local specificities and differences to influence them?

For almost 20 years it has been well recognised that creative design
solutions are no longer the product of single genius. 'The essence of
architecture is that it centres on creativity' (Blau, 1984: 28) and architects
are hired by clients to provide novel solutions to spatial problems (Jones
and Thornton, 2005). Yet, as creativity is a social process, the architect's
work is fundamentally collaborative and asks for communication and
interactions among different actors and stakeholders (Yoo *et al.*, 2006;
Hargadon and Bechky, 2006; De Fillippi *et al.*, 2007).

Existing literature and professional experiences have also pointed out
how encouraging creativity is a critical strategic choice (Amabile, 1996),
requiring practice management processes and systems orientated
towards the nurturing of creativity. At an organisational level, creativity
is a function of the creative outputs of its component groups and
contextual influences, such as the organisational culture, the reward
systems, the resource constraints and the larger environment outside the
system (Woodman *et al.*, 1993).

Project-based organisations are typical of creative contexts (Gunnarson
and Levitt, 1982). Organising architecture by projects teams is alternative
for departmentalisation, creating connections, engaging in different tasks

and commitment (Blau, 1984). It happens therefore that in HOK multiple offices sometimes form a single project team, as for the New Doha International Airport or for the King Abdullah University project illustrated in the chapter. It also happens that teamwork is encouraged with a tripartite system of responsibilities (management, delivery and design) on large projects.

In addition, different management practices are suggested for creative contexts. Mumford (2000), for example, argues that interventions intended to enhance creativity have to take into account the individual, the group, the organisation and the strategic environment and proposes some of them. First, select for breadth and depth of expertise and skill when recruiting people to work on a creative project. This is the reason why at HOK architecture, town planning, interior design, landscape architecture and graphics are mixed, as well as specialists and generalists, and diversity is a challenge for the future, too. Second, periodically review work progress and foster collaborative design innovation. Weekly reviews at HOK become more than assessment occasions, being forums for broader discussion of architectural philosophy and direction, where external insights are welcomed. Third, guarantee multiple career tracks for advancement. In HOK, a healthy mix of specialists and generalists is in fact kept, also in terms of promotion and career development: project and delivery specialists are offered managerial positions, only after having developed technical ones. Finally, actively pursue strategic hires. This is typical of the global practices in general for which globalisation is also about headhunting and accessing talented architects (Faulconbridge, 2009).

All these practices fostering and nurturing creativity are, however, effective only in the presence of an organisational culture orientated towards innovation, collaboration and shared endeavour and seeking to ensure, quoting Malcic, that 'every project and design achieves its full potential'.

References to Postscript Comment

Amabile, T. M. (1996) *Creativity in Context*, Westview Press, Boulder.

Blau, J. R. (1984) *Architects and Firms: a sociological perspective on architectural practice*, MIT Press.

Cody, J. W. (2003) *Exporting American Architecture, 1870–2000*. London: Routledge.

Coxe, W., Hartung, N. F., Hochburg, H. H., Lewis, B. J., Maister, D. H., Mattox, R. F. and Piven, P. (1988) *Success Strategies for Design Professionals*, John Wiley & Sons, New York.

DeFillippi, R., Grabher, G. and Jones, C. (2007) Introduction to paradoxes of creativity: managerial and organizational challenges in the cultural economy, *Journal of Organizational Behavior*, 28, 511–521.

Faulconbridge, J. R. (2009) The regulation of design in global architecture firms: embedding and emplacing buildings, *Urban Studies*, 46(12), 2537–2554.

Ghemawat, P. (2005) Regional strategies for global leadership, *Harvard Business Review*, December, 98–108.

Gunnarson, S. and Levitt, R. E. (1982) *Is a Construction Project a Hierarchy or a Market?* 7th Internet Congress.

Hargadon, A. B. and Bechky, B. A. (2006) When collections of creatives become creative collections: a field study of problem solving at work, *Organization Science*, 17(4), 484–500.

Jencks, C. (2006) The iconic building is here to stay, *City*, 10(1), 3–20.

Jones, C. and Thornton, P. H. (2005) Transformation in cultural industries, *Research in the Sociology of Organizations*, 23, ix–xix.

Larson, M. S. (1994) Architectural competitions as discursive events, *Theory and Society*, 23(4), 469–504.

Mintzberg, H., Otis, S., Shamsie, J. and Waters, J. A. (1988) *Strategy of design: a study of 'architects in co-partnership'*, *Strategic Management Frontiers*, Grant, J. (ed.), JAI Press, Greenwich, 311–359.

Mumford, M. D. (2000) Managing creative people: strategies and tactics for innovation, *Human Resource Management Review*, 10(3), 313–351.

Rimmer, P. J. (1991) The global intelligence corps and world cities: engineering consultancies on the move, *Services and Metropolitan Development*, Daniels, P. W. (ed.), Routledge, London, 66–106.

Yoo, Y., Boland, R. J., Lyytinen, K. Jr. (2006) From organization design to organization designing, *Organization Science*, 17(2), 215–229.

Winch, G. M. (2008) Internationalisation strategies in business-to-business services: the case of architectural practice, *The Service Industries Journal*, 28(1), 1–13.

Woodman, R. W., Sawyer, J. E., Griffin, R. W. (1993) Toward a theory of organizational creativity, *Academy of Management Review*, 18, 293–321.

12 Innovation in the construction sector

Jeremy Watson

What is innovation?

A frequently used word, employed rather interchangeably with invention, although it implies much more, is innovation. Innovation can be thought of as a system of processes spanning concept to commercialisation. Innovation includes a range of activities, which are set out in Table 12.1.

Several or all of these processes can be applied to a particular project, and their relevance depends on the class of good or service being developed. In the construction sector these might range from a component to a building.

Types of innovation

Generations of innovation process

Since the 1950s, sophistication in innovation methods has developed from *technology push*, where R&D outputs were expected to create markets (e.g. the Sony Walkman), to *demand pull*, where known or anticipated market demand triggers and steers R&D inputs (e.g. MP3 players) (Dodgson *et al.*, 2008). More advanced models such as *concurrent innovation* are increasingly used in some sectors, where much of a supply chain is stimulated in parallel, perhaps through a strong industry association, to create solutions of mutual commercial benefit – the classic example being advanced ICT equipment, where a comprehensive industry roadmap orchestrates development of a diverse set of technology and market enablers (SEMI Association, 1970). This approach has great potential for improving the responsiveness, adoption and hence market potential of new technologies (e.g. sustainable energy solutions for the built environment).

Managing the Professional Practice: in the built environment, First Edition. Edited by Hedley Smyth.
© 2011 by Blackwell Publishing Ltd. Published 2011 by Blackwell Publishing Ltd.

Table 12.1 Innovation from concept to commercialisation

Research	Ideation/invention	Design
Feasibility studies	Intellectual property diligence	Market analysis
Business planning	Funding	Venture capital raising
Proofs of concept and pilots	Production set-up	Market preparation
Beta prototypes and testing	Production	Launch
Assessment	Post-purchase services	

Open innovation

Open innovation is growing in popularity. It describes ideas traded in an open marketplace, a mode made practical by the internet. Would-be intellectual property (IP) buyers place their technology needs on a brokerage website, while technology providers add their emerging technologies. Both communities communicate via the site, making bids for needs or new technology. Two current open innovation brokerage companies are Yet2.com (Yet2.com 2009) and Innocentive (Innocentive, 2009).

This is a potentially disruptive approach, with possible outcomes including the abolition of corporate R&D facilities (already apparent in some sectors) and the growth of one-man innovators in distributed, web-enabled 'cottage industries'. Although this is a vision of a limiting case, small to medium-sized enterprises (SMEs) are now taking the R&D role in much of the pharmaceuticals industry, where the investment needed to run a central R&D facility is prohibitive given regulatory constraints and product success rates.

Characteristics of the construction sector

Size profile

The construction sector is characterised by a few large corporate contractors, some with international operations, and many (85% +) small operations of less than 10 permanent employees, almost all locally based.

This frustrates possibilities for business and technology development, also training, as SMEs inevitably operate on very tight time frames, with strong focus on current projects rather than capabilities which may be needed in the future. The ability to absorb external technological knowledge to realise innovation is thereby hampered.

Absorptive capacity

The ability of a company to receive and use innovation is termed *absorptive capacity* (Abreu *et al.*, 2008). It governs the value of interaction with technology partners. Lack of absorptive capacity can result from a company having a staff profile focused only on immediate operational activities. In a small organisation (81% of UK construction companies have four or fewer employees) this is inevitable. However, recent UK government interventions can assist in improving SME absorptive capacity. For example, in the UK the Knowledge Transfer Partnership (KTP) scheme funds up to 66% of the salary cost of technically qualified temporary staff who are employed by a host university and seconded to a target company, providing an 'interpretive bridge' between specialist knowledge and application.

Risk aversion

Associated with small company size and the consequent limits in absorptive capacity, the construction sector has a reputation for conservatism with respect to adopting new technologies. An unadventurous approach to 'risk versus reward' leads to the continuation of proven practices, the use of mature materials and components, and possibly unexciting business performance. Recent and new building codes and regulations are challenging this approach, as in the case of building energy efficiency, and targets cannot be met through the use of standard methods and technologies. Emerging UK government interventions promise to help change behaviours in the Sector. Strategic procurement (for example under the Technology Strategy Board's SBRI scheme) can provide 100% funding for companies developing new capabilities through research and technology transfer, essentially de-risking the deployment of newer technologies.

These factors present real challenges for professionals working in the construction sector. However, improvement in adoption of innovation practices may be achieved if managers receive appropriate training, and if they are exposed to company cultures outside their sector. It is also helpful for them to stay in touch with best practice via relevant professional institutions.

Professionals operating in built environment professional services firms can also stay abreast of developments in practice through linkages with university partners, and by sharing best practice with networks and associations such as the TSB's Modern Built Environment Knowledge Transfer Network (MBE KTN).

Value from innovation

Market position

Innovation very often has a step change impact on a company's market position. Case studies are available in the consumer electronics world where, for example, Apple's market position was hugely advanced by the technical innovation made in the iPlayer in combination with the complementary business model of iTunes. A similar success story can be told of Rolls Royce when it moved from the sale of aero engines to fees for 'power by the hour' services. In construction, large companies are increasing their R&D and product capabilities, and investigating new business models – directly or through the growth of innovation partner networks. As an example, building operation management (or facilities management) may become a service offering of construction companies. Significant market advantage can be anticipated through the outcomes of some of these innovations.

Baseline capability and performance improvements

A culture and practice of innovation does more than add new product offerings; it can also benefit the underlying baseline capabilities of a company. This can be through process improvements as well as products or services delivered. Categories in which innovation can assist profitability include: client requirements capture, validation and visualisation; supply chain management ('just in time', logistics, minimising site waste); construction processes; and materials and components. Work by Laing O'Rourke on sustainable concrete and prefabricated, off-site manufactured components, provide an example of innovation in construction processes.

It is notable that few professional practices are involved with such processes directly or through the innovation partner networks cited above, despite their earlier involvement in the supply chain. Perhaps this is due to the rather 'siloed' nature of most professional service firms. To make an impact on baseline and performance, a broader and more holistic approach is indicated.

Intellectual property (IP)

Not usually associated with built environment (BE) sector companies, intellectual property (UK IPO 2009) is nevertheless a hidden capital asset of BE engineering and construction companies. By no means limited to patents, IP describes any idea of commercial value to a company, from copyright designs through patents to trade secrets. IP can be traded (e.g. sold or licensed) in the form of patents, or just protected and used to create commercial advantage. Historically, 'trade secrets' encompassing methods and skills have been of great commercial importance to construction companies. Tradable IP is typified by patents describing unique physical products or processes. Professional practices involved in specification and design for the construction sector have potential to directly develop such IP or to gain value indirectly by promoting routes to market with third parties, especially in components and subsystems. Value can be realised by direct sale of the IP, licensing, joint ventures or spin-out companies.

Client value and corporate social responsibility (CSR)

Successful innovation usually gives rise to value perceived by clients (directly or via their own clients), often in novel or improved functionality, or in price reductions. In other cases, clients may benefit from the cachet of the innovation; a classic example is 'Intel Inside™' which benefits generic PCs makers as well as the chip manufacturer (see also Chapter 15).

Innovation can also support improved CSR, creating better customer perceptions and an intangible differentiator, for example in environmental performance through reduced resource consumption and lower operational energy needs. The corporate sustainability credentials of a company are enhanced if it introduces a product with zero or ultra-low standby power requirements.

Professional practices are frequently leaders in pursuing social and broader ethical consideration from education and training and through institutional support and professional codes. For the professional practice, improving clients' CSR position presents a valuable business opportunity, bridging as it can, management and technical consultancy, and raising the strategic profile (hence value) of the technical element through intangible value addition.

Promoters of innovation

Culture

An appropriate culture is essential in fostering innovation. This should allow free but focused time, adequate funding of new ideas, access to appropriate information, (perhaps most importantly concerning client needs) and mentoring. Examples of innovative companies, 3M and Google, allow employees between 15% and 20% of work time to develop commercial ideas of their own.

Management support is vital in nurturing innovation. Without this and the 'championing' of innovations by senior management they are almost certain to fail for want of resource and finance. An example of this effect was demonstrated in the commercialisation of Apple's iPod. The concept was developed in a major European consumer electronics company, but success was not achieved there (or in other companies) until adoption by the visionary Steve Jobs, who gave personal backing to the product.

Research

Research is a key element of innovation. It may involve the identification and application of existing knowledge, not previously used by the practice, or in the creation of new basic or applications knowledge. Research is typically driven by 'pull' – a need arising from a gap in practice capability to satisfy a market need, or 'push' – the emergence of a new capability.

Few professional practices support a dedicated R&D department, although R&D is frequently conducted by individuals and in project teams. On occasions research may be outsourced to universities or other specialist consultancies. In order to maximise the opportunities presented by research, the practice requires absorptive capacity to translate research outputs into activities, products and services. This usually implies a need for a 'technology translator' within the practice who can interface between internal teams, departments and, where relevant, external experts. UK government has recognised this need through KTPs (KTP, 2009).

Expectations from research need to be managed carefully. An ad-hoc piecemeal approach is not ideal; a research portfolio designed to fill knowledge gaps is better. The portfolio may be designed by roadmapping market drivers and trends into business opportunities, identifying market gaps then specifying research needs.

Managing the innovation process

A variety of methods and tools are available to facilitate innovation; this section covers roadmapping, TRIZ and quality function deployment tools, partnerships and cultural implications for managing innovation.

Tools

Roadmapping

Effective research will be driven by a rational agenda; this can be a time-ordered hierarchical priority list, or 'roadmap'. Linking the emerging regulatory, economic and environmental drivers and trends (top level), through business opportunities, to scoping and detailed research topics (bottom level), roadmaps are a valuable tool. Roadmapping (IfM, 2009) is typically undertaken in a workshop context using a cross-sectional focus team of business development and operations executives from the company. Where the area being studied is new to the organisation, external experts may be called in to present a state-of-the-art picture at the start. Several levels are then mapped by brainstorming against short-, medium- and long-term timescales (perhaps one, three and ten years). A sticky note, grouping and voting approach is frequently used to capture ideas at each level of detail. One valuable side effect of roadmapping is that it secures team buy-in from the participants, as well as creating a strategy. Roadmapping services can be bought in from certain consultancies and universities. Arup has used this technique in management and for undertaking research commissions.

TRIZ

TRIZ aims to generate innovative ideas and solutions via a combination of algorithmic method, an established knowledge base and models. Offering tools and methods for problem formulation, analysis and system evolution (both in analysis and synthesis), TRIZ contrasts with other techniques such as brainstorming (which tends to yield ideas in an unstructured way), in employing a methodology for inventing new, and refining old, systems. TRIZ is an automatable method, which, using laws of the physical world, attempts to solve problems posed in structured ways. Perhaps more suited to product design and simple functionalities, TRIZ may be applicable to subsystems of the built environment, and to construction processes.

Quality function deployment (QFD, house of quality)

QFD was developed by Japanese industry to allow comparison of the effectiveness of design solutions in meeting specification requirements. A novel feature is that it also shows the positive and negative interactions of potential solutions, thereby facilitating design trade-offs (Shillito, 1994). A further refinement allows mapping competitor solutions onto the same specification set, providing a point-by-point comparison. Although currently not widely used in built environment professional services, QFD offers significant potential advantages in this field when several solutions are available to satisfy a specification.

Partnerships

Partnerships are an effective way of enhancing the culture and practice of innovation. These can be hierarchical, as in a supply chain where collaboration is between suppliers and consumers (hence is inherently non-competitive and serves a common end-product or service), or peer-to-peer, where firms collaborate at a pre-competitive level. The latter is potentially very powerful in achieving rapid market and capability development, but also requires a maturity of approach in managing the relationships between partners. Peer companies are often very sensitive to leakage of IP or their client base, so peer-to-peer innovation agreements are likely to be more successful if established early in the development cycle, for example at the stages of basic or early integrative research. Partnerships can take several forms – see Table 12.2.

Delivery of the participants' output can take place concurrently (in parallel) or they may have interdependencies, in which case activities may need to take place in series.

Table 12.2 Types of innovation partnership

Type	Participants	Outcomes	Delivery
Supply chain	Suppliers and customers	Improved processes, cost reduction	Parallel
University	Knowledge provider	New product concepts, improved processes	Usually serial
Funding agency	Funding provider	Collaborative research with universities	Enabling
Peer	Company in same market space	Enabling methods and technologies, market creation/education	Parallel
Network	Mix of above	Multiple benefits, relationship-forming	Usually serial

Many of the above partnership types attract government funding under various interventions in the UK, Europe and the rest of the world. In the UK, the Technology Strategy Board plays a key role in promoting most of these types of partnership. Similarly, substantial funding is available from the European Union under framework programmes and public-private partnerships. Where delivery is parallel (i.e. the collaborators work on concurrent threads of activity, and combine the outcomes) there is considerable potential for reducing time to market of developed concepts.

Culture

Creating a culture of innovation is a subtle issue with few basic guidelines. At minimum, senior practice management must strongly support the desire to create that culture and the opportunities for innovation. There is a cost associated with supporting the culture, as staff need time to think, with pressure removed, to facilitate the creative process. Case studies (3M and Google) have indicated the requirement for 15–20% uncommitted time for personally championed projects. Associated with time cost is the cash cost of consumables, capital kit and external services, but this may not be demanding for most professional services. Market requirements and consultation can be used to select ideas. It is helpful to establish a ring-fenced budget for innovation.

A company's expectation to innovate may be strongly influenced by past performance and market expectation (e.g. Arup); this can drive an allocation of internal research and innovation funding, perhaps part-nered with research councils. Staff rewards are often cited as a way to stimulate innovation, but simple financial benefits have been shown to be less effective than reputational growth and the formation of a posi-tively competitive peer group of innovators. For example, BOC Edwards created an 'Inventors Club' by awarding all inventors a small fixed cash sum on the filing of a patent, following this up with a corporate dinner invitation and the presentation of a plaque if and when the patent was granted. It should be noted that in some jurisdictions, profit-linked rewards are mandatory (e.g. Japan and Germany). In these cases any reward scheme must factor in potential long-term payments to staff innovators.

An innovation support team (IST) can strongly influence the positive outcomes of investment in R&D. A typical IST, as deployed by Arup, will be 'lean' and comprise a few full-time staff, typically an innovation expert and an IP manager plus an administrator. The last can usefully be a trainee patent agent. A steering committee reporting to the management board with membership representing marketing, legal and research communities can provide tight focus, underpinning innovation and its exploitation. The business of the IST will typically be to encourage, identify and sift ideas coming from the company, prioritising and putting them forward for funding. Officers of the committee may advise inventors, helping them articulate their ideas and prepare patent applications. The IST may also have the important role of selecting routes for exploitation, identification of external partners and key clients.

Example innovations from professional practice

The Blade of Light

Opened in 1999, the Blade of Light a.k.a. the 'wobbly bridge' is a footbridge over the Thames, situated in the City of London. Designed to maximise the impression of lightness and elegance, it was the project engineered by Arup. One of the consequences of the initial design was good vertical, but relatively low lateral stiffness. This gave rise to a disconcerting sideways sway, particularly when footfalls fell into synchronism.

An urgent need to fix the problem led the Arup team to engage in high-intensity problem analysis and innovation, rapidly identifying the issues and evolving a distributed passive damping system based on visco-elastic elements attached to an outer frame. Having solved the problem, it was quickly recognised that this type of distributed damping solution could be very effectively applied to other types of structure, and the technique was soon deployed in the design of very tall buildings, to counter sway effects due to wind and seismic disturbances. When distributed dampers are used this way, towers can be made thinner and lighter, using less material. They can therefore be more efficient in terms of embodied energy. The client benefits are clear: the design can be slimmer and more elegant and there can be significantly lower building costs. A business model based on licensing dampers was evolved and put into practice by the IST, to return value to Arup.

Watercube

For the Watercube, which was designed by architects PTW for the 2008 Beijing Olympics, the architects sought to capture the essence of a three-dimensional foam in its structure. A semi-regular array of interconnected structural cells provides the structural integrity of the rectangular prismatic building, and it also offers interesting functional and aesthetic properties. Innovation was demonstrated in the use of design tools for aesthetics, closely coupled with analytical tools for structural performance modelling. This gave great flexibility with added benefits of high confidence in the workability and engineering margins associated with the design. The lead designer, Tristram Carfrae, won the 2009 Royal Academy of Engineering MacRobert award for the design and modelling work.

Thames Gateway Institute for Sustainability

A charity and a company limited by guarantee, the Institute of Sustainability (IfS) was formed as a result of UCL, Imperial College and Southampton University eco-city study collaborations with Tongji University, Shanghai. This began with focus on learning outcomes from the development of an eco-city on Chongming Island, at the mouth of the Yangtze estuary. Arup facilitated and contributed to the collaboration. Innovation was demonstrated through partnering and convergence of thinking. The UK's Engineering and Physical Sciences Research Council funded initial workshops and the formation of an academic network to identify a research agenda and support network activity. This led to close collaboration with Chinese funding agencies (MOST, CAUPD and STCSM) and local support for Tongji's collaboration.

A pair of twinned collaborative research centres was envisaged and initiated in Shanghai and in the Thames Gateway, London. In the UK, shared vision led to a convergence of activity on institutes for sustainability by the South East of England Regional Development Agency and the London Thames Gateway Development Corporation. The resulting company, which is limited by guarantee and registered as a charity, promotes close-to-market integrative research, development, demonstration and deployment, with concurrent research activities shared by industrial and academic partners. The outcomes will be to accelerate the adoption of sustainable systems, components and materials for the built environment.

Conclusion

Innovation is a vital element, which can strongly contribute to the success of professional practices. In the built environment sector, where innovation is less typical of corporate cultures, professional practices serving the sector can have a transformational and disproportionate impact on business fortunes.

The delivery of impact from innovation requires the need for culture change, the provision of catalysts for innovation – tools and staff time, and perhaps most significantly, strong support for new thinking and practices from senior management.

References

Abreu, M., Grinevich, V., Hughes, A., Kitson, M. and Ternouth, P. (2008) *Universities, Business and Knowledge Exchange*, Council for Industry and Higher Education, and Centre for Business Research.

Dodgson, M., Gann, D. and Salter, A. (2008) *The Management of Technological Innovation*, Oxford University Press, Oxford.

IfM: http://www.ifm.eng.cam.ac.uk/ctm/trm/resources.html

Innocentive (2009): http://www.innocentive.com/

Knowledge Transfer Partnerships (2009): http://www.innovateuk.org/deliver-inginnovation/knowledgetransferpartnerships.ashx

SEMI Association (1970) http://www.semi.org/en/About/.

Shillito, L. M. (1994) *Advanced QFD; linking technology to market and company needs*, John Wiley & Sons, Chichester.

UK IPO (2009): http://www.ipo.gov.uk/

Yet2.com (2009): http://www.yet2.com/app/about/home

Postscript Comment to *Innovation in the construction sector* by Jeremy Watson

Antti Ainamo

The most creative and innovative architects prefer to work with the most innovative construction engineers. Ove Arup was a pioneer of this breed of engineers. The firm still carrying his name is one of the leading global design engineering firms in the area of the built environment. Knowledge about processes of organising innovation in this firm is of obvious interest to those interested in innovation in the built environment. Below, I provide information on why and how Jeremy Watson's account of the Arup way of organising adds to research knowledge about innovation streams in the built environment.

Design research has begun to specify how world-class architects and engineers can be a model for other innovators in the built environment; historical research has uncovered why innovation is made difficult in the built environment, despite such creative professionals as engineers and architects. Today, it is largely construction engineers who decide how to develop and implement the conceptual design of architects. In just about any country, construction engineers now generally have more influence than architects in deciding how to choose between any local optima (Guillén, 2006). This has always not been the case.

During the first half of the last century, architects were the most influential specialists in determining the shape of the built environment (Guillén, 1997). Many architects such as Peter Behrens in Germany at the beginning of the 20th century became celebrities on their own right, influencing the mental models of subsequent designers and inhabitants of the built environment (Buddensieg, 1984). The growth in the volume of work in the built environment and the rise in its economic value towards the end of the 20th century contributed to the rise of construction engineers as the 'master builders' for technologies to realise designs on constructions sites. With requirements for technical efficiency and economic effectiveness, engineers have since been in a strong role vis-à-vis architects. Within this context, innovation tends to remain a scarce resource in the built environment of the 21st century. The signature practices of architects tend to place most emphasis upon the creative rather than the technical dimensions of their solutions. Engineers are educated and trained to analyse and to optimise, using established relationships with many signature architects, and using impersonalised information and communication technologies (ICT) to standardise interaction and to increase efficiency. Most engineers and architects have to subordinate their priorities to deliver service to clients, whose main value proposition is one of volume and efficiency. Such propositions constrain technical innovation (Simon, 1996).

A small group of architects and engineers represents a pocket of innovation in the built environment, however (see also Chapter 2 by Graham Winch; cf. Chapter 9 by Stephen Pryke). These practices are successful in securing resources to focus on overcoming aesthetic and technical challenges and to creative freedom (Jones and Lichenstein, 2002). Research on the architect Frank Gehry and his studio has specified how such an architect can be a bridge across a diverse set of stakeholders (Boland and Collopy, 2004; Weick, 2003; Boland *et al.*, 2007). The consistent finding across these studies is that, over time, Gehry has developed expertise and accumulated significant competence in how to challenge conventions and break new ground in terms of aesthetics. The takeaways from this research include guidelines as to how to dynamically balance free-flowing creativity and new technologies. Focusing on only one major project at a time Gehry has become an exemplar, the *primus inter pares*, or first among equals, of an innovator in the built environment. Gehry's team has channelled the new technologies into the built environment from other sectors of industry, such as the aircraft industry.

The same that applies to Gehry also applies to Ove Arup in the early days of the modern movement, putting in place the values and practices that still guide Arup as an engineering and multidisciplinary professional practice. Arup remains a pre-eminent practice in this regard, serving a significant yet small segment of the market as a whole.

What is new in the studies of Gehry's work is the idea that his innovative methods can be emulated, even successfully mimicked, by other professionals in the built environment. Indeed, many researchers and professionals in the built environment have embarked on the innovation journey in the model of Gehry. Even if locality may never be fully abandoned, the new vision is one of a built environment that is increasingly global in nature (Boland *et al.*, 2007). They apply competencies from their practice to structures around the world. Design engineers such as Arup are a subgroup of engineers that developed competences to break away from the 'decision attitude' (Boland and Collopy, 2004) that traditionally had dominated the mindset of many engineers, their management and clients. Personal, intense face-to-face interactions remain essential in the process of creative and innovative design engineering, whereas these have been in retreat amongst many construction engineers, working closely with architects and their clients. The lesson of Gehry may be applicable to engineers, which could improve innovation management if applied more widely.

The advantage of a 'design attitude' (Boland and Collopy, 2004) in engineering is that this can facilitate in the translation of innovative ideas of architects so that architects can afford to successfully develop these ideas further, and from which engineers can further develop their innovative ideas (Salter and Gann, 2003). Design engineers can bridge fundamentally different kinds of worldview that exist among professionals in the built environment: some professionals are more analytic than others, while others tend to be more synthetic. Such bridging is necessary, for example, to diffuse innovative engineering into projects that are otherwise less challenging in design terms. Arup has spanned a range of client requirements and worldviews in its workload. The management challenge at Arup is to ensure that knowledge diffusion occurs across its projects and organisation.

The value of design by engineers is more than technical competence and experience. Besides these individual and team-level competencies, organisational competencies also matter (Leonard-Barton, 1992). Development of organisational competence can benefit from hiring specialists educated or trained in design engineering, learning from experience, and developing process knowledge (Ainamo, 2005). Competencies from experience and process knowledge need to be captured in the organisation. This is part of organisational management and poses a challenge to all practices, including Arup, who have been at the industry forefront of developing knowledge management competencies for example.

In sum, Jeremy Watson's chapter describes how good design engineers in a firm such as Arup can facilitate innovation internally and in others, such as world-class architects, giving them the means to create concepts that are more radical than in the past and sometimes more radical than needed from a pure technical or functional viewpoint; that the innovators can flow with the ideas of their predecessors, the heritage from the past and the visions of the future. Good design engineers respect and facilitate the work of other professionals, some of whom may be less innovative than they themselves are. A role of a design engineering firm such as Arup is akin to that of a mid-wife, facilitating the delivery of the new born safely and soundly into the built environment. Yet, its role is also to be that of a broker of innovations; it is both a match-maker and partner.

References to Postscript Comment

Ainamo, A. (2005). Coevolution of knowledge management processes: Drawing on project experience in a global engineering consulting firm, *Research in Management Consulting*, 5, 107–129.

Boland, B. J., Lyytinen, K. and Yoo, Y. (2007) Wakes of innovation in project networks: The case of digital 3-D representations in architecture, engineering, and construction, *Organization Science*, 18(4), 631–647.

Boland, R. G. and Collopy, F. (2004), *Managing as Designing*. Stanford University Press, Stanford.

Buddensieg, T. (1984) *Industriekultur: Peter Behrens and the AEG*, translated by Iain Boyd Whyte, MIT Press, Cambridge.

Guillén, M. (2006) *The Taylorized Beauty of the Mechanical: Scientific Management and the Rise of Modernist Architecture*, Princeton University Press, Princeton.

Guillén, M. (1997) Scientific management's lost aesthetic: Architecture, organization, and the Taylorized beauty of the mechanical, *Administrative Science Quarterly*, 42, 682–715.

Jones, J. and Lichenstein, B. (2002). Architecture of careers: How career competencies reveal firm dominant logic in professional services, In: *Career Creativity: explorations in the remaking of work*, Peiperl, M., Arthur, M., Goffee, R. and Morris, T. (eds.), Oxford University Press, Oxford, pp. 153–176.

Leonard-Barton, D. (1992) Core capabilities and core rigidities: A paradox in managing new product development, *Strategic Management Journal*, 13, 111–125.

Salter, A. and Gann, D. (2003) Sources of ideas for innovation in engineering design, *Research Policy*, 32(8), 1309–1324.

Simon, H. (1996). *The Sciences of the Artificial*, 3rd edition, MIT Press, Cambridge.

Weick, K. (2003) Organizational design and the Gehry experience, *Journal of Management Inquiry*, 12, 93–97.

13 Managing a project management division

Andrew McSmythurs

Introduction

At every level, whether managing your own personal finances or those of a multinational plc, information is essential. Whether this is a simple bank statement with credit card slips, salary notifications or the full range of management information from all areas of a business, such information must be both timely and accurate. It is more complex than simply having more money coming in than money going out. For example, work is carried out in month one, then payment for that work may be received 30–90 days later. Combine that with salaries being paid monthly and other creditors expecting their payment at different times – the management of cashflow, debtors and creditors – and it can be seen there are many aspects to be managed. The multiple resources needed to carry out multiple tasks, and their costs, all need to be measured accurately and regularly. In a competitive environment the need is to measure efficiency and profitability, to identify trends and look at means of providing continuous improvement, using management information systems as an essential tool.

To manage we need to set goals, directing and communicating to our teams the means of achieving those goals, measure performance and reassess against our original targets. What this chapter describes therefore is a constantly evolving methodology, which has been born out of a combination of key commercially available management tools and bespoke supplements, which provide the detail to match generic systems to the particular business model of Cyril Sweett and the project management activity within the overall business.

Fundamentally, management information provides us with a means of translating strategy into action.

Managing the Professional Practice: in the built environment, First Edition. Edited by Hedley Smyth.
© 2011 by Blackwell Publishing Ltd. Published 2011 by Blackwell Publishing Ltd.

The Cyril Sweett business model

To understand the 'why' as well as the 'how' and 'what' is measured it is first necessary to understand the nature of the organisation being measured. Cyril Sweett is a multidisciplined international construction and property consultancy. It employs approximately 750 staff in 29 offices throughout the UK with over 60% of employees being shareholders. With a minority stock market flotation on the Alternative Investment Market in October 2007, the business had a capitalisation of £57.2 million with forecast sales of over £70m for 2008. It has four key areas of service: cost consultancy, project management, specialist services and management consultancy.

Cyril Sweett is a professional services organisation, its product being the provision of the intellectual knowledge and the skills of its staff. The matrices measured and the targets reflect the principles involved. This chapter will concentrate on the reports and management information systems that inform Cyril Sweett, and in particular those generated by the London and South East division.

The management reports are based on detailed information produced at work level, in this case the project management unit providing the detailed focus, and then cascaded through business units into operations units, then regional divisions to the executive board. The situation is further complicated when work-streams carried out by individual units can involve input from other units both within and across regions. This reinforces the need for accurate and timely information, as well as its gathering and reporting being on a consistent basis.

Within Cyril Sweett each business unit has direct profit and loss responsibility for its activities, accountable directly to the main board for its performance. Understanding performance, costs and income incurred by its own unit and other supporting units in multi-functional tasks is critical too, since each business leader manages their units by setting and monitoring targets and related necessary actions.

What do we measure?

The starting point for any model is the business plan. The business plan identifies and defines the services and/or products with short-, medium- and long-term goals and targets for each of these within overall forecast growth and market conditions. Resource levels are assessed. To support this, any good business management toolkit provides consistent information needed by the reviewer, when required. That information should also enable consideration of where a business is, and comparisons between where it was planned to be.

In month one, each individual business unit leader will prepare a first draft of the short-term, that is, one-year and three-year rolling review of their business area. This will include:

- a review of the sector within which they operate;
- existing clients and potential for increasing workload;
- existing commissions;
- potential future income from identified opportunities that have yet to be secured;
- income to find from sources yet unidentified;
- resources necessary to deliver the services;
- risks and opportunities associated with their sector.

This paper is released to the operational unit directors for consolidation into a regional model during month two. During month two the various regional models will be consolidated and rolled up into a UK model for review at UK board level during month three. Once approved, and subject to any amendments and/or changes to targets that the main board wish to require of the business unit leaders, this information is then transferred into a budget sheet which sets out all the key financial criteria that form the basis of the year's budget.

Tools available

The choice of tools available will largely depend upon the nature of the business, its size and company structure. Cyril Sweett has elected to follow a balanced scorecard approach, which provides a flexibility of information, whilst allowing it to address and match reports to service-based issues. The balanced scorecard was developed in Harvard in the late 1990s, and has since become established as an internationally renowned structure against which data can be collated, sorted and reported. More particularly, this approach allows an organisation to be more dispassionate concerning subjective issues, and provides a means for measurement of hard and soft data, including performance, cost, service levels and client attitudes, on a consistent basis throughout the business. This provides a comprehensive snapshot to those from whom decisions are required, and factual detail for those whose job it is to run the individual business, measuring their performance against targets.

The balanced scorecard forms the core of all management communication, communicating information up and down the management

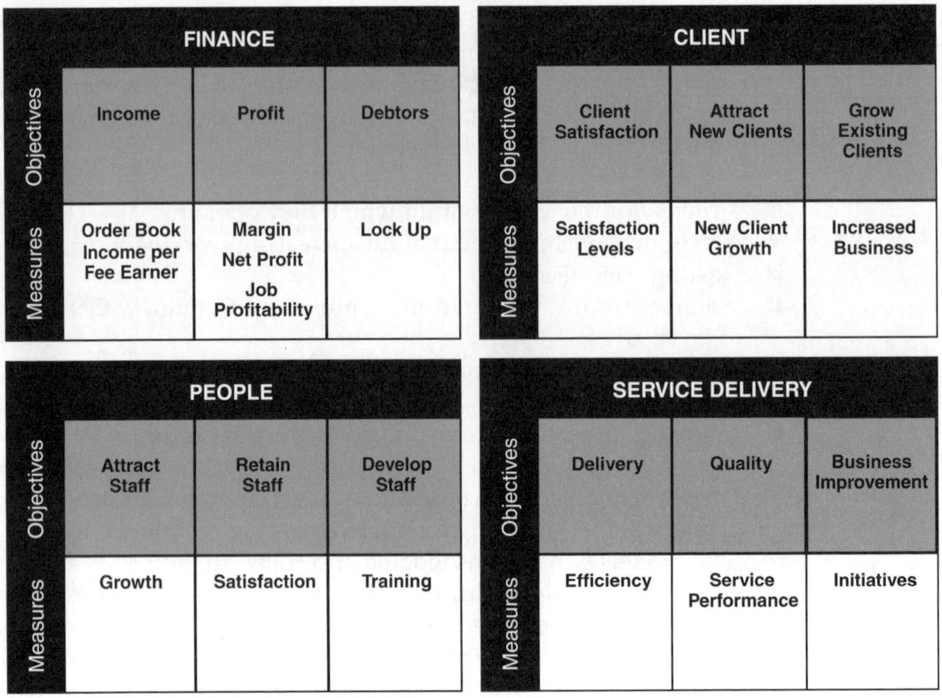

FINANCE			
Objectives	Income	Profit	Debtors
Measures	Order Book Income per Fee Earner	Margin Net Profit Job Profitability	Lock Up

CLIENT			
Objectives	Client Satisfaction	Attract New Clients	Grow Existing Clients
Measures	Satisfaction Levels	New Client Growth	Increased Business

PEOPLE			
Objectives	Attract Staff	Retain Staff	Develop Staff
Measures	Growth	Satisfaction	Training

SERVICE DELIVERY			
Objectives	Delivery	Quality	Business Improvement
Measures	Efficiency	Service Performance	Initiatives

Figure 13.1 Structure of the balanced scorecard

ladder. The reports highlight success, and identify areas of concern with recommended courses of action. The reporting level starts at business unit level. Typically this is a group of 8–10 professionals led by a director or business unit leader who then reports to an operations director through to the UK board. The balanced scorecard addresses four core elements and provides a holistic overview of the business: finance, people, client and service delivery – see Figure 13.1.

Each of the four core elements is supported by various separate reports collated from a range of applications and activities. For the balanced scorecard to be successful, we established several objectives and measures relevant to our particular business of professional services:

- For each objective there is a measure against which progress can be measured.
- To focus attention and effort only key areas are addressed.
- For each measure a specific target is given – if not achieved then remedial action or review is put in place.
- The measures reflect those items that require to be continuously monitored and managed.
- Consistency is provided through all levels of management.

Management information systems

It is the information systems that provide the raw data that underpins the quality of the balanced scorecard management process. The reports require people to take ownership of quality, timeliness and consistency of the data. Everyone is involved, from the completion of weekly timesheets whereby staff allocate time to individual projects, through evaluating team performance to departmental performance – in this case project management – to collating the data for the business as a whole. IT systems help, though over-reliance on such systems is to be avoided. Software inter-relationships are often difficult to analyse, and human interpretation and interrogation provide the common-sense assessment. In some areas issues are offering the opportunity to cross-check data, as well as challenge the accuracy of different sets of information.

A typical monthly report is shown in Figure 13.2.

People

For Cyril Sweett and other similar professional service-based organisa-tions people are their most valuable resource; there is no specific product other than the sale of our intellectual and professional skills. In produc-ing the balanced scorecard reports for the people category, we look at the following matrices:

- *What people are doing* – we collate information on everyone's activities through time sheets that identify in half-hour increments every activity during the week against a series of individual projects or other tasks such as marketing, business development, financial reporting and administration. In addition to retrospectively looking at what people have undertaken, we also match this information with future projections on resource planning. This ties in with other elements of the scorecard report when we look at future levels of business activity and the level of resource needed to provide that activity level.
- *Allocation* – correctly identifying individual staff to work on spe-cific projects is equally critical. We need to identify both available resource, and those with the appropriate skills and experience. In addressing this aspect we maintain a skills database for all typical staff in the business. It identifies professional qualifications, service delivery skills against discipline (such as project management, cost management) and the extent of experience in a range of individual sectors. In addition, and linked to a resource plan, we anticipate which projects will demand which particular skills and individuals, and, where possible, provisionally 'reserve' staff against projects.

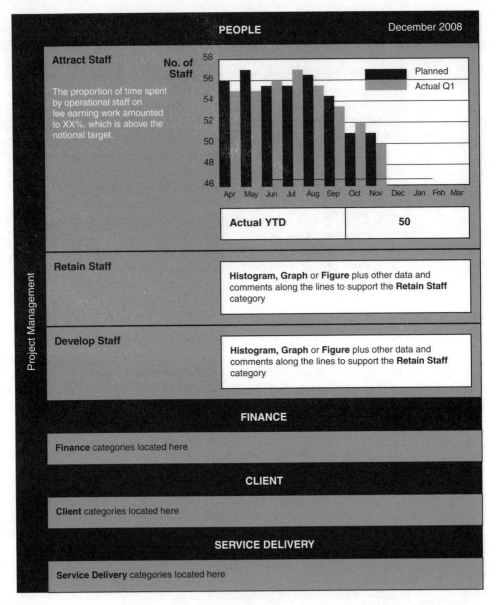

Figure 13.2 Indicative reporting format used in Cyril Sweett

- *Training* – ensuring that our staff are properly trained and fully abreast of the latest developments is a business-critical issue, and we look to identify training programmes we can offer throughout the business, and matching these against individual requirements. This is largely undertaken through individual appraisal process.
- *Career progression* – it has been Cyril Sweett's policy to develop and promote from within its business all grades of staff, but this

can only provide part of our resource pool, and we look here to measure the numbers of leavers and joiners in any one reporting period or 'churn'. New thinking brought by new staff is important, but too high a 'churn' rate can be indicative of a more fundamental dissatisfaction.

- *Appraisals* – all staff have their performance reviewed on a regular basis, such performance being measured against past targets for personal and professional growth as well as service delivery, and it also provides opportunity to set future goals.

Finance

Whilst people are the most critical aspect of our business provision, making a profit is the core reason to be in business. In formative years we have measured our financial performance based upon income and outgoings on relatively simplistic spreadsheets, managed on an individual discipline basis but not linked in any way other than through a manual reporting package. Clearly, this is inadequate for a business of our size and growth potential, and we have established a range of software systems that allow us to individually control specific tasks, whilst providing the real management data to populate the scorecard reports. Care has been taken to balance IT-generated reports with human input and checking.

An IT-based internal system referred to as an MIS (management information system) forms the core of our project-based financial control system. Each project is given a unique identifying number, and for each such project the MIS compares costs with income based upon:

- time;
- disbursements;
- sub-consultants;
- fee transfers.

Figure 13.3 sets out a typical MIS front sheet, and Figure 13.4 shows the data input sheet identifying and comparing projected costs and income against actual costs and income.

For each project, a project leader is identified who has the responsibility for populating the MIS for that project, identifying firm or projected income, and the resources necessary for effective delivery. It is that project leader's responsibility to maintain and update the MIS on a monthly basis, reviewing and where necessary amending the projections. On this basis, we are able, at a project level, to manage individual task profitability. The MIS can provide reports on profitability levels across all projects, together with detailed time analysis of the man-effort required to deliver the service, which can support and inform the

Details for Project no. XXXX									
Job Name:	YYYY		Start Date:		01/08/2004	Finish Date:	23/05/2010	Status:	Firm
Director:	Andrew McSmythurs		Leader:	Richards, Scott				Client:	ZZZZ plc
Sector:	Residential		Region:	PM-GIR-Transport				Country:	UK
BCIS Region:	Greater London		Work-in-Progress:		0				

Comment:	Provision of intrasfrtucture for new green field residential development
Notes:	Budget uplifted from spreadsheet Projected Revenue: £100k, Constuction Cost: £7m

Forecast Fee:	223,500.00		Forecast Cost:	71,054.16		Forecast Factor:	-4.1

Department	Time	%	Cost	%	Fees	%	Costs	Amount
PM-GIR	443	23.98	16161.85	22.75	-3800	-1.7	Disbursements	4934.84
PM-GIR-Commercial	135.5	7.34	4234.08	5.96	-64260	-28.75	Time Costs	71054.16
PM-GIR-Education	332.5	18	18994.73	26.73	-43210	-19.33	Total Costs	75989
PM-GIR-H&S	135.5	7.34	3963.62	5.58	0	0	Net Shares	-100970
PM-GIR-Health	219.5	11.88	7340.08	10.33	0	0	Factor	1.61
PM-GIR-PFI/PPP	156	8.45	5834.68	8.21	0	0		
PM-GIR-Transport	43	2.33	2580	3.63	218500	97.76	Master and Sub-Projects	
PM-LCM-Central H&S	4.5	0.24	155.25	0.22	0	0	Master Project	0
QS-CAM	7.5	0.41	277.03	0.39	0	0	Sub-Project 1	0
QS-GIR	47	2.54	1664.58	2.34	-1477.46	-0.66	Sub-Project 2	0
QS-GIR-Commercial	77.5	4.2	2538.07	3.57	5000	2.24	Sub-Project 3	0
QS-GIR-Transport	2	0.11	134.78	0.19	0	0	Sub-Project 4	0
QS-NOR	243.5	13.18	7175.52	10.1	8277.46	3.7		
Total	1847		71054.27		119030			

Staff and Date Last Worked:	Andrew McSmythurs		17/11/2008	Invoice Date	Fee No.	Amount
				19/01/2009	Net Shares	-104470

Figure 13.3 Indicative project details sheet for Cyril Sweett

people-report element of the scorecard, and this starts to generate profitability measurements for that particular operational unit, in this case project management. Income is raised through invoicing, and again using the MIS, the value of monthly invoicing can be identified and future cashflows established. Debtors can be tracked and 'lock up' figures established, 'lock up' being a factor calculated by the product of accounts outstanding and the period, in days, that payment is overdue. Through the MIS we are also able to identify work-in-progress fees in allowance (WIP/FIA), which allows us to identify the impact that

Budget Entry Details								
Job Name:	YYYY		Start Date:		01/07/2004	Finish Date:	01/07/2010	
Director:	Andrew McSmythurs							
Probability percent:	50							
Note:	Fees £112,500 PM; £7,500 PS							

	Firm Fees	Total Cost	Factor	Time £	Expenses	S-Cons	Fee Share Out
Forecast Outcome	223,500	176,959	1.61	71,054	4,934	0	100,970
Total Installments	223,500	176,959	-	71,054	4,934	0	100,970
Actuals to 31/12/08	223,500	176,959	1.61	71,054	4,934	0	100,970

				Date				
Actual	Month 1-8	Month 9	Month 10	Month 11	Month 12	Month 13	Month ...n
Fees	21,000	10,000	7,000	7,000	7,000	9,000	xxx
Time £	14,434	1,995	1,371	1,476	1,207	1,558	xxx
Expenses	384	23	40	0	43	42	xxx
S-Cons	0	0	0	0	0	0	xxx
Net Fee Share	0	0	0	0	0	0	xxx

Forecast							
Firm Fees	0	0	0	0	7,000	9,000	xxx
Probale Fees	0	0	0	12,000	0	0	xxx
Total Costs	0	0	0	0	3,000	6,000	xxx
Time £	0	0	0	0	3,000	6,000	xxx
Expenses	0	0	0	0	0	0	xxx
S-Cons	0	0	0	0	0	0	xxx
Fee Share Out	0	0	0	0	0	0	xxx
Notes	abc						

Figure 13.4 Indicative budget entry details sheet for Cyril Sweett

unbilled works have on monthly accounts. The future order book is split into two elements: 'probables', which we define as potential schemes with the estimated percentage of secured income that have got at least to the fee bid stage; and potential work that is more speculative or earlier in the business development pipeline.

At this level – that is, operational delivery – all information is project based; the fixed costs and overheads are not reported. Consistent with core principles of the balanced scorecard, only that which can be controlled and changed is reported at that particular level; fixed costs such as accommodation, bank charges and other direct overheads, which can only be influenced in the medium- to long-term by the main executive are excluded at this level.

Client

Clients or customers provide the business with the opportunity to survive and grow. Once the business development pipeline converts targets and prospects into bid opportunities, keeping clients is important for fees, repeat business and market reputation. We measure client perceptions under this element of the scorecard. We identify and measure client satisfaction, identifying any remedial actions and opportunities for adding service value along the following lines:

- *Client satisfaction reports on service* – against a standard set of questions, clients are regularly asked to provide their views on the overall service delivery provided by the business. Such reports can be anonymous if required, and are not usually meant to identify the shortcomings of one individual but rather the overall service provided.
- *Key account management* – within our business we have identified that over 60% of our business comes from less than 10% of our clients, measured numerically. For these few, yet business critical, clients, we have established a key account management process, from which we are able to directly measure the views and levels of activity of our key clients.
- *New clients secured* – for the business to grow, it must both maintain existing levels of operation and grow beyond those on this matrix, identified from the MIS, which allows us to review the number of new clients secured in a reporting period.
- *Repeat business* – securing new and future commissions from existing clients is important, and we measure two aspects here: maintaining the existing level of business and discipline services provided, whilst looking to broaden the level of support provided to individual clients into other business discipline areas, that is cross-referrals.

Service delivery

There is a direct link between client satisfaction and service delivery. Under this heading we specifically limit our reports to the provision of technical service content rather than measuring dimensions such as client activity and new commissions. Coverage includes the following:

- *Client satisfaction reports on technical and professional content* – a different dimension or level or satisfaction with our overall service. From such measurement we continually identify opportunities for improvement.
- *Efficiency* – under this heading – which is linked with people and costs – we look to measure utilisation of all technical members of staff, that is, the percentage of productive time spent during any reporting period. This information comes from time sheets measured under the MIS and is another example of where specific measurements cross between various headings of the scorecard.
- *Quality* – this comes from both internal QMS reports and audits and the client satisfaction reports providing a direct measure against a mathematical scale of satisfaction of the technical service that we provide.
- *QMS audits* – these are both internal and external measures and are undertaken both to maintain compliance for insurance and service delivery purposes, and also to ensure that we are providing the service that we were commissioned to do. Such audits cover all aspects of the service from the tracking of emails, and filing, through to whether there is a formal appointment in place and compliance with our own internal procedures and protocols.
- *Intranet* – this operates throughout the Cyril Sweett business, providing the opportunity to establish standard pro-forma, experience profiles, training sessions and guides. It is important to note that these are for guidance, and are not direct instructions.

Thoughts of a user – does it work?

The system appears to be generating accurate and consistent reports. This provides important information, which has to be evaluated, and informs decisions to improve business efficiency and to deliver our overall business planning targets.

It is a work in progress and will be refined and possibly developed. It is reliant upon everyone providing their input at the right time and accurately. It needs IT capacity across all elements and it needs those IT systems to be accurate although not necessarily individually integrated.

The balanced scorecard approach has given us the ability to provide consistent information to those responsible for taking business decisions, and that addresses all key aspects of our business at any one time. It also provides trends, and specifies weaknesses that we need to address in order to remain competitive in the marketplace.

Conclusion

The chapter has considered the way in which a division of a larger professional practice is managed, emphasising the information provided through a balanced scorecard approach. This management method is practice-wide and the division follows the method. Therefore, the method is part of the management strategy, and the information is used to implement other elements of our strategy for the firm and for the division. Good information is a prerequisite for good strategy implementation. The balanced scorecard approach provides the necessary information to monitor and control activities at a tactical level and to see where actions need to be taken to keep in line with the strategy, and where emergent trends may require some refinement of the strategy.

Whilst the balanced scorecard has a common approach in business, in Cyril Sweett the approach is central to management, whereas in many businesses it is a supplementary tool. The way in which it is implemented is unique in shape and in organisational context. The general lesson is that every large professional practice should benefit from having a comprehensive information system to aid management. Growing practices should consider what their requirements will be as they prepare for the next step-change in growth.

Postscript Comment to *Managing a project management division* by Andrew McSmythurs

Stephen Pryke

The chapter explores the application of the balanced scorecard. Andrew McSmythurs does so through an in-depth analysis of one professional practice that uses it more extensively for management purposes than many. This commentary attempts to provide a theoretical classification of the chapter and identifies some issues from published sources that might complement the case study. The aim is to guide the reader towards developing practice management in their context rather than particularly commenting on the firm in question.

McSmythurs started by emphasising the importance of information in financial management, in particular its timeliness and accuracy. The importance of the management of the firm's efficiency and profitability is stressed alongside the need to look at trends and continuous improvement in service provision. These management functions are accessed through a management information system. Management in the context of the professional service provider is defined as goal-setting and performance measurement, directing and communicating. There is recognition that this is a knowledge-based business, which firms can develop in explicit forms with links to knowledge management systems or can place reliance upon tacit knowledge exchange rather than an explicit system. This business is structured into business units and 60% of staff are shareholders. The chapter emphasises the link between the business plan for each business unit and the management tools necessary to manage the business units. The balanced scorecard provides the focus for management monitoring and communication. Data is gathered weekly from all staff, which gives total hours worked against each project by each member of staff. This data is essential to provide an audit trail against client invoices which acts as solid guidance for any practice.

Observations on the system described

Freud maintains (Holmes, 1965) that work serves two psychic purposes – to provide an outlet for some of our most basic and aggressive needs and to 'bind men together'. Czander (1993) observes that most workers are employed in hierarchical organisations, and gratification follows from the ability to respond to instructions and to develop relationships with superiors. The business unit model described a hierarchical structure rather than the non-hierarchical network model favoured by some of the large management and accountancy practices. The management system outlined in the chapter has two main elements. First, there is an accounting system to provide the financial information to generate cashflow into the business and to monitor profitability, project by project. Second, there is a more complex and sophisticated balanced scorecard system that provides a link between the business strategy of Cyril Sweett and the management of the business units. The principles behind the balanced scorecard system (BSC) were first identified by Kaplan and Norton (1992) and are cited in Brandon (2004). The four main metrics – financial, internal business perspective, learning and growth; and finally, customer perspective (Brandon, 2004) – are reflected in the BSC used by Cyril Sweett – finance, service delivery, people and client, respectively and show scope for firms to adapt to their own management context.

Perhaps the bipartite system described has benefits to the practice in some other ways. The Hawthorne Studies conducted at the Western Electric Company Works in Illinois, USA involved experiments with groups of workers and variations in lighting levels (Robbins and Coulter, 2009). The counterintuitive results demonstrated the importance, in motivating higher output, of the perception by staff that management is monitoring worker activity. Management systems are like national defence – their very existence has positive effects. Also, is there a link to culture perhaps? Client organisational culture, project and supply chain culture, internal organisational culture, industry culture and national culture all impact upon each other and the behaviour of managers and their staff within an organisation (Fellows, 2009). To some extent the system described is a product of the practice's history and the various layers of culture within which the organisation is embedded. Firms take different approaches towards motivating staff, and the balanced scorecard offers one option only and may be one of several applied.

From Maslow's viewpoint individuals in the workplace are motivated by a hierarchy of five personal needs:

1. *Physiological needs* – food, drink, shelter, sex and other physical requirements.
2. *Safety needs* – security and protection from physical and emotional harm, as well as assurance that physical needs will continue to be met.
3. *Social needs* – affection, belongingness, acceptance and friendship.
4. *Esteem needs* – internal esteem factors, such as self-respect, autonomy and achievement, and external esteem factors, such as status, recognition and attention.
5. *Self-actualisation needs* – growth, achieving one's potential and self-fulfilment; the drive to become what one is capable of becoming (Robbins and Coulter, 2009:358).

The hierarchy is effectively presented in an inverted form, human beings' most basic needs being located at the top of the list. The skilled, experienced and highly educated staff required to offer a credible service to large, experienced clients in construction would not be motivated by physiological and safety needs because the absence of either is not a concern for the group generally. It follows that social, esteem and self-actualisation needs are important in motivating this group. The BSC approach adopted in the case study organisation provides the framework within which to monitor and celebrate such motivational needs, although this is clearly not the primary function of BSC yet firms can explore such linkage.

Is there anything not dealt with?

The following issues are offered as potential areas for consideration:

1. *Project and business strategy* – Project management as a function is *value creating* (Kaplan and Norton, 1996), not *asset based*, and the key to creating value for a client is through developing employee knowledge, identifying and maintaining the customer base and relationships with customers, and access to innovation (Brandon, 2004). The classic model of BSC envisages that learning and growth feed into the internal business perspective, which in turn flows down into the customer, resulting in financial benefits for the business. The BSC system in use in Cyril Sweett can be seen as an opportunity to learn more about the needs of the clients. The BSC was originally designed with a focus upon the business case for the *firm* as its focus. For it to be effective for a project management service provider, surely the BSC system needs to feed on the strategic needs of the *client's* business as a next step in development, which this firm and others may seek to explore?

2. *Leadership* – the widely accepted four main areas of management are planning, organising, leading and control (Robbins and Coulter, 2009). The system that forms the basis of this case study does not immediately highlight the role of leadership. It is possible that this is the subject of a separate series of activities outside the remit of the chapter: perhaps the regular use of 'away days' and a number of symbolic gestures, perhaps celebrating the examples of excellence and success. Once again, the balanced scorecard offers linkage to other management issues as well as valuable information for management.

3. *Design management* – if Rimmer (2009) is correct and cost is directly related to design, and to the management of design, dealing with financial management without recourse to the use of independent design management may be a further avenue for firms to examine. Collaboration with the designer and the function of design management in the activities of Cyril Sweett broadens the consultancy remit and moves towards management consultancy in the built environment domain.

4. *Core competencies for creating value for clients* – the identification, management and maintenance of the customer base is clearly given a high priority in Cyril Sweett, and these activities are identified and presumably appropriately rewarded within the framework under review. But employee knowledge and access to innovation are not quite so explicitly covered. This may be because many professional bodies (RICS, for example) require their members to

undertake a prescribed number of hours of continuing professional development study, as part of the condition of membership.

5. *Innovation* – this is the subject of other chapters (9 and 12). Of all the disciplines serving the construction industry, the ex-QS professional service providers have been most active in discovering new services to offer their clients (product innovation). One wonders how product innovation is dealt with within the system outlined.

6. *Value management of professional services* – QS practices have diversified very effectively and now provide project, risk, value and, most recently, supply chain management alongside the original independent financial management role. In the face of some very tough negotiation by clients, many professional service providers have been prompted to apply a value management approach to their own professional service provision. What function is performed by each of the activities that comprise the service provided to the client?

I have speculated about some of the perhaps unintended consequences (or undeclared benefits) of Cyril Sweett's bipartite system described in the case study – Freud's (Holmes, 1965) binding together of people; the motivational effects identified in the Hawthorne Studies (Robbins and Coulter, 2009); and the relationship of the system with Maslow's hierarchy of needs (Robbins and Coulter, 2009). I then turned my attention to analysis of the potential gaps between the case study and issues suggested by published theory. For most consultants innovation proceeds along complex paths at and between organisational levels and information can facilitate and steer this. I looked at the creation of value and its relationship with the clients' overall business strategies; the importance of leadership within the practice; linking financial management with design management; managing knowledge and knowledge acquisition at the level of the individual, the project and the supply chain; and value management of the professional service provider's own services to clients. These points are raised to open up the discussion and promote debate in this interesting subject area.

References to Postscript Comment

Brandon, D. M. Jr. (2004) Project Performance Measurement, *The Wiley Guide to Managing Projects*, P.W.G. Morris and J. K. Pinto (eds.), John Wiley & Sons, New Jersey.

Czander, W. M. (1993) *The Psychodynamics of Work and Organisations: theory and application*, The Guilford Press, New York.

Fellows, R. (2009) Culture in Supply Chains, *Construction Supply Chain Management: concepts and case studies*, S. D. Pryke (ed.), Blackwell Publishing Ltd., Oxford.

Holmes, D. (1965) A contribution to the psychoanalytic theory for work, *Psychoanalytic Study of the Child*, 20, 384–391.

Kaplan, R. S. and Norton, D. P. (1992) The balanced scorecard: measures that drive performance, *Harvard Business Review*, 70(1), 71–79.

Kaplan, R. and Norton, D. (1996) *The Balanced Scorecard: translating strategy into action*, Harvard Business School Press, Cambridge, Mass.

Rimmer, B. (2009) Slough Estates in the 1990s – Client Driven SCM, *Construction Supply Chain Management: concepts and case studies*, S. D. Pryke (ed.), Blackwell Publishing Ltd., Oxford.

Robbins, S. P. and Coulter, M. (2009) 10th Edition, *Organizational Management*, Pearson Education Inc., New Jersey.

14 Developing capacity in an emergent market

Robert McIntosh

Introduction

This chapter discusses the establishment of a new division within a well-established company in what may be described as an emerging market. The objective is to highlight some of the different issues and objectives associated with such an enterprise.

Background

CB Richard Ellis describes itself as 'the world's premier, full-service real estate services company'. It has some 29,000 employees located in more than 300 offices in 50 countries providing a broad range of services including asset management, brokerage, consulting, finance, development and investment, facilities management, global corporate services, investment management, leasing, project management, research and valuation and advisory services. Many of these are broken down into specific sectors such as offices, retail, industrial and hotels. The focus of this chapter is on the hotel division in the Asia Pacific region.

The company has been well established in the region for many years and, by any standards, is a major real-estate company with an extensive network of personnel and offices (89 excluding affiliated offices in Asia Pacific), extensive contacts and a strong reputation, in addition to well developed systems. Like many real-estate firms it developed and was, historically, managed geographically. Intimate knowledge of specific locations was often the key to a successful business. This has been gradually changing, particularly over the past 20 years. In many firms, there has developed an increased focus on particular skills and knowledge that apply across geographical boundaries. This enables the

Managing the Professional Practice: in the built environment, First Edition. Edited by Hedley Smyth.
© 2011 by Blackwell Publishing Ltd. Published 2011 by Blackwell Publishing Ltd.

companies, and individual practitioners, to develop these attributes to levels that are impossible within narrowly defined regional and local markets. An essential element of a global or regional real-estate organisation is its ability to apply these competencies and capabilities and ensure that they are embedded in the business. This also reflects client requirements, where many investors and occupiers are now regional or global in their business needs. In addition, building types and industries have become more specialised, requiring increasingly detailed knowledge of the specific industry on the part of advisors.

This phenomenon is particularly the case in respect of hotels and the related leisure industries such as casinos, conference centres, pubs and theme parks. In response to this, a number of firms have either created specialist divisions or built their entire business around this sector. In the case of CB Richard Ellis there were well-established divisions in North America and Europe as well as in Australia and New Zealand. The broad objective was to establish a hotel focused business in Asia to complement that elsewhere and to help create a truly global business for the sector.

Initial issues

There were a wide range of matters to be investigated and understood before progressing and establishing the division within Asia. Some of the matters to be addressed included:

- understanding the market (or, in the case of Asia, numerous geographical markets, sources of demand, number and types of accommodation and the varied opportunities);
- the extent and nature of the competition;
- building relationships with the key stakeholders including the leaders of the other parts of the hotel division, the leaders of the relevant businesses in each geographic region and each complementary business, as well as management;
- obtaining information on the existing track record, clients, systems and relationships;
- obtaining from those in the industry, such as owners, operators, financiers and developers, an understanding of their needs and expectations.

At the time of commencing this task (early 2007) the business environment was extremely positive. In particular, the outlook in Asia was for extraordinary growth, and with it the rapid development of the hotel industry. However, even in very buoyant times, there were numerous challenges in relation to the market as a whole:

- Asia is not a homogenous market; each country has different characteristics whether they be language, religion, economic or socio-political structures.
- There was a real shortage of appropriately skilled personnel. Hotel advisory firms need those with a good understanding of both the hotel and real-estate industries. At the same time there was a rapid expansion in the number of hotels in the region with large numbers of developments taking place in locations which had a very limited previous exposure to the tourism industry. The personnel shortage problem extended to hotel operators, developers, builders, architects, financiers and competitors.
- Many markets were immature in terms of infrastructure. Ease of access is vital to tourism, and knowing when and if improvements are to be made to roads and airports is essential.
- There was, and is, a lack of information in relation to many locations. This is due largely to the immaturity of many markets. For example, there is a long history of tourism in cities such as Singapore, Hong Kong and Bangkok, and therefore detailed data is readily available – there are numerous existing reports on these markets. Newly developing locations such as second-tier cities in China or resorts in Cambodia present very different challenges.
- A lack of understanding of the benefits of professional advice is widespread in immature markets. Clients have more difficulty in seeing the value added by external consultants or of justifying the often substantially higher fees charged by specialists compared to locally based advisors.

It was necessary to understand both potential client requirements and the competitive environment before developing a business plan. Some features became apparent which indicated differences from more established markets and businesses. These included a lack of homogeneity between different markets: the range of potential clients tended to be less institutional in nature than in, say, North America and Europe, bankers were less directly involved in the business decision-making, and were relatively more focused on client relationships than the details of specific projects, and competitors were fewer numerically. The last point was one that required consideration in order to understand how and why other businesses had been successful and what unique attributes could be developed to not only differentiate the service offering but also perform better for clients – a goal which tends to lead to financial success.

Consideration of the competition showed that those who were most successful had a real focus on the tourism industry. There were numerous smaller, local, boutique operations. Many of these were successful and served well the niches in which they were positioned. However, a regional or global presence assisted in the establishment of a dominant market position. The key features of the successful real-estate businesses

included the marketing of the service as specialised and therefore superior, the use of skilled and specialised personnel, a long-established
reputation and a focus on a consulting business as a foundation for
other work.

There were the normal multitude of practical issues in starting a new
business in a new location including work permits and licensing. In
addition, there were choices to be made such as which country should be
chosen as the main office, where other personnel should be placed, and
whether to transfer existing personnel into the division or start afresh
and review who were the best available (including existing staff). Some
of the issues related to matters such as where clients were located, ease of
access (in particular to an airport hub with a wide range of flights),
security, cost of living and the socio-political environment.

The opportunity

An analysis of where the existing CB Richard Ellis business was positioned indicated areas for improvement and where opportunities existed
to create a point of difference which would assist clients. These included:

- the very significant existing business and reputation in the region for
  general real-estate advice;
- a perceived lack of skills and experience in respect of hotels in the
  region;
- a network of personnel and offices with excellent local knowledge
  and contacts but not necessarily a detailed understanding of the hotel
  industry;
- a considerable history of consulting and valuation work in respect of
  hotel properties within Asia;
- a strong and established name in the hotel industry in North
  America, Europe, Australia and New Zealand;
- a lack of any central point of focus, coordination and marketing in
  relation to hotels in Asia;
- varying standards of client service across the region;
- the chance to start with a relatively clean slate.

It was also apparent that there was a new, and large, market developing
with many new hotels. In the longer term, both leisure and business
tourism looked set to grow. At the same time, there was relatively limited
competition due to a number of factors such as many regions being
emerging markets with limited skills and experience, the fact that there
were only three existing competitors with a regional presence and two of
these not offering a brokerage service.

Possible solutions

There were four alternatives:

1. Continue as is with an incremental development of capability over the long term in organic and perhaps haphazard ways.
2. Acquire an existing business.
3. Create a quite separate division with a hotel-related branding and an exclusive mandate to perform all work in the sector.
4. Create a division with a hotel-related branding and an exclusive mandate to perform all work in the sector but with an emphasis on working with the other divisions.

The first was not an option that would create any substantial or consistent value and no added value for clients, and nor would it develop significant capacity and profitability for CB Richard Ellis.

Serious consideration was given to acquiring an existing business. This would have potentially provided a rapid solution, but the options were very limited. CB Richard Ellis has had extensive experience in the integration of new business lines so that was not considered a problem internally. The lack of potential targets and the changing market prevented this being progressed.

Consideration was given to creating a hotel division across the region which operated separately from the existing businesses. This would have the advantage of having a complete focus on the specific types of properties; in addition, it would assist in creating the perception amongst clients that this was the case. It would also help to ensure that there was a consistent level of service provided by specialists. However, this approach was likely to result in a suboptimal solution for clients because a coordinated approach is essential between different service lines. For example, in Asia many properties have a mixed use, and single developments include offices, retail, residential and hotels, and investors tend to have a less specialised focus than in some other regions. Therefore relationships need to be reinforced on a cross-divisional basis. Leveraging off existing relationships, by working closely with those already in the general real-estate business, rather than recreating those relationships, is preferable.

As a result, it was decided that all hotel work in the region should be coordinated by the new hotels division and allocated to those best able to carry it out. This requires a real emphasis on teamwork and communication as well as the establishment of mutual trust. The division has to show that it can add value by increasing the volume and value of instructions, reducing risk, improving the efficiency of production and giving clients and colleagues more confidence in the service. This needs to happen at all levels and not just with management. In other words, optimal solutions for clients were to draw upon a range of capabilities across the consultancy business and upon the business-wide skills and knowledge that are the core competencies of the business, and these are then coupled with the specialised skills as required.

It was apparent that the existing quantity of work was such that it could not all be controlled by a new division owing to the need to deploy resources and develop capacity. One solution was to utilise the existing, relevant personnel and give them better tools and assistance. Those with existing client relationships should be encouraged to develop these further by indicating that a broader range of services is available, including the hotel division. The relevant personnel can then be brought in as required.

A couple of examples may assist. First, a specialised leisure facility is to be constructed in a relatively undeveloped location. The client requires both demand and feasibility studies and advice on the appropriate operator to be appointed. The skill sets needed include local, operational, design, costing and hotel operator knowledge. It is most unlikely that these will exist in one person and therefore a team approach is necessary. Second, a long-established client of a local office wishes to buy a hotel. The existing relationship with a real-estate operative, who may have no understanding of hotels, may be essential to winning the work and should be reinforced. This person can then bring in advice as necessary.

It was therefore decided to create a division that would add value to the existing business and operations by having specialists who would work with the existing personnel. The emphasis is on leveraging the local market knowledge and contacts by adding skills and knowledge as appropriate. It is not practical, or necessary, to provide the services at all locations but rather to develop core teams in the key markets. For example, Singapore is a fairly central location for the whole of South East Asia, and many of the hotel operating companies have their regional bases there. The intention from early on was to build the business by adding locations as demand grew. Obvious candidates were Hong Kong for the region that includes Taiwan, Shanghai and/or Beijing for China; Tokyo for Japan; and either New Delhi or Mumbai for India. Personnel in these locations may have a focus on that immediate area but if a particular skill is required it can be used anywhere in the region. In some instances existing personnel have been transferred into the division but, when starting in 2007, there was such a shortage of experienced people across all aspects of real-estate that it was necessary to bring in operators from elsewhere. It is expected that this will change as greater experience and training is provided within the region.

Resultant issues

Undoubtedly, problems can arise in circumstances where there is a disparate team involved. However, these are mainly internal. Financial matters such as how to split fees and at what stage work should be passed on are examples of such challenges. The introduction of a new business line is not necessarily seen as a positive initiative by everyone in an established business. Some are comfortable with the status quo, while others can see a loss in fee income within their area as they are potentially excluded from some opportunities, and such changes affect the power structure and career paths. Therefore it is essential to develop an understanding of the existing structures and situations and explain and demonstrate the benefits of the proposed changes to all those involved, to try to ensure their support rather than their resistance. This is not always achieved quickly or easily.

Working in a team can mean some loss of control, especially where team members are from different divisions and have different goals and expectations. Perhaps more importantly it can be difficult to ensure that there is a full and frank exchange in relation to opportunities as individuals have tended to be protective of their own work. However, working in teams is a principal way to develop capacity and mobilise skills and experience to optimise the service and hence solutions for clients. Ultimately, it is in the interest of CB Richard Ellis to optimise fee income and profitability.

An important, additional (and hopefully short-term) issue has been the global financial crisis. This has undoubtedly slowed the growth and development of the division. The transaction market has almost dried up, there is far less interest in obtaining valuations and the previously strong market for feasibility studies has almost ceased to exist. This is exacerbated by the relatively strong impact on global investors, often European or North American funds, which were target clients. High-net-worth individuals have been active but have less need for the service offering being provided. However, the slowdown has provided time to focus on the building of client relationships.

Conclusions

Inevitably, managing a practice, even a single division, is a work in progress. Some of the issues identified are general, some relate to emerging markets and some are Asia specific. Those that appear essential include:

- an absolute focus on what is best for the client;
- strong support from management;
- the maintenance of an environment that engenders mutual trust and obligation;
- a differentiated product offering and the marketing to inform clients appropriately;
- a good understanding (or at least an attempt to have a one) and respect for differences such as cultures, languages and personalities;
- patience.

Staff who commenced work in a firm in which all the professional staff were chartered surveyors and had very similar training and socio-economic background have seen some massive changes during their working lives, particularly the need to draw upon and develop a broader range of knowledge and skills in order to assess and interpret the specific surveying skills in the context of each client and their investment opportunities. There is no doubt that these have been for the better. It is difficult to imagine a more inclusive and varied environment than working and developing capacity in a professional firm in Asia.

Postscript Comment to *Developing capacity in an emergent market* by Robert McIntosh

David Shiers and Hedley Smyth

CB Richard Ellis (CBRE) has been established in the real-estate market for hotel consultancy in the Asia Pacific region for many years. Management of the activity has centred on Sydney. Two changes of significance have been described: (i) the move towards a more holistic real-estate consultant service that shares many of the characteristics of management consultancy and (ii) the growth areas geographically have become and will increasingly be in the Asian heartland cities, and these locations are steeped in regional culture that requires the development of local management capacity to be effective long-term.

This raises four questions:

1. How do you develop your business capacity in this emerging market context?
2. What understanding and research are needed to address capacity building?
3. What strategy options are available?

4. How are decisions made, progress monitored and refinements to strategy made?

Taking each in turn, we will make a few points that demonstrate the degree of difficulty underlying the issues raised in the chapter by referring to the wider literature.

Developing business capacity is clearly a learning issue – professional training and expertise – yet more than this, it takes place in a different cultural setting and this will pose challenges for alignment with CBRE strategy, systems, procedures and norms. Drawing upon the work of on organisations in national settings (Hofstede and Hofstede, 2005), CBRE largely has its origins in the USA and the UK, which are both cultures characterised as predominantly individualistic and masculine values (not gender per se) in cultural terms (Hofstede, 2010). Australia is the origin for the regional hotel service, which shares the same individualistic and masculine dimensions, although it is recognised that Sydney is more multicultural, with an Asian influence culturally. Singapore is the new centre for managing these activities, which is based primarily on power distance and masculine values with a long-term orientation. Some of the key markets for current activity and expansion are Japan, which is masculine in cultural values with uncertainty avoidance and a long-term orientation, Malaya and the Philippines, which both value power distance and masculine values, and China, including Hong Kong, which values power distance with a long-term orientation. Therefore building local management capacity in these and other national markets across the region from Singapore is not merely a matter of bringing up the level of professional expertise and experience with the strategies, systems and procedures in the respective markets, it is also a matter of making sure that these are implemented in ways that accord with the intent of CBRE, even if local adjustment to the management processes is necessary to maintain intent and accommodate the cultural differences. It is an important senior management job to understand these dynamics in order to build capacity and monitor the way it is being shaped.

This brings us to the matter of the information and data needed to develop capacity in these markets. It is easier to direct resources and to channel efforts into target markets where a plethora of data exists. For example, in European markets information is more abundant and success is more a function of performance of the consultant practice, especially risk management, where the information available aids probability assessment. In many developing nations, data is scarce and the risks extensive, so uncertainty and ambiguity are high. Service success is therefore not such an accurate indicator of consultant performance in management terms, an issue that may not be so clearly understood outside the region by CBRE management and some clients.

In overall terms, the first strategic goal is to understand the market and the management issues to work effectively and efficiently in the markets – easily said, yet a complex set of issues faced, as the chapter demonstrates. It takes time, and the experience will be uneven across the region, but that is the management task to bring the service up to a professional level congruent with the practice as a whole. The long-term goal must be to look towards services of competitive advantage and in these markets there is exactly that mentality, so very fertile ground exists. In meeting the first strategic goal, the seeds for service enhancement may emerge, for example (i) through the adjustment of the systems and procedures to fit the culture, and this may yield ways of doing things that are particularly effective, which the literature calls dynamic capabilities (e.g. Teece *et al.*, 1997), and (ii) service components that go the extra mile to deliver added value, which the literature calls core competencies (e.g. Hamel and Prahalad, 1996). These may entail enhanced expertise through knowledge management (e.g. Nonaka and Takeuchi, 1995) and relationship management (e.g. Gummesson, 2001).

The final point concerns how decisions are made. All management decisions are in one sense about 'taking a view'; that is, different people in different organisational settings could have exactly the same information yet come to different views. This is (i) partly a function of the current organisational goals and context, (ii) partly a matter of interpretation based upon the (combined) view of management which is derived from experience from the past, and projection of how consequences of varying options, plus (iii) a view of the future in the light of the strategic organisational goals. It is a key function of management to bring these issues to bear on making such judgements, which are frequently managed as much intuitively as cognitively, because this is the value of experience. Ensuring that the decision-making process lines up the goals is important, and avoiding short-termism – taking decisions that move things forward quickly is not always in the best medium and long-term interest, for example sourcing local staff with international experience takes longer yet addresses cultural issues. It is therefore important to have half an eye on the long-term strategic competitive advantage, which will strongly influence the success of the professional practice. As capabilities are built, senior management gets embroiled in day-to-day decision-making, sometimes at the expense of the long-term. Managing the decision-making process in line with the strategic goals remains a constant issue.

More tactical issues are worth mentioning at this point. In organisations, there is frequently the propensity for middle management and more junior employees not to share valuable information or important viewpoints. In western settings, this can be because people do not feel sufficiently valued in the workplace by management, the power play of cliques and empires within the organisation can prove disruptive to optimal decision-making as can career-motivated thinking that is not in the best interests of the organisation, or simply that they will get blamed for anything that goes wrong that might link back to their contribution

(Bachrach and Baratz, 1970). It is a management function to facilitate sharing such information and viewpoints, yet in eastern settings two other issues can be prevalent. Deference arising from power distance can contribute to what Bachrach and Baratz (1970) call non-decision-making, whereby power structures and self-interest, in this context 'face' in particular, can lead to avoiding difficult decisions completely or in a timely way. Agreement needs to be sought amongst key actors, which leads to the second issue, the mobilisation of bias whereby decision-makers either have too narrow a view that can be distorted and reinforced by the group, or internal and external relations within the decision-makers' network leads to self-interest and, in the worst case, unethical and corrupt decision-making.

These are some of the key issues that management faces in building capacity, especially management capacity within the professional practice in general and in the Asian region in particular. The chapter has clearly set out the process, and this postscript has tried to tease out some of the underlying challenges that arise along the way.

References to Postscript Comment

Bachrach and Baratz (1970) *Power and Poverty*, OUP, Oxford.

Gummesson, E. (2001) *Total Relationship Marketing*, Butterworth-Heinemann, Oxford.

Hamel, G. and Prahalad, C. K. (1996), *Competing for the Future*, Harvard Business School Press, Boston.

Hofstede, G. (2010) Geert Hofstede™ Cultural Dimensions, itim International, http://www.geert-hofstede.com, accessed 26 March.

Hofstede, G. and Hofstede G. J. (2005) *Cultures and Organizations; software of the mind*, New York: McGraw-Hill.

Nonaka, I. and Takeuchi, H. (1995) *The Knowledge-Creating Company*, Oxford University Press, Oxford.

Teece, D. J., Pisano, G. and Shuen, A. (1997) Dynamic capabilities and strategic management, *Strategic Management Journal*, 18, 7, 509–533.

15 Branding professional services
Making the intangible tangible

Kate McGhee

Introduction

Over the past 20 years, the understanding of the application of company and corporate branding has evolved: 'It is only recently that we have realised that its real value lies outside of the business itself, in the minds of potential buyers' (Kapferer, 1992: 15). This is particularly so in the context of business-to-business and professional services branding, where the corporate brand has assumed a more significant and prominent role in overall company strategy.

A brand is no longer simply associated with a tangible product, logo or typeface; it represents and is expressed in all potential touch-points: its people, its actions and behaviour, its communications. While many of these are within the control of a company, without clear articulation and support of central guiding principles, there is a risk of inconsistency or the potential for an external and possibly distorted viewpoint, which may supplant the company view and ultimately destroy business value. Wally Olins stated:

> *Everything that an organisation does must be an affirmation of its identity. The products that the company makes or sells must project its standards and values. The buildings in which it makes things and trades, its offices, factories and showpieces – their location how they are furnished and maintained – are all manifestations of identity. The corporation's communication material, from its advertising and instruction manuals, must have a consistent quality and character that accurately and honestly reflect the whole organisation and its aims. (Olins, 1990, p7)*

A recognisable and well-articulated brand supports corporate strategy across interactions with all key stakeholders from customers and influencers to employees and business partners throughout the supply chain. Furthermore, groups who may observe or scrutinise the business from a

Managing the Professional Practice: in the built environment, First Edition. Edited by Hedley Smyth.
© 2011 by Blackwell Publishing Ltd. Published 2011 by Blackwell Publishing Ltd.

distance can also be influenced constructively by the power of a corporate brand: including pressure groups, the investment community, government, regulatory bodies, relevant media representatives, the academic world, corporate peers and, of course, the general public.

In the built environment, potential opportunities for branding are numerous, but it is acknowledged that this industry from design to construction, to ongoing maintenance and facilities management has been one of the slower to embrace the discipline of branding and to fully leverage the advantages of a strongly communicated corporate brand.

This chapter seeks to understand the main barriers that can prevent companies from wholeheartedly adopting a strategic approach to brand and communications. In addition, it will explore the key advantages of building a strong brand in the context of a business-to-business offer, using BPRI's experience of working with business-to-business marketing teams across a variety of industries.

Understanding the barriers

The discipline of branding developed and grew in the context of consumer packaged goods. The core function of companies such as Unilever, Proctor & Gamble, Nestlé is to disseminate their products as widely and profitably as possible, based on innovation and research, efficient operations, distribution and the application of world-class marketing. This is a deliberately simplistic overview, but what is key is that in these companies, marketing and brand sit at the heart of business activities, firmly tied to tangible products, families of products and the overall customer experience.

The overarching barrier for business-to-business service brand is one of mindset. In the world of professional services, the majority of successful organisations were, at the outset, created and built up by talented individuals, often a charismatic founding figure that remained with business and shaped its path to growth and strategic goals. Looking at the professions of law, accountancy, management consultancy and the design and creative industries, to a great extent the partnership model prevails, often preceded by a phase of leadership via a founding 'guru'. Value is created by a group of talented individuals who build relationships on a one-to-one basis with clients (see also Chapter 7 by Smyth and Kioussi). At the stage where the principals are bigger than the company entity itself, these personality-driven organisations are highly fragile. The departure of a founding partner or key member of the client-facing management team can result in the erosion of business or loss of client relationships. Brand is one of the weapons in the arsenal that can help businesses to mitigate this risk by distilling the essence of these individual working relationships into an experience that can be emulated and expanded to a wider arena of operation. However, in businesses with a dominant founder partner or partnership base, it requires a degree of selflessness and enlightenment and in the short term, and potentially a short-term loss of a known competitive advantage, to remove or downplay the role of individual or individuals, to identify and transfer the social capital that they represent, and recreate the brand minus those individual/s, without losing credibility or long-standing stakeholder relationships. This fundamental mindset issue is at the core of decision-making around spend on brand and marketing activities in the business-to-business markets.

Other interrelated challenges to the adoption of a clear strategy around branding include:

- *Ownership and resources* – brand and marketing activity needs to be endorsed from the top of the business and supported throughout; a lack of physical bandwidth in terms of resource and expertise within the business is the biggest constraint in this area.
- *Cultural antipathy between client and agency* – tension between creative organisations and more hard-nosed businesses can also bring viable marketing activity to an impasse; these industries require education, credible proof-points and a pragmatic adviser who understands the industry context and talks their language.
- *Prioritisation* – in the built environment and many other sectors, cost is critical, particularly in areas where there is significant pressure on margins, so marketing activity is often a victim to the spending axe, because without a proper understanding of the benefits or investment in infrastructure and monitoring vehicles, it is difficult to see the return on investment.
- *Lack of competitive impetus* – in a world where the majority of revenue is generated through successful acquisition of contracts via transparent bidding procedures, many firms deploy development investment against these specific opportunities, rather than a wider umbrella brand and marketing strategy; in a sector with no 'first mover' in marketing, a conformist attitude prevails: 'If no-one else is doing it, why should we...?'.
- *The invisible brand* – there is potentially a question-mark around the opportunities to leverage brand effectively in this space. Successful delivery of facilities management, for example, often requires a seamless integration with client activities, which inhibits the ability to outwardly express the FM brand. Within consortia built of multiple partners in PFI/PPP vehicles, use of one proprietary corporate brand may not be politically acceptable to the end-client or partners. If a business does not acknowledge or recognise sufficient value in the outward expression of brand, this is not likely to be an area where they fight for share of voice.

These challenges vary in importance according to the size, ownership model, culture and longevity of the business in question. For instance, in a small architectural practice, issues of bandwidth and resources, and creative tensions may represent the biggest barriers. In a large facilities management company, pressure on margins and the ability to deliver a low-cost but quality service to clients is imperative; in this context is spend on marketing and branding an out-of-reach luxury?

Why should you brand...?

Given the barriers outlined above, it is clear that businesses in this space require persuasive reasons to believe in the benefits of branding activity. How can the intangible benefits of a brand be made more tangible and its impact made measurable? Any branding activity needs to be firmly grounded in intelligence about what customers need and what the organisation is capable of delivering to the marketplace. While this is an excellent starting point, the requirement for a strong brand capable of sustainable growth is to build and communicate a proposition that not only resonates with a target audience, but is durable, relevant and unique.

A brand acts as a powerful short-hand symbol which encapsulates the image and purpose of the company, its culture and its value in the marketplace around which awareness, consideration and preference can be built. A well-managed corporate brand allows all stakeholders to understand an organisation's core business, guiding principles and ambitions and when strongly articulated, allows the business to:

- differentiate its offer on factors other than price;
- help its management and workforce understand business USPs and hence contribute to improved strategic management and execution;
- recruit and retain the best talent and supply partners in the industry;
- position itself more effectively during crises.

There is a question mark in the construction and built environment sector as to the worthwhile nature of investment in corporate branding initiatives, particularly in the context of increasingly standardised procurement processes and bid-specific relationship building. However, in the context of professional services, a brand with strong promise and reputation can actually help to create a 'licence to bid' and in some cases can give companies the opportunity to provide input to specifications at an early stage, or at least ease their journey through the early stages of the procurement process. The main advantages are detailed below.

A strong brand:

- gets your company on the initial long- or shortlist;
- opens doors in the procurement process, where perception is an important first hurdle to overcome;
- can allow you a seat at the table to shape tender specifications and in some cases policy, in a process where open dialogue can often be discouraged;
- secures the attention and acts as a comfort factor for key influencers in the buying process, who may be less familiar with the minutiae of the sector and its key players.

The process of branding

In order to create a viable branding platform, refresh or reposition an existing brand, an organisation needs to examine three main areas: its internal capabilities, its customers and its competition now and in the near future. This can be achieved via an integrated holistic research programme or on a modular basis, depending on resources available. The three central question areas cover:

1. *Capabilities*: What do you do and how/where do you do it?
2. *Customers*: Who are you targeting and why?
3. *Competition*: Who else is competing for the same client base?

An initial list of areas to explore is included below (Table 15.1). The same areas should be considered for both internal capabilities and any competitive assessment in order to benchmark performance. It is also important to consider how best to communicate with the target audience and which messages and channels considered to be most effective.

Table 15.1 Information-needs map for b2b service branding (Source: BPRI)

Understand Capabilities	Understand Customers	Understand Competition
Size	Size and segments	Size
Footprint	Needs	Footprint
Calibre of projects	Location	Calibre of projects
Calibre of people	Commercial vs public	Calibre of people
Scope of offer(s)	Profitability	Scope of offer(s)
Future growth potential	Cultural fit	Future growth potential

Depending on the scale of activity and the level of commitment, the business may elect to use internal or external resources to deliver all or elements of the programme. The benefits of handling this internally are proximity to, and detailed knowledge of, the issues, and use of internal resources at potentially a lower cost compared to committing spend externally. Support from external sources can bring objectivity, an impetus and focus (which may be lacking if internal resource is insufficient or if the task is treated as a bolt-on to an existing internal day-job), expertise in areas outside the capability of the commissioning business, and also scalability. Both approaches have their advantages and disadvantages and need to be evaluated on a case-by-case basis and traded off according to the size of the task and resources available.

Information is likely to be acquired through multiple sources, including internal management information and forecasts, staff and management interviews and workshops, customers, prospect and external stakeholder interviews and competitor intelligence. It is important to take account of published company news, stakeholder viewpoints and research of competitor-originated communications materials, including company reports, online presence and other published material.

Once the initial information-gathering stage is completed, a simplified but illustrative process map is shown below (Figure 15.1) to demonstrate how the brand strategy is defined, refined and executed. Depending on the complexity and dynamics of the market, this process can be iterative, with review and redirection as necessary and monitoring and tracking vehicles to monitor the effectiveness of the brand strategy and overall brand health over time.

The use of research and targeted communications to understand, access and engage with senior-level stakeholders and influencers who have the ability to scan the industry horizon and shape future trends is a proven method used by high-profile corporates in the business-to-business space. This approach is one that can be scaled up or down as appropriate and can be used by organisations of different sizes to shape corporate and brand strategy.

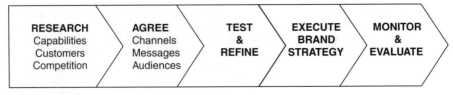

Source: BPRI

Figure 15.1 Brand strategy process map

The key success factors for branding in this context are:

- deployment of sufficient resource and senior buy-in to the task;
- strong project management and focus;
- the collective will and ability to achieve coherence and consistency;
- strong partnership between the business and any external support;
- an understanding of the business USPs and where it competes.

All of these factors together contribute to the creation of a brand, supported by action that can 'walk the talk'.

Building capacity

In order to deliver an effective strategy on brand, businesses must be prepared to commit internal resources and, where necessary, external resources in areas which fall outside the skill sets of its internal team. Activity needs to be supported and endorsed from the top of the company and aligned with the overall corporate strategy. When businesses are attempting this activity for the first time, there is a need for a walk-before-you-run approach, but the principles remain the same in terms of defining your market and understanding its needs. Risk can be managed by initiating on a modular basis, e.g. piloting internally, in a single geographical territory or with a carefully chosen customer segment, prior to a major roll-out of activity across the whole organisation.

The scale of activity depends on the size of the company and the size and scope of market within which it operates. A business that sells to a predominantly domestic public sector client base will differ in need and sophistication from a multidisciplinary global consultant. The former will benefit from a highly targeted programme of activities geared to understanding the needs of policy makers and implementers and the latter may ultimately need to build an intricate international multi-stakeholder approach with a broad-brush communications strategy at the global level complemented by more targeted activity within core client segments.

Regardless of size of budget, the primary benefits of a successfully executed brand strategy are consistent: they allow a business to understand and align around customer needs, prepare for a sustainable future and, if communicated effectively, face external and internal marketplaces with a strong and clearly articulated proposition. The benefits of this are improved targeting with greater efficiency around transactions and partnerships. In an increasingly competitive environment where the buying cycles are long and relate to high-value engagements, it is imperative that good matches are identified early in the process and that business offers evolve to match the future needs of customers.

Acknowledgement

Our thanks go to BPRI's clients since 2001, whose challenges and feedback have contributed to the growing body of intellectual capital around business-to-business branding, and to Vikki James of BPRI for her invaluable encouragement, and the input to this chapter from her own client portfolio.

References

Kapferer, J-N. (1992) *Strategic Brand Management: new approaches to creating and evaluating brand equity*, Kogan Page, London.

Kapferer, J-N. (1997) *Strategic Brand Management: creating and sustaining brand equity long term*, Kogan Page.

Olins, W. (1990) *Corporate Identity: making business strategy visible through design*, Harvard Business School Press. p7.

McGhee, K. and BPRI (2003) *Not the Poor Cousin: a view of b2b advertising research*, White Paper, BIG Conference, 14–16 May, BIG (Business Intelligence Group), Marriott St Pierre, Chepstow, UK.

Postscript Comment to *Branding professional services* by Kate McGhee

Hedley Smyth

It is poignant to note the emphasis that Kate McGhee places upon mindset as one of the principal barriers to the adoption of brand management in professional practice. Her experience and the position of BPRI as a member of WPP plc, as one of the leading global advertising and media consultants, lend tremendous weight to this emphasis. The academic literature refers to the commercial disdain held by the professions, for example architects, to marketing matters (e.g. Kotler and Conner, 1977; see also Chapter 7). Whilst this provides a historical justification where the professions, especially those with chartered status and the associated restraints of soliciting for work, this is largely of a bygone age. Whilst some residual social inheritance may prevail in professional cultures and some institutions, most professional practices have become overtly commercial and have done so in very professional ways. Marketing is increasingly becoming explicit and more adequately resourced. Whilst it is still the subject of cutbacks in recession, the strategic agendas remain, although the entire palette of marketing has yet to be pursued even amongst the most sophisticated industry players. This is certainly the case for branding. So, perhaps the barrier is less about the profession and professional disdain for commercialism and more about the mindset of the individual practice founders and management, a point well made in the chapter.

A lack of understanding of branding prevails (Kioussi and Smyth, 2009), and this chapter makes a significant contribution to clarifying content and dispelling myths. This is timely. It is over a decade ago that many contractors, using the UK as an example, lost many branding opportunities. The construction site represented a huge billboard and activity centre of interest to the passing population, frequently situated in high-profile locations. Contractors used hoardings and cranes as advertising media, yet overlooked opportunities for a more powerful presence, which many clients realised and have imposed conditions on their suppliers to promote their own company. The supermarkets and major developers were in the forefront of this move. It is surely time for the professional consultants in the built environment to harness branding opportunities. Professional practices require softer approaches than contracting counterparts, although this makes the out-working and benefits of brand management less tangible, yet this chapter provides a sound basis to argue the case for brand management and seeking tangible outcomes. Paradoxically, the so-called 'credit crunch' – indeed any recession or downturn – provides excellent opportunity. Those practices that have found themselves on a comparatively sound financial footing are best placed to grow market share especially on the upturn (see Chapter 1), and branding provides one means.

Branding is conceptually part of the intangible social capital of the firm, which is frequently recorded as goodwill in accountancy terms and generally perceived as reputation in the professional marketplace. Brand management is more than simply the recognition of this; it seeks to enhance the value of the brand. In professional terms this is more than receiving reward on merit, the historic professional position that is largely passive because of restriction on promoting, soliciting and advertising for work, but seeks to actively inform client markets and other key stakeholder markets (Christopher *et al.*, 2006) of the capabilities of the practice as Kate McGhee unpacks in the chapter. Branding is therefore part of a range of important marketing and sales tools, added to such outputs as editorials and articles, web pages and brochures, b2b relationship building amongst clients and other influencers. Most people need to get the same message from several different sources before they really start taking notice. Brand management can be seen as both a separate source in itself, and also reinforcing the other sources. This is the message that this chapter has conveyed, demonstrating that branding is currently underestimated and undervalued by the professions.

How is branding best adopted? Senior management need to designate a single point of responsibility, perhaps a partner or board director. Where practices have a 'marketing function' that is confined to business development roles, it is suggested that this is too narrow for brand management as well as other aspects of marketing as a discipline. Brand permeates all activities, and therefore a senior point of responsibility is needed working closely with marketing strategy and sales functions. The person with responsibility to champion brand management is essentially a facilitator who is required to (i) inculcate branding into the culture, (ii) embody branding as a consideration at decision points within implementing the practice systems and procedures, and (iii) lever the resources to develop the tangible expression of branding in the marketplace.

As discussed in the chapter, brand management is implemented internally, starting with the responsible person, yet can benefit from the skills, experience and network of an external specialist consultant. This has the advantage of freeing up staff to focus on what they do best and can have the added advantage of ensuring that the firm takes brand management seriously as the external consultants engage with the practice staff. Conversely, it can also make implementation seem distant and can result in a lack of commitment to, and adoption of, the messages and actions to be projected into the market required from staff. The context needs strategic evaluation by senior practice management.

To conclude, it is important to return to senior management hiding behind professional disdain as a pseudo-justification for rejecting brand management and marketing. Marketing and brand management are not – or at least should not be – hype. As the chapter clearly indicates, it must be founded on the reality of practice – making the most of what is already achieved. Brand management may even be a stimulus and indirect motivator for staff as it becomes part of practice culture. Marketing and brand management form a professional activity in itself and therefore the professional practices should feel greater affinity to these management activities than has hitherto been the case. This chapter has helped to convey this, and has helped to improve understanding of brand management as well as hopefully provide a future stimulus for greater dialogue with brand managers and those with brand management responsibilities.

References to Postscript Comment

Christopher, M., Payne, A. and Ballantyne, D. (2006) *Relationship Marketing: creating stakeholder value*. Butterworth-Heinemann, Oxford.

Kioussi, S. and Smyth, H. J. (2009) Brand management in design-led firms: the case of architecture practices in the design-construction-development market, *Proceedings of the 5th Thought Leaders International Conference on Brand Management*, 6–7 April, ATINER, Athens.

Kotler P. and Connor R. A. (1977) Marketing professional services. *Journal of Marketing*, 41(1), 71–76.

16　The first 20 years

Mike Nightingale

The beginning

This is a personal account that led to establishing Nightingale Associates as a leading UK and international architecture practice, initially in healthcare. I hope there is encouragement and guidance, and lessons for others in setting up and managing a practice.

Having a family background that includes medicine and nursing, and a twin brother who is a doctor, I decided at the beginning of my architectural career to specialise in healthcare design. Starting with a community hospital in Cirencester and culminating in the design of the 650-bed Royal Hospital in Oman, at 42 I felt I had learned enough to create my own firm embodying the design ethos and core values that I hoped would result in a successful business that would produce memorable architecture.

The central idea was to help transform and uplift the quality of healthcare architecture by example. By achieving this I hoped to realise three goals, namely to:

1. have delighted and enthusiastic clients giving repeat commissions;
2. maintain loyal, highly motivated staff eager to progress in the firm;
3. create a reputation for design excellence, reliability and top-quality, friendly service.

I was very keen to move back to my roots in Oxford and to bring up my family outside London. Another catalyst for this was the re-establishment of links with past colleagues from the Oxford Health Authority now in a position to commission architects. Also, I had close links with a commercial practice, the Carnell Green Partnership, who were keen to diversify into healthcare design. Having initially had an understandably negative response from the practice in which I was a partner in their London office to setting up an Oxford office, I hatched a plan with David Green and Chris Carnell and the Carnell Green

Managing the Professional Practice: in the built environment, First Edition. Edited by Hedley Smyth.
© 2011 by Blackwell Publishing Ltd. Published 2011 by Blackwell Publishing Ltd.

Partnership Oxford was launched at our newly acquired design studio at the Cherry Barn, Harwell in May 1989. The firm started with two people, myself and David Clarke, a former colleague from the former practice, bringing with him his cutting-edge knowledge of MicroStation, our chosen computer platform. Our first recruit was Richard Harrington, another former colleague who lived in Oxfordshire, just behind the Cherry Barn.

Unbeknown to us, we were weeks away from the beginning of the second worst recession in the 20th century. Strangely, the new practice benefitted from this. Falling workloads, especially in London, meant bright young architects were more prepared to take a risk with a new outfit, especially if it meant avoiding commuting. The beauty of the Harwell location is that it is five minutes from the Didcot–London rail link, so the area is full with high-calibre professionals who had been working in London.

As the recession began to bite in earnest, public sector clients responded by demanding cutthroat fee tendering that meant that well-established offices with high overheads were seriously disadvantaged as they were forced to take on work for ridiculously low fees, sometimes just in order to survive. Fees as low as 2% for full architectural services were common. Luckily, our only large overhead was the Cherry Barn, which was owned by the partners. We offset this by letting part of it to a friendly structural engineer and quantity surveyor.

We were at the cutting edge of CAD, health planning, master planning and healthcare design innovations that made us very attractive to local clients for two reasons: relatively advanced computer skills and our ways of working; these made us competitive on fees yet we maintained a reasonable profit, and clients benefitted from the latest ideas. In this way, we quickly built up a base of local commissions allowing us to build a small but extremely effective local design studio. The continued recession enabled us to cherry-pick the most experienced architects and students to join our team. Another factor was the determination of the Thatcher government to single-mindedly purge central and local government in-house architectural teams. We were also able to recruit the most talented public sector architects who were looking for career moves and had experience of client bodies.

From the very beginning we were determined to be in a position to compete for major suitable commissions without risking building an unsustainably large design studio too early. Thus, we concentrated on creating a talented core design team with strong management skills, whilst in London we forged links with gifted 'big building' architects in the Carnell Green London studio. In the event of landing a large commission they would provide vital backup to Harwell, especially in the design of external envelopes. This policy of collaboration with talented non-health-specialist architects was a deliberate part of our design excellence aim to lift the design quality of public sector healthcare buildings in Britain.

Towards becoming a main player

Large hospitals need an almost unparalleled level of detail design. The catch-22 for small and medium-sized practices aspiring to design such projects is how to be able to build up talent that can realise this, in-house, before reaping the fee rewards from large commissions.

While we were with our former practice, Richard Harrington, David Clarke and I worked on large healthcare projects from the relatively small London office of 25 people. The enormous design throughput of this talented team was made viable by the effective and extremely profitable 'internal outsourcing' methodology developed by the firm from the early 1970s onwards.

Government policy had led to evolving standardisation of hospital briefing data and its universal application to practically all new hospital building in England and Wales. The Department of Health research and development teams, led by Howard Goodman, first produced the standard Harness hospital in 1972, with its baby brother, Nucleus, spawned by the energy crisis, following in 1976. The former practice in which I had been a partner in the London office had developed a centralised function in response to the demands of standardised designs to serve its regional offices. It later offered this service on the open market as Insight Services. The third strand of our strategy to be able to compete for large hospital projects was then a project-by-project link-up with Insight Services to do the 1:50 scale room layouts and internal room elevations. This provided the means for a small practice to bid for large commissions.

In the autumn of 1989, six months after our new company started trading, we entered a design competition, organised by St Thomas's Hospital in London to provide a mixture of facilities on the site of Riddell House, their original home for nurses. Our entry was submitted at the end of January 1990. We were asked to present our submission in mid February and to our huge delight we won the competition and had to start work in earnest almost immediately. This exciting win of a £35,000,000 project was 'manna from heaven' for the emerging practice and gave us the confidence to further strengthen our team.

Although the 1989–1993 recession proved a beneficial market in the health sector if you were 'lean and mean' enough to compete for low fees whilst maintaining high design standards, it proved disastrous for many commercial practices. Carnell Green was no exception and this brought our experiment of combining healthcare and commercial architecture to an abrupt end. In 1993 Nightingale Associates severed connections with Carnell Green and made a determined focus on healthcare design as their core expertise and key strategy for coping with the worsening recession.

We too explored work opportunities not affected by the UK downturn. We had understood, from the beginning, that it was vital for our survival to have a global outlook in both the public and private markets if we were going to narrow our client base to healthcare and closely related commissions. Another key advantage of an international approach was the attraction of students and young architects from around the world interested in gaining healthcare design experience. This not only enriched design capabilities, but it enhanced global healthcare design credentials of the firm when the students returned home.

We were fortunate in the lean start-up years of 1989–1994 to have several experienced partners and staff with direct experience of designing BUPA private hospitals in the UK, and several members of the team had extensive experience in designing very large hospitals internationally, mainly in the Middle and Far East. This in-house expertise and the right client contacts led to several lucrative commissions at a difficult time in the UK market.

There are tangible downsides to developing an architectural firm based on healthcare design and we needed clear strategies to address them. With regard to hiring excellent staff, a few things must be noted. Students and young architects, especially in times of economic prosperity, are often more attracted to practices designing simpler, more glamorous buildings than hospitals. It takes years to train an experienced healthcare architect so it was vital to have strategies in place to retain them. Also, the vigour and application needed to produce high-quality designs for multi-headed institutional clients with low budgets on difficult sites required very hard work and dedication from staff.

The other severe challenge to hiring that faces firms specialising in healthcare is that generally, fees for public sector work are lower than fees achieved by commercial architects even though healthcare work is far more complex and therefore time-consuming to design. To combat these factors, Nightingale Associates decided that it was important to always place a very strong emphasis on staff welfare and to pay particular attention to the individual motivation of everyone in the firm. Nightingale Associates was the first architectural practice to receive an Investors in People award, in 1998, which has always been championed at senior management level.

This emphasis on staff welfare remains important today. Individuals are actively encouraged to take as much responsibility as they feel comfortable with and are given as much freedom as possible to develop their design skills. The firm deliberately does not have a 'house style' and does not encourage a culture where all the key design decisions are confined to a limited number of design specialists.

Project architects are encouraged to conduct the client interface work themselves, and from these briefing meetings develop their own design solutions. Design quality is protected by formalised design reviews by peer groups from the project architects' own studio and relevant specialist reviewers from other Nightingale Associates studios. Because of the very large range of size and type of healthcare projects, from small ward conversions up to full-scale teaching hospitals, project architects and their teams can progress by either working in teams on large projects or heading up smaller schemes.

This emphasis on development of individual careers as a way of maximising job satisfaction to counter relatively modest salaries yet extremely good benefits has greatly influenced the manner of practice growth. The model for growth has evolved around design studios of 30 and 50 people each with a strong local client base. Offices of this size are straightforward to manage and develop a supportive social culture, which is difficult to replicate in large offices of 100 or more staff. They are carefully located to optimise communication between studios, maximising client access and being conveniently located for staff. Between 1993, when the firm had 12 staff in Harwell, and 2002 with 100 staff in Harwell, London and Brighton, the firm gained a very strong reputation for the design and delivery of well-designed health buildings, predominantly in the public sector in the UK.

Moving with the market

In 1997, when Labour gained power, the government made a massive commitment to modernise the building state of the NHS, and to transform schools and higher education premises. Using the Private Finance Initiative (PFI), 100 new hospitals were promised, and by 2000, Building Schools for the Future (BSF) earmarked £6bn to 'rebuild or refurbish every state secondary school in the country'.

These long-term commitments from the UK government were the key stimuli for the dual strategies of expansion and design quality enhancement at Nightingale Associates. The PFI programme is one of the largest healthcare building programmes in the world and, as such, attracts world-class architects keen to gain a share of this lucrative market. The projects have been large – between £50m and £800m – and needed to be delivered fast and efficiently. The PFI bidding process was and still is notoriously lengthy and onerous for architects brave enough to be involved. It was essentially a design competition lasting over a year funded by 'at cost' fees with the incentive of a massive bonus for the winner. Only large, well-funded firms with sufficient 'design clout' to compete with international healthcare designers stood a chance in this market. Some UK firms chose to make associations with American or European architects to broaden their appeal and spread the risk of competing – for example, Anshen Dyer.

By 1995 the firm had established a strong research and development service as a means to ensure that its growing network of offices benefitted from coordinated information and innovation initiatives. The R&D team also started taking on external commissions, for example drafting hospital building notes and technical memoranda for NHS Estates. The core aim to promote quality of healthcare design was achieved by partners taking an active role in the RIBA Health Client Forum and Architects for Health. In 1995, I was commissioned to edit the design guide, Better by Design, that set out healthcare design principles that were endorsed by the Minister of Health, Tom Sackville, and sent to all NHS Hospital Trusts.

In 1998, the practice set up a Sustainable Design R&D Team that has played a very active part in formulating NHS policy on the promotion of sustainable health buildings. The team leader was a key member of the NHS Estates think tank that created NEAT (the NHS Environmental Assessment Tool) and is currently involved in the monitoring and evaluation of its successor, BREEAM Healthcare. The R&D Team has developed a specialisation studying the relationship between sensory perception and design. The central premise that all key design decisions should emanate from client satisfaction to reactions from all our senses (sense sensitive design) is at the core of the Nightingale Associates design ethos.

Securing the future

A key watershed in the development of Nightingale Associates was reached in 2002. We were a partnership with 100 staff in three studios with 90% of its workload in the UK public healthcare market and an enviable healthcare design reputation. There was a full order book with no more capacity to exploit the rapidly expanding UK healthcare and education market. Clearly, a new direction was needed for this highly successful, yet potentially vulnerable firm with the following characteristics:

- a very profitable business, historically, with an exemplary performance track record and high staff morale;
- a privately owned partnership forced to take to very real financial, organisational and design risks competing in the healthcare PFI market – 'the only show in town' in our core market;
- a practice led by a 55-year-old entrepreneur with a strong vision to position the firm to exploit strengths and overcome weaknesses.

The next stage of development was triggered by two events. First, we were approached by a young, rapidly expanding management consultancy called Tribal. Already an AIM (Alternative Investment Market) company, Tribal was an exciting new company, offering a wide range of educational, health and governmental consultancy services, in support of the Labour government's huge expansion in education and health investment.

Secondly, Nightingale Associates became 'preferred bidder' on the £300 million Coventry Hospital PFI. Winning Coventry as a 100-person-strong partnership demonstrated graphically that the firm was 'punching above its weight'. In order to maintain its impeccable reputation for successful project delivery it either had to expand rapidly or outsource a large proportion of the work. Winning Coventry also demonstrated to Tribal that Nightingale Associates was a serious player worthy of investment. Tribal convinced Nightingale Associates that if they were to agree to an investment from them then their independent development, including retention of their very successful brand name, would be honoured, and that their business model was to finance and support successful consultancies for the mutual benefit of parent company and subsidiary.

The partnership was very attracted to becoming a member of a 'tribe' of likeminded firms with closely related and relevant expertise, and one that would supply the vital financial umbrella that would enable Nightingale Associates to grow and compete globally in their chosen speciality of healthcare architecture. The fact that Tribal owned Secta, a very well respected firm of health planners that had a long history of working with Nightingale Associates, was a key factor in making the decision in May 2002 to join Tribal. The benefits for Nightingale Associates in joining Tribal have been tangible. Funding was immediately made available to expand the business by acquisition and natural growth. Nightingale Associates set itself clear expansion and targeted diversification goals as compatible as possible with its Tribal parent company:

- *Ash Design*: Tribal started out developing a wide range of educational consultancy services, including project management and architectural design. In 2000, they purchased Ash Design, a 20-person firm of architects based in Kent, specialising in further education and schools design. By the time Nightingale Associates joined Tribal, Ash Design were 40 people based in Dartford and satellite offices in Bristol and Leeds. In 2006, the decision was made to incorporate Ash Design as part of Nightingale, and by 2008, almost 50% of the firm's workload was coming from education commissions.
- *Derek Hicks and Thew*: A well-established education and community health specialist firm was purchased in 2005 and became the Liverpool office of Nightingale Associates.
- *h2M and Studio Baad*: There was a clear objective to improve the geographical spread of the firm to take advantage of local markets and to perpetuate the successful federal model of studios of between 30 and 50 people. Before joining Tribal, new studios had been created as starter offices, usually based on managing local projects, and their

organic growth was encouraged. The constraint is providing a complete service until they gain a critical mass of at least 15 people. The more structured approach, based on strategic acquisition, facilitated by Tribal, notably through h2M in Cardiff and the Studio Baad health team in Rochdale, was used to achieve both the desired geographical spread and dramatic increase in capacity and expertise to satisfy the expanding market.

Between 2002 and 2008 Nightingale Associates grew to be one of the top five architectural practices in the UK with over 300 people based in 11 studios. The integration of Ash Design and the establishment of the Liverpool studio made up half the growth and quickly established Nightingale Associates as a major player in education alongside the core speciality of healthcare design (see Image 16.1). A third and related expert field, science buildings design, also emerged during this period. Maintaining top-quality design and delivery at all times is vital for specialist firms because any loss of reputation can be rapidly conveyed through the narrow client base. Therefore, the design quality strategies,

Image 16.1 Clinical Education Centre, Keele University

including strong centralised R&D and rigorous design reviews by peers, developed early in Nightingale Associates, have been further developed and refined to reflect the larger scale of the practice.

Management issues

One potential downside of a federal practice structure with studios of a maximum of 50 people could be the failure to service very large projects with maximum efficiency. Having everyone in a studio working on one enormous project can distort and inhibit studio development and demoralise many people. Nightingale Associates explored three main alternative strategies to address this challenge:

1. The practice studied ways of splitting £100m+ projects between studios either by building blocks or by allocating plans and interiors to one studio and external envelope design to another.
2. Worldwide outsourcing organisations were explored to assess the quality and appropriateness of their services to Nightingale Associates' requirements.
3. An exercise was performed to explore the viability of setting up an in-sourcing centre designed to meet the particular needs of the practice.

The first option was rejected as a primary way of alleviating capacity problems because of logistical inconsistencies that could compromise quality of delivery. The second option could not meet the quality of delivery needed for the highly specialised Nightingale projects. The idea of a Nightingale Associates in-sourcing centre was, therefore, developed in detail. Cape Town in South Africa was chosen as a location because it combined a time zone advantage of only one hour's difference from the UK with the availability of top-quality architects and technologists trained in RIBA-accredited colleges.

Setup began in 2005 from the Harwell office. A lot of thought was put into the most appropriate projects and aspects of these projects that would best benefit from remote execution. The design of complex healthcare buildings and to a lesser extent larger education projects requires enormous attention to detail on a room-by-room basis. Extremely sophisticated computer software, called CodeBook, has been developed to enable expert CAD operators to capture and manipulate all the complex medical equipment and services information, for example in an operating theatre, and to produce 2D and 3D plans, room elevations and 3D images.

Today, the Cape Town in-sourcing centre has 40 staff: half are dedicated to producing CodeBook-driven health and educational detailed designs and production information, and half are producing a wide variety of working drawings for the UK design studios. The centralised facility maximises the efficient use and development of cutting-edge CAD software such as CodeBook and Revit, facilitating ongoing research into, for example, standard rooms, and provides valuable practice-wide production information quality control. This in-sourcing centre empowers the design studios to confidently pitch for very large and complex projects that would be beyond their ability to resource on their own.

Having established the goal of a network of medium-sized design studios serving most of the UK and maximising efficiency and quality control by developing a dedicated practice in-sourcing centre, the next challenge for Nightingale Associates was to replicate this model world-wide. The aim is to stick to the firm's three areas of design expertise, healthcare, education and science, and offer an expanded in-sourcing centre in support of new international design studios. The first of these opened in Cape Town in 2008. This is a 26% black-owned fully accredited Broad Based Black Economic Empowerment (BBBEE) design studio targeting sub-Saharan Africa. Each new office needs to be fully established with a track record in winning new work before further design studios planned for Australia and Canada are set up.

Conclusion

It is interesting to reflect on the pros and cons of the decision in 2002 for Nightingale Associates to join Tribal as part of a publicly limited company (PLC). Being part of Tribal has given Nightingale Associates the financial strength and stability to expand by acquisition, establish a viable in-sourcing centre, and offer staff very attractive benefits, including private healthcare cover and stakeholder pensions for all. Arguably the strict financial reporting demanded by the PLC environment has led to much less financial 'firefighting', leaving time for the Nightingale Associates management team to concentrate on the firm's core objectives of raising design standards, improving project delivery and seeking new clients.

On the other side, the prime aim of all PLCs is to maximise profit to satisfy shareholders. This emphasis on short-term, annual profit that can be positively reported to the city to bolster share price, can siphon off money that could be well spent on improving company infrastructure. Fortunately, Nightingale Associates has a strong management team able to argue its case with a generally enlightened PLC board that recognises the importance of sustainable company development.

There is a perception in the architectural profession that the PLC environment is not as conducive to design excellence as the partnership and limited liability company models. In the case of Nightingale, excellent design is a prerequisite for competing at the highest levels with international architects for flagship projects, and the design capability has been enriched by the inflow of new talent from acquisitions.

Building on the solid foundations of the past 20 years, we feel well-positioned to extend our design and management philosophy worldwide.

Editor's note

Since this chapter was written the Tribal Group reviewed its business and Nightingale Associates was bought by Canadian architects, IBI Group.

Postscript Comment to *The first 20 years* by Mike Nightingale

Andrew Edkins

The rise of Nightingale Associates from a barn in the idyll of the Oxfordshire countryside to a significant part of Tribal plc in the space of 20 years is a testament to the need for all the forms of strategy as would be espoused by the likes of Henry Mintzberg (Mintzberg and Waters, 1982) and the development of the organisation as developed by Mary Jo Hatch (Hatch, 1999). However, the particular success of Nightingale Associates is that it achieved a major position, as measured both by size and reputation, without compromising on its core set of values (Porter, 1985). It is what the company does, and what these values are, that mark this case as one worthy of note.

The starting point of a technically excellent professional wanting to 'branch out' is not unusual, indeed in professional design and creative markets (for example architecture, specialist engineering, advertising) there is a clear organisational genealogy that shows how parent firms spawn new start-ups (often small partnerships) that exploit location advantage (in this case, the appeal of the area around Oxford), particular specialist skills (in this case, healthcare), and good relationships (in this case, with healthcare authorities). Having taken the bold step to start up, the issues then become ones of initial survival and then growth, (Eisenhardt and Schoonhoven, 1990).

What becomes clear from this case is that Mike Nightingale and the other leaders of the firm recognised that they had to take the best from two possible alternative growth strategies. The first is to become fully corporate, with the layers of management, introduction of formalised systems and procedures, and the focus on developing the range of component parts (departments and/or divisions) that provide an attractive market offering. Another alternative is to model growth strategies based on a form of cloning – we see this as franchising (Brickley and Dark, 1987; Caves and Murphy, 1976). Here, regional or otherwise geographically disparate units operate in regularised ways, often following standard operating procedures (SOPs) and aiming to achieve minimum targets and key performance indicators (KPIs) with rewards being offered for out-performing. The reality was for organic growth followed by both merger and acquisitions with the final result being a business model based on a form of in-sourcing, with the parts of Nightingale themselves becoming part of the Tribal business.

It is this creation of a larger network – indeed now a network of networks – which demonstrates the arguments for the changing business paradigm, where the relationships between the client and their suppliers is neither obvious nor straightforward (Moller and Halinen, 1999). This is particularly relevant when the focus is the generation and development of creative knowledge – as health and education building design is. With the design being a fundamental part of the project, it is now, more than ever, expected that the building's designers will consider and cater for many different needs as considered from many differing perspectives.

If we take two areas that are highly topical, we have from the world of PFI and PPPs the clear need for cost to be considered over the full life of the project, this typically being the minimum period of the contract, which is often 25 years or longer. To be able to predict the way that healthcare or education will be delivered over this timescale is foolish, but the architect has to consider the likelihood that there will be the need to change, so both adaptability and flexibility are needed in order that operational efficiency and effectiveness can be ensured (Nutt and McLennan, 2000; Blyth and Worthington, 2001).

If we then move from functional considerations to that of the aesthetic, we have to then consider the need for taking into account the views of those that are seen as custodians of the 'urbanscape'. In the UK, this has increasingly fallen to CABE (Commission for Architecture and the Built Environment – www.cabe.org.uk) and its role is considered as an important stakeholder in maintaining and improving the 'quality' of the design.

In addition to the challenge of delivering functional value over the longer term and making a positive aesthetic contribution, designers such as Nightingale Associates have to aggressively attack the carbon footprint of healthcare and education facilities, provide constructors with opportunities to deploy modern methods of construction, such as prefabrication and modularity, and cope with an ever-changing technological landscape, now moving to integrate highly sophisticated computer aided design with computer aided manufacture and computer aided facility management (CAD/CAM/CAFM). It is little wonder that, given this level of complexity, a firm such as Nightingale Associates has sought to build its range of organisational competencies as it has.

One hopes that the way the parts of this complex professional services firm, now part of Tribal plc, continues to develop will positively reinforce the success to date and prove to be cooperative. The danger, particularly in economically hostile times, is that this is replaced by internal fighting for attention or resource and becomes inherently competitive. Given Mike Nightingale's track record and the management and leadership ethos he has built up over the past 30 years this risk is considered low on the corporate risk register.

References to Postscript Comment

Blyth, A. and Worthington, J. (2001) *Managing the Brief for Better Design*, Spon, London.

Brickley, J. A. and Dark, F. H. (1987) The choice of organizational form: the case of franchising, *Journal of Financial Economics*, 18, 401–420.

Caves, R. E. and Murphy, W. F. (1976) Franchising: firms, markets, and intangible assets *Southern Economic Journal*, 42, 572–586.

Eisenhardt, K. M. and Schoonhoven, C. B. (1990) Organizational growth: linking founding team, strategy, environment, and growth among US semiconductor ventures, 1978–1988 *Administrative Science Quarterly*, 35, 504–529.

Hatch, M. J. (1999) Exploring the empty spaces of organizing: how improvisational jazz helps redescribe organizational structure, *Organization Studies*, 20, 75–100.

Mintzberg, H. and Waters, J. A. (1982) Tracking strategy in an entrepreneurial firm, *The Academy of Management Journal*, 25, 465–499.

Moller, K. K. and Halinen, A. (1999) Business relationships and networks: managerial challenge of network era, *Industrial Marketing Management*, 28, 413–427.

Nutt, B. E. and McLennan, P. E. (2000) *Facility management risks and opportunities*, Blackwell Publishing Ltd., Oxford.

Porter, M. E. (1985) *Competitive advantage: creating and sustaining superior performance*, Free Press, New York.

17 Reflection on the redevelopment of the University of Tokyo Hospital

The last 26 years

Shinichi Okada and Makoto Nanbuya
(translated by Junko Iwaya)

Origin of the University of Tokyo Hospital (UTH)

The origin of the Medical School of the University of Tokyo goes back to 1858 at the end of the Edo period. The school pioneered the establishment of teaching hospitals in Japan. After the Kanto earthquake disaster in 1923, a master plan for the university campus reconstruction project was designed by architect Shozo Uchida and the hospital was rebuilt.

In the 1950s a new hospital master plan was designed by Professor Yasumi Yoshitake, a mentor of Shinichi Okada, who developed Uchida's master plan. By the 1980s the hospital building could not accommodate the new medical technologies any longer. Dr Seiichi Mishima, the chief executive of the Hospital, approached Professor Seibun Suzuki at the Department of Architecture of the University of Tokyo for advice on the redevelopment of the hospital. This was how the large hospital redevelopment project started: the number of beds was 1301 (including the branch hospital) and the design brief called for the following:

1. *Functional* – most advanced and innovative hospital for teaching at an advanced level of medical practice.
2. *Continuity* – harmony and identity of the Hongo campus of the University Tokyo in the historical urban context.
3. *Improved efficiency by automation* – auto-distribution system, instead of increasing staff numbers.

Managing the Professional Practice: in the built environment, First Edition. Edited by Hedley Smyth.
© 2011 by Blackwell Publishing Ltd. Published 2011 by Blackwell Publishing Ltd.

Image 17.1 Aerial view of the hospital

Architect appointment

Professor Seibun Suzuki recommended Shinichi Okada as a consultant for the Hospital and Estate Department of the University, based upon the attitude and approach applied in architectural planning and the design of prestigious projects including the High Court of Justice. And so started the University of Tokyo Hospital (UTH) Redevelopment project in 1982, comprising four completed phases over 26 years. Okada proposed at the beginning of the planning process that the 'system master plan' should be implemented, which sets 'streets without change' to allow flexibility for other changes and development for the hospital – inspired by John Weeks, a British healthcare architect. Weeks's studies of Ashmore in Dorset, where the main streets had not changed in over 800 years despite repeated rebuilding, which Weeks applied at Northwick Park Hospital in North London, were the influence.

In Japan, it is very rare for the same architect to undertake a whole government programme consisting of multiple projects extending over as much as 26 years. Consistent design, in line with the system master plan, was considered important by the client. Okada and Associates (OA) have been retained throughout, which is not just the result of producing successful design but also of successful client management.

We proposed the system master plan as our unique design method when we started the project. And 26 years later, we can see that it also worked as a communication tool between us and the client to understand a design principle which could last such a long period of time.

Normally, a master plan is something that proposes the architectural form, size, and design, but our system master plan neither proposed a form, nor defined the size. Instead, it was a basic concept, which considered the future timescale. For hospital planning, it is impossible to predict the environments in five years' time because new functions and newly invented medical technologies are constantly developed. In order to accommodate such developments, a flexible system with flexible rules are required. This defined the principle of the system master plan. We have proved that the rules we set initially worked well over 25 years as anticipated. The system master plan we invented originally was our unique design method and it became a key for the client to keep us retained on the project throughout all phases.

Office management

A project of this significance and duration has management implications for an entire office. The UTH project has been one of the core projects in our office, and was one of the largest-scale projects we worked on following the High Court of Justice and the Police Headquarters. The UTH project can be classified as a national project. This project made a great contribution to shaping our office management from research and development, project team organisation, resource management to marketing methods.

Research and development

The UTH is a top national teaching hospital, which sets benchmarks for the other teaching hospitals owned by the Ministry of Education and Science. Therefore, the design process started from a stage to establish new sets of standards for room sizes, functions and specifications. The UTH set up a project room within the hospital, where our staff worked every day over a year in order to research the functions in detail, design needs and design criteria. Based on these researches, we prepared our proposal and submitted it to the Ministry of Education and Science. We proposed a future profile of the new UTH by incorporating our research of the existing conditions, usage and activities within the hospital. We also carried out precedent studies of most advanced hospitals within the country and abroad to reflect onto our design. For example, for the ward block design on the Phase III, we visited the USA for case studies of intensive care/critical care units (ICU/CCU) and accident and emergency departments; and for the new diagnostic and treatment centre (the second phase) on the Phase IV, we visited the USA again with medical doctors in the project team for case studies of operating theatres. In collaboration with the researchers at the Architectural Planning Units of the University of Tokyo, we designed the UTH with a multidisciplinary approach by extending our design activities extensively to research and development. We believe that a hospital is not a simple building but like a complicated creature that requires a systematic solution.

Project team member

The development project at the UTH involved the following four entities:

1. Client: the Ministry of Education and Science (the Estate Department at the University of Tokyo)
2. Users: the University of Tokyo Hospital
3. Hospital planning: Architectural Planning Units at the Architecture Department of the University of Tokyo, supervised by Professor Yasumi Yoshitake, Professor Seibun Suzuki and Professor Yasushi Nagasawa
4. Architect: Shin'ichi Okada and Associates

During the period of the project, the UTH had 14 chief executives, and the government hospital organisation was reformed to be an independent administrative institution. The project staff were replaced each time within the client body. These personnel changes made it more important for the practice to keep the same staff on the project in order to realise the plan 'without losing focus'. This was aided by practice rules and principles regarding design, which are the mission statements of the practice.

Project team organisation

Okada acknowledges a dilemma within the organisation between the enormous amount of creative energy and achieving a holistic design. Our organisation is challenging this difficult dilemma. We select skilled personnel who can design in a holistic sense. It is difficult to find the right person with not only qualifications but also skills. The organisation nurtures such designers and the design team members deal with the subdivided tasks depending on the professional skills in their speciality. Our organisation does not have a pyramid type of hierarchy. We aim for an organic form of organisation. Skilled designers with a holistic approach have creative input across the whole organisation. Other project designers and those with technical professional expertise focus upon specific roles and tasks on projects.

There are a number of project team organisation types depending on the project from the 'Individual type' where one person covers all professional skills (diagram 1 in Figure 17.1); to 'Organisational type' where each professional skill team covers the extremely subdivided areas of work (diagram 3 in Figure 17.1). Among those, the 'Team type' is most frequently used. This can be illustrated for the UTH project team (see diagrams overleaf) with Okada as 'A'. The team organisation changes, depending on the phase, as the design progresses.

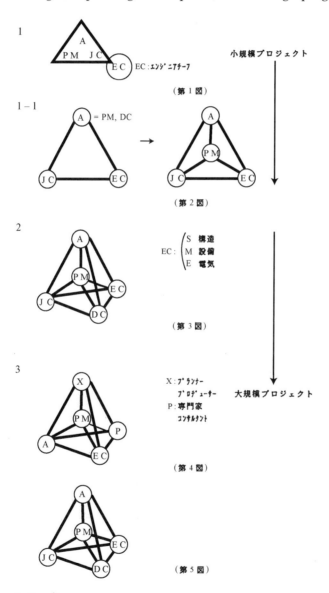

Figure 17.1 Organisation diagrams

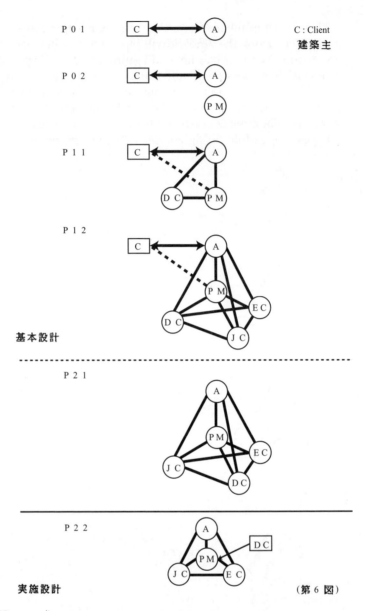

P 0 1

C : Client
建築主

P 0 2

P 1 1

P 1 2

基本設計

P 2 1

P 2 2

実施設計   （第 6 図）

Figure 17.1 *(Continued)*

The skilled architect with the holistic approach, called the 'Architect', leads the 'Total Design', integrating the whole design from programme, outline proposal to detailed design with the different professional specialities.

The 'Project Manager' (PM in Figure 17.1) specialises in managing the team and the work together with the skilled or lead architect and others in negotiation and in meetings with clients. Functions include preparation and arrangement for design team meetings, coordination within the practice, design programme management such as the design process. The role is to assist the smooth progress of the design process, and overall quality depends upon this role.

Design is to 'transform product information into a form of space'. The 'Project Manager' is in charge of managing the process of product information and the quality of design across the professional disciplines: architects, structural, mechanical and electrical engineering staff. 'Design Captain' (DC in Figure 17.1) is in charge of outline proposal and 'Architect' serves this role depending on the scale of the project. 'Job Captain' (JC) is in charge of product and production information.

The 'Engineer Captain' (EC) is responsible for structure, mechanical and electrical engineering for each outline proposal and detailed proposals. They generally play a role similar to project management, depending upon the balance of requirements for a project. Architects or other specialists can lead the 'Total Design' for the project, which requires broader knowledge and experience on the large scale rather than just architecture.

Communication

In order to make the best of individuals within the organisation described above and thinking together, we have an 'Information Centre'. This plays a key role for communication. We believe that each individual is connected with the organisation through the Information Centre, from formal 'Design Work' (job review) to informal coffee breaks. For example, Shin'ichi Okada attends a 'Design Work' every week for a design stage project and a site meeting every month for construction stage projects in order to communicate with each individual.

We facilitate and support our communication through an archive system, which is uniquely personalised, based on individual 'study'. In addition, the centre acts not only as a bank of information, but as a workshop, which becomes a node on our design process. Through this workshop, we expect the staff to communicate with each other beyond the hierarchy or the specialities in their professional skills. Therefore, we expect all staff to understand the meaning of the 'Information Centre' in depth and make the most of it.

Resource management and marketing methods

The demands on resources, especially people, have been considerable and have had to be managed carefully according to the inputs required for the UTH project, whilst other projects are managed effectively too. The relationship between this project and others goes beyond resources. The reputation and network that the office gains from successfully completing a project of this significance affects the ability to attract other clients and stimulating projects. The past chief executives of the UTH spread our good reputation and have had influence on architects' appointments on the other hospital projects across the country. As a result, we have built up our experience in this field which has fed back into each succeeding phase of UTH as well as the other projects within the practice. Consequently, we recently published a book to share the knowledge with the others.

Conclusion

On reflecting over the redevelopment of UTH project for 26 years, we realise that the project made our office management grow in both scale and quality to ensure good quality works required for a national project of a top level. For the long period of time, we had a hard time ensuring the good quality of the design due to systematic changes of architect appointment, scope of works and fee. However, we made considerable efforts because of our belief – at the cost of time and profit. We believe that our mission is to inherit the spirit of the architecture from the past and pass it on to the next generation with a long-term vision. The UTH project proved that our office management completed the circle of producing good works, keeping good reputation and improving the office management to produce better works over a quarter of a century.

Postscript Comment to *Reflection on the redevelopment of the University of Tokyo Hospital* by Shinichi Okada and Makoto Nanbuya

Andrew Edkins

Shinichi Okada and Makoto Nanbuya simply encapsulate their involvement on the University of Tokyo Hospital (UTH). In one way their description underplays the richness of useful and illustrative content which comes into focus when viewed through an academic lens.

We should start with the question of categorising what form of entity UTH is, when considered by those in the space of 'project management'. The answer is squarely that the expansion and adaptation of UTH is clearly a programme. The argument for this is derived from the activities of those organisations such as national defence (e.g. The US Department of Defense – DoD), space and aeronautical engineering (NASA), and complex engineering (companies such as Bechtel, Fluor, KBR – Kellogg Brown and Root). In terms of significant written contributions to the subject, there is, from the UK, the Office of Government Commerce (OGC) *Managing Successful Programmes* – MSP (Great Britain) (Office of Government, 2007). Whilst some may argue that programme management is just glorified project management, this chapter reveals that the complexity and temporal endurance of the *programme* requires a number of other issues that would commonly fall outside the traditional area of project management to be considered. This has been historically the case as described in both the Project Management institute's (PMI) Body of Knowledge (PMBOK) and the equivalent for the Association for Project Management (APM). Both organisations have sought to rectify this, but it is telling that this has occurred in more recent years, well after projects and their management were first described and discussed (Project Management Institute, 2008; Association for Project Management, 2006). The first of these is the issue of relationships as discussed in the context of service-based marketing by Grönroos (2000) and in the project context by Pryke and Smyth (2006).

It is clear almost from the outset of the UTH case that a vital part of the solution to the need of growing and improving UTH would come from the appointment *suitable* individuals and organisations. The issue of suitability or compatibility is one that can be, and indeed traditionally has been, dominated in the project management field by reviews of technical and financial viability. Such things as skills, qualifications, relevant experience, banking and accounting reviews are all important, but in this case they may be considered as necessary but not sufficient. Why is such tangible and explicit testing not sufficient? The answer is that in managing a programme the critical individuals and organisational actors, such as the lead architect, have to be trusted to deliver now and into the future the client's vision of success. In a working hospital of national repute the classic 'iron triangle' of delivery to the technical requirements as specified, within budget and on time are going to be couched in many more subtle concerns. For example, how does an architect ensure the character (the sense of place) when the plan is to expand and remodel? The answer here was to think long-term and strategically, and use the evidence (in this case drawn from historical town layouts) of the enduring nature of 'vital' streets. Whilst there is much written on the potency of such visual cues to layout (see for example Hillier, 1996). But, whilst this appears to have been a successful design strategy, the client will not just be considering 'What is the proposal?', but will be considering 'Do I believe this person?'. To be believable is a judgement that requires many informational feeds. In this case there would presumably have been written and graphical submissions, models and existing examples, and formal and informal presentations. We are therefore, at this point of our reflected analysis, able to differentiate between those elements that are capable of rigorous and objective assessment, and those where the decision is made on subjective assessment and by individuals drawing upon very subtle cues. This would typically get wrapped in statements such as 'I didn't warm to them', 'I liked the way they engaged me – I felt they really understood my situation', 'There was something just not right' (see Chapter 7). These are illustrative quotes, but ones that are heard often. In certain transactions it really doesn't have much of an impact, but as short-term and clearly described projects become amorphous long-term programmes, so the issue of trust in the people involved becomes more critical (Smyth *et al.*, 2010). This point is amplified when the focus of the relationship is a service, and in this case one can see the role of the architect as providing a clear translation service, turning the clients' needs into a series of realistic solutions. The fact that the architect produces numerous drawings and other tangible design output is secondary to the service they are providing.

The final critical area that this case highlights is one that is highly topical – that of knowledge management. This is a large and growing area of research, consultancy, literature and software. However, as this case shows, we are still fundamentally solving knowledge management challenges in the same way as our distance ancestors did before the invention of the written word. It is clear from the various anthropological studies and archaeological investigations of ancient civilisations in locations such as Africa and Australia, that knowledge was passed down using visual depictions such as drawings and pictograms but also, and vitally, by close relationships between individuals with a common bond or set of interests (tribes). Whilst in the modern age we are able to archive vast amounts of explicit information, it is through the more ancient art of recruiting the younger to adopt the role of the older through learning to blend the knowledge and wisdom of the elders with the new approaches that the younger generations have. In this case, although not stated, it is assumed that the younger generations of architects joining Okada and Associates would be taught as part of their formal education about modern building technologies and such things as computer aided design systems. They would therefore be entering the job market with significant sets of technical competence, but they will have no sense of the richness of the relationship built over the many years that the founding architects would have, both with the client and the many others that are involved in delivering a working hospital facility. To learn this knowledge still requires a mix of learning to which one would ascribe the term *experiential*.

The three academic areas addressed in the above review can be summarised as:

1. The complexity of managing programmes.
2. The role of relationships in delivering complex projects and programmes.
3. The challenge of managing knowledge.

Peter Morris was the first to begin to write on this subject (Morris, 1994), which led to a school of thinking called the 'management of projects' that proposes that there is much in common between projects and programmes when looked at from the strategic perspective, as well as understanding the importance of the 'front-end' of a project/programme where strategy and relationships are critical. Equally importantly, the learning from projects is vital and this then raises both the issues of knowledge management and organisational learning. This set of arguments, backed by copious evidence, convinced others, and in 2004 resulted in a mighty tome where a large collection of disparate writers contributed to what can be considered as a compendium of best in theory and best in practice (Morris and Pinto, 2004).

In summary, it is refreshing for an academic reviewer to look at what is clearly a case study written by a highly respected practitioner who has provided such rich and high-quality testimony that allows academe to dissect, analyse and identify some core themes and topics that can then be communicated to a wider audience with the sole intention of improving our understanding of, and the performance of, projects and programmes.

References to Postscript Comment

Association for Project Management (2006) *APM Body of Knowledge*, 5th ed., Association for Project Management, High Wycombe.

Office of Government Commerce (2007) *Managing Successful Programmes*, 3rd ed., TSO, London.

Grönroos, C. (2000) *Service Management and Marketing: managing customer relationships for service and manufacturing firms*, 2nd ed., John Wiley & Sons, Chichester.

Hillier, B. (1996) *Space is the Machine: a configurational theory of architecture*, Cambridge University Press, Cambridge.

Morris, P. W. G. (1994) *The Management of Projects*, Thomas Telford, London, (1997 [reprint]).

Morris, P. W. G. and Pinto, J. K. (2004) *The Wiley Guide to Managing Projects*, John Wiley & Sons, Hoboken, NJ.

Project Management Institute (2008) *A Guide to the Project Management Body of Knowledge (PMBOK Guide)*, Project Management Institute, Inc., Newtown Square, PA.

Pryke, S. D. and Smyth, H. J. (2006) *The Management of Complex Projects: a relationship approach*, Blackwell Publishing Ltd., Oxford.

Smyth, H., Gustafsson, M. and Ganskau, E. (2010) The value of trust in project business, *International Journal of Project Management*, 28(2), 117–129.

18   Beyond the first generation

David Stanford

Introduction

The majority of new practices are established by comparatively young people at relatively early stages in their careers, usually with an unbounded enthusiasm for the creative aspects of their work, frequently with a degree of naivety of the business needs associated with running a practice and almost never with a plan for how the practice, or their involvement in it, will end 20, 30, 40 or even 50 years later.

The issues surrounding a change from first to second generation should be considered as early as possible in a practice's history – its future success will be inextricably linked to the way in which change is managed. It is likely that the partners or directors of a first-generation practice will be of similar age, and therefore may wish to leave or retire at a similar time.

The challenges surrounding the transition from first to second generation are likely to be felt less in future transitions because:

- it has happened before;
- there is likely to be a greater age range of partners or directors and therefore the time over which change can take place will be longer.

Of course, it is possible to simply close the doors on a particular day and retire to the sun-soaked island of your dreams. However, few professionals choose this route and the large majority wish to see the practice that they have established and nurtured to success continue beyond its first generation. Whilst wishing to see the practice succeed in its second and subsequent generations, the founding partners and directors will usually wish to realise a personal financial return on the investments they have made, the risks they have taken and the inherent value of the business they are passing on.

Managing the Professional Practice: in the built environment, First Edition. Edited by Hedley Smyth.
© 2011 by Blackwell Publishing Ltd. Published 2011 by Blackwell Publishing Ltd.

There are therefore three key aspects that need to be resolved if a practice is going to successfully survive beyond its first generation:

1. Transfer of roles and responsibilities.
2. 'Reward' for the outgoing partners or directors.
3. Transfer of ownership.

All of these issues are most simply resolved by being considered at the time that the practice is first established, and the mechanisms for future transfer being embodied early and understood by both those leaving and those taking over. When this is well planned at an early stage in the practice everyone understands how change will take place and the basis on which it will do so. It becomes then a matter of 'when' and 'how much' – both issues that should be considered and are perfectly capable of resolution in the planning stage.

This chapter assumes that this has *not* been done and that mechanisms have yet to be put in place to permit the smooth transfer from first- to second-generation practice. It is informed by the experience of Reid Architecture, a practice that had been in existence for almost 30 years and chose the route of merger with 3D Architects to form 3DReid and thus effect this transfer and facilitate the retirement of the former majority shareholder. 3D Architects and Reid had a common heritage, similar aims and objectives and complementary client and location bases, all key benefits in the bringing together of two practices, as we will see later in this chapter and encapsulated in the logo transition and assimilation – see Image 18.1.

Roles and responsibilities

A practice structure will have evolved throughout the first generation of a practice and, with that, roles and responsibilities for the key people in it. Some will have evolved by design and others just grown through need and natural evolution! These roles and responsibilities need to be identified as the practice moves forward and reallocated appropriately to the succeeding partners and directors, or others within or outside the practice. Included in these will be:

■ business responsibilities, such as financial control, human resources, marketing;
■ design and design quality responsibilities;
■ client management responsibilities.

Many first generation practices set out with the founders taking responsibility for all of the above. At 3DReid, we argue that the large majority of

Image 18.1 Logo evolution during the 3D Architects and Reid Architecture merger to form 3DReid. Source: © 3DReid, reproduced with permission

architects are not good accountants, marketers, HR or IT managers and that we should employ the best we can in these business management roles and allow architects to get on with design and client management. The changeover between first and second generation of practice presents a good opportunity to follow this philosophy through, and ensure that all the staff and directors are utilising their skills, experience and concerns in the best interests of the practice, trusting them and giving them sufficient licence to perform their functions to maximum effect.

The handing on of design-related responsibilities is especially important, particularly if the departing partner or director has been the key figure in producing designs, especially where they have single-handedly created the design reputation of the practice. The careful nurturing of talent over the years – and this is likely to take years – leading up to the handover of responsibility is vital.

A practice's reputation also often stands or falls by the manner in which it executes its designs: clients rarely sue practices over the appearance of a building and are equally unlikely to do so if it is performing as intended. Good-quality control systems are therefore also important, and need to be operated to the stage where they have become a part of the culture of the business rather than being the domain of a single person.

Client management responsibilities are of crucial importance to the future success of the practice – ensuring the best chance of an ongoing workflow beyond the first generation of partners/directors. Putting sufficient time and effort into ensuring that each client is fully content with the continuing partner or director after the founding one has retired/moved on is fundamental.

It is of essence, having identified those to assume roles in the second-generation practice, that partners or directors are coached and supported to be successful in these roles. The departing partners or directors should ensure that they empower the succeeding people sufficiently to develop the necessary skills and relationships, and give them an adequate amount of 'space'. Empowering others will lead to the greatest chance of success for the practice in its second and subsequent generations.

This needs particularly careful handling in the situation where two practices come together to form a new entity by means of merger or acquisition. Both are likely to have identified those with the potential for advancement within their respective practices and to have commenced some sort of mentoring – even if only to tell those people that they 'have potential'. This may lead to two groups of talented people having similar expectations, but without space for them all in the new practice.

There are, regrettably, often causalities in these situations, but it is best to review this as early as possible in the life of the new practice and give each of these people a fair and honest evaluation of their likely future. Some will leave, but better to allow this and get on with the process of ensuring the success of the new practice than to have a top-heavy management structure with individuals working in competition with one another as they fear that others may be promoted to the positions that they had felt would be theirs.

Reward

Departing partners or directors will usually wish to receive financial recompense for their contribution to the practice over time, typically selling their share or equity to the incumbent and next generation of directors or partners.

Establishing a value is rarely straightforward, but in the end it is what one party is prepared to pay and the other is prepared to accept – it will usually come down to a tough negotiation. Assuming that the intention is to transfer ownership to those remaining within the practice, the basis for agreeing a figure should be negotiated as early as possible in order that other aspects of the smooth transition to the next generation can be effected. The figure should be acceptable to the departing partners or directors and affordable by the practice and its new partners.

There are a variety of sums that might contribute towards such a payment that, if planned early and 'cash-flowed' over time, need not put undue strain on the practices and individual resources. These may include:

- equity purchase of the departing partner or director's interests;
- enhanced pension contributions;
- dividend or bonus payments out of future profits;
- ongoing paid consultancy or non-executive directorship;
- an *ex gratia* payment – any such payments are tax free up to limits set under national income tax rules.

Payment for a departing partner or director's interests can be made in a single tranche or in a series of payments, either in cash or possibly in cash and equity. It may be that an initial payment is made, with the balancing payments calculated based on the financial performance of the practice following the departure of the founding partners or directors. Indeed, they may be involved for an agreed period of time to assist in the smooth transfer of clients and workload to the new directors or partners.

The payment that is agreed will represent a number of aspects including some or all of the value of the premises, furniture and equipment that are owned by the departing partners or directors and to be acquired by the new ones, an allowance for the fees that are due and owing to the practice at the time of departure and an element attributed to the goodwill built up by the departing partners or directors that will assist in the continuing success of the practice in its new iteration.

Of course, it may be that agreement cannot be reached between the parties and that the departing partners or directors then have to consider other options, which will principally be a 'trade sale' of the practice to new owners. Whilst this has the benefit of bringing new investors into the practice, it should ideally be done with the agreement of those key people who will remain within the practice. Failure to secure their buy-in to a new ownership structure is likely to see an exodus that is, in turn, likely to affect its future success and thus, potentially, the practice's value and the amount paid if this is dependent on future earnings or profits.

Allied to a financial settlement – and particularly one where the 'departing' partners or directors will have some sort of ongoing involvement with the practice – is what role will they play, if any, and what authority and responsibility they will have for the practice.

Image 18.2 Gunwharf Quays. Source: © 3DReid, reproduced with permission

It is imperative that these matters are fully discussed and recorded to ensure that there is no uncertainty in the future. The question of 'run off' professional indemnity insurance for the departing parties also needs to be resolved.

Transfer of ownership

This is possibly the key issue in the successful transfer of a practice from its first generation to the second. The future success of the practice, and therefore potentially the value that departing partners or directors might get for their equity if payment is phased over time, will be directly related to the commitment of the remaining partners and directors, and it is therefore of great importance that they feel motivated by the situation that they will be in.

There are fundamentally three options:

1. Ownership remains in whole or in part with the founders – remaining and/or new partners or directors direct the practice and gain reward via salaries, bonuses and dividends, whilst the founders continue to derive income via dividends related to their equity.
2. Ownership passes to those within the practice, for example through management buy-out, employee trust or share ownership scheme.
3. Ownership passes to people outside the practice, for example external purchase through acquisition or a form of merger.

Whichever of these options is pursued, specialist advice should be sought, in particular relative to legal and taxation issues, where a decision to transfer ownership by one mechanism or another can have significant implications, some of which can be highly positive and some unexpected or even unwelcome.

Clearly option one is the simplest of the above to effect and carries the potential for least change. However, it is amongst the more difficult to ensure motivation for those remaining, and will rely on an ongoing excellent relationship between the owners and those running the practice.

Option two involves the transfer of ownership internally. This option is likely to motivate the remaining senior management team the most, provided that they do not feel constrained by a financial arrangement with the departing partners or directors that put too much strain on the future performance of the practice. At an early stage, plans need to be made to identify those people who will participate in the future ownership of the practice. Will it be restricted to a small number of senior managers or will it be broadened to include many, or indeed all, staff? There are a number of major practices, Arup and Make to name two (see Chapter 10), who operate wide ownership across all staff and distribute their profits, less an agreed amount for future investment in the practice, to the wider practice via dividends – a tax-efficient way to reward people in the UK – which represents a significant incentive.

Acquisition, the third option, has become increasingly common within the design-related professions over recent years, both major acquisition programmes to form large conglomerates, for example SMC/Archial, or the coming together of high-profile firms, for example Aukett/Fitzroy Robinson in the UK. There are a number of reasons why one practice may wish to come together with another, but underlying the detailed reasons will always be the belief that the new business will be stronger than the businesses that are being brought together. These reasons need to be very clear and will influence the ways in which the new practice behaves following its formation.

For instance:

- is it purely for financial reasons: increased turnover, rationalisation of overheads and thus lower cost and increased profit?
- is it to acquire an 'instant reputation': for example, by acquiring specialism in certain sectors, a 'high design' reputation, higher market presence through increased market share?
- is it to be able to present a broader appeal: wider geographical spread, wider range of skills and experiences?

A number of factors need to be considered if the new practice is to achieve such 'greater than the sum of the parts' ambitions, including:

- cultural fit;
- geographical fit;
- sector fit;
- skills fit;
- new practice structure.

Of these the cultural aspects are the most important – critically, do the senior players in the new business share the same ideals? It is only by having clear vision of the long-term objectives that the new practice will be able to present itself convincingly to its potential client base and motivate its staff. There is inevitably some fall-out amongst staff in the first couple of years following a change of ownership, particularly senior staff because personal comfort zones and career structures are challenged. Yet the best chance of retaining those important to the future success of the practice is by ensuring a clear vision bought into wholeheartedly by the new partners or directors, which is communicated and effectively modelled to all employees.

3D Architects and Reid Architecture came together to form 3DReid in 2007, having agreed to 'merge' for mutual benefit and to enable the passage of Reid from first into second generation and facilitate the retirement of the principal owner. Of critical importance was the cultural fit, which was facilitated by half of the 3D shareholders having formerly been part of the Reid senior management team, and the working practices they had introduced into 3D mirroring many of those within the Reid organisation. The result was a comparatively easy bringing together of two similar-size firms.

Even with this advantage, the systems and procedures had differences. It took a year to identify agreed common practices and more than two years to fully implement these practices seamlessly in their own terms and in relation to the way the culture had developed. Of course, an initial

12 months of unparalleled growth followed by 18 months of recession did not make this task any easier!

However, the underlying ambition to achieve a singular entity at the earliest opportunity is unlikely to be achieved if the individual parts of the new practice are competing with one another, between staff, by teams or offices covering the same markets in terms of geography or sector.

The objective is to create a seamless organisation, with a culture of sharing for the common good. There will be opportunities for cross referrals and client introductions from one part of the new organisation to others across teams, office locations and sectors and these must be identified and exploited to the full. This helps facilitate knowledge transfer across design teams and, in the longer term, skills and experience transfer may also occur between offices and across sectors too.

The skills present in one organisation that can be introduced to another part of the new practice need to be recognised and made available to the whole of the new practice. At 3DReid an excellent track record in airport and commercial work at Reid was complemented by an equally impressive array of education and hotel work at 3D, and cross fertilisation rapidly led to developing design skills and work opportunities across the breadth of the new practice. The highly developed knowledge management process that had been developed at Reid was rapidly and enthusiastically absorbed by the former 3D Architects staff to mutual benefit.

Any significant overlap of skills also needs to be identified and will frequently lead to the redundancy of one or other of the 'experts' following the commencement of the new practice. Reid Architecture had adopted 'Workspace' as its document management/database system, whilst 3D Architects utilised 'Archetype' – clearly the newly merged practice had to select one, resulting in the 'redundancy' of the other. Similarly both practices had different legal and benefits advisors – resulting in the interview and invitation of proposals from both, but ultimately the selection of one of each.

If the 'fit' of all of the above is good and the acquisition is to go ahead, the structure of both management and ownership of the

Image 18.3 RIBA-award-winning Farnborough Terminal. Source: © 3DReid, reproduced with permission

second-generation business must be considered. It is almost inevitable that there will be some duplication of roles when two practices come together and therefore some jockeying for position. The new partners or directors should look ahead and predict it, agree what the preferred structure is for the particular aspect of the practice, set skills' needs, and assess the possible candidates for suitability for the role. It is best to deal with any potential issues swiftly and positively, however difficult this may appear initially. A percentage of individuals within the two organisations will feel threatened by an acquisition and the subsequent merging of activities and functions. The quicker that potential areas of difficulty can be dealt with and communicated fully to all concerned, the better. The most important thing, however, is to make sure that the right people have the right roles within the new structure and this can create positive opportunities for some staff.

At 3DReid both former practices had a management structure that involved directors, a second tier known as divisional directors at 3D Architects and project directors at Reid and associate directors. Whilst the roles differed slightly between the two practices, the similarities in structural arrangement facilitated integration.

Reid Architecture and 3D Architects had offices in six locations between them, but only one city where there was any significant overlap – Glasgow. This meant minimal issues arose when dealing with matters such as premises, support services and suppliers in five locations. It is significant to note that issues that were resolved rapidly in the five locations took significantly longer and required more input in Glasgow.

Genuine mergers are rare. An acquisition is sometimes presented as a merger for PR reasons. The matters listed above need to be considered prior to finalising the arrangements, and carried out diligently. In practice, a carefully considered acquisition not only tries to reconcile functional overlaps and role duplication, but also tries to build on the strengths of the two organisations in creating a fit. Therefore some functions are merged and some become dominant from each of the former practices in an emergent form. A straight acquisition may simply impose control of one organisation on another, both strengths and weaknesses. In the case of 3DReid, the good level of fit from the outset made it easier to agree and build upon the strengths and address certain weaknesses in resolving the areas of overlap and duplication.

Promoting the new practice

The way in which the new business promotes itself should be carefully considered and a plan made, well in advance, for announcing the transfer and structure of ownership to existing and potential clients as well as the 'world in general'. The 'message' that the new partners or directors want to impart must be particularly carefully thought about, with the aim of promoting strengths, building reassurance and confidence, and setting out long-term aims in positive yet realistic ways.

The practice name should be considered. Should it remain the same as the previous iteration to demonstrate 'business as usual', or should it change to demonstrate a 'new beginning'? If a change is contemplated, when should this happen? If the current name is clearly identified with an individual, the succeeding partners or directors might want to consider changing it to be less personalised. This is best done a little while prior to the founder's departure. This is in order that clients, consultants and other industry figures with whom they have historically dealt have time to get used to the new identity prior to their departure. In the case of Reid Architecture we were frequently asked, 'Is there a Geoffrey Reid?' and, 'Is he still an active member of the practice?' well before his retirement. These are good signs in that clients making such comments clearly have confidence in the younger generation and are not relying on historic associations as the bedrock of their relationship with the practice.

The decision to give the name '3DReid' to the newly merged practice arose from the desire to demonstrate a new entity born out of two roughly equal constituent parts that each had its history and track record of success. The large majority of clients clearly understood this and embraced the new practice without hesitation.

If the name is to change, marketing and promotional material should be available to explain the extent of changes that are about to occur and what the aims and ambitions of the practice in its new incarnation will be.

The image or brand (cf. Chapter 15 by Kate McGhee) that the new practice wishes to create for itself is important and will, to an extent, dictate the method of promotion and the type of promotional material used. In general an attitude of 'evolution rather than revolution' is the one likely to find favour with the broadest group of people.

Amongst the first actions following the formation of 3DReid was the establishment of a logo and visual image for the practice combined with an 'awareness campaign' both internally and externally to reinforce the aims and objectives of the newly merged practice and to establish it within the minds of all staff and key clients. This campaign took the form of a series of small brochures issued over the first 12 months of the new practice – see Image 18.4.

The main objective is to deliver a smooth transition and 'no shocks' to the clients who will feed the new practice with work. It is best to select particularly important clients and for the old and new partners or directors to visit these clients together to explain the changes that are about to occur. Formal announcements by letter and in the press can follow.

Q. Will my job be safe?
A. Yes. 3DRaid will take all existing contracts of employment and will honour all the obligations contained in them including payment, holidays. benefits and date of commencement.

Q. Will the Terms & Conditions of my employment change?
A. No. You will be transferred under TUPE regulations. Any changes in the future will be made in full consultation with all employees.

Q. How will I benefit personally from this?
A. There will be significant opportunities created from the merger through the larger practice, the more varied workload and the wider range of skills and experiences within the increased numbers of staff. There will be opportunities for advancement through the flat structure of the practice and its wider ownership base and investment.

Q. Will this mean I will be surrounded with more bureaucracy and lose authority or autonomy in making decisions?
A. No. Every effort will be made to simplify procedures through one single business with no geographic or other barriers. We aim to create more freedom within the company.

2 what does it mean for me?

Image 18.4 Communication about the merger. Source: © 3DReid, reproduced with permission

Conclusions

There are no rights and wrongs as to how to plan for a practice move from initial construct into a second generation. Each practice is different, but the key message is that it must be thought about as early as possible during the practice lifecycle. As has been indicted – 'the best time to plan the exit strategy for the founders of a practice is at its inception, the second best time is now!'

For each context, certain decisions may be better than others, therefore carefully planning for succession when it comes is important. Every eventuality cannot be anticipated nor every detail known in advance, yet careful consideration can aid efficient, effective succession to the next generation, leaving the practice in the best possible shape to continue its success.

In conclusion, the following should be considered as early as possible in the life of a practice:

- the mechanism by which the founders will come to retire or otherwise leave, and the manner in which they will release their equity in the practice;
- a method of calculating the value that the founders are passing on to the next generation;

- identification of those individuals who will be the 'next generation', and their grooming over time to be ready to excel in the role;
- ways of ensuring that the goodwill of the founders will be passed on to the new generation;
- the methods by which those remaining in the practice are incentivised and rewarded if the agreed mechanisms involve outside finance;
- strategies that will ensure that the new practice is more than the sum of the two former practices if the agreed mechanisms involve a merger or purchase by another practice;
- how the new practice will present and market itself to its client base.

Postscript Comment to *Beyond the first generation* by David Stanford

Hedley Smyth

There are two main themes in this chapter: the succession issue and a merger. The succession issue will be addressed first and merger second.

Succession is under-researched and not always understood by those experiencing this process. Under the best circumstances it is an uneasy transition, and David Stanford has set out clearly some of the key issues to be addressed. Yet there are many tensions and several taboos that hold back open discussion and the development of clear strategies for transition.

Probably the greatest tension and most taboos surround the strong idea firms, as defined by Coxe *et al.* (1987) and Winch and Schneider (1993). On the one hand, the founding guru of the strong idea firm, who has built up the reputation of the practice and may be closely associated with the brand, wants to leave a legacy of success that goes beyond the buildings designed. On the other hand, they may feel that there is probably nobody else who can step into their shoes. This is less of problem for strong idea practices and strong service firms that are not designers and thus they will probably have an even greater desire to leave a legacy in the shape of the firm. In practice, though, this tension will either mean that the issues are not talked about or are insufficiently addressed – the taboo subject – or if someone is brought on to step into their shoes, they may be left in mid air later as the founder has second thoughts about them. A team may be identified to succeed. In many cases the founding owner will tend to keep too much equity, which can be understandably important for securing their future yet it can make it difficult for the successors to be able to raise the capital to buy them out.

This may have been one of the issues for Reid Architecture, albeit as a strong service firm developing its strong ideas capabilities and hence value of the firm too. Concentrated ownership can be one driver towards finding a suitor. A gradual transfer of equity is needed over several years, especially during expansion years. Successors can acquire equity as part payment through a salary or profits distribution scheme in addition to outright purchases of existing equity.

Lord Foster has taken an interesting path as the founder of the strong idea firm, Foster Associates. First, he founded a large internationally renown practice with a brand based around his distinctive design approach. Strong idea firms tend to become strong service firms over time without creative refreshment as yesterday's innovation becomes tomorrow's generic palette adapted to different contexts (Coxe *et al.*, 1987). Without the founder, the distinctiveness of design is lost and the brand weakened. New blood can refresh the creativity, but may not be given sufficient head by the founder. Foster's solution was to bow out and demand that his name be removed from the firm's name in time. Perhaps Foster wants his buildings to speak for themselves or perhaps he lacked confidence in the practice's ability to sustain the legacy. Yet this approach is tantamount to recognition that his firm is likely to become a strong service firm, which it could be argued is under way.

All firms, regardless of market position, experience something of these issues concerning succession. The tensions and taboos lead to the issues being addressed late in the day. Yet as the legal and financial demands set out by David Stanford show, timely consideration is important for the health of the firm, particularly for retaining clients and staff.

People do not follow strategies; they follow people. If they like those in charge and the practice strategy seems reasonable, then they will adhere to the strategy, perhaps develop it where they closely identify with the firm (cf. Chapter 7 by Hedley Smyth and Sofia Kioussi). To the extent that this is the case, succession may mean that many key staff will move to rivals. While some key staff may not actively dislike the new leadership, they may not identify so closely with them, and hence see the change as a stimulus to seek pastures new and explore new challenges. Others who felt favoured will feel less favoured under the new regime and seek to satisfy career ambitions elsewhere. The extent to which succession has been inadequately addressed, and kept a taboo subject, is likely to increase staff churn.

Senior management may not always be aware of these tensions amongst staff, especially middle and junior management. These people are an important part of the social capital of the firm (Ghoshal and Nahapiet, 1998), and hence of the value of the equity bought by successors. Uncertainty and tension amongst staff can also lower morale, which reduces the effectiveness and efficiency of staff remaining in the practice. One way of managing this problem is to allow for some devaluation of the equity at the point of sale. Another common approach is to phase the payments to the founders over several years after they have left in ways that are linked to future performance. This acts as an encouragement to founders to address these succession issues in a timely way, manage the social capital by creating opportunities through succession and also take account of market volatility in the economic cycle.

It is best for the founder to sell at the peak of the market, but the worst time to buy – see Chapter 1. It is best for successors to buy in the downturn, not so much because they can buy cheap, although they might, but because staff are more likely to stay and the management can control more directly whom they want as core staff and whom to make redundant. In many ways the best time for the founder to sell is in the upturn with equity stage payments linked to performance over several years of growth. False or overoptimistic expectations of the value of the practice are unlikely at this time, growth creates hope and career options for existing staff, and helps retain clients in positive trading conditions with least disruption.

The other main theme in David Stanford's chapter is merger. There has been an increased level of research into mergers and acquisitions amongst professional practice in recent years (e.g. Empson, 2000; Bröchner *et al.*, 2004) and consolidation has been proceeding apace in recent years, particularly with the emergence of conglomerate professional practices, such as AECOM in built environment services. (see Chapter 1 by Hedley Smyth and Chapter 19 by Jim Meikle).

Many of the same issues apply to mergers, such as staff churn, the effect of change on morale, and the consequential value of the social capital and hence of equity. Yet mergers tend to induce greater levels of change, for example a challenge of organisational cultures. In the case of 3DReid, there were senior personnel who had worked in both practices. This clearly helps. Assuming the market position is the same – both 3D Architects and Reid Architecture were strong service firms (cf. Coxe *et al.*, 1987: Winch and Schneider, 1993) – the organisational culture and norms may be different. Mergers tend to intensify the negotiation process, power struggles emerging between cultures, and the consequence being that most mergers end up as acquisitions where one firm's norms become dominant overall. This can accelerate the rate of churn and adversely affect morale, hence destroying social capital, the result being that the full benefits of merger do not materialise. Paradoxically, this might stimulate the search for other targets to acquire. The larger resource base and diminishing social capital can be used to buy in new capabilities and expand geographical spread. This may lead to the homogenisation of services – strong service firms becoming strong delivery firms (Coxe *et al.*, 1987) – unless other capabilities are added (Helfat *et al.*, 2007). It has led to conglomerate consultancies with global reach, such as AECOM, Atkins and WSP, where capabilities include multidisciplinary service provision and the ability to service international clients in almost any geographical region.

Part of the capability in relation to culture is the formal and informal routines or norms (Nelson and Winter, 1982). David Stanford has drawn attention to the difficulties of harmonising formal routines such as IT systems and informal processes. This is crucial for effective working, yet dominance does not provide best guidance to adoption. For example, the merger of two major real-estate consultancies in the UK resulted in the firm with the most corporate or bureaucratic systems emerging as the dominant partner. Yet, the other practice had the lighter touch to systems management with higher levels of informal systems. This was the profitable player and this market advantage was lost post-merger.

In conclusion, successions and mergers are amongst the most difficult management issues. The way in which they are managed is critical to the long-term success of the practices concerned.

References to Postscript Comment

Bröchner, J., Rosander, S. and Waara, F. (2004) Cross-border post-acquisition knowledge transfer among construction consultants, *Construction Management and Economics*, 22, 421–427.

Coxe, W., Hartung, N., Hochberg, H., Lewis, B., Maister, D., Mattox, R. and Piven, P. (1987) *Success Strategies for Design Professionals*, McGraw Hill, New York.

Empson, L. (2000) Merging Professional Service Firms, *Business Strategy Review*, 11(2), 39–46.

Ghoshal, S. and Nahapiet, J. (1998) Social capital, intellectual capital, and the organizational advantage, *Academy of Management Review*, 22, 242–266.

Helfat, C. E., Finkelstein, S., Mitchell, W., Peteraf, M. A., Singh, H., Teece, D. J. and Winter, S. G. (2007) *Dynamic Capabilities: understanding strategic change in organizations*, Blackwell Publishing Ltd., Malden.

Nelson, R. R. and Winter, S. G. (1982) *An Evolutionary Theory of Economic Change*, Harvard University Press, Boston.

Winch, G. M. and Schneider, E. (1993) The strategic management of architectural practice, *Construction Management and Economics*, 11, 467–473.

19 Changes in UK construction professional services firms in the late 20th century

Jim Meikle

Until the 1970s, professional services firms in the UK construction sector were mostly single-discipline traditional partnerships and firms with more than ten partners or more than 100 staff considered large. Today, in the late 2000s, there are many firms of many hundreds of people in a variety of corporate forms providing a wide range of construction-related services. Why have things changed so much in such a relatively short time? What does it say about the way these firms have been, and are being, managed and about the environment in which they operate?

In some ways it is a continuation of a trend; in others, it is a result of step changes in both the immediate industrial environment, and the wider social, economic and regulatory environment. Before World War II, UK professional firms were rarely more than 20 strong with, typically, two to four partners, and they rarely worked from more than one location. Economic conditions were precarious in the 1920s and 1930s, and most firms were content to remain small and local. After the war there were 25 years of generally steady demand for construction works and services, much funded by the public sector and most on mandatory fee scales set by the professional institutions. More or less guaranteed workload encouraged firms to grow in size and in the number of locations they operated from, but, by today's standards, they still remained relatively small and largely focused on a core discipline. It all began to change in the 1980s.

This chapter discusses three interrelated themes in the construction professions that began to emerge strongly in the 1980s in the UK: deregulation, growth and consolidation and diversification. The first is a 'cause' or driver of change, the second and third are 'effects' or results. The chapter focuses on firms whose core activity is quantity surveying or cost management. Many of the ideas come from personal experience as a partner in what was Davis Langdon LLP and, more particularly, research for a recent published history of the firm

Managing the Professional Practice: in the built environment, First Edition. Edited by Hedley Smyth.
© 2011 by Blackwell Publishing Ltd. Published 2011 by Blackwell Publishing Ltd.

(Meikle, 2009). The chapter is in six parts, including this introduction. The second section describes the recent development of Davis Langdon in the UK while the third, fourth and fifth discuss the three themes in turn. A final section draws some conclusions for construction professional services firms.

The origins and development of Davis Langdon

Davis Langdon is the result of a merger in 1988 that brought together two of the largest quantity surveying firms of the day. The main rationale for the merger was a perceived need for increased size and strength in depth in a number of markets. The nine national partners in Davis Belfast & Everest, and the five in Langdon & Every, saw the advantages and potential of merging but it was market conditions and the new firm's response to these that created a firm in the UK and the Middle East alone with more than three times the people and almost ten times the turnover in 2008 than there had been 20 years earlier (the turnover values have not been adjusted for inflation).

Over that period, the construction industry saw two major booms and busts, but most of the period (1994–2008) was a healthy market for professional services firms in construction. The merger was consummated at the tail end of the 1980s boom – and almost certainly would not have taken place if the timing had slipped by a year or two; by 1990 the industry was in steep decline and it was three or four years before there was the beginning of a recovery in business confidence. The first decade of the merged firm, therefore, comprised two or three years of continuing growth, followed by four or five years of declining workload and revenues, then two or three years of cautious recovery.

In 1998, ten years after the merger, Paul Morrell became senior partner and rapidly set in train a programme of radical change. The merger had been of two traditional professional partnerships; Morrell was determined to create a modern business. The merger had generated the need for the new firm to rethink itself in terms of management and structure, and the merged firm had much more formal organisational arrangements than either firm had previously. It had a management board that endeavoured to represent all sides of the business, at least geographically, and functional managers were appointed for finance, HR, IT and business development. Initially, the latter two were quantity surveyors who had reinvented themselves.

Morrell built on the initial moves after the merger towards a more business-orientated structure and culture. The finance partner was now an equity partner (the first non-RICS member), the provincial offices were grouped into regions to help generate critical mass and the London office developed specialisms, for example, offices, tall buildings, retail

Table 19.1 Davis Langdon mergers, 1999 to 2002 (Source: Meikle, 2009, reproduced with permission of Black Dog Publishing Ltd)

Original name of firm	Locations	Date of merger	Notes
National			
Leighton & Wright	South Wales	1999	Quantity surveyors
Poole Stokes & Wood	Manchester, Birmingham, London	1999	Established 1965; quantity surveyors
Mott Green & Wall	London	1999	Established 1970; mechanical and electrical services quantity surveyors
Schumann Smith	Stevenage	2000	Established 1986; specification consultants
NBW Crosher & James	London, Birmingham Glasgow, Edinburgh	2001	Crosher & James established 1935; Napier Blakely & Winter, 1988; NBW Crosher & James, 2001; construction taxation consultants
Stockings & Clark	East Anglia	2001	Quantity surveyors
International			
Farrow Laing & Partners	South Africa	1999	Established 1922; quantity surveyors
Adamson Associates	USA	1999	Established 1974; cost consultants
Knapman Clark & Co	New Zealand	1999	Established 1954; quantity surveyors
Patterson Kempster & Shortall	Republic of Ireland	2002	Established 1860; quantity surveyors

and sports. Another of his achievements, in a three-year period from 1999, was to complete a series of ten mergers – six of which were in the UK – that increased the firm's QS resources, broadened its services and supplemented the firm's presence both nationally and internationally (Table 19.1).

The mergers increased the size of the partnership but diluted the personal links among partners. The pure quantity surveyors (Leighton & Wright, Poole Stokes & Wood and Stockings & Clark) were absorbed into the main firm more or less immediately although, over time, some partners and staff left; the specialist firms (Mott Green & Wall, Schumann Smith and NBW Crosher & James) tended to retain their own procedures, partners and cultures.

The international mergers joined an international practice that was a network of practices with the same or similar names but with no shared ownership and relatively little shared management. Cross shareholdings were abandoned in the late 1990s and an international *verein* structure introduced because of the practical (exchange rate, tax and regulatory) difficulties of assessing revenues and profits. A *verein* is a Swiss form of business organisation combining a number of independent entities, each of which has limited liability vis-à-vis the others. The main purpose of the *verein*, in the context of Davis Langdon internationally, was to establish common standards across the practice without the complications of shared management, ownership and finances. Its main disadvantage is its lack of corporate 'glue', but it has the advantages of simplicity of establishment and operation and non-controversial business relationships. The *verein* structure has been adopted by a number of major international professional services firms, including, for example, Deloitte Touche Tohmatsu and Baker & McKenzie.

Other changes during Morrell's five-year tenure included company-wide QA registration and accreditation as Investors in People (IIP), the introduction of formal business plans, and staff and partner performance reviews. Some of these were the result of client demand (e.g. QA registration) but all of them reinforced a more corporate approach to organising the firm and doing business.

Rob Smith took over as senior partner in 2003 during booming market conditions. He continued the moves to the more corporate structure, management and image introduced by Morrell. The firm moved to MidCity Place in High Holborn, a modern prestige location and building and, shortly after, the firm became a limited liability partnership (LLP). LLP status reduced the professional liability of individual partners and led the way to increased spread of ownership, with salaried partners taking a share in the equity.

In 2008, a 'One Firm One Future' initiative reordered the firm into a single national practice along sectoral lines defined by building type specialisations (Eccles and Simpson, 2008). The old geographical organisation as a primary management structure was abandoned, although the regional offices remained. There had been debates on ownership and profit sharing in the early 1990s but these were largely overtaken by a preoccupation with survival. Now the cost management, project management and various specialist teams – such as construction taxation, management consulting and legal support services – were grouped together and, where possible, their work, income and profit were allocated to sectors.

In late 2008, the credit crunch struck and workload dropped dramatically. The impact of the resulting recession on the QS profession generally was immediate and substantial. The firm's management response included redundancies, salary cuts for staff, movement of UK staff overseas, mainly to the Middle East, and reduced drawings for partners. By mid 2009 staff numbers had fallen by more than 10% and across-the-board payroll cuts of some 15% were introduced.

Deregulation of the professions

There had been critical comments about professional monopolies since the 1960s and a 1977 Monopolies and Mergers Commission report (House of Commons, 1977) led to major revisions in the RICS bye laws: fixed or mandatory fee scales were abolished, and restrictions on fee competition, advertising and permissible company structures were relaxed. The Conservative government that came to power in 1979 under Margaret Thatcher finally ended the common use of set scale fees. Initially the booming market through the 1980s reduced the impact of abolition but, progressively, fee competition became commonplace and firms responded with a combination of reduced fees and services and an increase in the number of services offered for which they could charge fees.

After the recession of the early 1990s, the normal scope of services offered by QSs was radically different from the standard service set down in the RICS fee scales. In particular, the use of bills of quantities and the standard method of measurement declined markedly, and the focus moved to early project cost advice and cost planning, particularly in the larger firms. Project management and other non-core services became a significant component of some of the larger firms' range of services; these provided new income streams and allowed firms to charge for services, some of which had often previously been provided as part of the core service. Other services also offered scope for ambitious and far-seeing quantity surveyors to utilise their education and training across a broad spectrum of construction services.

At the same time, the new rules on advertising led to a much more commercial approach to marketing, and press advertising, sponsorship and corporate entertainment became increasingly mainstream. In the 1990s, Davis Langdon sponsored a sailing race and an expedition to Mount Everest, before the Everest name was dropped from the firm's title. Davis Langdon retained their partnership structure but took advantage of the relaxation on partners' qualifications to appoint their first non-RICS partner, an accountant and, effectively, the firm's finance director.

Growth and consolidation

After the recovery from the 1990s recession, there was a steady trend to growth and consolidation in the larger construction professional services firms, including quantity surveyors. There is also some evidence that construction projects became progressively larger; the average job size in the UK increased markedly between 1994 and 2008. Table 19.2 shows the top ten quantity surveying firms by chartered (RICS qualified) staff in 1988 and 2002. In what was the first *Building Magazine* survey of quantity surveyors in 1988, the ten largest firms that submitted data had combined UK chartered staff of 1169. The top ten firms in 2002, the last year that the feature had a table dedicated to quantity surveyors, had combined UK staff of 4248 an average growth over 14 years of more than 10% per annum, much higher than the growth in demand for QS services.

Table 19.2 Chartered (RICS) staff in the top ten QS firms in the UK, 1988 and 2002 (Source: Building Magazine, 1988 and 2002 and the RICS)

Rank	1988		2002	
	Firm	Chartered staff	Firm	Chartered staff
1	Gleeds	190	Atkins	810
2	Faithful & Gould	175	EC Harris	668
3	Davis Langdon & Everest	153	Davis Langdon & Everest	618
4	Franklin & Andrews	134	Atkins Faithful & Gould	600
5	Currie & Brown	102	Franklin & Andrews	510
6	Monk Dunstone	110	Gleeds	320
7	WT Partnership	90	Turner & Townsend Group	230
8	Turner & Townsend	75	Capita Property Consultancy	195
9	Northcroft Neighbour & Nicholson	73	Systech Group	150
10	Bucknall Austin	67	Cyril Sweett	147
		1169		4248
All chartered quantity surveyors		21,461		24,670*
Top ten as a percentage of all		5.4%		17.3%

*This is the 2008 total; the 2002 RICS figures do not separate QS members. It is probable that the total number of chartered quantity surveyors in 2002 was around 23,500. The percentage would then be 18.1%.

Growth was largely at the expense of medium-sized firms as predicted in an RICS report of the early 1990s (Davis Langdon & Everest Consultancy Group, 1991). In addition to deliberate growth strategies there has been a financial, regulatory and client-driven preference for larger firms through demands for formal registrations (e.g. for quality assurance and Investors In People accreditation), requirements for published accounts and strong balance sheets, high professional indemnity insurance limits and increases in the use of framework arrangements for client programmes of work. (Framework agreements involve firms bidding to secure limited positions as suppliers to regular construction clients; once secured, framework contracts provide access to work streams that may or may not require further competitive bidding.) All of these trends tended to present barriers to market entry for new and smaller firms.

Size brings with it issues of ownership, organisation and management. All of the big firms were private unlimited partnerships until the mid 1980s, because institutions such as the RICS required that. The rules were relaxed in 1984, and some firms took the opportunity to become private or even limited companies, but most of the large firms remained as traditional partnerships until the more recent limited liability partnership form was introduced in 2001.

But even though the traditional partnership structure stayed, with growth in turnover and staff numbers, the number of partners in Davis

Langdon increased. In 1988, before the merger that created Davis Langdon, Langdon and Every had five UK partners and Davis Belfield & Everest had nine, for a combined staff of some 300. In 2008 Davis Langdon had over 70 principal equity-owning partners and another 120 shareholding partners but they had over 2000 staff. It was relatively simple and straightforward to manage a firm with less than 20 partners and a few hundred staff; it is much more complex to structure and manage 200 owners and 2000 staff.

Growth and structural change led to changes in management style and form. Not all partners could be involved in all decision-making, and increasingly partnership became a form of ownership and profit-sharing but with much less involvement for most partners in strategy and decision-making. Mergers also tended to create business, rather than traditional personal relationships among partners. A management board and management board committees were introduced in 1988 but individual partners still largely maintained control over their offices or teams.

Diversification

The firms listed in the 2002 column of Table 19.2 are, of course, also becoming more diversified and less tied to historic QS origins. Half of them appear in both 1988 and 2002 but the firms that were dedicated quantity surveying firms now call themselves construction consultants, or some such non-specific descriptor, and provide a range of services. Of the others, Atkins was originally an engineering consultancy that had accumulated a large number of quantity surveyors in their takeovers of local authority technical departments; they had also taken over a long-established QS firm, Faithful & Gould that appears separately in Table 19.2. Capita's origins were in financial management and it grew rapidly, as had Atkins, on the back of the outsourcing of public services; its roster of QSs was entirely from acquisition.

Specialist firms, for example on legal services (James R Knowles) and taxation (Crosher & James) emerged in the 1970s. Project management emerged in the 1980s, partly introduced from the USA, partly from the process engineering industries – particularly North Sea gas – and partly as a result of architects' withdrawal from their traditional role as leaders of the building team. Value and risk management came out of project management and in part were the result of it being promoted by the Association of Project Management.

Diversification into new or different services could be 'home grown' or 'bought in', and buying in could involve employing individuals or acquiring firms. Davis Langdon has diversified using both methods: management consulting and legal support services were home grown; project management, risk and value management and construction taxation were started by buying in employees, although construction taxation was subsequently reinforced by a major merger. Specification was the result of another merger; a building surveying group was also formed by pulling together a number of individuals and groups around the firm.

The rationales for these services varied. Some were new and fashionable; some were niche and became mainstream; and most were the result of individuals pursuing personal interests. One general driver towards diversification was that the demise of scale fees and fierce fee competition created an impetus for new sources of revenue. Services that had been included in the larger firm's general offerings – quasi-legal or accountancy advice and market or economic research, for example – were now seen as discrete fee earners.

Diversification was also the result of a more business-like approach to the management and organisation of construction professional services firms. Traditionally there had been a place for technically expert, and business savvy, partners but these had usually been in single discipline practices. Multidiscipline firms needed to be large enough and sufficiently business minded to actively pursue a range of parallel offerings.

Service diversification came relatively late to Davis Langdon. At the time of the merger in 1988, over 95% of Davis Langdon's fee income came from traditional quantity surveying or cost management services, while the balance was in project management and management consulting. The only specialist group was the consultancy group, the predecessor of Davis Langdon Management Consulting; Davis Langdon Management appeared in 1990 some time after Gardiner & Theobald Management Services and specialist project managers. Over the next 20 years, project management grew to be a core service, representing around a quarter to one-third of total fee income and other non-core services represented 15% of total income.

Davis Langdon's initial reluctance to diversify was mainly due to inherent conservatism, risk aversion and a concern that their architect colleagues would not approve. Legal support and taxation advice gradually emerged in the 1990s. Other specialist services came from or were reinforced by mergers (see Table 19.1).

Commentary

Some, but not all, of the factors discussed in this paper are common to other built environment professions. The large engineering firms have increased their scope of services but architects have tended to be more focused on their core skill of building design. Quantity surveyors have always tended to respond to the economic and legal environment that they find themselves in, rather than endeavour to shape it.

Changes in the structure, operation and management of all built environment professional services firms over the last 20 or so years have been extensive, wide ranging and possibly, but not certainly, long lasting. The big firms are much larger than before and command a bigger share of their markets (see Table 19.2). The firms with their roots in quantity surveying provide a much wider range of services and operate both nationally and internationally. Most of the large firms have company or LLP structures and are managed as corporate businesses, not traditional partnerships.

Changes have been prompted by both external and internal factors with the former probably being more significant, although the drive and ambition of individuals has also been important. Regulation, privatisation and market conditions have all had impacts. Regulatory effects have been about both the lifting and the imposition of rules and regulations. The most significant for chartered surveying firms was almost certainly the removal of set fee scales that led inexorably to fee competition, but registration and certification requirements have also had significant effects. Privatisation provided opportunities for professional firms to acquire resources and secure business.

Market conditions included the effects of both booms and busts. The property market collapse in 1989/90 shortly after the removal of set fee scales paved the way for a 'triple whammy' for many firms: falling demand for their services, reduced percentage fees due to competition and reduced contract values on which *ad valorem* fees were based. Those firms that survived became more effective at providing reduced cost management/quantity surveying services and providing and charging for other services.

There is a law or rule of unintended consequences that follows many government and other official policies. It is certain that removal of mandatory scale fees and the accompanying relaxation of restrictions in practice in the 1980s led to a reduction in fee levels and an increase in competition. But they also led to reduced services and stricter interpretation of the services and an increase in 'new' services for which 'new' fees could be charged. This, combined with requirements for strong balance sheets, high professional indemnity insurance and demands for regulatory compliances, all tended to favour larger established firms able to offer core services efficiently and to diversify into other services that produce good rates of return. It is increasingly difficult for small or new firms to gain entry to major public or private sector built environment commissions.

Growth in the scale and scope of construction professional services firms has come from both mergers and acquisitions, and from organic growth. Interestingly, while manufacturing and contracting, and some services firms have tended to focus on 'core business', firms like Davis Langdon have deliberately diversified. It is worth noting, however, that diversification has largely been within, rather than beyond, the world of construction projects; it has provided additional revenues but basically that revenue still comes from the same market.

Although structure and management have changed since 1988, ownership has remained within the firms. With some notable exceptions, most built environment professional firms are still privately owned by partners or directors, but the numbers of partners or directors have grown at least in line with the overall size of the firms. When ownership is spread across many people, individual responsibility is inevitably diluted and individual partners' involvement in policy and strategy is necessarily limited.

Either a small partnership (less than, say, 15 partners) or wider ownership (for example, all employees with more than a minimum period of employment) is probably preferable to a large partnership. In a large partnership the more junior partners have had their abilities recognised but often that has not led to a more strategic role in the firm, only more responsibility and financial risk.

The architects of the Davis Langdon merger, although bold, could not have foreseen what the firm would become – and possibly would not have wished it. They would have been impressed by the size of the firm but concerned about the spread of ownership. They would no doubt have been amazed at the turnover but worried about percentage fee rates. And they would not have recognised what quantity surveyors do nowadays. But what the firm has become flowed inexorably from what those 14 partners of Davis Belfield & Everest and Langdon & Every set out to do in 1988. Arguably, if the firm had not done what it has it would not have grown in size and reputation, and it would have lost market share to its competitors. Time alone will tell whether the firms like Davis Langdon will grow and prosper in the future.

Editor's note

Since this chapter was written Davis Langdon agreed to by acquired by AECOM, the US professional services group.

References

Meikle, J. (2009) *Thinking Big: a history of Davis Langdon*, Black Dog Publishing, London.

House of Commons (1977) *Surveyors' Services: a report on the supply of surveyors' services with reference to scale fees*, 5 November, London.

Eccles, R. and Simpson, K. (2008) *One Firm One Future at Davis Langdon*, Harvard Business School, Boston.

Building Magazine (1988) League tables of quantity surveying firms, 29 July.

Building Magazine (2002) League tables of quantity surveying firms, 27 September.

Davis Langdon & Everest Consultancy Group (1991) *The Future Role of the Quantity Surveyor*, QS 2000, RICS QS Division, London.

> **Postscript Comment to *Changes in UK construction professional services firms in the late 20th century* by Jim Meikle**

Hedley Smyth

The nature of enterprise management is that there are sensitivities in the marketplace. On the one hand, firms need to build confidence in their markets. This is essentially a moral question for society and an ethical issue for business. Frequently overlooked is the moral functioning of markets, which underpins their survival (Smyth, 2008a; 2008b; 2009; cf. Kramer, 2009); particularly overlooked in economic models and also ideologies such as monetarist views that shareholder views are the only ones that matter (e.g. Friedman 1970; 2000). Such views were and are unsustainable as recognised by Adam Smith (1984). Confidence arises from degrees of openness as evidence of good financial and moral practices accumulates.

On the other hand, firms operate on the basis of trust, whereby openness is limited by the cost of being transparent or by the sensitivity and confidentiality of information. Trustworthiness is a sense that actors are operating with ethical concern for other parties and society at large most of the time. Opportunistic self-interest with guile, at the level of the firm and its dealings in the marketplace, can prevail for periods and for particular transactions, but such firms run the risk of losing market share as a result of loss of reputation and diminution of social capital derived from the goodwill that confidence and trust bring. This picture, particularly the time frames in which reputation and market share is lost, is moderated by frequency of transaction, the specificity of assets and bounded rationality cited in transaction cost economics.

Professional practices are no different from other firms in these respects within the marketplace. Indeed, it could be argued that the professional status and values give rise to higher levels of social capital derived from trust and confidence, and hence value. Where this social capital is high in general terms, it is hard to quantify in financial terms, to which economists and accountants would testify. This potentially renders any professional practice undervalued in the market and thus subject to a bid from rivals seeking expansion to grow in size, geographical coverage, multidisciplinarity and hence, market share. Whilst growth motives from predatory practices may seek acquisitions that are motivated by a range of criteria (see also Chapter 18 by David Stanford), the social capital element is one that is assessed as goodwill. Acquisitions and mergers are particular infrequent and asset-specific transactions that require high levels of confidentiality to succeed or resist. Acquisitions test confidence and trust in the market and can erode the value of the actors if managed badly; indeed, one aim is for parties to increase the value of their companies through a more complete realisation of their market value. For the acquirer is the recognition amongst shareholders that they are buying a company that will increase their value – the new whole being worth more than the sum of the parts. The acquirer may also be able to argue that the target is undervalued; therefore, a further enhancement will arise to the acquirer. The company being acquired will try to maximise value for its owners, hoping the bid will raise the share value on sale or help it to ward off the bid if it is contested.

This chapter by Jim Meikle has set out the extent to which Davis Langdon has grown over the years, including by acquisition. Chapter 1 has also shown the importance of acquisition as a growth strategy for professional practices in the built environment. At the time of writing, Davis Langdon is itself subject to a bid from the US-based multidisciplinary practice, AECOM. This bid is part of the trend to grow market share at the bottom of, and coming out of, recession (see Chapter 1 by Hedley Smyth). More generally it is a sign of:

- the growing trend of globalisation;
- the increasing emergence of the large multidisciplinary practices;
- the importance of London as a world cluster for the built environment.

At the time of writing the draft, the outcome of the bid was unknown (but has subsequently been finalised) therefore this dimension is not explored further. There are a few general points that can be drawn out and this Postscript particularly wishes to focus upon the final bullet points above.

Large multidisciplinary professional practices in the built environment will particularly want a strong base in London, especially if their home base is outside the UK. London is currently the premier world cluster for the built environment (see Chapter 1 by Hedley Smyth). It is a prime location for the national, European and global market for all disciplines. There have been a range of acquisitions of UK practices based in and around London, one of the earliest being the takeover of the engineering consultant Sir Alexander Gibb & Partners by the US firm, Jacobs, in 2001. Quantity surveying (QS) and cost consultant practices from the UK have distinct features, and the Royal Institution of Chartered Surveyors (RICS) has been investing in the internationalisation of their disciplines with some success. This renders major QS and cost consultant practices important targets for aggressive global practices.

Consultants from the USA that acquire UK-based – and particularly London-based – practices are especially significant. The media and advertising groups were largely based in New York. There was a British invasion of New York's leading world cluster, led by Saatchi & Saatchi and by WPP in the 1980s and early 1990s (Grabher, 2002; see also Chapter 2 by Graham Winch). Today, UK media and advertising groups dominate, and London has become a more important world cluster for that sector as a result. It is possible that a similar trend in reverse is under way, whereby US firms are trying to secure greater dominance through acquisitions in the London world cluster of the professions in the built environment.

There have been criticisms of acquisition strategies, stating that the benefits do not always accrue to the acquirers, and there is truth in this as many bids turn out to be optimistic, especially where staff and clients are the primary assets, and both can 'walk' in service industries. Yet some benefits accrue from undervalued social capital such as the moral components of trust and confidence in the market that is historically embedded in professional practices. Whilst Chapter 1 questioned whether the large consultants with global reach can become too self-interested and neglect the ethics of their professional roots, acquiring practices rich in these, both lends greater confidence to any acquisition and replenishes the stock of social capital derived from trust and confidence.

References to Postscript Comment

Friedman, M. (1970) The social responsibility of business is to increase its profits, *The New York Times Magazine*, 13 September, New York.

Friedman, M. (2000) *Capitalism and Freedom*, University of Chicago Press, Chicago.

Grabher, G. (2002) The project ecology of advertising: tasks, talents and teams *Regional Studies*, 36, 245–262.

Kramer, R. M. (2009) Rethinking trust, *Harvard Business Review*, June, 69–77.

Smith, A. (1984) *The Theory of Moral Sentiments*, Liberty Fund, Indianapolis.

Smyth, H. J. (2008a) *Developing Trust, Collaborative Relationships in Construction: Developing Frameworks and Networks*, (eds. H. J. Smyth and S. D. Pryke), Blackwell Publishing Ltd., Oxford, 129–160.

Smyth, H. J. (2008b) The Moral Economy and the Management of Projects, *Paper presented at Euram 2008*, 14–18 May, Ljubljanna, Slovenia.

Smyth, H. J. (2009) Trust and the Moral Economy, *Trust in and across Organizations*, Keynote address, Arctic Workshop 2009, Finnish Doctoral Program in Industrial Engineering and Management, 12–13 November, Helsinki University of Technology, Espoo.

Conclusion

Professional practices are founded and will continue to be founded by people leaving established firms and college, especially at the bottom of the economic cycle and in the upturn. Some fail, some stay small and some become the next generation of leaders. Leadership can be in terms of inspiration, innovation, relationship development and influence, size and global reach. In all cases success is always a combination of (i) being excellent in terms of the discipline and having a clear position on the areas of excellence, and (ii) being effective in the marketplace, whether that market is formed of a network of influential individuals or organisations or whether the markets are also more disparate and diffused in client type and location. In between the discipline and the market lies management, and this has been the focus of this book.

One of the main aims of the book was to set out the diverse approaches to management and also to consider how certain issues that arise can be decisive in the form and direction that a practice takes. I hope that aim has been achieved and offers a complementary yet contrasting approach to the more standardised approaches to management set out by many books. While there are patterns of significance and importance for management, they provide an inadequate recipe for success because of their homogenous nature. Diversity needs to be celebrated and provides distinctiveness and sometimes distinction in the marketplace. What can be distilled from this that is of summary and concluding value? A hard call, and inevitably a personal synthesis of points, and so I am choosing to select merely a few on the grounds that long lists tend to become too much to grapple with or come to look bland. I have separated them into points of value for practice and research, but in each case there are overlapping implications.

■ While practice management has become very sophisticated in many ways, there still remains a residual sense in practice that management is a necessary (if unfortunate) add-on to each discipline rather than being an integral part of that discipline. This split remains in education and training, and it comes through in practice. The consequence is that opportunities are lost to enhance the substantive discipline and its attendant service to clients, and these are issues that come through in several of the chapters from academics and practitioners.

Managing the Professional Practice: in the built environment, First Edition. Edited by Hedley Smyth.
© 2011 by Blackwell Publishing Ltd. Published 2011 by Blackwell Publishing Ltd.

- Professional practice relies heavily on being effective in the substantive areas of the discipline, yet what is necessary to be head and shoulders above direct competitors is increasingly more than professional expertise and competence. Rather, it is increasingly the knowledge and process management that goes beyond these disciplinary boundaries, that is, the organisational dynamic capabilities and core management competencies, whether this is innovation, relationship management or knowledge management, for example.
- Professional practices will continue to grow and consolidate, especially at the upper end of the market. Clients are demanding more sophisticated services to meet new demands of large and highly complex facilities, which abound in uncertainties and ambiguities – the needs and risks that require expertise. With growth come not only the need for practices to effectively manage their clients and projects through studio teams and programme management, and cross-functional and inter-organisational management, but also the need to manage their organisations to new levels of excellence. Successful practices, especially those working on the global scale, will be those that take organisational management seriously in terms of rigour and in terms of sensitivity to their professional disciplines.
- Internationalisation is placing new demands upon the built environment professional practices, and new technologies are creating new information and coordination possibilities. How these will be managed in the future is open to question, as addressed in the book, but the growing size and capability of some practices compared to the institutional arrangements and ownership structures of practices brings into sharp focus the role of the 'professional' in terms of ethics, codes and thus values, which will be faced over the coming decade or two.
- Academia has begun to understand much more about the creative and problem-solving processes, but to date, and as reflected in this book too, most of the management tools are indirect in the sense that structures and processes are put in place to facilitate creativity and problem solving rather than being the generation of creativity and problem solving per se. Research needs to move to the socio-psychological process of creativity in order to know how better to manage the process for the long-term improvement of this aspect of managing the professional practice.
- Research will continue on specific issues that practice faces, sustainability and carbon footprint being a high profile set of issues. However, the technical dimensions of such research have thrown up the potential of various solutions, yet feedback makes clear that people and the organisations do not always use facilities in the way anticipated and thus the benefits are compromised at best and corrupted at worst. More research is needed into the management

of techniques and technologies in their development and in application to understand and improve this dynamic.

- Research has begun to look at client needs and client management at a more detailed level and this needs to continue. Most emphasis has been on the practice side rather than the client side. A socio-psychological research towards clients would help client and relationship management for the long term.
- The research into world clusters, internationalisation and competitive advantage of practices, especially at the upper end of the market by size of professional practice is developing apace, and this is a fast-changing picture that needs tracking. The informal dimensions of those processes that are not organisationally bound are poorly understood in research and there will be benefit from analysing the importance of the industrial and service networks that are formed and used by key actors from professional practices in the capturing and delivering of value into projects and across projects.

Four practice-based and four research-based ideas are summarised above that come out of the chapters presented in this book. They are only a few of the issues that could be drawn out, but it is hoped that they are specifically pertinent to many readers and will provide a stimulus to explore other issues amongst most if not all readers.

The past 15–20 years have seen an unprecedented focus on 'what' issues, no more so than in accountability measure, such as key performance indicators (KPIs). These are important yet, if dominant, tend to constrain the development of the profession at an organisational level. The professions are fundamentally about 'how' and have a great deal to offer in addressing markets where clients are essentially looking for assurance and confidence in the quality of service at the time of appointment and trust and confidence as the service experience unfolds. These aspects are less easy to measure, but like confidence in financial markets, are essential to their operation. This focus upon 'how' issues is important and will continue to be so for it addresses 'why' the professions are needed. Addressing 'how' issues is perhaps the most important part of managing the professional practice.

Acronyms

3D	Three dimensional
AIA	American Institute of Architects
AIM	Alternative Investment Market
APC	Assessment of professional competence
APM	Association for Project Management
B2B	Business-to-business
BAA	British Airports Authorities
BBBEE	Broad based black economic empowerment
BE	Built environment
BIM	Building information modelling
BoK	Body of knowledge
BREEAM	Building Research Establishment environmental assessment method
BRIC	Brazil, Russia, India and China
BSC	Balanced scorecard system
CABE	Commission for Architecture and the Built Environment
CAD	Computer aided design
CAFM	Computer aided facilities management
CBRE	CB Richard Ellis
CCOTS	Customised commercial off-the-shelf
CDM	Construction and design management regulations
CERF	Civil Engineering Research Foundation
CIC	Construction Industry Council
CPD	Continuing professional development
CRM	Customer relationship management
CR	Corporate responsibility
CRC	Carbon reduction commitment
CSR	Corporate social responsibility
CV	Curriculum vitae/résumé
DECs	Display energy certificates
EEIG	European Economic Interest Group
EMS	Environmental management systems
EPCs	Energy performance certificates
ERP	Enterprise resource planning
EU	European Union
FIA	Fees in allowance

Managing the Professional Practice: in the built environment, First Edition. Edited by Hedley Smyth.
© 2011 by Blackwell Publishing Ltd. Published 2011 by Blackwell Publishing Ltd.

FM	Facilities management
GIC	Global intelligence corps
HR	Human resources
ICT	Information and communications technology
IIP	Investors in people
IP	Intellectual property
IST	Innovation support team
IT	Information technology
KAM	Key account management
KPIs	Key performance indicators
KTP	Knowledge transfer partnership
LEED	Leadership in energy and environmental design
LLP	Limited liability partnership
MAC	Move, add and change
MBE KTN	Modern built environment knowledge transfer network
MIS	Management information system
MSP	Managing Successful Programmes
NEAT	NHS environmental assessment tool
NHS	National Health Service
OGC	Office of Government Commerce
PI	Professional indemnity insurance
PFI	Private Finance Initiative
PLC	Public limited company
PMBOK	Project Management Body of Knowledge
PMI	Project Management Institute
PPP	Private Public Partnerships
PR	Public relations
PruPIM	Prudential Property Investment Managers
PSFs	Professional Service Firms
QA	Quality assurance
QFD	Quality function deployment
QMS	Quality management system
QS	Quantity surveyor
R&D	Research and development
RFPs	Requests for proposals
RIBA	Royal Institute of British Architects
RICS	Royal Institution of Chartered Surveyors
RPMS	Resource planning and monitoring system
RPBW	Renzo Piano Building Workshop
SBRI	Small business research initiative
SDP	Silcock Dawson & Partners
SMEs	Small to medium-sized enterprises
SOPs	Standard operating procedures
SPOC	Single point of contact
SRI	Socially responsible investment
STEP	Sustainability training and education programme

TRIZ	TeoriyaResheniyaIzobretatelskikhZadatch – a problem solving, analysis and forecasting tool
TSB	Technology Strategy Board
UKCMRI	UK Centre for Medical Research and Innovation
UKGBC	UK Green Building Council
USPs	Unique selling points
UTH	University of Tokyo Hospital
WIP	Work-in-progress

Index

Managing the Professional Practice: in the built environment, First Edition. Edited by Hedley Smyth.
© 2011 by Blackwell Publishing Ltd. Published 2011 by Blackwell Publishing Ltd.